Student's name: _____ Assignment date: _____

Math Contest Preparation, Problem Solving Strategies, and Math IQ Puzzles for Grades 3 and 4

顶级
英文奥数, 解题策略, 及 IQ 思唯训练宝典

小学三, 四年级

Frank Ho　　Amanda Ho

何数棋谜 培训

Ho Math Chess Learning Centre

只见棋谜不见题　劝君迷路不哭涕　数学象棋加谜题　健脑思维眞神奇

Table of Contents

2016 My story of creating this unique 3-in-1 workbook 2016 我写此独特, 三合一書的故事 9

2014 Preface 2014 前言 **10**

How to use this workbook? 如何使用这本教材教课? **11**

How to use this workbook to prepare for the Kangaroo math contest? 如何用本書準備袋鼠奥数考? **14**

Part 1 Prerequisite of using this workbook assessment 学生能力评估 **18**

　Lower grades math ability assessment 低年级数学能力评估 19

　Mixed operations minutes math 四则混合计算 23

　Quotient assessment 除法的评估 26

　Basic knowledge required for preparing math contests 奥数的基本功 27

　The basic knowledge test for lower grades 低级数学能力评估 28

　Basic 4 operations test for multiple grades 多年级多功能计算题 31

Part 2 Problem-solving strategies **32**

Changing data types to whole numbers or small numbers 转换数为正整数 ... **33**

Marking or writing intermediate answers on the sentences 一边唸题一边写答案 ... **34**

Corresponding method 对应法 **36**

　The corresponding method in different data types 对应法在不同数型的应用 ... 45

Horizontal computation vs. vertical computation 横向及垂直计算 **52**

Line Segment Diagram – universal problem-solving method 线段图 – 万能解法 ... **53**

　Line Segment Diagram review 线段图基夲複習 54

　ABCD line segment ABCD 线段 55

　The universal word problem solver – Line Segment Diagram 用线段图解数学文字题 ... 56

　Is the algebraic method always easier than the arithmetic method? 代数解永比算術好吗? ... 56

Work backwards 倒算法(还原问题, 逆退问题) **58**

　Mysterious work forward and backward problem 神秘的向前算法及倒算法 ... 65

Combination problems 组合题 **73**

　Using multiplication to solve Combination problems 以乘法解组合题 73

　Combination with different conditions 一对多, 多对多组合 73

　Using addition and table to solve Combination problems 以加法或表解组合题 ... 75

　Using the list to solve Combination problems 以列舉法解组合题 76

Box method for nCr Combination problem 盒子法解 nCr 组合问题 **78**

　nCr with no repeating digits 無重複数字 79

　nCr with 0's but no repeating digits 有 0 無重複数字 81

Student's name: _____ Assignment date: _____

NCR WITH 0'S AND REPEATING DIGITS 有 0 有重複数字 82
SUMMARY OF THE COMBINATION PROBLEMS 组合問題的总結 83
PROBLEMS OF USING BOX METHOD TO SOLVE COMBINATION PROBLEMS 以盒子法解 组合题 86
MIXED COMBINATION problem 混合组合题 87

Sequence 排序 **92**
Patterns and sequence 規律 **93**
NUMBER PATTERN 数的規律 93
FIGURE PATTERN 图形的規律 93
THE PATTERN IN WORDS 文字描述的規律 93
PATTERN PUZZLES 数谜的規律 93
TABLE PATTERN 表的規律 94
COMPUTING PATTERN 计算的規律 94
CIRCULAR PATTERN 95
THE ACCUMULATED SUM OF PATTERN 累積規律合 97
HIDDEN PATTERN TO GET SUM 隐藏性的規律 98
NUMBER PATTERN 数的規律 99
NUMBER PATTERN IN COMPUTATION 数字運算的規律 100
MULTIPLYING BY MULTIPLES OF 11 11 的倍数乘法 107
PATTERNS DESCRIBING IN SYMBOLS OR WORDS 以图形或文字表述的規律 108
THE ACCUMULATED SUM OF PATTERN 累積規律合 110
TWO-COLUMN PATTERN 二列規律 111
MIXED PATTERN PROBLEMS 混合規律問題 112

Pascal triangle 楊輝三角形数 **119**
Arithmetic sequence and series 算術序列及级数 **122**
USING THE ARITHMETIC SERIES FORMULA TO FIND ITS SUM 以算術级数公式计算和 123

Even and odd numbers 偶奇数 **137**
Operational math 操作式数学 **140**
Part 3 Chinese classic math contest word problems and Geometry 中国奥数范题及几何 **143**
Chickens and Rabbits 雏兔同笼 **144**
Surplus and Shortage problem 盈不足术, 盈亏问题 (紅利分配问题) **149**
Expansion of Surplus and Shortage problem 盈亏问題举一反三 **151**
Advanced problem **155**
USING MULTIPLE NUMBERS METHOD 156

Hidden information in Sum and Difference **168**
Sum and Difference problem 和差問題 **170**
BASE VALUE 基本值 171
METHOD 1, USE A STORY (RECOMMENDED METHOD) 171
TRANSFERRING SUM AND DIFFERENCE PROBLEM INTO A STORY 转化和差问題为情景问題 171
METHOD 2, USE THE LINE SEGMENT DIAGRAM (MUST LEARN) 172

METHOD 3, USE THE SYSTEMS OF EQUATIONS...173
METHOD 4, USE FORMULAS 173
SUM AND DIFFERENCE EXPRESSED IN SYSTEMS OF EQUATIONS 联立方程解和差问题.............174
SUM AND DIFFERENCE PROBLEMS USING FORMULAS 用公式解和差问题 175
CHANGING SUM AND DIFFERENCE TO TWO BASE VALUES 转化和差问题为二个标准值.............176
NON-STANDARD SUM AND DIFFERENCE PROBLEMS 178
SUM AND DIFFERENCE PROBLEM CONNECTING TO SUM AND MULTIPLIER PROBLEM 180
MORE THAN 2 VARIABLES SUM AND DIFFERENCE PROBLEM 181

Sum and Difference applications 和差問題举一反三.. **183**
PERIMETER AND AREA PROBLEM 183
AGE PROBLEM 183
WORK PROBLEM 184
DISTANCE AND SPEED PROBLEM 185
SUM AND DIFFERENCE IN DIFFERENT DATA TYPES 不同数性的和差问题.................................188

Sum and Multiplier 和倍问题 **189**
USING THE BOX METHOD FOR COUNTABLE OBJECTS 191

Difference and Multiplier 差倍问题 **192**
USING THE BOX METHOD FOR COUNTABLE OBJECTS 194

Sum, Difference, and Multiplier **195**
SUM AND DIFFERENCE WORD PROBLEMS 和差文字問題 196
SUM AND DIFFERENCE, SUM AND PRODUCT, REMAINING QUANTITY 和差, 和绩, 餘数 197
TRANSFERRABLE SUM, DIFFERENCE, AND MULTIPLIER 198
DIFFERENCE AND MULTIPLIER OF AGE PROBLEM 198
DIFFERENCE AND MULTIPLIER OF PERIMETER PROBLEM. 198
DIFFERENCE AND MULTIPLIER OF WORK PROBLEM...199
SUM AND MULTIPLIER OF AGE PROBLEM 199

Sum and Difference Distance and Speed problem **200**
SUM AND MULTIPLIER DISTANCE AND SPEED PROBLEM 200
DIFFERENCE AND MULTIPLIER DISTANCE AND SPEED PROBLEM 201

Mixed Sum, Difference, and Multiplier **202**
SUM/DIFFERENCE AND MULTIPLIER 和差倍問題 204
SUM AND DIFFERENCE 和差問題 205

Word problems using Line Segment Diagrams **206**
USING LINE SEGMENT DIAGRAM – AGE PROBLEMS 年齡問題 206
USING LINE SEGMENT DIAGRAM – WEIGHT PROBLEMS 重量問題 208
USING LINE SEGMENT DIAGRAM – MIXED PROBLEMS 混合题 209
SUM AND DIFFERENCE, SUM AND MULTIPLIER, DIFFERENCE AND MULTIPLIER LINK TO MATH CONTESTS 211

Travelling problem 行程問題 **212**

Give and Take 取捨問題 **217**
GIVE AND TAKE IN DIFFERENT DATA TYPES 不同数型的取捨問題 218

Complementary numbers 互補数 **219**

Arithmetic factoring 算術共因子 **219**
  DISTRIBUTIVE LAW 分配律 219
  NUMBER PATTERN AND DISTRIBUTIVE LAW 数的规律及分配律 221
Order of operations 先乘除後加减 **224**
Geometry 几何 **230**
  BAR GRAPH 柱狀图 230
  DIVIDING SHAPES 分割图形 232
  SOLID NETS 立体图平面分解 233
  PARALLEL LINE 平行线 234
  QUADRILATERAL ATTRIBUTES 四边形特质 235
  COUNTING DIGITS 数数字 236
  COUNTING LINE SEGMENTS, SHAPES 数形狀 237
  MIXED COUNTING PROBLEMS 混合数奌, 线, 形 239
  COUNTING DIAGONALS 数对角线 240
  TETROMINO 四连方 241
  TETRIS 俄罗斯方塊 242
  A TRACEABLE GRAPH WITHOUT LIFTING THE PENCIL 一筆画 245
  SOME PERIMETER PROBLEMS 周長問题 248
  TRANSFORMATION 图形的转换 250
  CONGRUENT FIGURES (FIGURES WITH THE SAME SIZE AND SHAPE) 等樣形 260
  GEOMETRY WITH ARITHMETIC 几何计算题 261
  3 DIMENSIONAL PERSPECTIVE DRAWINGS 265
  3 DIMENSIONAL PERSPECTIVE DRAWINGS 266
  3 DIMENSIONAL PERSPECTIVE DRAWINGS 267
Venn diagram 思維图 **268**
  DIAGRAM VS. VENN DIAGRAM 卡罗尔图及维思图 272
Metric Measurement 度量衡公制 **273**
Likelihood 可能性 **274**
Probability 机率 **275**
Standard and expanded forms 标准数及展開式 **276**
  NUMBER FORMATS 数的表示法 277
Estimating 估算 **280**
Rounding 四捨五入 **281**
Pages and sheets 頁数及纸张数 **288**
Scale problems 秤量问题 **289**
Clock problems 时鐘問题 **290**
  TIME 时間問题 291
  METRIC TIME (Y, M, D) 公制的时间 294

Spinner problems 旋转器 297

Sum partition with no restrictions 没限制和的分解 298

Sum partition with restrictions 有限制和的分解 299

Logic and reasoning 邏輯思唯 300

Consecutive numbers 连續数 302

Inequality 不等式 303

Systems of equations 联立方程 - 二元一次方程 306

Part 4 School math mixed English word problems 学校数学混合文字应用题 309

    BASIC FACTS WORD PROBLEMS 四则基本計算应用题 310

    SUM AND MULTIPLIER OR PARTITION OF SUM 和倍的分項 312

    MIXED WORD PROBLEMS 混合文字題 313

    + − × ÷ 329

Part 5 Mixed computations and number puzzles 混合计算技巧及数迷 330

Shortcuts for number computations 331

It is multiplied by 5. 331

Multiplied by 25 332

Multiplied by 125 333

Multiplying an even number by a number ending with 5 334

    MULTIPLYING TWO NUMBERS WITH THE SAME TENS OR HUNDREDS DIGIT AND THE SUM OF ONES DIGITS IS 10 335

Multiplied by 11 336

Shortcut for adding numbers ending with 0's 337

Shortcuts for mixed operation 340

Numbers, digits, place values 数, 数字, 位数值 341

Basics concepts review 基本計算观念複習 342

    GCF AND LCM 最大公約数及最小公倍数 342

    DIVISIBILITY 約数 343

Multiplication and divisions facts 乘除恒等式 346

Multiplication review 乘法複習 347

Multiplying numbers ending in 9 尾数是 9 的乘法 354

Cross multiplication 交义相乘 356

Smallest and largest products 最小及最大乘積 379

Finding missing digits – multiplication 乘的数字迷 383

Division review 除法複習 390

    DIVIDING BY 0 除以 0 390

Finding missing digits – Division 除的数字迷 399

Using operators to make math sentences 用+, −, ×, ÷ 或 小括号造数学等式 401

Using operators to create an equation 造算式 405

Roman Numerals 罗馬数符 409

Decimals 小数 **410**

DECIMAL MULTIPLICATIONS 小数乘法 410

DECIMAL DIVISIONS 小数除法 411

MIXED DECIMAL DATA TYPE CALCULATIONS 混合小数型的计算 412

DECIMAL WORD PROBLEMS 小数文字题 413

DECIMAL WORD PROBLEMS AND CALCULATIONS 小数文字应用题 414

MIXED DECIMAL PROBLEMS 小数混合题 417

Fractions 分数 **418**

PIE CHART AND FRACTIONS 圆形图及分数 418

SHADED FIGURES AND FRACTIONS 阴影图及分数 419

FRACTION DRAWINGS 画分数图 420

FRACTIONS REPRESENTED BY FIGURES 以图形代表分数 421

EQUIVALENT FRACTIONS 等值分数 422

ORDER FRACTIONS FROM LEAST TO GREATEST 分数小到大的排列 423

FRACTION 3-MODEL PROBLEMS 三个分数模式的计算 424

CONVERTING FIGURES TO FRACTIONS 由图转分数 425

CONVERTING FIGURES TO FRACTIONS 由分数转图 426

FRACTIONS REPRESENTED BY FIGURES 以图形代表分数 427

PICKING THE LARGEST FRACTION 选最大的分数值 428

SPLITTING UNIT CIRCLE INTO EQUAL PIECES 分数单位园的等分 430

Fraction calculation for advanced students 学霸分数计算 **432**

FRACTION WORD PROBLEMS 分数文字应用题 433

Decimals, fractions match 小数分分数配对 **437**

FRACTION, DECIMAL, PERCENT 分数, 小数, 百分比 439

Decimal and fraction conversion 小数及分数的转换 **440**

Ratio 比 **441**

ONE RATIO PROBLEM 3 METHODS 一比例题 3 解 442

Mixed computations ＋－×÷混合式计算 **444**

Mixed multiplication and division 乘除混合计算 **445**

Mixed puzzles operations 数字迷混合计算 **446**

Mixed operations 混合题计算 **449**

Mixed 4 operations 混合四则计算 **463**

Part 6 Ho Math Chess Puzzles for the Creative Minds 棋谜式智趣题 **471**

NUMBER PUZZLE 数字谜 472

DOMINO NUMBER PUZZLE 骨牌数字谜 473

FRANKHO CUBE MATH™ 何数棋谜 FRANKHO 方块数学 474

FRANKHO HAPPY MATH™ 何数棋谜 FRANKHO 快乐数学 475

Number puzzles using figures 图形数字迷 **479**

ENGLISH AND MATH 英文数学...480
ROBOT MATH 机器人数学...487
＋－×÷...490
Magic square 幻方 **491**
Introducing Ho Math Chess in Chinese 介紹何数棋谜......................... **548**

2016 My story of creating this unique 3-in-1 workbook 2016 我写此独特, 三合一書的故事

Frank's background and experience

I wrote this workbook with a vision that is I wanted to create a workbook that I think will be good and useful for children. This workbook was created based on my personal, educational background and teaching experience and my own chess coaching experience with my own son. All these experiences and observations tell me that a student who has a higher IQ and has a higher than average math score does not mean necessarily that this student will do well in math contests. Everybody can learn math, but the results could be very different. Other than to have a smart brain and the ability to learn math faster than the other children, a child needs other "qualities' to do well consistently in math contests. These special qualities include perseverance, patience, and willingness to take time to think. The ability to be able to draw a conclusion, make comparisons, expand and use learned knowledge onto other problems, can follow and write procedures or steps neatly and logically; organize and list data; visualize spatial relations. The student could be trained vigorously, but without real interest and willingness to work on problems, then the enthusiasm of training on math contests will not last long, so we know to use one pure math contest workbook alone is difficult to achieve the effect of "all-around" training. This is my vision of creating this integrated workbook.

Why is this workbook so huge (What unique is about this workbook?)?

How to train a child to be more patient? How to train a student to observe and compare? One way of achieving these is to use puzzles. This is the main reason that puzzles are included in this book. Further, puzzles can increase a child's IQ. How to train a child to think "out of the box" and be creative? The integrated chess, Sudoku, and math computational puzzled can help. When considering all of the above purposes, the result is that this workbook has become a huge workbook.

How did I get started to create this workbook?

I received my university education in Taiwan and later received my Science of Statistics master's degree in the US. My working in teaching and research math at my own learning Centre Ho Math Chess based in Canada has offered me insights on how math is taught differently in different countries. The integrated game is a good way of learning math; in our case, chess is integrated into our worksheets, not a totally separate subject. This is one uniqueness of our Math Contest workbook. Since our math contest workbook has many different parts, so students could pick other materials other than math contest.

Why teachers, coaches, parents, or students should buy this workbook?

We need a workbook which not only just teaches math contest. It should also be fun for children and enhance their brain power. This is the vision that leads me to create this workbook, and if you agree with my idea and view, then this world's first integrated math contest, problem-solving strategies and fun math IQ workbook is for you and your student or child.

Frank Ho

December 2016

2014 Preface 2014 前言

We have been very much interested in creating a "perfect" workbook that could cover students' day schools' math curricula in many countries for elementary students, and it must be fun for students to use; ideally, it also should offer challenging problems for very intelligent students.

This "ideal" workbook should cover a variety of topics such that it can be used by average students to gifted students. In the past, such a workbook must be created by using a few workbooks: one for school math, one for word problems, and one for puzzles etc.; the problem of using multiple workbooks is it is difficult for a teacher to teach by using three or four workbooks in once a week session of after-school learning centre.

Through many years of research and teaching, Ho **Math Chess** has finally had a breakthrough. We have created a workbook *Problem Solving and Math IQ Puzzles* for different levels of students. To meet the requirement that this workbook can be used to teach day school math curricula for different countries, our workbook contents levels are very high standard, and at the same time, this type of workbook also adds fun into math learning by incorporating puzzles. We also included many of our own intellectual and copyrighted puzzles in the workbook.

For students who are interested in preparing math contests, we have produced a math contest preparation workbook. For students who are interested in learning chess, we also have produced a chess learning workbook. We also have a Frankho ChessDoku 何数棋谜算独 specifically designed to train students in a combination of math computation, chess, and logic. FrankhoMaze is a special type of maze which offers the feeling of 3-D maze play using chess moves. For those students who like to review math materials for test purposes, we have a "review workbook" produced just for that purpose.

Frank Ho
Amanda Ho

January 2014

The above was our view on creating our workbooks, but as you can see in the 2016 preface, we have changed the direction since the new edition was published in 2016 – 2017.

How to use this workbook? 如何使用这本教材教课?

This workbook belongs to a series of *Ultimate Math Contest, Problem Solving Strategies, and Math IQ Puzzles*. This series of books is a special collection of math problem-solving workbooks, which not only raises a student's word problem-solving ability, it also raises a student's IQ because of many mathematical IQ puzzles are included in these workbooks. The series of workbooks do not necessarily consist of only two parts: word problems and puzzles because many workbooks also contain school assessment problems, so preparation and study of these workbooks become extremely important for teachers or instructors in advance of teaching.

Most parents found it is difficult for them to help their children with these workbooks at home, so it is also important that teachers attempt only to teach this workbook in class instead of assigning problems in this workbook as homework unless they are just computation problems or students are exceptional. Only assign to students whose parents are willing and capable of helping their children at home. Some parents try to teach their children using algebra to solve the Chinese classic model problems such as chickens and rabbits or Sum and Difference problems. There is nothing wrong with teaching algebra, but do children understand algebra before they were taught?

I have found that teachers normally do not do good teaching if they did not study this workbook in advance, the good thing is teachers only must prepare once then the teaching becomes easier each time. My observations on the problems teachers face when they are not prepared in advance are explained below.

1.　Many problems in these workbooks contain challenging problems other than run-of-the-mill problems. Without advanced preparation, teachers tend to pick run-of-the-mill calculation problems during the teaching period with very little dialogue with the students and then the students are not challenged and may feel bored.

2.　Teachers do not know how to teach students how to tackle the problem but simply just tell students the steps on how to do it. For example, the following problem

$$0.1234 = \boxed{} \times \frac{2}{3}$$

One teacher just told the grade-6 student to solve it the following way.

$$0.1234 = x \times \frac{2}{3}$$

There is nothing wrong with doing it in algebra to solve the equation, but if this grade-6 student has not learned how to solve the equation using algebra, then it will be a problem for the student. So, without assuring a student's ability and just use algebra, the students still did not know how to solve a similar problem after teaching.

How to teach the above problem to a grade-6 student without knowing algebra? The teacher only must explain from a different angle by replacing the fraction to a small whole number using such as the following:

Let's say if the problem is $6 = ? \times 3$, the student can find the answer easily, but the more important question should be to ask the student to think about how the answer was found. The student will answer it is because of $6 \div 3 = 2$. So, the teacher can immediately point out to the student to compare these two problems (One has only whole numbers, and the other has a fraction and a decimal.). then the answer could be found by the student.

$$0.1234 = \boxed{} \times \frac{2}{3}$$
$$6 = ? \times 3$$

Ask students to think before giving out answers is important. Guide students on how to think or tackle the problem are more important than just giving out answers. Without an explanation of why or how a problem is done is the wrong way of teaching.

3. If the teacher feels a lot of problems are difficult for students, then it is true because we have produced a workbook to meet the challenging of higher level of thinking to challenge students in countries such as China, Korea, Japan, and Singapore etc. and to meet the expectations of challenging programs such as IB program or gifted program. Teachers do not have to teach in a sequential sequence page after page, and this is a wrong way of organizing a teaching class. Instead, the teacher should always ask what the student is learning at school, then to see if some problems in this workbook could be found to match what is learning at school.

4. Some teachers always go with the easy way of teaching problem solving by suggesting the Trial and Error method. There is not much time for students to use Trial and Error in math contest without some direction. Therefore, we do not include Trial and Error in our math strategies when they get to know this method at schools. We suggest changing the data types or using small whole numbers to figure out.

All in all, teachers must teach from a student's view by observing if the student really understand what has been taught and if not, the teacher should try to find an alternative way of explaining the problem, do not just give out the answer and then thinking the teaching is over. The worst is to blame the student's ability is not up to the level to understand without trying to find out how to help a student to catch up.

For example, I taught a grade-8 student on the following problem:

$$2(x-2) - 3(-1-x) = 3(x-3)$$

I sensed she had trouble in attempting to solve this problem by looking at her facial expression, so I gave her some simple problems to try such as $-2(-3-2)-3(-3)$-. She seemed to have difficulties in getting the correct answers, so I immediately hand-wrote and asked her to do 20 similar styles of basic integers, then she felt better. Her problem was that she really had not mastered the basic integer operations, so she encountered problems when she attempted to solve more advanced equation solving problems. The teacher needs this kind of ability to find out what is the source of problems and know how to fix the student's problem.

With online teaching or computerized teaching, the above of teaching strategy is difficult to implement successfully if the teacher is not able to see how a student works on paper.

This workbook has imported the idea of Chinese classic model word problems and then combined with western's problem-solving strategies to have come up with an East meets West integrated workbook. Many examples have shown multiple ways of solving the same problem such as arithmetic and algebra. Many problems also show one method can be applied to different data types, such as the method of using "Quantity divided by its corresponding value" whether it is fraction, percent or ratio.

The following gives a comparison table on how to use this workbook.

	Has to experience in training math contest	No experience in training math contest	Comments
Teachers or parents	Still, we need to study Chinese model word problems.	Need to work on Problem-solving strategies and Other word problems first.	Teachers or parents need to study this workbook before teaching.
Students	Can work on Chinese model problems and problem strategies.	I need to work on computations, then a mixture of problem-solving strategies and other word problems.	Students need to have a solid background in computation.

If you encounter any problems when using this workbook or have any comments and suggestions, please contact us at homathchess@outlook.com.

Frank Ho

December 18, 2016

How to use this workbook to prepare for the Kangaroo math contest? 如何用本書準備袋鼠奥数考?

The Contest-Game "Math Kangaroo" originated in France in 1991 and quickly became very popular among students in many European countries. Several years later, the association "Kangourou sans frontieres" was founded, and it now organizes the event. The contest's main purpose is to promote mathematical thinking and stimulate an interest in math by providing students with an opportunity to compare their abilities against the abilities of other students from different countries around the world. In the past, several years, the geography of the participating countries has been extended outside Europe, to the USA, Paraguay, Mexico, Canada, etc.

In 2011, over six million students and hundreds of mathematicians from 46 countries played the game worldwide. More information about the contest is available at www.mathkang.org

The contents of the Kangaroo math contest

There are a few characteristics of the Kangaroo Math Contest, so to prepare for it, we must understand its uniqueness.

1. It is international math contests

Since it is an international math contest, so Kangaroo Math Contest does not have as many computational types of problems as other national or local math contests. Different countries may have different math curricula, so the Kangaroo Math Contest contains many problems requiring a lot of thinking skills.

2. Preparing some model problems but learn to analyze problems

Some basic model problems are required in any math contests, but the training should also be on strategies and deep analysis also. Knowing the model problems can speed up the finding of solutions. Many classic Chinese model problems such as Chickens and Rabbits, Sum and Difference, Sum and Multiplier are helpful in finding answers.

3. Geometry problems

Many geometry problems do not require advanced geometry knowledge, but understandings.

4. Do not confuse the way of solving problems when doing homework and math contests

The procedures required to do math contest must be efficient and fast, so some homework types of solving problems like Trial and Error may not be suitable. Students must learn the most efficient way of solving problems after learning a multi-way of solving the same problem.

The training of the Kangaroo Math Contest is different from the school math because Kangaroo Math Contest does not really follow any school curriculum.

We like Kangaroo Math Contest. We like kangaroo Math Contest because the problems in the Kangaroo math contests are ingeniously created, students not only need to have good training, they require some creativity and deep understanding of math concepts as well as to be able to link, organize, and compare, and summarize information. Kangaroo Math Contest problems foster student's creativity, understanding of math concepts. It steers the training direction to an overall understanding of many math concepts and interconnects them together. Some Math Kangaroo Contest problems are mathematical puzzles in nature, which are in line with Ho Math Chess teaching philosophy. We have included one sample of our math, chess, and puzzles integrated worksheet at the end of this preface for the reader's reference. Good math contest contestants not only care about getting the correct answer, but they also enjoy the process of thinking on how to solve the problem.

For example, the following problem appears in the 2007 Canada Kangaroo Math Contest grades 7 and 8.

Table 3 × 3 contains nine natural numbers (see the picture). Nick and Peter erased four numbers each such that the sum of the numbers erased by Nick was three times as great as the sum of the numbers erased by Peter. What numbers remained on the table.

4	12	8
13	24	14
7	5	23

Nick: 12, 13, 23, 24
Peter: 4, 5, 7, 8
Remaining number: 14

This problem is interesting because, in fact, the numbers are placed in a 3 by 3 square, but they have nothing to do with the square at all, and students must be able to spot it. Second, the guess and check are not a good method in solving this problem, so the solution is not to find what numbers have been selected by two persons, the number of persons does not matter to the solution either.

This problem also gives a feeling that an excellent math contest student must also be well versed in language so he or she can analyze the language to be able to understand the problem from a math point of view. A student who is not good at language then the chance of doing math contest well is not very high.

The problem is to find out what number should be left behind such that the sum of the remaining number is a multiple of 4 after one number is chosen. The problem has been worded such that the English language sounds to direct students to find the 6 numbers instead of finding one number. Students must be able to decide what strategy to take instead of blindly following what the English states in the problem to attempt to find an answer.

I used to tell students that one of the big difference between chess and math is when playing chess, you have an opponent who prevents you from winning, but there is no one there causing trouble for you to think a solution when working on math contest problem, but this problem has proved me wrong.

You cannot just do only school math and to be able to do well on Kangaroo Math Contest because the nature of Kangaroo Math Contest problems integrates all kinds of knowledge (even games) and only when possessing this integrated and inter-linked knowledge can you solve some problems quickly.

One type of Kangaroo Math Contest problem is to ask students to use pattern knowledge, then from there to use the concept of place values, and then use the factoring knowledge to find the sum. The pattern may come from a student's understanding of combination or even a pre-processed knowledge.

I present the following Kangaroo Math Contest problem to help the reader understand my point of view. This solution is provided in this book.

Five boys weighed in pairs in all possible combinations. The measured weights were 43 kg, 40 kg, 39 kg, 37 kg, 38 kg, 36 kg, 35 kg, 33 kg, 32 kg, and 30 kg. What was the total weight of the 5 boys?

See *Hidden Pattern to Get Sum* section for the answer.

We have analyzed past Kangaroo Math Contest problems and compared them with problems from other math contests and school math to see the differences. Chinese model word problems offer one of the world's best model problems for preparing math contest problems, so we also incorporate Chinese model math contest problems as a training base to offer some suggestions, ideas, or tips etc. on how to prepare Kangaroo Math Contest. This is how this book was born.

Kangaroo Math Contest may consist of problems that do not have any book problems strategy or method to follow. For example, the following problem needs students to estimate the answers without any method or equation to follow.

Problem

Ella and Ola had 70 mushrooms altogether. $\frac{5}{9}$ of Ella's mushrooms are brown and $\frac{2}{17}$ of Ola's mushroom are white. How many mushrooms did Ella have?

Normally we teach students to match the quantity to its corresponding fractional number, but in this example, there is no reasonable fraction number to match the quantity 70.

One way of solving this problem is to find a quantity to see if it is divisible by 17.

Ola's white mushroom must be multiple of 17.

Ola's number of mushrooms	Ola's number of white mushrooms	Ola's number of brown mushrooms	Ella's number of mushrooms
17	2	15	70 - 17 = 53 which is not multiple of 9.
34	4	30	36
51	6	45	19, which is not a multiple of 9.
68	Not available	Not available	Not available

Teachers are encouraged to select materials that suit student background.

Frank Ho
Amanda Ho

January 2015

Part 1 Prerequisite of using this workbook assessment 学生能力评估

Not everyone should be trained in math contests because it could be very unpleasant for some students. For example, for those students who have short memory may not want to be trained because they have difficulty to remember what had been taught to them.

Some parents were surprised at some of their children who could not do even after they themselves taught their own kids just a few days ago. The reasons could be that the students understood simply by memorizing the steps and by repetitive working on similar problems but did not truly understand the concepts. The other reason could be that they have short-memory and were not able to draw their own observations and conclusions on what they had been taught.

So, it is important a student should be assessed on some very basic computation abilities

Lower grades math ability assessment 低年级数学能力评估

Calculate the following. 计算题

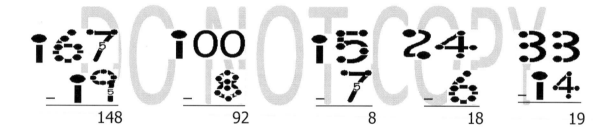

$$170 - 6 = 164$$
$$123 - 15 = 108$$
$$103 - 18 = 85$$
$$613 - 19 = 594$$
$$23 - 16 = 7$$

$$167 - 19 = 148$$
$$100 - 8 = 92$$
$$15 - 7 = 8$$
$$24 - 6 = 18$$
$$33 - 14 = 19$$

$$45 - 19 = 26$$
$$223 - 114 = 109$$
$$\square\square\square - 12 = 221 \quad (233)$$
$$43 - \square\square = 29 \quad (14)$$
$$175 - 17 = \square\square\square \quad (158)$$

Student's name: _____ Assignment date: _____

Lower grades math ability assessment 低年级数学能力评估
Mixed operations minutes math 四则混合计算

$4 \times 3 = 12$	$18 \div 3 = 6$	$26 - 9 = 17$	$43 + 8 = 51$
$3 + 9 = 12$	$17 - 9 = 8$	$24 \times 5 = 120$	$16 \div 2 = 8$
$15 - 4 = 11$	$12 \times 9 = 108$	$23 + 8 = 31$	$12 \div 4 = 3$
$25 \div 5 = 5$	$26 - 9 = 17$	$24 \times 3 = 72$	$21 + 3 = 24$
$4 \times 4 = 16$	$45 \div 9 = 5$	$18 + 7 = 25$	$19 - 8 = 11$
$14 \times 5 = 70$	$18 + 7 = 25$	$15 - 7 = 8$	$25 + 9 = 34$
$16 + 5 = 21$	$14 - 9 = 5$	$17 \times 4 = 68$	$21 \div 3 = 7$
$23 + 8 = 31$	$23 - 9 = 14$	$14 \times 6 = 84$	$48 \div 6 = 8$
$14 \times 7 = 98$	$16 \div 8 = 2$	$23 - 7 = 16$	$17 + 8 = 25$
$14 \div 7 = 2$	$23 - 9 = 14$	$18 \times 3 = 54$	$23 + 5 = 28$
$26 \times 3 = 78$	$24 + 8 = 32$	$23 - 9 = 14$	$28 \div 4 = 7$
$12 \div 6 = 2$	$15 - 9 = 6$	$17 \times 3 = 51$	$77 + 8 = 85$
$4 \times 9 = 36$	$25 \div 5 = 5$	$14 - 8 = 6$	$55 + 8 = 63$
$13 - 4 = 9$	$24 \times 8 = 192$	$23 + 8 = 31$	$27 \div 3 = 9$
$4 \times 3 = 12$	$36 \div 6 = 6$	$27 - 9 = 18$	$29 + 8 = 37$
$18 - 9 = 9$	$14 \times 7 = 98$	$33 + 7 = 40$	$21 \div 3 = 7$
$24 \times 3 = 72$	$15 \div 5 = 3$	$24 - 9 = 15$	$23 + 8 = 31$
$23 + 8 = 31$	$13 - 9 = 4$	$23 - 6 = 17$	$49 \div 7 = 7$
$40 \div 8 = 5$	$24 \times 5 = 120$	$31 - 9 = 22$	$34 + 5 = 39$
$24 \times 5 = 120$	$13 + 8 = 21$	$27 - 8 = 119$	$54 \div 9 = 6$
$15 - 9 = 6$	$36 \div 9 = 4$	$24 \times 5 = 120$	$29 + 8 = 37$

Lower grades math ability assessment 低年级数学能力评估
Assessment of word problems – addition and subtraction

If Andrew gives 3 sheets of lined paper to Wendy, then each of them has an equal number of sheets. Altogether they have 28 sheets. How many sheets does each have originally?

$28 - 6 = 22$ to remove the extra sheets $22/2 =$ **11**   **Wendy**
Andrew $= 11 + 6 =$ **17**

If I add 4 and subtract 5 then add 7, I will get 22, what number am I?

22

If I subtract 5 and add 17 then subtract 6, I will get 39, what number am I?

33

Meghan and Coco together have 24 cookies. If Coco gives Meghan 5 cookies and Meghan gives 3 cookies to Coco, then each of them has the same number of cookies. How many cookies does each of them have in the beginning?

Work backwards to get the answer with 12 for each person.
The difference is really 4 between 2 persons (Use a T-table of $+5, -5; -3, +3; +2, -2$ to find out or work backwards 12, 12; 17, 7; 14, 10 to find out.) So, $24 - 4 = 20$, $20/2 = 10$ this is the   amount each person has an equal number of cookies, and it is also **Meghan's cookies, so it is 10**. **Cock's cookies** $= 10 + 4 =$ **14**.

In 5 years, Andrew will be 12 years old. Five years ago, Meghan was 5 years old. what is the total age of both Meghan and Andrew now?

Andrew's age now is $12 - 5 = 7$ Meghan's age now $5 + 5 = 10$, $10 + 7 =$ **17**

Lower grades math ability assessment 低年级数学能力评估
Assessment of word problems – mixed word problems

Jennifer has 2 more than five times as many as Andrew's cookies. Together they have 1208 cookies. How many cookies does each one of them have?

$$\text{Andrew} = \frac{1208-2}{6} = \textbf{201}$$
$$\text{Jennifer} = 201 \times 5 + 2 = \textbf{1007}$$

Adam has 3 balls less than Bob. Bob has 96 balls less than Cathy. Cathy and Bob altogether have 110 balls. How many balls does each of them have?

C+B=110
C-B=96

$$\text{Bob} = \frac{110-96}{2} = \textbf{7}$$

Cathy = 96 + 7 = **103**
Adam = 7 − 3 = **4**

Adam gave 13 balls to Meghan, then Meghan still had 12 balls more than Adam. What was the number of difference between Adam and Meghan originally?

14 balls

If each student gets 2 balls, then there will be 1 ball left. If each student gets 3 balls, then there will be 2 balls short. How many balls are there?

7 balls

This problem has 2 equations, so we use 2 T-table to solve it.

student	ball
1	3
2	5
3	7

student	ball
1	1
2	4
3	7

Mixed operations minutes math 四则混合计算

$14 \times 3 = 42$	$12 \div 3 = 4$	$96 - 9 = 87$	$13 + 8 = 21$
$32 + 9 = 41$	$12 - 9 = 3$	$44 \times 5 = 220$	$36 \div 2 = 18$
$55 - 4 = 51$	$14 \times 9 = 126$	$13 + 8 = 21$	$12 \div 4 = 3$
$55 \div 5 = 11$	$21 - 9 = 12$	$14 \times 3 = 42$	$69 + 3 = 72$
$24 \times 4 = 96$	$27 \div 9 = 3$	$18 + 8 = 26$	$19 - 8 = 11$
$34 \times 5 = 170$	$17 + 7 = 24$	$23 - 7 = 16$	$15 + 9 = 24$
$56 + 5 = 61$	$91 - 9 = 82$	$15 \times 4 = 60$	$69 \div 3 = 23$
$43 + 8 = 51$	$41 - 9 = 32$	$34 \times 6 = 204$	$72 \div 6 = 12$
$14 \times 7 = 98$	$24 \div 8 = 3$	$21 - 7 = 14$	$37 + 8 = 45$
$84 \div 7 = 12$	$33 - 9 = 24$	$14 \times 3 = 42$	$53 + 5 = 58$
$16 \times 3 = 48$	$74 + 8 = 82$	$26 - 9 = 17$	$72 \div 4 = 18$
$72 \div 6 = 12$	$21 - 9 = 12$	$14 \times 3 = 42$	$78 + 8 = 86$
$14 \times 9 = 126$	$75 \div 5 = 15$	$16 - 8 = 8$	$85 + 8 = 93$
$47 - 4 = 43$	$24 \times 8 = 192$	$33 + 8 = 41$	$24 \div 3 = 8$
$24 \times 3 = 72$	$96 \div 6 = 16$	$77 - 9 = 68$	$23 + 8 = 31$
$28 - 9 = 19$	$14 \times 5 = 70$	$73 + 7 = 80$	$81 \div 3 = 27$
$84 \times 3 = 252$	$25 \div 5 = 5$	$24 - 9 = 15$	$93 + 8 = 101$
$93 + 8 = 101$	$23 - 9 = 14$	$33 - 6 = 27$	$42 \div 7 = 6$
$40 \div 8 = 5$	$34 \times 5 = 170$	$81 - 9 = 72$	$64 + 5 = 69$
$34 \times 5 = 170$	$93 + 8 = 101$	$77 - 8 = 69$	$54 \div 9 = 6$
$35 - 9 = 26$	$36 \div 9 = 4$	$34 \times 5 = 170$	$39 + 8 = 47$

Student's name: _____ Assignment date: _____

Mixed operations minutes math 四则混合计算

$24 \times 3 = 72$	$39 \div 3 = 13$	$42 - 9 = 33$	$53 + 8 = 61$
$33 + 9 = 42$	$12 - 7 = 5$	$34 \times 5 = 170$	$36 \div 4 = 9$
$53 - 6 = 47$	$24 \times 9 = 216$	$23 + 8 = 31$	$54 \div 6 = 9$
$45 \div 5 = 9$	$12 - 9 = 3$	$24 \times 3 = 72$	$59 + 4 = 63$
$14 \times 4 = 56$	$36 \div 9 = 4$	$28 + 8 = 36$	$91 - 8 = 83$
$33 \times 5 = 165$	$27 + 7 = 34$	$13 - 7 = 6$	$35 + 9 = 44$
$57 + 5 = 62$	$92 - 9 = 83$	$16 \times 4 = 64$	$96 \div 3 = 32$
$25 + 8 = 33$	$43 - 9 = 34$	$32 \times 6 = 192$	$36 \div 6 = 6$
$13 \times 7 = 91$	$40 \div 8 = 5$	$23 - 7 = 16$	$39 + 8 = 47$
$63 \div 7 = 9$	$23 - 9 = 14$	$41 \times 3 = 123$	$57 + 5 = 62$
$18 \times 3 = 54$	$75 + 8 = 83$	$27 - 9 = 18$	$32 \div 4 = 8$
$84 \div 6 = 14$	$28 - 9 = 19$	$17 \times 3 = 51$	$77 + 8 = 85$
$17 \times 9 = 153$	$85 \div 5 = 17$	$17 - 8 = 9$	$85 + 8 = 93$
$20 - 4 = 16$	$16 \times 8 = 128$	$34 + 8 = 42$	$21 \div 3 = 7$
$23 \times 3 = 69$	$84 \div 6 = 14$	$75 - 9 = 66$	$24 + 8 = 32$
$28 - 9 = 19$	$14 \times 5 = 70$	$73 + 7 = 80$	$84 \div 3 = 28$
$83 \times 3 = 249$	$75 \div 5 = 15$	$31 - 9 = 22$	$95 + 8 = 103$
$92 + 8 = 100$	$28 - 9 = 19$	$21 - 9 = 12$	$49 \div 7 = 7$
$48 \div 8 = 6$	$35 \times 5 = 175$	$83 - 9 = 74$	$63 + 5 = 68$
$32 \times 5 = 160$	$99 + 8 = 107$	$71 - 8 = 63$	$45 \div 9 = 5$
$23 - 9 = 14$	$45 \div 9 = 5$	$30 \times 5 = 150$	$33 + 8 = 41$

Student's name: _____ Assignment date: _____

1.	Calculate $400089 - 38998$. **361091**
2.	Calculate $410012 - 367898$. **42114**
3.	Calculate 3098×4109. **12729682**
4.	Calculate $31 \cdot 218$. **6758**
5.	Calculate $213(987)$. **210231**
6.	Without calculating 0.4×0.9, how do you know the result is less than 0.4 or 0.9? Explain **Less than 0.4. Because of times a number less than 1, the result will be less than the original number.**

Ho Math Chess   何数棋谜   英文奥数, 解题策略, 及 IQ 思唯训练宝典
Frank Ho, Amanda Ho © 2020   All rights reserved.
Student's name: _____ Assignment date: _____

Quotient assessment 除法的评估

0 at the beginning of quotient	0 in the middle of the quotient	0 at the end of the quotient
$120 \div 24$ 5	$120120 \div 24$ 5,005	$1200000 \div 24$ 50,000
$200 \div 4$ 50	$200020 \div 4$ 50,005	$4000000000 \div 8$ 500,000,000
$2040 \div 40$ 51	$2000\ 040 \div 40$ 50,001	$2040000000 \div 40$ 51,000,000
$36036036 \div 6$ 6,006,006	$3600000036 \div 6$ 600,000,006	$3600000000000 \div 600$ 6,000,000,000

Basic knowledge required for preparing math contests 奥数的基本功

There are some basic concepts or math knowledge required before taking the contest, these concepts may not be tested in every math contest, but they are important to serve as background information to prepare for Kangaroo Math Contest. This background information includes Prime, Factors, Even or Odd number, LCM, GCF, Divisibility, and Multiples etc.

For lower grade students, we suggest students master the four basic operations even it means for grade one students, and only students master the basics, can they start enjoying the happiness of working on math contest problems.

Below is a collection of problems that can be used to discuss or review the basic math concepts required for preparing math contests.

The basic knowledge test for lower grades 低级数学能力评估

What is the smallest positive integer from 100 and 200 consisting only 1's and 2's? The number is divisible by both 3 and 8.

For a 3-digit number between 100 to 200, the numbers divisible by 8 are
104, 112, 120, 128, 136, `144, 152, 160, 168, 176 184, 192, 200
Which one of the above its sum of digits is a multiple of 3?
120, 144, 168, 192

What is the smallest positive integer consisting only 3's and 2's with at least one of each? The number is divisible by both 3 and 2.

2232

What is the smallest positive 4-digit integer and is divisible by 2, 3, 4, 5, 6, 8, 9, and 10?

The LCM of 2, 3, 4, 5, 6, 8, 9, and 10 = 360
$3 \times 360 = $ **1080**

What is the smallest positive 5-digit integer and is divisible by 8 and 9?

$72 \times 139 = 10008$

43?55 is divisible by 3 and 9. Identify the missing digit.

1

Student's name: _____ Assignment date: _____

617?8 is divisible by 4. Identify all the possible missing digits.

2, 4, 6, 8, 0

How many even numbers are there from 2 to 100 inclusive?

50

From 10000 to 20000 inclusive, how many numbers are divisible by 2, 5, and 10?

$$\frac{20000-10000}{10} = 1000$$

1001

Anna has some marbles. If she counts them by 2's, there is 1 left. If she counts them by 3's, there are 2 left. If she counts them by 4's, there are 3 left. If she counts them by 5's, there are 4 left. How many marbles does Anna have?

Method 1 List some multiples and then find the LCM

Use multiples with remainders to find one common multiple which suits all conditions.

2's with 1 left: 1, 3, 5, 7, 9, ..., all odd numbers.
3's with 2 left: 2, 5, 8, 11, 14, 17, 20, 23, 26, 29, 32, 35, 38, 41, 44, 47, 50, 53, 56, 59, ...
4's with 3 left: 3, 7, 11, 15, 19, 23, 27, 31, 35, 39, 43, 47, 51, 55, 59, ...
5's with 4 left: 4, 9, 14, 19, 24, 29, 34, 39, 44, 49, 54, 59, ...

The common multiple is 60. 60 -1 = **59**

Method 2 Use GCF and LCM

The LCM works for dividing by 2's, 3's, and 4's is 11.
To find the LCM works for dividing by 5's: 12k + 11
When k = 4, the answer is **59**.

Method 3 is to find LCM then subtract 1 = **59**

List the first number greater than 500, which is divisible by 2, 5, and 10.
Explain your strategy. _____　　**510**

If you multiply any whole number by 12, will the product always be divisible by 2, 3, 4, and 6?

Explain why or why not. _____　　**yes**

Ho Math Chess　何数棋谜　英文奥数, 解题策略, 及 IQ 思唯训练宝典
Frank Ho, Amanda Ho © 2020

Student's name: _____ Assignment date: _____

Find LCMs for the following pair of numbers.

Pairs of numbers	LCM	Three other common multiples other than the left LCM
8, 12	24	48, 72, 96
40, 6	120	240, 360, 480
13,2	26	52, 72, 104

Justin wants to buy some green, blue, and red-light bulbs for his holiday tree decoration. Green lights come in a package of 5, blue lights come in a package of 6, and red lights come in a package of 8. What is the lowest number of packages of each colour Justin must buy if he wants to have an equal number of coloured lights to decorate?

The LCM of 5, 6, and 8 is 120, so he must buy 120 light bulbs for each colour.

120 ÷ 5 = 24 green packages
120 ÷ 6 = 20 blue packages
120 ÷ 8 = 15 red packages

Basic 4 operations test for multiple grades 多年级多功能计算题

只见棋谜不见题　劝君迷路不哭涕　数学象棋加谜题　健脑思维眞神奇

You are a chess piece located at c3.

	5		●		▢	
	4	▲	▲	▢	(two ▢)	●
	3		▲	(piece)	▭	
	2	●	○	○	▭	▭
	1		○		●	
		a	b	c	d	e

	(piece)	▢	▭	○	▲
Fraction	$2\frac{2}{5}$	24	$3\frac{2}{3}$	$4\frac{2}{3}$	$5\frac{3}{4}$
decimal	0.0024	0.024	10000	0.0048	0.001
Whole	12	36	45	72	90
%	100	25%	10%	$33\frac{1}{3}\%$	0.05%

Whole number

$\div$ = _____ $\div$ _____ = 3	$\div$ = _____ $\div$ _____ = 6
$\times$ = _____ $\times$ _____ = 540	$\times$ = _____ $\times$ _____ = 1080

Decimal

$\div$ = _____ $\div$ _____ = 10	$\div$ = _____ $\div$ _____ = 2
$\times$ = _____ $\times$ _____ = 24	$\times$ = _____ $\times$ _____ = 0.0000024

The fraction of multiplication and division [Do not need to have the same measuring unit (denominator).]

$\times$ = $24 \times 2\frac{2}{5} = 57\frac{3}{5}$	$\times$ = _____ $\times$ _____ = $8\frac{4}{5}$
$\div$ = $4\frac{2}{3} \div 2\frac{2}{5} = 1\frac{17}{18}$	$\div$ = _____ $\div$ _____ = $2\frac{19}{48}$

Fraction of addition and subtraction [Must have the same measuring unit (denominator).]

$+$ = _____ $+$ _____ = $26\frac{2}{5}$	$+$ = _____ $+$ _____ = $6\frac{1}{15}$
$-$ = _____ $-$ _____ = $2\frac{4}{15}$	$-$ = _____ $-$ _____ = $3\frac{7}{20}$

%

$\times$ = _____ $\times$ _____ = 25	$\times$ = _____ $\times$ _____ = 10
$\div$ = _____ $\div$ _____ = $\frac{1}{300}$	$\div$ = _____ $\div$ _____ = 5

Student's name: _____ Assignment date: _____

Part 2 Problem-solving strategies

Many problem strategies we have mentioned in the previous two publications of Grades 1 and 2, Grades 3 and 4, including the universal problem-solving tool – the Line Segment Diagram are still workable in higher grades. The data types such as decimals or fractions etc. may get more complicated when entering the higher grades.

As you study this workbook, you can see it is impossible to completely divide the math problems into one using just one problem-solving strategy or a problem, which is just a model problem. Often a word problem needs a strategy, and the problem itself is also a model problem. For example, the Sum and Difference problem is a model problem, but it can be easily solved using the Line Segment Diagram strategy.

Changing data types to whole numbers or small numbers 转换数为正整数

Introduction

The first type of data students learned and mastered is the whole number, so if the student could not understand how to work on some problems with different types such large numbers, fractions, or percents etc., one way of teaching is to convert the numbers to small whole numbers or think the numbers as small whole numbers.

Example

How many times is 0.2 of 6?

This mixed data types had lots of students confused about what to do. What happens if we change the above problem as follows?

How many times is 2 of 6?

$$\frac{6}{2} = 3$$

With the above solution in mind, we can figure out the solution to the problem, "*How many times is 0.2 of 6?*" is as follows:

$$\frac{6}{0.2} = 30$$

There are many other examples illustrated in this workbook. Without limiting to the following sections, please see the following for more examples.

The corresponding method in different data types 对应法在不同数型的应用
Give and Take used in different data types 取捨问题应用於不同的数型
Sum and Difference in different data types 不同数性的和差問題

Student's name: _____ Assignment date: _____

Marking or writing intermediate answers on the sentences 一边唸题一边写答案

We can write intermediate answers as we are reading each sentence of a read word problem. This method helps the student develop the mental ability to figure out word problems.

Example 1

Jennifer is twice as old as Thomas. David is three times as old as Jennifer. If Thomas is 15 years old, how old is David?

15 x 2 = 30　　　　　30 x 3 = 90

Jennifer is twice as old as Thomas. David is three times as old as Jennifer. If Thomas is 15 years old, how old is David?

By writing the answer right beside each sentence, we can figure out that David is 90 years old.

Example 2

140 x 3 = 420　　　　　121+19=140

Tyson won three times as many chess games as Harry did. Harry won 19 more games than Frank. Frank had 121 won chess games. How many games did Tyson win?

Problem

Marvin has 13 stamps. Calvin has 3 times as many stamps as Marvin. How many do they have altogether? Method 1: There are 4 times 13, so the answer is 4 x 13 = 52. Method 2: 13 x 3 + 13 = 52
Elvin has $5. Tiger has $23 more than Elvin. Coco has twice as much as Tiger. How much money does Coco have? 　　　　23+5=28　　　　　28 x 2 = 56 Elvin has $5. Tiger has $23 more than Elvin. Cico has twice as much as Tiger. How much money does Cico have? $56

Student's name: _____ Assignment date: _____

Isaac and Maria get $40 from their dad. Isaac gets 4 times as much as Maria. How much does Maria get?

$40 \div 5 = \$8 \ldots$ Maria

Caroline spent $650 on Chinese New Year shopping and food. She spent $269 on clothing and $60 more than the clothing on a computer. How much did she spend on food?

Caroline spent $650 on Chinese New Year shopping. She spent $269 on clothing and $60 more than clothing on a computer. How much did she spend on food?

269 + 60 = 329

650 - 269 - 329 = $52

answer

Mrs. Spring made 47 spring rolls. She gave 5 rolls to each of her students and had 2 rolls left. How many students did she give?

$\frac{47-2}{5} = 9$ students

Adam had $14. Bob had $2 more than Adam. Cathy had $2 less than three times as much as Bob.
How much do three people have altogether?
answer

14 + 2 = 16   16 x 3 - 2 = 46

Adam had $14. Bob has $2 more than Adam. Cathy had $2 less than three times as much as Bob.
How much do three people have altogether?

14 + 16 + 46 = $76

answer

Corresponding method 对应法

The Corresponding Method is to use the resulting Quantity divided by its corresponding value, and we can use it as a universal method to solve word problems before using algebraic equations. But this Corresponding Method shall not be viewed as the only universal method to solve word problems for math contests purpose; instead, other methods such as line segment (bar chart) method or algebraic equations all shall be learned.

Example

1. Melissa spent $\frac{2}{3}$ of her money and had $60 left, how much did she have originally?

   The amount of $60 corresponds to its fraction $\frac{1}{3}$, so the original amount is $60 \div \frac{1}{3} = 180$.

2. Melissa had a 25% discount and paid $60 left; how much was the original price?

   The amount of $60 corresponds to its percent 75%, so the original amount is $60 \div 0.75 = \$80$.

3. In Jennifer's class, there are two girls for every three boys. There are ten girls in Jennifer's class, how many students in total are in Jennifer's class?

   $10 \div \frac{2}{5} = 25$

The *Quantity divided by its corresponding fractional number* method is faster in solving math fraction remaining problems.

Why does it work?

1. Explanation from working backwards of a multiplication operation.

When a piece of datum is changed, it can only have three conditions: enlarged (> before), shrunk (< than before), or the same as before (= as before). For example, if the result (R) is $\frac{3}{2}$ of the original amount then when R $\div \frac{3}{2}$, it performs two arithmetic operations. The first operation is to ÷ 3, then × 2.
The following are two examples.
If paid $30 after 50% price increase, then the original price is _____. $30 \div \frac{3}{2} = \$20$.

If paid $30 after $\frac{1}{3}$ price discount, then the original price is _____. $30 \div \frac{2}{3} = \$45$.

2. Explanation using a line segment diagram

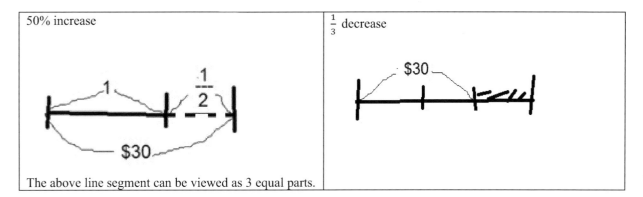

50% increase

$\frac{1}{3}$ decrease

The above line segment can be viewed as 3 equal parts.

The Corresponding Method is very powerful in solving world problems involving fractions. There are a few important concepts we shall be familiar with when using the Corresponding Method. The idea of using the Corresponding Method is to identify two variables: quantities and its corresponding value, but sometimes both are not all that clear to identify. In this case, your job will be to make both quantity and its corresponding value clear and then do the calculation.

Single variable		Quantity	
		clear	unclear
Corresponding values	Clear	Owen bought a hat, and it cost $125 after $33\frac{1}{3}$% discount. What was the original price? $$125 \div \frac{2}{3} = \$187.50$$	Owen bought a hat with $33\frac{1}{3}$% discount. Later He returned it and got $66\frac{2}{3}$% off with $40 returned to him because of the defect. What was the original price? $$40 \div \frac{2}{3} \div (1 - 33\frac{1}{3}\%) = \$90$$
	Unclear		

Two or more variables (System of equations)		Quantity	
		Clear (Looking for a variable that is not changed.)	unclear
Corresponding values	Clear (looking for fractions which have the same standard 1 as a base.)	Owen and David have 120 apples altogether, and Owen has $\frac{2}{3}$ of David. How many apples does each of them have originally? D:O = $1:\frac{2}{3}$ = 3: 2 $\frac{120}{3+2}$ = 24 D=24× 3 = 72 O=24× 2 = 48 Owen has as many apples as $\frac{2}{7}$ of David's. The number of difference between their numbers of apples is 2520. How many apples does each of them have? $\frac{2520}{7-2}$=504 Owen = 504 × 2 = 1008 David = 504 × 7 = 3528	
	Unclear (Transfer fractions with different standard 1's to the same 1.)	Owen has as many apples as $\frac{2}{3}$ of David's. After David sells 1521, then David has $\frac{3}{4}$ of Owen's apples. How many apples does each of them have originally? David's apples are $\frac{3}{2}$ of Owen's apples. $1014÷\left(\frac{3}{2} - \frac{3}{4}\right) = 2028$ … David's $2028 × \frac{2}{3} = 1352$ … Owen's	

1. The corresponding value may not be clear at first.

Example 1

The total length of 3 metal wires is 48 m. The length of the first wire is $\frac{1}{3}$ of the second and the length of the first wire is also $\frac{1}{4}$ of the third. What is the length of each wire?

Arithmetic method

Change the fraction to ratio so we can convert fractions to have the same unit.

The corresponding values have different "Base Values" of unit 1. So, we must change the corresponding values to have the same measuring unit.

$A : B = \frac{1}{3} : 1 = 1 : 3$

$A : C = \frac{1}{4} : 1 = 1 : 4$

$A : B : C = 1 : 3 : 4$

The value of each ratio unit is $\frac{48}{1+3+4} = 6$

A = 6 m, B = 18 m, C = 24 m.

Student's name: _____ Assignment date: _____

Example 2

In Carmen's class. The number of female students is $\frac{4}{9}$ of the entire class and later 6 male students transferred out and the number of female students is now $\frac{1}{2}$ of the entire class. How many students were there in Carmen's class?

The number of female students never changed, so we use it as the corresponding value.

Algebraic method	Arithmetic method
Let the total number of students = x $$\frac{4x}{9} = \frac{x-6}{2}$$ $x = 54$	$\frac{1}{2}$female now $= \frac{4}{9} female\ then$ Female now $= \frac{4}{9} female\ then \times 2 = \frac{8}{9} female\ then$ It means male now $= 1 - \frac{8}{9} female\ then = \frac{1}{9} female\ then$ $6 \div \frac{1}{9} = 54 =$ total students
	Line segment method

The fraction of male student is $1 - \frac{4}{9} = \frac{5}{9}$

$$6 \div \left(\frac{1}{2} - \frac{4}{9}\right) = 50 - 45 = 5$$

Example 3

There are 84 students in class A and class B. The total number of students of $\frac{5}{8}$ of class A and $\frac{3}{4}$ of class, B is 58. How many students in class A and B separately?

Arithmetic method	Algebraic method
	A+B=84 $$\frac{5A}{8} + \frac{3B}{4} = 58$$ A 40, B 44

2. The quantity value may not be clear at first (Looking for some unchanged quantity.).

Example 4

Carmen has 60 students in her class. The number of female students is $\frac{5}{12}$ of the entire class and later some more female students transferred in and the number of female students is $\frac{6}{13}$ of the entire class. How many female students got transferred to?

The number of male students never changed, so we use it as the quantity.
The number of male students = $60 \times \frac{7}{12} = 35$. Later the fraction of its corresponding value changes to $1 - \frac{6}{13} = \frac{7}{13}$ $35 \div \frac{7}{13} = 65$ … The total number of students after more female students got in.
$65 - 60 = $ **5** …. The number of female students got in later.

Practice

Carmen has 45 students in her class. The number of female students is $\frac{4}{9}$ of the entire class and later some more female students transferred in and the number of female students is now $\frac{1}{2}$ of the entire class. How many female students got transferred to?

Algebraic method	Arithmetic method
	The number of male students did not change before and after more female students got in, but its fraction changed. $$45 \times \left(1 - \frac{4}{9}\right) \div \left(1 - \frac{1}{2}\right) - 45 = 50 - 45 = 5$$

Example 5

At the Chinese student camping party, one person used one rice bowl, two persons shared one soup bowl, and three persons shared a salad bowl. If 55 bowls were used all together at the party, how many students were there at the party?

Method 1 – arithmetic

$$55 \div \left(1 + \frac{1}{2} + \frac{1}{3}\right) = 30 \ (student)$$

Method 2 – algebra

Let x be the number of persons.

$$\frac{x}{1} + \frac{x}{2} + \frac{x}{3} = 55$$
$$x = 30$$

Method 3 – LCM

$[1, 2, 3] = 6$ people …. Per table
The number of bowls per table is $\frac{6}{1} + \frac{6}{2} + \frac{6}{3} = 11$ (bowls)
The total number of desks $= \frac{55}{11} = 5$
Total number o people $= 5 \times 6 = 30$

3. Transfer fractions to shares

We do not really want to work with fractions, so if we can transfer fraction word problems to whole numbers, then we should do so.

Example 6

The female students are $\frac{4}{5}$ of the number of male students in a school, and there are 525 more male students than female students. How many male and female students are there separately?

The corresponding method in different data types 对应法在不同数型的应用

Problems	Whole number	fraction	%	ratio
The fraction has 1 and % has 100% as the assumed original amount or whole. How to get back the original amount? **For percent,** partial quantity ÷ % = original quantity **For multiple,** new amount ÷ multiple = old amount **For difference** new amount ÷ multiple difference= old amount **For sum** new amount ÷ multiple sum= old amount **For a remaining fraction, %, the ratio** new amount ÷ remaining fractional number = old amount	Jocelyn has triple as many white blocks as black blocks. The number of red blocks is four more than the number of white blocks. There are 15 white blocks, how many blocks of each colour are there? W=15 R=19 B=5 Decimal Jocelyn bought an ice cream cone for $2.50 and spent double that amount on lunch, and she then spent $2.50 playing games. If she had $4.95 left, how much did she have in the beginning? $14.95	Adam ate $\frac{2}{5}$ of his apples, and he had 36 apples left. How many apples did he have in the beginning? $36 \div \frac{3}{5} = 60$ Adam had $\frac{2}{3}$ more apples than Bob, but if Adam gave 150 apples to Bob, then they each had an equal number of apples. How many apples did each of them have in the beginning? $300 \div \frac{2}{3} = 450$. Adam $450 - 300 = 150$. Bob B=450, A=750 On Monday, Adam sold 10 more than half of all his apples. On Tuesday, he sold 20 more than half of the remaining apples, and there were 90 apples left. How many apples did he have at the start of Monday? Use the line segment Diagram. 90+20=110 110× 2=220 220+10=230 230×2=**460**	Bob ate 35% of his apples, and he had 260 apples left. How many apples did he have in the beginning? 260÷0.65=400 Adam's apples are 5 more than three times of Bob's apples. Together they had 169 apples together. How many apples did each of them have in the beginning? 169-5=164 164÷ 4=41. Bob Adam 41× 3+5=128 After a 20% sales tax, Steven bought his Notebook for $139. What was the original price? 139÷1.2=115.83 Use fraction. 139 corresponds to 120%. $\frac{139}{120} \times 100 = 115.83$	The ratio of seated to unseated seats in a classroom is 3:2. (There were 3 seated seats to 2 unseated seats in a classroom.) There were 24 unseated seats in the classroom, how many seats were seated in the classroom? $\frac{seated}{unseated} = \frac{3}{2} = \frac{36}{24}$ 36 There are 15 more girls than boys in Jim's class, and the ratio of the number of girls to the number of boys is Jim's class is 5 to 2. How many boys and how many girls in Jim's class? 15 corresponds to 5 – 2 = 3 units Each ratio unit is 5. Girl = 5 × 5 = **25** Boy = 5 × 2 = **10**

Example

Gina sold $\frac{1}{3}$ of her apples and then sold $\frac{2}{5}$ of her remaining apples. Later, she sold $\frac{1}{4}$ of the remaining apples, she had 120 apples left.

Note that there are 3 remaining quantities.
1st sold $\frac{1}{3}$
2nd $\frac{2}{5}$ of the remaining 1st.
3rd $\frac{1}{4}$ of the remaining 2nd.

Method 1 Work backward in steps

$120 \div \frac{3}{4} = 160$ which is the amount of 4 parts (denominator) $(120 \div 3 \times 4 = 160)$
$160 \div \frac{3}{5} = 160 \times \frac{5}{3} = \frac{800}{3}$ **(Do not convert to decimal since it is not divisible.)** $(160 \div 3 \times 8 = \frac{800}{3})$
$\frac{800}{3} \div \frac{2}{3} = 400$

Method 2 Use one division statement

$120 \div \frac{3}{4} \div \frac{3}{5} \div \frac{2}{3} = 400$

By using the above division method, then we can get the answer easily.

Problem

1	On the first day of harvesting apples, Adam picked two-fifths of his apples. On the second day, he harvested half of the apples that were left. On the third day, he harvested the remaining 150 apples. How many total apples did he harvest? 300+200 =500 500 apples.
2	Bob spent half of his money at the grocery store. He then spent half of what was left at the mall. Of the remainder, he spent half at the gift shop. He had \$13 left. How much money did he start with? \$13 × 2 × 2 × 2= 104 One remaining one division, so if there are 3 remaining, then there will be 3 divisions.

Example

Customer 1 bought 1 more than $\frac{1}{2}$ of all Adam's apples. Customer 2 bought 1 more than $\frac{1}{2}$ of all Adam's remaining apples. Customer 3 bought 1 more than $\frac{1}{2}$ of all Adam's remaining apples. Customer 4 bought 1 more than $\frac{1}{2}$ of all Adam's remaining apples. Customer 5 bought 1 more than $\frac{1}{2}$ of all Adam's remaining apples. Customer 6 bought only the remaining apple. How many apples did Adam have in the beginning?

	Apples left	Apples before bought
Customer 6	0	1
Customer 5	$1 = \square - \frac{\square}{2} - 1$	$\square = 4$
Customer 4	$4 = \frac{\square}{2} - 1$	10
Customer 3	$10 = \frac{\square}{2} - 1$	22
Customer 2	$22 = \frac{\square}{2} - 1$	46
Customer 1	$46 = \frac{\square}{2} - 1$	94

Example

Adam gives Bob as many apples as Bob has, then Bob gives Adam as many apples as Adam has. in the end, each has 32 apples. How many apples did each have at the beginning?

	Adam	Bob
Apples at end	32	32
Previous round	16	48
Apples at start	40	24

Problem

Adam gives Bob and Cathy as many apples as each already has, then Bob gives Adam and Cathy as many apples as each of them has. Finally, Cathy gives as many apples as each has. In the end, each has 32 apples, how many apples did each have at the beginning?

	Adam	Bob	Cathy
Apples at end	32	32	32
Previous round	16	16	64
Previous round	8	56	32
Apples at start	52	28	16

On Monday, Adam gave Bob twice as many candies as Bob already had. On Tuesday, Cathy gave Bob as many as $\frac{1}{3}$ of Bob's. On Wednesday, Bob gave Cathy as many candies as Cathy already had. In the end, each person had 48 candies. How many candies did each have at the start of Monday?

	Adam	Bob	Cathy
At end	48	48	48
Wed	48	72	24
Tue	48	54	42
Mon	84	18	42

Example

Most of the time, problems can be solved by using work backwards or forward, but can you solve the following problem by using work forward?

A basket has 15% of rotten apples. Of the rotten apples, $\frac{2}{3}$ were golden delicious, and the remaining 8 were Macintosh. How many apples were not rotten?

Work forward

$0.15 - 0.15 \times \frac{2}{3} = 0.15 - 0.1 = 0.05$
$8 \div 0.05 = 800 \div 5 = 160$ ......total apples
$160 \times 0.85 = 136$ .... not rotten apples

Work backwards

$8 \times 3 \div 0.15 = 160$
$160 - 24 = 136$

Problem

Mandy paid \$57.50 for a skirt with a tax of 15%. What is the price of the skirt before tax?

$57.5 \div 1.15 = \$50$

At a party, there were 224 guests left after $\frac{3}{4}$ guests had left. How many guests were at the party in the beginning?

$224 \div \frac{1}{4} = 896$

After finishing 224 days of work, William still has $\frac{5}{9}$ of work needs to be finished. How many days does William originally plan to finish all his work?

$224 \times \frac{9}{4} = 504$

At a party, there were 273 more children than adults. $\frac{1}{5}$ of guests were adults. How many were children?

$273 \div \left(\frac{1}{4} - \frac{1}{5}\right) = 455$
$455 \times \frac{4}{5} = 364$

At a party, there were 320 more children than adults $\frac{2}{5}$ of guests were adults. How many were children?

$320 \div \left(\frac{3}{5} - \frac{2}{5}\right) = 1600$
$1600 \times \frac{3}{5} = 960$

$\frac{3}{4}$ of all the guests had left the party. How many guests were at the party in the beginning if there were still 24 guests left in the party?

$24 \div \frac{1}{4} = 96$

Jaden now weighs as $\frac{6}{7}$ of his last year's weight, but if he gains 5 kg more than last year, Jaden will weigh as much as his last year's weight. How much did he weigh last year, and how much did he weigh now?

$5 \div \frac{1}{7} = 35$ kg ...... last year

$5 \times \frac{6}{7} = 30$ .... this year

Student's name: _____ Assignment date: _____

Horizontal computation vs. vertical computation 横向及垂直计算

Students at a day school math curriculum normally spend the first 4 years to work on horizontal way of computation such as mixed addition, subtraction, multiplication, or division so most students would think when doing math, it is just calculated in a way from left to right especially with the idea of order of operations being taught to do it that way. However, the most powerful way to solve computational problems is to do it vertically and horizontally at the same time in a fractional way simply because a fraction involves multiplication and division itself. This situation is more evident when students learn rational computation in high schools. Students must master the skills of computing fractions.

Example 1

Evaluate $17 \times 3 + 17 \times 7$

Example 2

Evaluate $19 \times 21 - 19 \times 19$

Example 3

Evaluate $23 \times 21 \div 46 - 23 \times 19 \div 46$

Example 4

Evaluate $23 \div 21 \times 42 - 41 \times 19 \div 82$

Line Segment Diagram – universal problem-solving method 线段图 – 万能解法

What is a Line Segment?

A straight line without two arrows at two ends is called a Line Segment.

How many straights lines (line segments) intersecting at one point are there in the following diagram?

For example, the following diagram has 2 straight lines.

How many straights lines are in the following diagram?

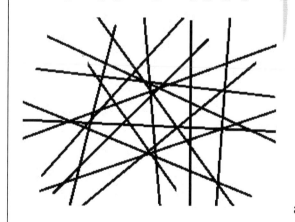

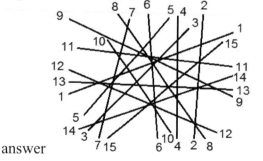

answer

The above diagram has _____ straight lines.   15

Multiplying and dividing by 10's power			
1 × 10 =	1.234 × 100 =	1 ÷ 10 =	12.34 ÷ 100 =
1 × 0.1 =	12.34 × 0.1 =	1 ÷ 0.1 =	12.34 ÷ 0.01 =

10,   123.4   0.1,   0.1234
0.1,   1.234   10,   1234

Line Segment Diagram review 线段图基夲複習

means to take away.

means to add.

30 ├ –19 ─┤ ├ 21 ▨ ├ = ?,

The answer is _____ . 28 = 30 + 19 - 21

****

42 ├─ 28 ▨ ─┤ then 2 of ├ –19 ─┤
=
?
The answer is _____ . 52 = 42 – 28 + 38

****

Look at the following line segment diagram and figure out what is the value of ▢ ? 35

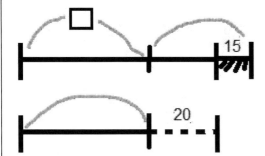

If I put in $34 into my piggy bank then my piggy bank would have doubled the amount I put in, how much do I have in my piggy bank originally?

34

****

If I take out $17 out of my piggy bank then my piggy bank would have $36 less than twice as much as I originally had, how much do I have in my piggy bank originally?
$19

(Hint: Draw line segment diagram backwards according to the above result and then figure out the answer from the line segment diagram.)

Step 1.
Draw the line segment diagram

Step 2.
Figure out the answer by looking at the line segment diagram.

The algebra method is easier.

ABCD line segment ABCD 线段

One type of problems appeared in Kangaroo Math Contest got our interest is as follows:

Points A, B, C, D are marked on the straight line in some order. It is known that AB = 13, BC = 11, CD = 14 and DA = 12. What is the difference between the farthest two points?

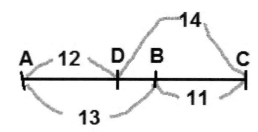

24

This problem only requires students to possess addition and subtraction ability. Further, students need the ability of visualization and can adjust line segment points to meet the requirement of line segment lengths. The line segment problem does not allow students to have an advantage of pre-acquired knowledge to get the answers, but a lot of thinking skills. We like this type of problem.

The way to solve is to find the largest line segment, to begin with.

The universal word problem solver – Line Segment Diagram 用线段图解数学文字题

In the US and Canada elementary math teaching, there is no universal problem-solving method offered. In China, there is a universal problem-solving method, and it is called the Line Segment Diagram method (线段图), which s a good way to solve many math word problems before students can use algebra. This method is most helpful in solving fraction remaining word problems and in some cases, it is much easier than using algebra. The Line Segment Diagram method is to use line segments to represent the relationship of equation or equations to find answers. The Line Segment Diagram method is often used in solving the Sum and Difference problem and its variations, and fractions with remainders.

Some readers may wonder if we have a universal method that is the Line Segment Method, then do we still need the Algebraic method, or why not just learn algebra as the universal method instead of introducing the Line Segment Method? The answer is we need both methods. The reason is as follows.

Is the algebraic method always easier than the arithmetic method? 代数解永比算術好吗?

From the following computation comparison, we can see clearly that the algebraic method is not always easier than arithmetic to get the answer, especially when the work backward strategy is used.

Example 1

Together, Tom and Jerry have 76 marbles. Tom gives half of his marbles to Jerry and then 14 more marbles. At this moment, Jerry then has three times as many marbles as Tom has. How many marbles did Jerry have originally?

Method 1- an arithmetic method using T table
The total 76 was never changed so $\frac{76}{4} = 19$.

Tom	Jerry
19	57
76 - 43 = 33	43 = 57 - 14
66	10

Jerry originally had 10.

Method 2 - algebraic method
$$3\left(x - \frac{x}{2} - 12\right) = 76 - x + \frac{x}{2} + 14$$
$$x = 10$$

Example 2

The cats Kiko and have an equal number of cans. If Kiko gives 7 cans to Snow, then Snow will have twice as many cans as Kiko's cans. How many cans does Kiko have?

Method 1 – logical thinking

Read the question in reverse. It means if Kiko does not give 7 cans to Snow, then they have an equal number of cans. If Kiko all together 7 cans to Snow, then the difference will be 14 because they had an equal number of cans. At this time, Snow has twice as many as Kiko's cans. So, we know the number of "one time" is 14. So Kiko originally has $14 + 7 = 21$ cans.
For the majority of students, it is difficult to understand the above method.

Method 2 – Line Segment diagram

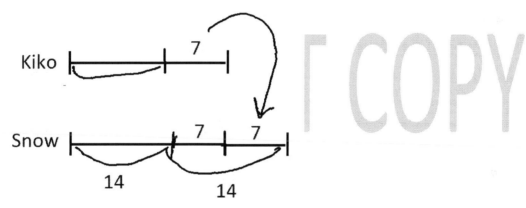

From the above Line Segment Diagram, we know Kiko originally has 14 cans.

Method 3 – Algebraic method

Since Kiko and Snow, each has the same number of cans, so there is only one variable,

$2(K - 7) = K + 7$
$K = 21$

Work backwards 倒算法(还原问题, 逆退问题)

Introduction

If students can learn only one problem-solving strategy, then we would suggest the strategy of working backwards. The simple reason is students learn to work backwards even in learning computation but without realizing it. For example, a kindergarten problem such as the following:

If $5 - 2 = 3$ then find out the number to replace the box with the following problem

$$\boxed{} - 2 = 3$$

Some students can find the answer by intuition because they already possess the mental math ability but the strategy to work out the problem is simply to work backwards. When students are in higher grades, then they are using the work backward method all the time without realizing it, and this happens even when they are doing computation work purely. The following examples demonstrate that students are doing the reverse of their times table calculations by reducing fractions.

$$\frac{10}{25} \times \frac{18}{20}$$
$$\frac{2 \times 3 \times 7}{5 \times 4 \times 6} \times \frac{18}{20}$$
$$\frac{2 \times 3 \times 25}{5 \times 4 \times 9}$$

By working backwards, students develop the ability to "seeing ahead" to get an answer. Students also develop their ability of "reverse thinking" in math to be able to find the original value.

One equation problem

Students should get used to the idea of working backwards in such a way that it is just like working forward other than reversing the operations. To work backwards on word problems is more than just reversing the operation sign.

One of the most and effective strategies for solving word problems is to work backwards. The "work backwards" method is most effective in solving some problems in fractions, percents, or ratios; the reason is some problems can be solved easily using work backwards.

Example 1

To get the whole (or original amount), we can use the reversing method or work backwards.

1. Through multiple to get the original amount.

Triple me and get 39. What am I? _____ 13

2. Through difference to get the original amount.

Double me and subtract 13 to get 13. What am I? _____ 13

3. In sum, to get the original amount.

Double me and add 13 to get 13. What am I? _____ 0

4. Through partial (discount or price increase) to get the original amount.

Halve me and subtract 13 to get 26. What am I? _____ 78

Student's name: _____ Assignment date: _____

Order of operations in the following examples do not apply.

Example 2

$$\square - 4, + 12, \div 7, \times 5 = 120, \text{ what is } \square ?$$

160

$120 \div 5 \times 7 - 12 + 4 = 160$

Example 3

$$4 + \square, + 4, \div 3, \div \frac{1}{5} = 120 \qquad\qquad 64$$

Example 4

Replace each letter with a number. Can you find all the answers?

$$\begin{array}{r} 1\ A\ 2 \\ -\ \ A\ 8 \\ \hline 9\ 4 \end{array}$$

Answer: A can be 0, 1, 2, 3, 4, 5, 6, 7,8, 9

Example 4

$$10 \times \square, \div 8, + 16 = 32 \qquad\qquad 12.8$$

Student's name: _____ Assignment date: _____

Two or more equations problem

Example 5

Adam and Bob together had 108 apples, and if Adam gave Bob 6 apples, then each of them had the same number of apples. How many apples did each one of them have in the beginning?

Work backwards	Sum and Difference
$\dfrac{108}{2} = 54$ Adam = 54+6=60 Bob = 54 – 6=48	A+B= 108 A – B = 12 $\dfrac{108+12}{2}$=60 108 – 60=48

Example 6

Adam and Bob together had 216 apples, and if Adam gave Bob 23 apples, then Adam still had 4 apples more than Bob. How many apples did each of them have in the beginning?

Work backwards	Sum and Difference
$\dfrac{216-4}{2} = 106$ Adam: 106 + 23 + 4= 133 (Think $\square$ – 23 –4 = 106) Bob: 216 – 133 = 83	Method 1 A+B= 216 A – B = 50 (23+23+4=50) 2A=266, A=133 B=216 – 133=83 Method 2 $\dfrac{216 + 46}{2} = 131, 131 + 2$ =133 $\dfrac{216 - 46}{2} = 85, 85 - 2$ =83

Example 7

Adam, Bob, and Cathy had 72 apples together. If Adam gave Bob 10 apples and Bob gave 8 apples to Cathy, then all of them had the same number of apples. How many apples did each of them have in the beginning?

$$\frac{72}{3} = 24$$

Adam 24 + 10 = 34
Bob 24 + 8 − 10 = 22
Cathy 24 − 8 = 16

Example 8

Adam had 3 times as many as apples as Bob. Cathy had 3 more apples than Adam after Adam ate 5. Cathy had 10 apples, how many apples did Bob have at the beginning?

4

Example 9

Adam, Bob, and Cathy exchanged their stamps. Adam gave Bob and Cathy every 7 stamps, Bob gave Adam and Cathy every 10 stamps, Cathy gave Adam and Bob every 11 stamps, then each ended up with 32 stamps. How many stamps did each of them have in the beginning?

Work backwards by using a table.

A	B	C
32	32	32
46	25	25
36	45	15
25	34	37

answer

Adam had 25 stamps, Bob had 34, and Cathy had 37.

Student's name: _____ Assignment date: _____

Adam, Bob, and Cathy exchanged their stamps. Adam gave Bob and Cathy every 7 stamps, Bob gave Adam and Cathy every 10 stamps, Cathy gave Adam and Bob every 11 stamps, then each ended up with 24 stamps. How many stamps did each of them have in the beginning?

Work backwards by using a table.

	A	B	C
distribution 1	17	26	29
distribution 2	3	33	36
distribution 3	13	13	46
result	24	24	24

answer

Adam had 17 stamps, Bob had 26, and Cathy had 29.

Adam, Bob, and Cathy exchanged their stamps. Adam gave Bob and Cathy every 11 stamps, Bob gave Adam and Cathy every 5 stamps, Cathy gave Adam and Bob every 10 stamps, then each ended up with 32 stamps. How many stamps did each of them have in the beginning?

Work backwards by using a table.

	A	B	C
distribution 1	39	21	36
distribution 2	17	32	47
distribution 3	22	22	52
result	32	32	32

answer

Adam had 39 stamps, Bob had 21, and Cathy had 36.

Work Backward Problem

Mabel spent some money. On the first day, she spent one-third of her money. On the second day, she got $6 from her mom. On the third day, she got the same amount from her mom again and then she had $24 left. How much did Mabel have in the beginning?

$18

What number belongs in the START circle?

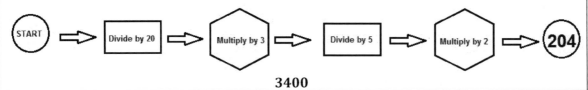

3400

Jasmin read the book at the speed of doubling every week. On week 6, she read 256 pages. How many pages did she read in week 1?

8 pages

When a ball is dropped from the top of a building, it bounces back to a new height that is half the height it last fell. If its fifth bounce is 1.5 m high, from what beginning height was it dropped?

48 m

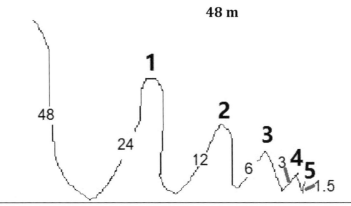

Mysterious work forward and backward problem 神秘的向前算法及倒算法

Problem 1

A turtle crawls up a 12-m hill after a heavy rainstorm. The turtle crawls 3 m but slides back $1\frac{1}{2}$ m when it stops to rest. How many tries does the turtle make before it reaches the top of the hill?

$12 - 3 = 9$ to reach 9 m

$$\frac{9}{3-1\frac{1}{2}} = \textbf{6 tries}$$

7th try reaches the top $9 + 3 = 12$ m.

Problem 2

A turtle crawls up a hill after a heavy rainstorm. The turtle crawls 3 m but slides back $1\frac{1}{2}$ m when it stops to rest. It takes the turtle 6 tries to reach the top of the hill. How tall is the hill?

$(3 - 1\frac{1}{2}) \times 5 = 7.5$
The hill is $7.5 + 3 = 10.5$ m.

Are the heights of hills different in problem 1 and problem 2?
The first problem takes 7 times, but the second time takes 6 tries.

How is this problem different from the still water and current water travelling problem?
The water problem has a continuous motion of current while travelling upstream or downstream. The turtle crawling problem does not have the continuous motion of the current.

Fill in value in ☐.

$$\boxed{} + 4 + 8 + 12 + 16 + 20 - 3 - 7 - 11 - 15 - 19 = 0$$
5

I jumped 3 times every 20 minutes. You jumped 5 times every 15 minutes. Together we jumped ___ times every 60 minutes.
29

$$\bigcirc + \bigcirc = \triangle$$

$$\triangle - 4 = \bigcirc + 4$$

Triangle = 16, circle = 8

Fill in each box with digit from 1 to 9, the same shape of box has the same number. There are 5 answers. Answers may vary.

$$22 = \bigcirc + \bigcirc + \triangle + \triangle = 1\square + 1\square \quad = 5 + 5 + 6 + 6$$

$$26 = \bigcirc + \bigcirc + \triangle + \triangle = 1\square + 1\square \quad = 6 + 6 + 7 + 7$$

$$30 = \bigcirc + \bigcirc + \triangle + \triangle = 1\square + 1\square \quad = 7 + 7 + 8 + 8$$

$$34 = \bigcirc + \bigcirc + \triangle + \triangle = 1\square + 1\square \quad = 8 + 8 + 9 + 9$$

Problem

Forward and backward thinking 前算及倒算思路

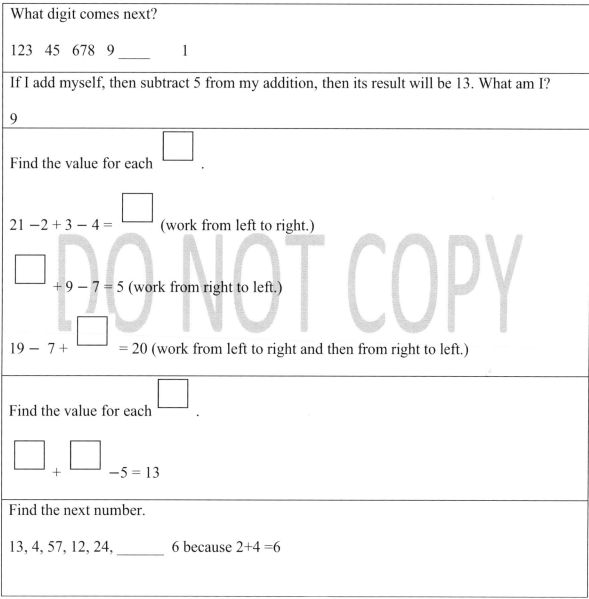

What digit comes next?

123　45　678　9 _____　　　1

If I add myself, then subtract 5 from my addition, then its result will be 13. What am I?

9

Find the value for each ☐ .

$21 - 2 + 3 - 4 = $ ☐ (work from left to right.)

☐ $+ 9 - 7 = 5$ (work from right to left.)

$19 - 7 + $ ☐ $= 20$ (work from left to right and then from right to left.)

Find the value for each ☐ .

☐ $+$ ☐ $- 5 = 13$

Find the next number.

13, 4, 57, 12, 24, _____　6 because 2+4 =6

Find the next two numbers.

02 46 81 01 21 41 ____ _____ 61 82

0246810121416182
02 46 81 01 21 41 61 82

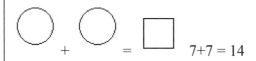

+ = 7+7 = 14

+ 8 = 22 14

If I add myself and then add 8, I will get 32. What number am I?

12

Kevin sold one of his baseboard cards to Henry, making a profit of $3. Henry sold it to Cleo and lost $3. Cleo sold it to Sam for $21 by making a profit of $4. How much did Kevin pay for his baseboard card?

Henry
21 - 4 + 3 - 3 = 17

21 − 4 = Cleo bought
answer

Kevin paid $17.

Student's name: _____ Assignment date: _____

Work forward first then backwards

Andy was counting birds in the Nature Park, and he noticed that there were 125 birds on three trees. While he was watching, 7 birds flew away from the first tree, 11 birds flew back to the second tree, and 15 birds flew away from the third tree. At this moment, he saw that the number of birds on each tree was the same. How many birds were there on the first tree in the beginning?

$125 - 7 + 11 - 15 = 114$, $\frac{114}{3} = 38$ There are 38 birds on each tree equally. $38 + 7 = $ **45**.

Tree A: $39 + 7 = 45$
Tree B: $38 - 11 = 27$
Tree c: $38 + 15 = 53$

Justin had a whole number. If Justin multiplied his number by either 5 or 4, subtracted by either 7 or 9, and finally divided by 7 or 9, the result was 63. What was Justin's number?

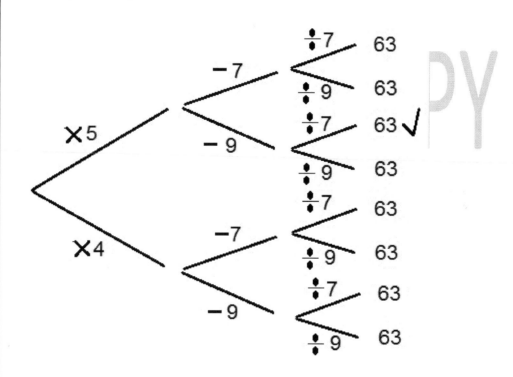

Work backwards using 63 on each path from the above tree structure and the answer is 90.

Student's name: _____ Assignment date: _____

Sold $\frac{1}{3}$ of apples, and there were 24 apples left. How many were in the beginning?

Sold $\frac{2}{3}$ of apples, and there were 54 apples left. How many were in the beginning?

Sold $\frac{2}{5}$ of apples, and there were 54 apples left. How many were in the beginning?

Sold $\frac{1}{3}$ of apples and then sold $\frac{3}{4}$ of the remaining, there were 24 apples left. How many were in the beginning?

What % of 125 is 62.5? 62.5 ÷ 125=50%

30% of what number is 18?
18 ÷ 0.3=60

Find the ?

Regular price	$28	? $16.95	$125	? $120	$885	? $38.65
% discount	? 25%	20%	? 20%	%15	15%	
Discount			$25	$18		$16.50
PST (tax)					6%	$1.58
GST (tax)					5%	$1.42
PST rate						? 7.13%
Sale price	$21	$13.56	? $100	? $112	? $752.25	$25.15

How much is interest earned after 4 years of $700 invested at a 12.5% simple annual rate?
700 × 0.125 × 4=$350

Math Contest Preparation, Problem Solving Strategies, and Math IQ Puzzles for Grades 3 and 4
Ho Math Chess　　　何数棋谜　　英文奥数, 解题策略, 及 IQ 思唯训练宝典
Frank Ho, Amanda Ho © 2020　　　　　　　All rights reserved.

Student's name: _____ Assignment date: _____

Finding the original number using backwards work method 倒算法找原数

Some geese were walking in the park. Now 7 of them flew away and later, 5 geese came back. At that moment, 21 geese were walking in the park. How many geese were there at the very beginning?

23

☐ - 7 + 5 = 21

Twenty-three geese were walking in the park. Now, some of them flew away and later, 7 geese came back. At that moment, 15 geese were walking in the park. How many geese flew away? **15**

Work backwards	Work forward
15-7=8	23 + 7 =30
23-8=15	30 − 15 = 15

Some geese were walking in the park. Now 9 of them flew down and joined the group. Later, 4 of them flew away. At that moment, 21 geese were walking in the park. How many geese were there at the very beginning?

17+9-4=21

21+4-9=16

16

The following is a 5 by 5 multiplication table. The products obtained by multiplying the vertical line number on the left by the horizontal line number at the top. For example, 4 × 8 = 32. Find the number for each empty cell.

				8
			6	
	28	7		
			4	
			10	
4	20			32

	1	4	5	1	2	8
1	1	4	5	1	2	
3	3	12	15	3		24
7	7		35		14	56
2	2	8	10	2		16
5	5	20	25	5		40
4		16			4	8

Half of Alex's age added by 3 and its result subtracted by 2 will be equal to Naomi's age subtracted by 7. Naomi is now 20 years old. How old is Alex?

14 years old, use work backwards method $\frac{A}{2} + 3 - 2 = 20 - 7 = 13$

Combination problems 组合题

Using multiplication to solve Combination problems 以乘法解组合题

Combination with different conditions 一对多, 多对多組合

1. **One condition to many conditions problem**

   Jessica has 3 different colours of hats, and she wears one style of uniform every day. How many different outfits can she have when she wears a uniform and hats?

   3

2. **Many conditions to many conditions problem**

   Jessica has 3 different colours of hats and three different styles of uniforms. She wears a uniform every day. How many different outfits can she have when she wears a uniform and hats?

   9

Student's name: _____ Assignment date: _____

Rain decides to order 1 sandwich and 1 drink from the menu. How many different meals can he order from this menu?

Menu

Sandwiches	Drinks
Beef	Tea
Chicken	Juice
Turkey	Milk

9

Meghan bought one of each item in the following menu. What was the total cost of what she could have ordered?

Menu

Sandwiches		Drinks	
Beef	$5.15	Tea	$1.25
Chicken	$4.50	Juice	$1.15
Turkey	$6.75	Milk	$0.95

5.15+4.5+6.75+1.25+1.15+0.95 = $19.75

Using addition and table to solve Combination problems 以加法或表解组合题

Fernando had some coins in 4 cents, 8 cents, and 12 cents. What are all the ways that he could make exactly 40 cents?

13ways

In the order of 4, 8, and 12 cents. 103, 212, 022, 402, 131, 321, 511, 701, 050, 430, 620, 810, 10 0 0

Balls are thrown at the target. What are the ways that you could score exactly 20?

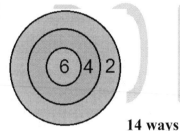

14 ways

In the order of 6, 4, and 2 cents: 301, 220, 212, 204, 131, 123, 115, 107, 050, 042, 034, 026, 018, 00 10

Elise got a total of 24 scores with target scores of 2 and 4 (no target 6). Show all the ways Elise could throw her balls if she threw at targets 2 and 4 each at least two times.

2	4
6	3
8	2
10	1

3   answer

Elise got a total of 32 scores with target scores of 4 and 6 (no target 2). Show all the ways Elise could throw her balls if she threw at targets 4 and 6 each at least two times.
2 times. 2 of 4 + 4 of 6, 5 of 4 + 2 of 6

Using the list to solve Combination problems 以列舉法解组合题

Caroline buys ice cream cones with one flavour on each ice cream. The available flavours are as follows:

- Strawberry
- Chocolate
- Vanilla
- Cherry
- Mango

How many ways can she buy?

5

Caroline buys one ice cream cone with two different flavours on each ice cream. The available flavours are as follows:

- Strawberry
- Chocolate
- Vanilla
- Cherry
- Mango

$$_5C_2 = \frac{5 \times 4}{2} = \mathbf{10}$$

How many ways can she buy if the order of flavours (top or bottom) on each ice cream does not matter?

- Strawberry
- Chocolate
- Vanilla
- Cherry
- Mango

10 = 4+3+2+1

Caroline buys a pizza with the choices of 3 toppings, 2 toppings, 1 topping, or no topping. The choices of toppings are as follows:

- Pepperoni
- Pineapple
- Ham

How many ways can she buy a pizza?

8 (0, 1, 2, 3, 12, 13, 23, 123)

What could be the 2-digit numbers if the sum of each 2-digit number is 3?

30, 12, 21

Emily bought three rubber bracelets with the following prices:

- Small bracelets cost 24 ¢.
- Large bracelets cost 36 ¢.

Show all the different amounts Emily could have bought. **4 $1.08, $0.96, $0.84, $0.72**

How much is a glass of milk? **C**

A. 2 mL
B. 20 mL
C. 200 mL
D. 2000 mL

Box method for nCr Combination problem 盒子法解 nCr 組合問題

The day school math also asks students to use the combination to list possible numbers by giving digits but rarely ask students to find their sum.

The following table gives a contrast to the school math and math contest problem.

Day School Math Problem	Kangaroo Math Contest problem
There are 3 digits 1, 2, and 3 written on three cards. Jocelyn picks up one card each time to make a three-digit house number. How many house numbers can she make?	There are 3 digits 1, 2, and 3 written on three cards. Jocelyn picks up one card each time to make a three-digit house number, no digit can be repeated. How many house numbers can she make? What is the sum of all these numbers? 6 house numbers. The total sum is 1332.
The list can be as follows: 123, 132, 213, 231, 312, 321 Students should list numbers in ascending order with the rightmost digit changes faster. The List Method is suitable for lower grades.	Here we introduce **Box Method,** so students can get the answer much quicker than the List method. `3` `2` `1`

nCr with no repeating digits 無重複数字

Condition	There are n distinct digits with no 0's and no repeating digits. For example There are 3 digits 1, 2, and 3.	There are n distinct digits with no 0's and no repeating digits. For example There are 3 digits 1, 2, and 3.
Problem	**nCn with no repetitions** **Create 3-digit numbers using digits 1, 2, and 3 with no repetitions. How many numbers can be created?**	nCr with no repetitions (r<n) **Create 2-digit numbers using digits 1, 2, and 3 with no repetitions. How many numbers can be created?**
Solution	Method 1 Factorial 3! Method 2 Box method **3 2 1** $3 \times 2 \times 1 = 6$ Method 3 List Method List them all. 123 132 213 231 312 321	Method 1 Box method **3 2** Method 2 List Method List them all. 12 13 21 23 31 32

nCr with no repeating digits

Condition	There are distinct digits with no 0's and no repeating digits. For example There are 3 digits 1, 2, and 3.	There are distinct digits with no 0's and no repeating digits. For example There are 3 digits 1, 2, and 3.
Problem	**nCn with repetitions** **Create 3-digit numbers using digits 1, 2, and 3 with repetitions. How many numbers can be created?**	**nCr with repetitions (r<n)** **Create 2-digit numbers using digits 1, 2, and 3 with repetitions. How many numbers can be created?**
Solution	Method 1 Box method Method 3 List them all.	Method 1 Box method Method 2 List them all.

Student's name: _____ Assignment date: _____

nCr with 0's but no repeating digits 有 0 無重複数字

Condition	**There are distinct digits with 0's and no repeating numbers.** For example There are 3 digits 0, 1, and 2.	**There are distinct digits with 0's and no repeating numbers.** For example There are 3 digits 0, 1, and 2.
Problem 1	**nCn with repetitions** **Create 3-digit numbers using digits 0, 1, and 2 with repetitions. How many numbers can be created?**	**nCr with repetitions (r<n)** **Create 2-digit numbers using digits 0, 1, and 2 with repetitions. How many numbers can be created?**
Solution	With 0 as one of the digits, then it is easier for students just to use the list method to list them all. List method	Box method
Problem 2	nCn with no repetitions Create 3-digit numbers using digits 0, 1, and 2 with repetitions. How many numbers can be created? Box method	nCr with no repetitions (r<n) Create 2-digit numbers using digits 0, 1, and 2 with no repetitions. How many numbers can be created? Box method

Student's name: _____ Assignment date: _____

nCr with 0's and repeating digits 有 0 有重複数字

Condition	There are distinct digits with 0's and repeating digits. For example There are 4 digits 0, 1, 1, and 2.	There are distinct digits with 0's and repeating digits. For example There are 4 digits 0, 1, 1, and 2.
Problem 1	nCn with repetitions Create 4-digit numbers using digits 0, 1, 1, and 2 with repetitions. How many numbers can be created?	nCr with repetitions (r<n) Create 2-digit numbers using digits 0, 1, 1, and 2 with repetitions. How many numbers can be created?
Solution	Box method $\boxed{3}\ \boxed{4}\ \boxed{4}\ \boxed{4}$ $3 \times 4 \times 4 \times 4 = 192$	Box method
Problem 2	nCn with no repetitions Create 4-digit numbers using digits 0, 1, 1, and 2 with no repetitions. How many numbers can be created? Box method $\boxed{3}\ \boxed{3}\ \boxed{2}\ \boxed{1}$ $3 \times 3 \times 2 \times 1 = 18$	nCr with no repetitions (r<n) Create 4-digit numbers using digits 0, 1, 1, and 2 with no repetitions. How many numbers can be created? Box method

Student's name: _____ Assignment date: _____

Summary of the combination problems 組合問題的總結

Problem	Results	Example 1	Example 2	Comments
There are n distinct digits with no 0's and no repeating digits.	nCn with no repeating digits	Create 3-digit numbers using digits 1, 2, and 3 with no repetitions. How many numbers can be created?	Same as left but find the sum of all numbers. $2 \times (1 + 2 + 3) \times 111 = 1332$	$(a + b + c) \times 111 \times$ *numberof digits on each place value* $= (a + b + c) \times 111 \times \frac{3!}{3}$ This type of problem often appears in Kangaroo Contest.
	nCn with repeating digits	Same as above but with repeating digits allowed.		Box method will give 27.
	nCr with no repeating digits	Create 2-digit numbers. 12, 21, 31, 13, 23, 33	Sum = $2 \times (1 + 2 + 3) \times 11 = 12 \times 11 = 121$	
	nCr with repeating digits	11, 12, 13, 21,22,23,31,32,33		Box method is $3 \times 3 = 9$

Problem	Results	Example 1	Example 2	Comments
There are n distinct digits with 0's and repeating digits.	nCn with no repeating digits	Create 4-digit numbers using digits 0, 1, 1, and 2 with no repetitions. How many numbers can be created? Box method is $3 \times 4 \times 4 \times 4 = 192$	Same as left but find the sum of all numbers.	This type of sum problem may not appear in Kangaroo Math Contest, but you never know.
	nCn with no repeating digits	Same as above but with no repeating digits allowed. Box method is $3 \times 3 \times 2 \times 1 = 18$		
	nCr with repeating digits	Create 2-digit numbers. Box method is $3 \times 4 = 12$	Sum = just use list method to add	
	nCr with no repeating digits	Create 2-digit numbers. Box method is $3 \times 3 = 9$	Sum = just use list method to add	

Problem	Results	Example 1	Example 2	Comments
There are n distinct digits with 0's and no repeating digits.	nCn with no repeating digits	**Create 3-digit numbers using digits 0, 1, and 2 with no repetitions. How many numbers can be created?** **102** **120** **201** **210**	Same as left but find the sum of all numbers.	This type of problem appeared in Kangaroo Contest.
	nCn with repeating digits	Same as above but with repeating digits allowed. Total of 18		Box method will give 18.
	nCr with no repeating digits	Create 2-digit numbers. 10, 12, 20, 21	Sum = just use list method to add	
	nCr with repeating digits	10, 11, 12, 20, 21, 22		Box method is 2 × 3 = 6

Problems of using box method to solve Combination problems 以盒子法解 组合题

Tara chooses three digits from 1 to 9 to make a 3-digit number with the following restrictions:

- Has to be an odd number.
- The hundreds digit must be from 1 to 4.
- The tens digit is as large as twice the ones digit.
- No digits can be repeated.

How many possible numbers could she make?

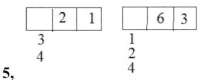

5,

Tara chooses three numbers from 4 to 6 to make a 3-digit number with no repeating digits. How many possible numbers could she make?

3 2 1

$3 \times 2 \times 1 = 6$

6 different numbers

Mixed Combination problem 混合组合题

Henry had 105 coins in 1 cent and 5 cents. The total value is $3.37. How many coins does Henry have for each coin?

The problem can also be solved by the Chickens and Rabbits method.
58 nickels and 47 pennies

A pizza can be added with 3 different toppings; 2 different toppings and just one topping; or no topping. The topping choices are:
A. Ham
B. Pepperoni
C. Double cheese
How many different combinations can a customer order from?

$$1 + 3 + 3 + 1 = 8$$

A, B, C, AB, AC, BC, ABC, none

At the Funfair, Dianna bought 24 tickets. Show all the ways Dianna could use her 24 tickets if she goes on each ride at least two times.

Bumper car ride
4 tickets each ride

Wagon ride
2 tickets each ride

Bumper car	2×4	3×4	4×4	5×4
wagon	8×2	6×2	4×4	2×2

1	

Jaayday saw ducks, swans, and herons in the Nature Park. For every heron, she saw 3 ducks; for every heron, she saw 2 swans. She saw 36 birds in all. How many of each bird did she see?

6 herons, 18 ducks, 12 swans.

2	

How many different ways can Terry change for 60 cents using 5 cents, 10 cents, or 25 cents?
1 quarter = 25 cents, 1 dime = 10 cents, 1 nickel = 5 cents.
1 quarter = _____ cents = _____ dimes _____nickel
            = _____ dime _____ nickels
            = _____ nickels
Each time, if one quarter is dropped, the 2 dimes and 1 nickel is added.
Each time, if one dime is dropped, hen 2 nickels are added.
13 ways

Nickels	0	2	1	3	5	7	0	2	4	6	8	10	12
Dimes	1	0	3	2	1	0	6	5	4	3	2	1	0
Quarters	2	2	1	1	1	1	0	0	0	0	0	0	0

3	

How many 3-digit numbers can you make from three digits 1, 5, and 9?

6

159, 195
519, 591
915, 951

4	

There are 4 letters A, B, C, and D. A and B must be together. C and D must be together. How many different ways that A, B, C, and D can be arranged?
8
2 x 2 x 2 = 8
ABCD   CDAB
ABDC   CDBA
BACD   DCBA
BADC   DCAB

Mixed Combination problem 混合組合题

Kelly walks her dog 5 times each week for about 45 minutes each walk. What is the estimated total time taken each week for her dog-walk?

About 225 minutes (answers may vary.)

Each pizza is cut into 7 equal pieces. Each child will eat about 2 pieces of pizza. How many pizzas are needed for a class of 27 children?

8 pizzas

Kelly got $25 change in one-dollar and two-dollar bills. Find out all different combinations of bills to make $25 change. 13 ways

$2	0	1	2	3	4	5	6	7	8	9	10	11	12
$1	25	23	21	19	17	15	13	11	9	7	5	3	1

Kelly got 25 ¢ change in 5 ¢, 10 ¢. Find out all possible ways that she can make 25 ¢ change.

3 ways

10¢	2	1	0
5¢	1	3	5

Student's name: _____ Assignment date: _____

Mixed Combination problem 混合組合題

Balls are thrown at the target. What are the possible scores that you could get if you throw two balls?

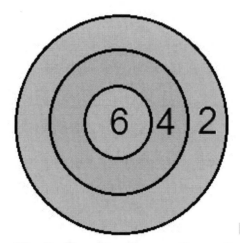

5 possible scores. 12 (6+6), **10** (6+4), **8** (6+2 or 4 + 4), **6** (4+2), **4** (2+2)

What are the different possible scores that you could get if you throw three balls?

6	8	10	12	14	16	18
222	224	622	642	644	466	666

7

What are the different scores that you could get if you throw five balls at target scores of 6 and 4 only?

44444 **20**
44446 **22**
44466 **24**
44666 **26**
46666 **28**
66666 **30**

$$20, 22, 24, 26, 28, 30$$

Mixed Combination problem 混合組合題

Andy chooses 3 different colours from a box of crayons, which only has 6 colours, red, blue, yellow, green, black, and white. How many different ways can Andy choose crayons from the box?

120 (6 $\times$ 5 $\times$ 4)

Andy participates in 2 running events in a track meet, which has 50-m, 75-m, 100-m, and 200-m dashes. How many different choices does Andy have?

6 choices

There are 28 identical square desks. A large rectangular table is created to use these squares. How many possible ways can a rectangular table be put together by these square tables?

3 possible ways:
1 by 28; 2 by 14; 4 by 7

Terry counted there were 21 bicycles and tricycles in the park. He got a total of 62 when he counted the wheels. How many bicycles and tricycles were there each?

20 tricycles and 1 bicycle

Sequence 排序

Take a look at the following number sequence and find out what term in the sequence is 198.
$4 \times$ Term $- 2$ is the pattern rule.

Terms	1	2	3	4	…	? **50**
Numbers	2	6	10	14	…	198

Take a look at the following number sequence table and find out under what letter will the number 80 appear? Use 80 divided by 5 = 16 rows. The 16th row is an even, so it goes from right to left. The pattern period is ABCDEEDCBA of 10. 80 divided by 10 = 8 with no remainder, so the letter is A.

A

A	B	C	D	E
.1	2	3	4	5
10	9	8	7	6
11	12	13	14	15
?	?	?	17	16

Take a look at the following number sequence and find out under what letter will the number 80 appear? 80 divided by 5 = 16 with the remainder of 2 rows as a set and no remainder. It is the 5th number of the second set row of a set. The pattern period is ACEDB of size 5. So, 80 divided by 5 = 16 with no remainder, so the letter is B. **B**

A	B	C	D	E
1		2		3
	5		4	
6		7		8
	10		9	

Take a look at the following number sequence and find out under what letter will the number 80 appear? 80 divided by 3 = 26 r 2. The 3 columns are A, C, E. All numbers are from left to right. The period size is 3 ACE. So, the letter is C with remainder 2. **C**

A	B	C	D	E
1		2		3
4		5		6
7		8		9
10		11		12

Patterns and sequence 规律

A **Sequence** is an ordered set of numbers or objects which are related to each other by a specific rule. This rule may involve repetitions, reasoning, logic, or shapes. A rule is called a **Pattern**.

A **Pattern** is a set of numbers or objects repeated in predictable manner numbers or objects and can be found in the sequence. A sequence can be created by patterns.

Patterns appear in many ways: figures, numbers, letters, tables, or words etc.

Number Pattern 数的规律
What is the next number (term)?
1, 4, 7, 10 _____ **13**

Figure Pattern 图形的规律
What are the total sides of the 20th figure?

$61 = 3n + 1$

The pattern in words 文字描述的规律

Andy gets his allowance as follows; 1 ¢ on day 1, 2 ¢ on day 2, 3 ¢ on day 3, and if this pattern continues, then what is Andy's total in 10 days?

55

Pattern Puzzles 数谜的规律

$34 + 17 = 51, 29 + 22 = 51, 13 + 38 = 51, \textbf{25} + 26 = 51$

Table Pattern 表的规律

A T-table is often used as a strategy to figure word problems.

Andy is 8 years old now, and his father is 34. In how many years will his father's age be exactly 2 times of Andy's age?

This problem can be solved by using a T-table to see the pattern.
He ages difference will be always 26. (34 – 8 = 26)
$2(8 + x) = 34 + x$
$16 + 2x = 34 + x$
$x = 34 – 16 = 8$

Andy's age	Father's age	Getting close to 2 times
8	34 (8+26)	No
13	39 (13 + 26)	No
14	40 (14 + 26)	no
15	41 (15 + 26)	no
16	42	no
20	46	
21	47	
22	48	
23	49	
24	50	Close
26	52	yes

Computing pattern 计算的规律

One of the most difficult problems in math contests is patterns. Math contest problem creators like to create pattern problems because they require keen observation and organization ability. Many Pattern problems have a combination of small problems and require the ability to solve multi-step problems. After inquiring about the basic knowledge of arithmetic series and the creation of pattern rules, the only way to thoroughly understand the way to solve pattern problems is to do many types of pattern problems.

This type of problem is presented in these books as Computing Patterns.

Student's name: _____ Assignment date: _____

A kitten continues to grow, as the following table shows. If the pattern continues, what would be kitten's mass be at the end of week 10?

Week	1	2	3	4	5	6	7	8	9	10
Mass	250 g	315 g	380 g	445 g	510g	575g	640g	705g	770g	835g

Lynn bought goldfish, guppies, and catfish. Her fish tank can hold 5 fish. Show all the combinations of fish she can put in. There must be at least one of each kind of fish.

Goldfish	1	1	1	2	2	3
Guppies	1	2	3	1	2	1
catfish	3	2	1	2	1	1

 There are 7 monkeys in a monkey family. The number of female monkeys is 1 less than the number of male monkeys. How many male monkeys are there?

4 males, 3 females

Kirsten has $140, which is 2 times of Elise's. How much do they have altogether?

Total of 210

Circular pattern
A group of children are evenly spaced sitting around a large circle. Each child has a number tag in consecutive numbers starting from 1. Number 3 is sitting opposite number 10. How many children are sitting around the circle?

14,
3 -10, 4 – 11, 5 -12, 6-13, 7-14, 2-9, 1-8

Kelly got $2.45 in 10 ¢ and 25 ¢ with more quarters than dimes. Find out all the possible ways of each coin that she can have?

9 quarters and 2 dimes

If the fence of a rectangular garden has a perimeter of 48 m and all sides are in whole number lengths. What are all the different areas you can get?

Length	23	22	21	20	19	18	17	16	15	14	13	12
Width	1	2	3	4	5	6	7	8	9	10	11	12
	23	44	63	80	95	108	119	128	135	140	134	144

A dog breeder sold 6 puppies that were either spotted or black in colour. Spotted ones were sold for $60 each and the black ones for $80 each. He sold all his puppies for $400. How many puppies did he sell for each colour?

$60 $80
spotted | black
  0   5

2 black and 4 spotted

How many 4-digit numbers that you can write using the digits 1, 2, 3, and 4. No digits can be repeated for each number.

24 ways

4 3 2 1

Student's name: _____ Assignment date: _____

The accumulated sum of pattern 累積規律合

Jocelyn is building a train with blocks. She used one block for the first train, 8 blocks for the second train, 15 blocks for the third train, and so on. If she continues to build the train this way, how many blocks will he use in the seventh train? **43** **1, 8, 15, 22, 29, 36, 43**
Jocelyn is building a train with blocks. She used one block for the first train, 3 blocks for the second train, 5 blocks for the third train, and so on. If she continues to build the train this way, at which train, will she use 25 blocks? **13th train** 1, 3, 5, 7, 9, 11, 13, 15, ... $\frac{25+1}{2} = 13$
Jocelyn made $20 the first week by working at the Fun Fair. Each week after that, she earned 10 cents more than the week before. How much money did she make in 7 weeks? **142.1** **20+20.1+20.2+20.3+20.4+20.5+20.6**

Students were surveyed to find out what were their favourite juices. How many students were surveyed?

	Apple	Grape	Cherry	Orange
	😊			
	😊			😊
	😊	😊		😊
	😊	😊		😊
	😊	😊	😊	😊

If 169 students were surveyed, how many students does each 😊 represent?

13

Hidden pattern to get sum 隐藏性的規律

Example

Five boys weighed in pairs in all possible combinations. The measured weights were 43 kg, 40 kg, 39 kg, 37 kg, 38 kg, 36 kg, 35 kg, 33 kg, 32 kg, and 30 kg. What was the total weight of the 5 boys?

Without knowing all possible paired combinations of weights, it is difficult for students to get a total.
The ten all possible pairs of combinations are ab, ac, ad, ae, bc, bd, be, cd, ce, de.

The sum is $\dfrac{43+40+39+37+38+36+35+33+32+30}{4} = 363$

Student's name: _____ Assignment date: _____

Number pattern 数的規律

Write the next 4 terms for the following number patterns:

1, 3, 6, 10, 15, _____, _____, _____, _____ **21, 28, 36, 45**

The pattern rule is _____ Add 2, 3, 4, 5, …

Start at 1, add 2 to get the 2nd number. Add 1, 2, and 3 to get the 3rd number. Add 1, 2, 3, and 4 to get the 4th number.
Nth number = 1 + 2 + 3 + … + (n-1) + n

2, 4, 8, 16, _____, _____, _____, _____ **32, 64, 128, 256**

The pattern rule is _____ **time 2 each time**

Observe the following table and replace each ? by a number.

The pattern rule is _____ **Starts at 3 and add**
1 to get next one, add 2, add3, …

day	# of pages
1	3
2	4
3	6
4	9
5	13
6	?18

Pattern

1, 4, 9, 16, 25, 36, _____, _____, _____, _____ **49, 64, 81, 100**

The pattern rule is _____ **Square 1, 2, 3, … etc.**

Student's name: _____ Assignment date: _____

.
Number pattern in computation 数字運算的規律

Observe the following pattern and relation. Fill in _____ with a number.

$$1 \times 5 + 4 = 3 \times 3$$

$$2 \times 6 + 4 = 4 \times 4$$

$$3 \times 7 + 4 = 5 \times 5$$

$$4 \times 8 + 4 = 6 \times 6$$

$$5 \times 9 + 4 = \square \times \square \qquad 5 \times 9 + 4 = 7 \times 7$$

$$6 \times \square + 4 = \square \times \square \qquad 6 \times 10 + 4 = 8 \times 8$$

$$\square \times \square + 4 = \square \times \square \qquad 7 \times 11 + 4 = 9 \times 9$$

Number pattern

Observe the following pattern and relation. Fill in _____ with a number.

$$8 \times 1 + 1 = 9$$

$$8 \times 12 + 2 = 98$$

$$8 \times 123 + 3 = 987$$

$$8 \times 1234 + 4 = \underline{\hspace{2cm}} 9876$$

$$8 \times 12345 + 5 = \underline{\hspace{2cm}} 98765$$

$$8 \times 123456 + 6 = \underline{\hspace{2cm}} 987654$$

Student's name: ________________________ Assignment date: ______________

Number pattern

Observe the following pattern and relation. Fill in _____ with a number.

$1 \times 9 + 2 =$ __________ $\mathbf{11}$

$12 \times 9 + 3 =$ __________ $\mathbf{111}$

$123 \times 9 + 4 =$ __________ $\mathbf{1111}$

_____ $\times\ 9 + 5 =$ __________

$\mathbf{1234 \times 9 + 5 = 11111}$

_____ $\times\ 9 + 6 =$ __________

$\mathbf{12345 \times 9 + 6 = 111\,111}$

_____ $\times\ 9 + 7 =$ __________

$\mathbf{123456 \times 9 + 7 = 1\,111\,111}$

Student's name: _____ Assignment date: _____

Number pattern

Observe the following pattern and relation. Fill in _____ with a number.

$37037 \times 3 = \mathbf{111\ 111}$
$37037 \times 6 = \mathbf{222\ 222}$
$37037 \times 9 = \mathbf{333\ 333}$
$37037 \times 12 = \mathbf{444\ 444}$
$37037 \times 15 = \mathbf{555\ 555}$
$37037 \times 18 = \mathbf{666\ 666}$
$37037 \times 21 = \mathbf{777\ 777}$
$37037 \times 24 = \mathbf{888\ 888}$
$37037 \times 27 = \mathbf{999\ 999}$

Student's name: _____ Assignment date: _____

Number pattern

Multiplying by 11

Observe the following pattern and relation. Fill in _____ with a number.

Equation	Hint and solutions
$11 \times 11 =$ _____ **121**	Do it by hand and then observe the patterns of the results. The results of any number multiplied by 11 have the pattern of placing the non-11 digits as "**copy 2 ends and then add every 2 digits one at a time.**". (carry over if the sum is over 10.)
$11 \times 12 =$ _____ **132**	1(1+2)1
$11 \times 23 =$ _____ **253**	1(2+3)1
$37 \times 11 =$ _____ **407**	
$56 \times 11 =$ _____ **616**	copy 2 ends and add then add every 2 digits one at a time. (carry over if the sum is over 10.) 5 6 5 11 6 6 1

Number pattern

Multiplying by 11

Observe the following pattern and relation. Fill in _____ with a number.

65 × 11= _____	**715**
78 × 11= _____	**858**
89 × 11= _____	**979**
99 × 11= _____	**1089**
97 × 11= _____	**1067**
77 × 11= _____	**847**
88 × 11= _____	**968**

Student's name: _____ Assignment date: _____

Number pattern

Multiplying by 11

291 × 11 = _____ **3201**	2 (2+1) (1+3) 3 copy 2 ends and add then add every 2 digits one at a time. (carry over if the sum is over 10.) 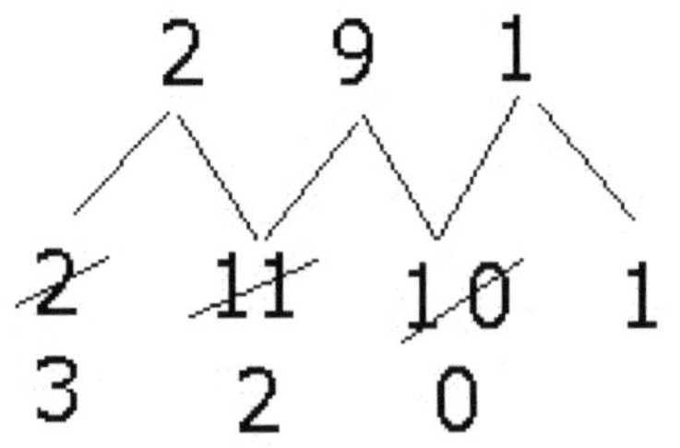 2 9 1 2 11 10 1 3 2 0
293 × 11 = _____ **3223**	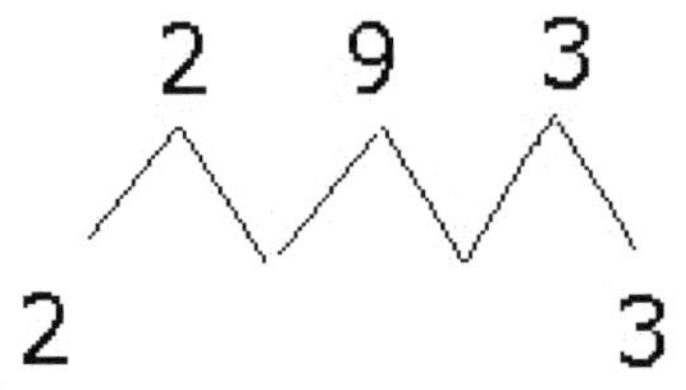 2 9 3 2 3
273 × 11 = _____ **3003**	
389 × 11 = _____ **4279**	
48393 × 11 = _____ **532323**	

Student's name: _____ Assignment date: _____

Multiplying by multiples of 11 11 的倍数乘法
Observe the following pattern and relation. Fill in _____ with a number.

Equation	Hint and solutions
11 × 11 = _____**121**	Do it by hand and then observe the pattern of the result.
111 × 111 = _____**12321**	Can you see the pattern?
1111 × 1111 = _____**1234321**	
11111 × 11111 = _____**123454321**	

Figure pattern

If the following pattern continues, what figure will be the sixteenth position?

position	1	2	3	4	... 6
figures	A	BB	CCC	DDDD	... **FFFFFF**

F

_____

What will be the one hundredth figure?

14N

_____

Patterns describing in symbols or words 以图形或文字表述的规律

If the figure pattern continues, what will be the 49th shape?

□ ○ △ ▽ □ □ ○ △ ▽ □ ···

▽ answer

	Grade 4 class put up 23 school fun fair day posters on Monday. They put up 7 more posters than the day before until Friday. How many posters will be put up on Friday? How many will be put up in total by Friday?

Monday	Tuesday	Wednesday	Thursday	Friday	Total
23	30	37	44	51	185

A wall clock strikes 1 chime at 1 o'clock, 2 chimes at 2 o'clock, 3 chimes at 3 o'clock, and so on. If this pattern continues, then how many chimes will continue the clock strike in one day?

(1+2+3+4+5+6+7+8+9+10+11+12)*2= 156

Caroline is starting a fitness club at her school. She is the only member right now, but she plans to ask every member to find 2 new members at each end of the month. How many members will be in the club at the end of 6 months?

The pattern is 1, 3, 9, 27, 81, 243, 729.

1x2+1, 3x2+3, 9x2+9, 27x2+28, 243,729

3   9   27   81

answer

The distance from Vancouver, BC, Canada to Phoenix, Arizona, USA, is 2509 km. Fernando drove from Vancouver to Phoenix and stopped in Boise, Idaho, which is a 1480 km drive from Phoenix. Estimate whether Fernando was closer to Phoenix or Vancouver when he stopped.

Vancouver

Student's name: _____ Assignment date: _____

The accumulated sum of pattern 累積規律合

Jocelyn is building a train with blocks. She used one block for the first train, 8 blocks for the second train, 15 blocks for the third train, and so on. If she continues to build the train this way, how many blocks will he use in the seventh train?

43

1, 8, 15, 22, 29, 36, 43

Jocelyn is building a train with blocks. She used one block for the first train, 3 blocks for the second train, 5 blocks for the third train, and so on. If she continues to build the train this way, at what train she will use 25 blocks.

5th train

1+3+5+7+9=25

Jocelyn made $20 the first week by working at the Fun Fair. Each week after that, she earned 10 cents more than the week before. How much money did she make in 7 weeks?

142.1

20+20.1+20.2+20.3+20.4+20.5+20.6

Students were surveyed to find out what were their favourite juices. How many students were surveyed?

	Apple	Grape	Cherry	Orange
	😊			
	😊			😊
	😊	😊		😊
	😊	😊		😊
	😊	😊	😊	😊

If 169 students were surveyed, how many students does each 😊 represent?

13

只见棋谜不见题　劝君迷路不哭涕　数学象棋加谜题　健脑思维眞神奇

Two-column pattern 二列规律

$9 \to \mathbf{16}$ $3 \to \mathbf{4}$ $2 \to \mathbf{2}$ $8 \to ?$ $A \times 2 - 2$	$9 \to \mathbf{1}$ $3 \to \mathbf{7}$ $2 \to \mathbf{8}$ $8 \to ?$ $A+B=10$	$6 \to \mathbf{5}$ $5 \to \mathbf{6}$ $7 \to \mathbf{4}$ $3 \to ?$ $A+B=11$	$4 \to 3$ $3 \to 2$ $2 \to 1$ $8 \to ?$ $A-1=B$	$8 \to \mathbf{13}$ $3 \to \mathbf{8}$ $2 \to 7$ $13 \to ?$ $A+5=B$
$9 \to 11$ $0 \to 2$ $1 \to 3$ $4 \to ?$ $A+2=B$	$5 \to 4$ $3 \to 2$ $4 \to 3$ $7 \to ?$ $A-1=B$	$6 \to 7$ $2 \to 3$ $1 \to 2$ $3 \to ?$ $A+1=B$	$5 \to 9$ $3 \to 5$ $8 \to \mathbf{15}$ $9 \to ?$ $A \times 2 - 1$	$9 \to 19$ $4 \to 9$ $5 \to 11$ $6 \to ?$ $A \times 2 + 1$
$0 \to 13$ $1 \to 14$ $2 \to 15$ $3 \to ?$ $A+13=B$	$6 \to 7$ $7 \to 6$ $2 \to 11$ $9 \to ?$ $A+B=13$	$5 \to 11$ $4 \to 9$ $2 \to 5$ $3 \to ?$ $A \times 2 + 1 = B$	$6 \to 10$ $3 \to 7$ $2 \to 6$ $5 \to ?$ $A+4=B$	$7 \to 15$ $8 \to 17$ $2 \to 5$ $1 \to ?$ $A \times 2 + 1$
$8 \to 6$ $4 \to 10$ $2 \to 12$ $6 \to ?$ $A+B=14$	$7 \to 12$ $3 \to 8$ $2 \to 7$ $5 \to ?$ $B=A+5$	$8 \to 12$ $3 \to 7$ $2 \to 6$ $9 \to ?$ $A+5=B$	Find the value of each shape. circle = _____ rectangle = _____ pentagon = _____ triangle = _____ 2, 5, 6, 3	
$3 \to 10$ $2 \to 11$ $6 \to 7$ $5 \to ?$ $A+B=13$	$4 \to \mathbf{15}$ $3 \to 14$ $5 \to 16$ $8 \to ?$ $A+11=B$	$7 \to 14$ $3 \to 6$ $2 \to 4$ $6 \to ?$ $A \times 2 = B$		

14, 2, 8, 7, 18
6, 6, 4, 17, 13
16, 4, 7, 9, 3
8, 10, 13
8, 19, 12

Student's name: _____ Assignment date: _____

Mixed pattern problems 混合規律問題

The corresponding numbers are arranged in four columns, as shown as follows. Under which column letter will 102 appear?

A	B	C	D
1	2	3	4
8	7	6	5
9	10	11	12
……		14	13

The corresponding numbers are arranged in four columns, as shown as follows. Under which column letter will 300 appear?

A	B	C	D	E	F	G
1		2		3		4
	7		6		5	
8		9		10		11
	14		13		12	
15		16		…		

Student's name: _____ Assignment date: _____

How many diagonals does a 10-sided polygon have?
3 sides,
4 sides,
5 sides,
6 sides,
10 sides,

Fill in _____ with a number by observing the following pattern.

1	5
2	12 (5 + 7)
3	26 (12 +14)
4	54 (26 + 28)
5	110 (54 + 56)
6	222 (110 +112)
7	446 (222 + 224)
8	894 (446 + 448)
9	1690 (894 + 896)
10	3482 (1690 + 1792)

Student's name: ______________________________ Assignment date: __________________

<table>
<tr><th>Table</th><th>Rule</th></tr>
<tr><td><table><tr><td>1</td><td>2</td></tr><tr><td>2</td><td>4</td></tr><tr><td>3</td><td>6</td></tr><tr><td>4</td><td>8</td></tr></table></td><td>column2 = column1 × 2</td></tr>
<tr><td><table><tr><td>1</td><td>3</td></tr><tr><td>2</td><td>5</td></tr><tr><td>3</td><td>7</td></tr><tr><td>4</td><td>9</td></tr></table></td><td>column2 = column1 × 2 + 1
______________________________</td></tr>
<tr><td><table><tr><td>1</td><td>4</td></tr><tr><td>2</td><td>5</td></tr><tr><td>3</td><td>6</td></tr><tr><td>4</td><td>7</td></tr></table></td><td>column2 = column1 + 3
______________________________</td></tr>
<tr><td><table><tr><td>1</td><td>4</td></tr><tr><td>2</td><td>5</td></tr><tr><td>3</td><td>6</td></tr><tr><td>4</td><td>7</td></tr></table></td><td>column2 = column1 + 3
______________________________</td></tr>
</table>

For every 4 boys, there will be one girl at Kevin's birthday party. How many children could be at Kevin's party?

(A) 13
(B) 14
(C) 15
(D) 16   **C**

Kevin earns as much as four times as Jessica's hourly rate, what amount could be the amount difference between Kevin and Jessica?

(A) $5
(B) $6
(C) $7
(D) $8   **B**

On day 1, Adam reads book 4 pages and Bob reads book 5 pages. On day 2, Adam reads 8 pages and Bob reads 10 pages. On day 3, Adam reads 16 pages and Bob reads 15 pages. What will Bob be reading when Adam is reading page 128.

Day	1	2	3	4	5	6
Adam	$2^2=4$	$2^3 = 8$	$2^4=16$	$2^5=32$	$2^6=64$	$2^7=128$
Bob	5	10	15	20	25	30

30

Adam, Bob, and Charles weighed together on the same scale, and it showed a total weight of 165 kg. When Adam got off, it showed 115 kg on the scale. When Bob got off, and the scale showed 63 kg on the scale. What was the weight of each boy?
Adam: **50 kg**
Bob: **52 kg**
Chatles: **63kg**

Student's name: _____ Assignment date: _____

3, 7, 16, 32, 57, _____, _____ 93, 142
Differences are perfect squares

3, 4, 11, 116, _____, _____ 13451, 180929396

36, 32, 28, 24, _____, _____ 20, 16

2, 6, 18, 54, _____, _____ 162, 486

7, 8, 10, 13, 17, _____, _____ 22, 28

77, 72, 67, 62, _____, _____ 57, 52

20, 21, 23, 26, 30, _____, _____ 35, 41

3, 7, 13, 21, _____, _____ 31, 43

36, 25, 16, 9, _____, _____ 4, 1

Triangular numbers are as follows:

Can you find the pattern in the triangular numbers?

n^{th} triangular number = $1 + 2 + 3 + \ldots + n$

Square numbers are as follows:

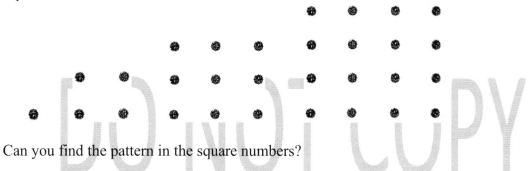

Can you find the pattern in the square numbers?

n^{th} square number = $2[1 + 2 + 3 + \ldots + (n-1)] + n$

Can you divide the above square number drawing to show that every square number is the sum of two triangular numbers?

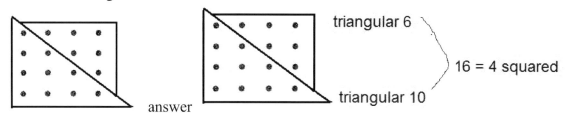

answer

triangular 6

triangular 10

16 = 4 squared

What 2-digit number is both square and triangular?

What happens when two triangular number clusters are put together?
For example, a triangular number of 10 are put together with another same number of a triangular number. They form a rectangle of the dimension of 4 by 5.

Pentagonal numbers are as follows.

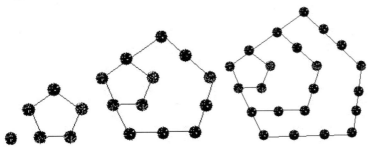

1+ 5n

Can you find the pattern in the square numbers?

Is it true that each pentagonal is the sum of a square and a triangle?

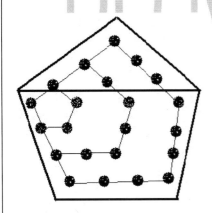

Pascal triangle 楊輝三角形数

Pascal's triangle has relationships to "Counting paths", base 2 numbers, base 11 numbers, binomial expansion coefficients, and binomial probability, triangular numbers, Fibonacci numbers, natural number sequence etc. The following diagram illustrates the details.

		Row	Base 2	Base 11
1		0	1	1
1　1		1	2	11
1　2　1		2	4	121
1　3　3　1		3	8	1331
1　4　6　4　1		4	16	14641
1　5　10　10　5　1		5	32	161051
1　6　15　20　15　6　1		6	64	1771561
1　7　21　35　35　21　7　1		7	128	19487171
1　18　28　56　70　56　28　8　1		8	256	

The row 1: $1 = {}_0C_0 = (x+y)^0 = 1$

The row 2 : $1 \quad 1 = {}_1C_0 \quad {}_1C_1 \Rightarrow (x+y) = x+y$

The row 3 : $1 \quad 2 \quad 1 = {}_2C_0 \quad {}_2C_1 \quad {}_2C_2 \Rightarrow (x+y)^2 = x^2 + 2xy + y^2$

The row 4: $1 \quad 3 \quad 3 \quad 1 = {}_3C_0 \quad {}_3C_1 \quad {}_3C_2 \quad {}_3C_3 \Rightarrow (x+y)^3 = x^3 + 3x^2y + 3xy^2 + y^3$

When the outcome of an event only has mutually exclusive two outcomes, then it is a binomial condition, and we can use binomial expansion to figure out its outcome depending on how many times it will happen. Lower grades students can also use the Pascal triangle pattern to figure out its coefficients.

The following explains the relation between binomial problems and how to figure out the solutions using various methods.

Student's name: _____ Assignment date: _____

Throw a coin x number of times.	Possible outcomes	Binomial expansion	Pythagoras triangle	Problems
1	H, T	$(H + T)^1$	1 1 ⇐ 1 2 1 1 3 3 1 1 4 6 4 1	What the possible outcomes are throwing a coin once?
2	HH, HT, TH, TT	$(H + T)^2 = H^2 + 2HT + T^2$	1 1 1 2 1 ⇐ 1 3 3 1 1 4 6 4 1	What are the possible outcomes after throwing a coin twice?
3	HHH, HHT, HTH, THH, HTT, HTT, THT, HTH, TTT	$(H + T)^3 = H^3 + 3H^2T + 3HT^2 + T^3$	1 1 1 2 1 1 3 3 1 ⇐ 1 4 6 4 1	A family has three children. What is the probability that there are 2 boys? $\frac{3}{8}$
4		$(H + T)^4 = H^4 + 4H^3T + 6H^2T^2 + 4HT^3 + T^4$	1 1 1 2 1 1 3 3 1 1 4 6 4 1 ⇐	A family has four children. What is the probability that there are at least three boys? $\frac{5}{16}$

Throw a coin x number of times.	Possible outcomes	Binomial expansion	Pythagoras triangle	Problems
5		$(H + T)^5$ $= H^5 + 5H^4T +$ $10H^3T^2 + 10H^2T^3 +$ $5HT^4 + T^5$	1 1 1 2 1 1 3 3 1 1 4 6 4 1 1 5 10 10 5 1 ⇐	A family has five children. What is the probability that there are at least 3 boys? $\frac{1}{2}$ Take a look at the binomial expansion and the Pythagoras then we know the probability is $\frac{1}{2}$.

If we do not use the binomial expansion, then we can use a combination, and the method is taught in Canada in grade 12.

$${}_5C_3\left(\frac{1}{2}\right)^3\left(\frac{1}{2}\right)^2 = 10\times\left(\frac{1}{2}\right)^5$$

$${}_5C_4\left(\frac{1}{2}\right)^4\left(\frac{1}{2}\right)^1 = 5\times\left(\frac{1}{2}\right)^5$$

$${}_5C_5\left(\frac{1}{2}\right)^5\left(\frac{1}{2}\right)^0 = 1\times\left(\frac{1}{2}\right)^5$$

Add the above 3 equations, we get $\frac{1}{2}$.

Arithmetic sequence and series 算術序列及级数

A list of numbers, letters, or objects is called a sequence. In this section, we only deal with numbers. The series is to add all the terms of a sequence. We are only interested in 2 kinds of sequences and series: the arithmetic sequence/series and the geometric sequence/series. We will also introduce the method of getting the sum of other series with patterns. It is a good idea to learn the notation of $\sum$ (pounced as Sigma) before working on series. $\sum_{i=1}^{5} i = 1 + 2 + 3 + 4 + 5$.

Arithmetic Sequence

A sequence is called an Arithmetic Sequence when the difference between any 2 terms is constant (the same value). The difference in constant is called Common Difference (d). For example, 2, 7, 12, 17, 22 are an arithmetic sequence, and the common difference (d) is 5. The general form of an arithmetic sequence is $a_1, a_1 + d, a_1 + 2d, \ldots, a_1 + (n-1)d, \ldots$ where $d = a_2 - a_1 = a_3 - a_2$ etc.

The arithmetic mean is different from the statistical mean (average). The arithmetic means mean the terms of the arithmetic sequence.

The arithmetic means between 2 and 12 is 7.
The 2 arithmetic means between 2 and 17 are 7, 12.
The 3 arithmetic means between 2 and 22 are 7, 12, and 17.

Arithmetic Series

The sum of an arithmetic sequence is called arithmetic series, $S_n = \dfrac{\text{first} + \text{last}}{2} \times n$ (Note that this means the sum is the midpoint (average) $\times n$.). The sum formula is the same as the area formula for a trapezoid. The nth term is $a_n = a_1 + (n-1)d$.

Special series:

$1 + 2 + 3 + 4 + \ldots + (n-1) + n = \dfrac{1+n}{2} \times n = \sum_{i=1}^{n} a_i$ (Sum of natural numbers, n^{th} triangular number)

$1 + 2 + 3 + 4 + 5 + 6 + 7 + 8 + 9 + 10 = 55$
$1 + 3 + 5 + \ldots + (2n-1) = n^2$

Using the arithmetic series formula to find its sum 以算術级数公式计算和

Find $1 + 2 + 3 +...+ 98 + 99 + 100$.
(first + last) times half of the number of terms.

$101 \times 50 = 5050$

Find $2 + 4 + 6 +...+ 98 + 100$.
$102 \times 25 = 2550$

Find $1 + 3 + 5 +...+ 97 + 99$.
$100 \times 25 = 2500$

Fine the next 2 numbers.
6, 11, 16, 21, 26, _____, _____ 31, 36

How to find the general formula for the next term? (Hint: think about "× common difference" first.

The next term = $5n + 1$.

If the number is 501, then what will be its term number?
          100th term.

Find the total of $6 + 11 + 16 + 21 + 26 + ... + 501$
$$\frac{6 + 501}{2} \times 100 = 25350$$

Find the total of $3 + 6 + 9 + 12 + 15 + ... + 579$

Hint: Is there a common difference?

$$\frac{3+579}{2} \times 192 = 55872$$

Student's name: _____ Assignment date: _____

Problem

Use 1, 2, 3, and 4 to create 2-digit numbers without repeating digits. How many numbers can be created? List them all.

12
12, 13, 14, 21, 23, 24, 31, 32, 34, 41, 42, 43

Four persons shake hands to each other. How many handshakes could there be?

6
3+2+1

Find the next term in the following pattern

2, 7, 11, 14, _____　　16

What is the next shape in the sequence?

the answer is a delimiter or limit

Angela has 30 chocolate cookies and likes to give the same number of cookies to each of her 7 friends. How many chocolate cookies are left over?

2

Student's name: _____ Assignment date: _____

Find the value for each (   )

1, 10, 3, 8, 5, 6, 7, 4, (   ), (   )   9, 2   1+10=11, 3+8=11, 5+6=11, 7+4=11, 9+2=11

2, 5, 10, (   ), 26, 37, 50   17

1, 4, 10, 22, (   )   46

Find a figure for each?.

 ?

?

 ?

The answer to "Find a figure for each?".

Observe the pattern and replace ? by a figure.

   ?   answer

Randomly take three digits from 1,2, 3, and 4. How many different sums you can get by adding digits of each of these three-digit numbers?

3 sums of 6, 7, or 8.
123 (6), 124 (7), 134 (8), 143 (8)

Replace each of the following ? by a digit such that the 3-digit number is divisible by 3. How many are there?

171	372	570	777
174	375	573	870
177	378	576	873
270	471	579	876
273	474	678	879
276	477		
279			

answer

$\boxed{? \mid 7 \mid ?}$

23 numbers

How many pairs of squares do not share any common sides?

1	2	3
4	5	6
7	8	9

1	2	3	4	5	6	7
(1,3) (1,5) (1,6) (1,7) (1,8) (1,9)	(2,4) (2,5) (2,6) (2,7) (2,8) (2,9)	(3,4) (3,5) (3,7) (3,8) (3,9)	(4,6) (4,8) (4,9)	(5,7) (5,9)	(6,7) (6,8)	(7,9)
6	**6**	**5**	**3**	**2**	**2**	**1**

6+6+5+3+2+2+1 = **25**

Student's name: _____ Assignment date: _____

There are two bags, and in each bag, there are numbers 1, 2, 3, 4, 5, 6, 7, 8, 9, 10 11, 12, and 13. If a number is drawn from each bag randomly and calculate their product, how many different products are divisible by 6?

In the natural numbers 100, 101, 102, …, 1996, 1997; how many natural numbers have the ones place equal to the hundreds place

How many numbers contain digit 2 from 100 to 500?

How many less than 1000 natural numbers have the sum of all digits of each natural number to be

How many different sizes of rectangles are there if the perimeter of each rectangle is 30, and all their widths and lengths are natural numbers?

Student's name: _____ Assignment date: _____

Use 0, 1, 2, and 3 to create 2-digit numbers without repeating digits. How many numbers can be created? List them all.

10, 20, 30
12, 21, 31
13, 23, 32
9

1-row pattern

Find the next term in the following number sequence.

5, 11, 17, _____   23

2-column pattern

Problem 1

Row	Chairs
1	4
2	7
3	10
4	?

What is the pattern rule? _____.
13, Start at 4, add 3 to get the next one.

Problem 2

Row (R)	Chairs (C)
2	7
3	10
4	13
5	?

What is the pattern rule? _____.
$C = 3 \times R + 1$

If renting a boat costs $15, then how much would it cost to rent 10 boats?

Can you write a mathematical expression for the cost of renting 10 boats? _____
$15 \times 10 = 150$

Student's name: _____ Assignment date: _____

Problem 1

input	Gap × Input	Output
1	5	6
2	10	11
3	15	16
4	? 20	? 21

Pattern Rule: Output = Input × 5 + 1

The gap is the number that multiplies the Input to get the Output.

Problem 2

input	Gap × Input	Output
1	? 6 × 1	3
2	? 6 × 2	9
3	? 6 × 3	15
4	? 6 × 4	? 21

Pattern Rule: Output = Input × 6 − 3

The gap is the number that multiplies the Input to get the Output.
The gap can be found by $\frac{9-3}{2-1} = 6$

Given the following pattern table, what is the price of each almanac?

Dictionary	Almanacs	Total price
1	1	$24
2	3	$61

$61 - 48 =$ **$13**

Edward reads 1 book on January 1st, 2 books on January 2nd, and 3 books on January 3rd, and so on until January 11th. How many books will Edward have read in total?

$1 + 2 × 2 + 3 × 3 + 4 × 4 + 5 × 5 + … + 10 × 10 + 11 × 11 = 516$

Given the following pattern table, what is the price of each almanac?

Dictionary	Almanacs	Total price
1	2	$38
2	3	$51

51-38=13
58-13=**25**

Given the following pattern table, what is the price of each dictionary?

Dictionary	Almanacs	Total price
3	2	$59
1	1	$24

$59 - 24 \times 2 = 59 - 48 = \mathbf{11}$

Jaden saves $50 in January and saves $5 each month after that. His sister Audrey saves $55 in January and then saves $3 each month after that. Who has saved the most money by the end of July?

Hint: You can use a T table to figure it out or just use multiplication and a pattern rule to solve it.
Jaden: $50 + 5 \times 6 = 80$
Andrey: $55 + 3 \times 6 = 73$

If the pattern of RRRYYRRRYY ... continues, then what would be the 143rd letter?

Do not write letters up to 143rd or use the chart. Use the division idea of periodic data to find it out.

$143 \div 5 = 23 \, r \, 3$
The letter is **R**.

Jaden is 425 km away from his home and if he rides 50 km each day towards home starting on Monday morning. How far will he be away from his home on Wednesday evening? When will he reach his home?

$50 \times 3 = \mathbf{150 \, km}$
$\frac{425}{50} = \mathbf{8.5 \, days}$

Student's name: _____ Assignment date: _____

Find the LCM for the following pairs of numbers. Do not use the method of listing multiples but using the division method.

14 and 24

5 and 14

6 and 9

2 and 8

12 and 26

Jaden has piano lessons every 5th day, and Issac has singing lessons every 7th day. Today is January 25th, and both have their lessons. When will the date both have their lessons on the same day?

Andrew made a volcano with baking soda, food colouring, and vinegar. For every tablespoon of red food colouring, Andrew used 4 tablespoons of baking soda and 6 tablespoons of vinegar. If Andrew had 18 tablespoons of vinegar, how many tablespoons each of baking soda and food colouring would Andrew need?

You can use the T table pattern or the ratio concept to solve this problem.

On Monday, a magic plant is 2 cm tall. Each day after Monday, the magic plan doubles its height from the day before. How high will the plant on Thursday?

.

Student's name: _____ Assignment date: _____

Selecting the part from a list nCr

For simple problems, to use the list is clear and easier for students to understand, but the Box Method is more suitable in the math contest.

Meghan can choose two events from a track meet. The events in the track meet have a 50-m dash, 75- m dash, 100-m dash, and 400-m relay. How many different choices can Meghan have?

Andrew can choose 3 colours from a box of red, blue, black, yellow, and red. How many different ways can Andrew choose from?

Find $1 + 2 + 4 + 8 + \ldots + 1024.$

The sum is $1+2+4+8+16+32+64+128+256+1024 = 2047$

Find $-1 + 2 - 3 + 4 - 5 + 6 - 7 + 8 - 57 + 58 - 59 + 60.$

6

What is $(3 + 7 + 11 + \ldots + 123) - (4 + 8 + 12 + \ldots + 120)$?

$123 = 3+4n$, n=30th term

$\dfrac{3 + 123}{2} \times 30 = 1890$

$120 = 4 + 4n$, n = 29th term

$\dfrac{4+120}{2} \times 29 = 1890 = 1798$

$1890 - 1790 = \mathbf{100}$

What is $1 + 3 + 5 + 7 + 9 + 11 + \ldots + 37 + 39 + 41$?

What is the remainder of $1 + 2 + 3 + 4 + \ldots + 11 + 12 + 13$?

$\dfrac{1 + 13}{2} \times 13 = 91$

Student's name: _____ Assignment date: _____

What is $2 + 4 + 6 + 8 + 10 + \ldots + 46 + 48$?

$$\frac{2+48}{2} \times 24 = \mathbf{600}$$

What is the 100th number in the following sequence?
1, 4, 7, 10, ….

$$1 + 3 \times 99 = 298$$

Student's name: _____ Assignment date: _____

Most of the following problems need Sum and Term formulas to find answers quickly. These problems are for advanced students only.

What is $3 + 7 + 11 + \ldots + 91 + 95$?

$\frac{3+95}{2} \times 24 = 1176$

Simplify $28 + 30 + 32 + \ldots + 84 + 86$.　　　　1710

Find the sum: $1 + 2 + 3 + 4 + \ldots + 48 + 49$　　　　1225

The sum of consecutive even integers $2 + 4 + 6 + \ldots + m = 2550$. What is the value of m?

$\frac{2+m}{2} \times \frac{m}{2} = 2550$
m(m+2)=10200=100× 102
m=100

Simplify $28 + 30 + 32 + \ldots + 54 + 56$
56=28 + (n-1)2, n=**15**
$\frac{2+56}{2} \times 15 =$**630**

Simplify $95 + 195 + 295 + \ldots + 995$

$\frac{95+995}{2} \times 10 =$**5450**

Order of term	1	2	3	4	...	N
Term value	2	5	8	11	...	449

What is the value of N?

Order of term	1	2	3	...	N
Term value	3	10	17	...	528

What is the value of N?

Order of term	1	2	3	4	...	100
Term value	7	10	13	16	...	?

What is the value of the 100th term?

7+99× 3 = 304

Order of term	1	2	3	4	...	50
Term value	4	7	10	16	...	?

What is the value of the 15th term?

4+49× 3 = 151

Even and odd numbers 偶奇数

Exercise (For grade 3 and above)

Elise wrote even numbers from 1 to 1000. How many even numbers did she write?
$500 = \frac{1000}{2}$

Elise wrote even numbers from 1 to 1000. How many digits did she write 1?

1-digit numbers	4 (2, 4, 6, 8)
2-digit numbers	45 (10, 12, 14, 16, 18) $9 \times 5 = 45$ 9 5
3-digit numbers	$9 \times 10 \times 5 = 450$ 9 10 5
4-digit numbers	1 (1000)

The number of digits = 4 + 45 + 450 + 1 = 500 of 1

Elise wrote even numbers from 1 to 1000. How many 0's did she write in all the even numbers?

0 appears at one's place, i.e., 10, 20, 30, 40.	$\frac{1000}{10} = 100$
0 appears at ten's place i.e., 100, 102, 104, 106, 108	100 200 300 400 …. 900 102 202 303 104 204 304 106 206 306 108 208 308 $9 \times 5 + 1 (1000) = 46$
0 appears at the hundred's place	1 (1000)

Total 0's = 100 + 46 + 1 = 147

Student's name: _____ Assignment date: _____

Kirsten wrote numbers from 1 to 100, how many even numbers did she write?

Kirsten wrote numbers from 1 to 100. How many digits did Kirsten write in all her numbers?

Kirsten wrote numbers from 1 to 100. In all the 2-digit numbers Kirsten wrote, how many numbers do they end in 2?

12, 22, 32, 42, 52, 62, 72, 82, 92

Kirsten wrote numbers from 1 to 100. In all the 2-digit numbers Kirsten wrote, how many numbers ending in 4 or multiple of 4?

Circle the following numbers, which are odd numbers.

223+24, 24+25, 24+24, 25+25, 679+871, 1234+4321,

6478 + 8746, 546 + 234, 100+ 201,

579+321, 444 + 555, 11111 + 22222, 4321 - 1234, 24- 23,

25 - 24, 25 - 25, 871 - 679, 4321- 1234,

7846 - 4678

Student's name: ______________________________ Assignment date: ________________

Circle the following numbers, which are even.

23×24, $25\ 25$, 31×13, 91×89, 371×43, 111×222,

679×872, 45675×25678, 1234×4321

For higher grade students.

Kirsten wrote numbers from 1 to 100. How many 0's did she write in all those even numbers?

9

10, 20, 30, 40, 50, 60, 70, 80, 90

Melissa created a set of all four-digit numbers using the digits 2, 3, 4, and 5 without repetitions. What is the sum of all the numbers of her set?

$(2+3+4+5) \times 6 \times 1111 =$

Student's name: _____ Assignment date: _____

Operational math 操作式数学

Introduction

Operation math is to ask students to use hands to operate operation using virtual manipulative and then come up with answers. Ho Math Chess has created a kind of operation math, which includes math, chess moves, puzzles, and robot figures etc. many of these kinds of problems include cubes, or paper folding, or even matchsticks, beads, paths etc. and solved by pattern or counting.

Here we include three examples that were created by the authors at Ho Math Chess.

Example 1

A squared paper is folded in into half from left to right in half and again is folded from the top to down in half, as shown below.

1. If the folded paper is cut along the line on all 4 papers, circle the cut line will give 2 pieces of paper.

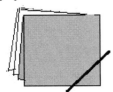   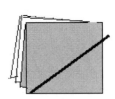

2 If the folded paper is cut along the line on all 4 papers, circle the cut line will give 3 pieces of paper.

 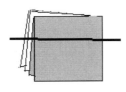  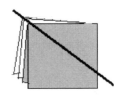

3. If the folded paper is cut along the line on all 4 papers, circle the cut line will give 4 pieces of paper.

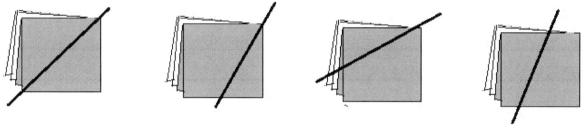

4. If the folded paper is cut along the line on all 4 papers, circle the cut line will give 2 pieces of paper.

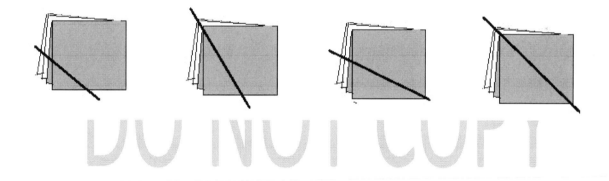

Example 2

A squared paper is folded in into half from left to right in half and again is folded from the top to down in half, as shown below.

A circle is cut out in the middle.

Circle the following figure, which should be the final figure after the cut.

DO NOT COPY

Chickens and Rabbits 雏兔同笼

Introduction

We have introduced the Chickens and Rabbits problems in the Grades 1 and 2, Grades 2 and 3 workbooks. Different methods are introduced at different grades. Lots of many Chinese math contest books use formulas to teach and solve Chickens and Rabbits problems. but we do not like the idea of using the formula and think it could be one reason that many students do not benefit from doing math contests. Lots of teachers use the Trial and Error method, but a very clear method using the exact steps could be taught to students that is the **Assumption method**.

Example of Assumption method 假设法

There are two types of tables in the library. One small table sits 4 students, and one large table sits 6 students. There are 38 students sitting at 7 tables in the library. How many of them are small tables? How many of them are large tables?

We do not know how many small or large tables, so we can assume, then make the adjustment. Let's assume all 7 tables are large tables (or small tables if you like), and then there will be 7×6 = 42 students. We only have 38 students, so we know we have got too many students. We need to change some large tables to small tables to reduce the number of students. Every time when we change a large table to a small table, then we reduce 2 students. How many students do we need to reduce from 42 to 38? The answer is 2 To reduce 4 students. We need to exchange 2 large tables to 2 small tables.

One statement to do all the above explanation is $\frac{7 \times 6 - 38}{6 - 4}$ = 2 small tables (2 could also be the number of large tables to be reduced, but this answer does not help to get the correct answer for the large table, so we use 2 for the small tables).

The number of large tables is $7 - 2 = 5$ large tables

Chickens and Rabbits problems follow the following basic four models $(++, +-, -+, --)$:

All variables are natural numbers. C = the number of chickens and R = number of rabbits.
In this workbook, we only deal with model 1. We will discuss other models and the variations of Chickens and Rabbits in higher grades workbooks.

Model 1 (+ +)

$$C + R = a$$
$$2C + 4R = b$$

Example

Melody has 10 chickens and rabbits on her farm. She counts 28 chicken legs and rabbit legs altogether. How many chickens and how many rabbits does she have?

C + R = 10
2C + 4 R = 28

C = 6, R = 4

Model 2 (+ −)

$C + R = a$ $2C - 4R = b$ Melody has 14 chickens and rabbits on her farm. She counts 4 fewer chicken legs than rabbit legs. How many chickens and how many rabbits does she have? C + R = 14 2C − 4 R = 4 R = 4, C = 10	$C + R = a$ $4R - 2C = b$ Melody has 10 chickens and rabbits on her farm. She counts 28 fewer chicken legs than rabbit legs. How many chickens and how many rabbits does she have? C + R = 10 4R − 2C = 28 R = 8 C = 2

Student's name: _____ Assignment date: _____

Model 3 (− +)

$C - R = a$ $2C + 4R = b$ Melody has 4 more chickens than rabbits on her farm. She counts 56 chicken legs and rabbit legs altogether. How many chickens and how many rabbits does she have? $C - R = 4$ $2C + 4R = 56$ R = 8, C = 12	$R - C = a$ $2C + 4R = b$ Melody has 4 fewer chickens than rabbits on her farm. She counts 64 chicken legs and rabbit legs altogether. How many chickens and how many rabbits does she have? $R - C = 4$ $2C + 4R = 64$ C= 8, R = 12

Model 4 (− −)

$C - R = a$ $2C - 4R = b$ Melody has 11 more chickens than rabbits on her farm. She counts 12 more chicken legs than rabbit legs. How many chickens and how many rabbits does she have? $C - R = 11$ $2C - 4R = 12$ C = 16, R = 5	$R - C = a$ $4R - 2C = b$ Melody has 5 fewer chickens than rabbits on her farm. She counts 30 fewer chicken legs than rabbit legs. How many chickens and how many rabbits does she have? $R - C = 5$ $4R - 2C = 30$ C = 5, R = 10

Student's name: _____ Assignment date: _____

Problem

Melody has 24 chickens and rabbits on her farm. She counts 74 chicken legs and rabbit legs altogether. How many chickens and how many rabbits does she have?   R = 13, C = 11
Melody has 12 chickens and rabbits on her farm. She counts 32 chicken legs and rabbit legs altogether. How many chickens and how many rabbits does she have?   R = 4, C = 8
Melody spent 64 cents and bought 10 stamps of some 8-cent stamps and some 4-cent stamps. How many 4-cent stamps and how many 8-cent stamps did she buy?   4 of 4-cent and 6 of 8-cent
Melody has 100 chickens and rabbits on her farm. She counts 256 chicken legs and rabbit legs altogether. How many chickens and how many rabbits does she have?   C=72, R = 28

Student's name: _____ Assignment date: _____

Problem

A restaurant owner sold 5 hamburgers that were padded with either ham or egg. The ham hamburger was sold for 80 ¢, and the egg hamburgers were sold for 90 ¢ each. The total sale was $4.30. How many ham hamburgers were sold? How many egg hamburgers were sold?

Egg hamburger(s)	4	3	2	1
Ham hamburger(s)	1	2	3	4
Total	$4.10	$4.20	$4.30	$4.40

2 egg hamburgers and 3 ham hamburgers

Are there any other possibilities? Explain how do you know?

No.

Mr. Ho told his class children to open their math books to the facing pages whose page numbers add up to 95. What are the two facing pages the children turn to?

47 and 48

Mr. Ho told his class children to open their math books to the facing pages whose page numbers add up to 117. What are the two pages the children turn to?

58 and 59

Surplus and Shortage problem 盈不足术, 盈亏问题 (紅利分配问题)

This kind of problem appears in grade 3 math contest books in China puzzled me a lot. For example, picking up any math contest book in China, you might see a problem which is similar to the following:

The Surplus and Shortage problem is very easy to solve using the algebraic method. The reason it appears in many grade-3 Chinese math contest books is that it was a classic Chinese word problem. The ancient Chinese were fascinated by the natural model $ax \pm b = cx \pm d$ ($equation1 = equation2\ with\ the\ same\ divisor\ x$). The + and – in the equation reflect the nature of surplus and shortage. This situation is very similar to the Plant problem, which has three natural models built in the problem.

This kind of Surplus and Shortage problem can also be thought of as a Distribution problem.
The dividend is distributed to some people, and the result is either even with a remainder or not enough to share.

Dividend = Quotient1 × divisor $\pm$ remainder1 = Quotient2 × divisor $\pm$ remainder2

被除数 = 商1 × 除数 ± 余数1 = 商2 × 除数 ± 余数2

We can teach this kind of problem using the Line segment diagram. However, I do not think it is very difficult for grade 3 or 4 students to solve using a very simple equation.

For example,

Max is short of 35 cents to buy 5 kg of apples, but he will have 15 cents left if he buys 4 kg. How much does each kg cost, and how much money does he have?

The cost of one kg does not change whether he buys 5 kg or 4 kg. So, we know from the above equation, the divisor is the cost per kg. Let's say it is x.

Max's money can be expressed in 2 ways, and they are equal. $5x - 35 = 4x + 15$
Both sides subtract $4x$. $5x - 35 - 4x = 4x + 15 - 4x$

$x - 35 = 15$
Both sides add 35. $x - 35 + 35 = 15 + 35$
$x = 50$
The cost per kg is 50 cents.
Max has $5 \times 50 - 35 = 215$ cents = $\$2.15$.

The following problem appeared in *Chinese Nine Chapters on the Mathematics Art* (https://en.wikipedia.org/wiki/The_Nine_Chapters_on_the_Mathematical_Art 九章算朮). The ancient book had recorded procedures on how to solve this type of problem without much reasoning explained.

今有共实物, 人出八, 盈三, 人出七, 不足四. 问人数, 物价各几何?

Example

If everyone pays \$8, there will be \$3 left. If everyone pays \$7, then there will be a short of \$4. How many people are there buying the goods and how much are the goods?

The ancient Chinese book used the concept of Systems of Equations, but it can be solved by a much simpler equation $ax \pm b = cx \pm d$ to solve it. The modern Chinese math contest books did not use the simple equation $ax \pm b = cx \pm d$. The reason is that the grade 3 students do not understand algebra. Rather, they offer a formula to calculate.

How to teach a grade-3 student the above ancient Chinese Surplus and Shortage problem without using algebra or formulas?

We use the Line Segment Diagram.

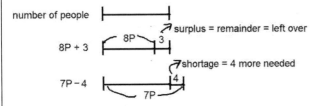

From the above 3-line segments, we know
$7p + 4 + 3 = 8p$
P = 7 …. the number of people.
$8 \times 7 - 3 =$ **53 …. the cost of goods.**

Expansion of Surplus and Shortage problem 盈亏問題举一反三

As we have mentioned that the Surplus and Shortage problem coming from the model of $ax \pm b = cx \pm d$, where x is the number of students and b and d (remainders) could be either surplus or shortage, so there are in total 6 different models, i.e., (surplus, surplus), (surplus, shortage), (shortage, shortage), (shortage, surplus), (surplus, 0), (shortage, 0). The problem is to find x, but we try to make the dividend equation.

The Surplus and Shortage problem may involve distributing goods to people or some problems similar to this nature. The results are either there is a surplus, or there is a shortage. We can find the number of people by using the concept of using the two remainders difference divided by each share difference, but to find the two remainders difference is not easy for the grade 3 students, so we use the Line Segment Diagram to give them the visual effect. The two remainders difference can be found by using the formulas. The two remainders difference is explained later in this section.

The algebraic method is the easiest method, but for those who do not know the simple algebraic equation manipulation, then the Line Segment Diagram can be used.

The formula method is the worst method because it relies on memorization, not understanding. It is also a wrong approach to teach math contests strategy and word problem-solving methods. However, if we use the diagram suggested in this workbook, then it is easy to find the two remainders difference.

Example

If everyone pays $8, there will be $3 left. If everyone pays $7, then there will be a short of $4. How many people are there buying the goods and how much are the goods?

The two remainders difference between the two distributions is $4 + 3 = 7$. The share difference (each person's payment difference) $= 8 - 7 = 1$. How many people will it take to make a $7 difference?
$7 \div 1 = 10$ people

How do we know the two remainders difference is $7 + 3 = 10$?

Using a diagram to find the remainders difference

By using the following diagram, students have no need to memorize whether the difference between surplus or shortage is addition or subtraction.

The central vertical line shows that the remainder is 0 after the distribution; the right hand of the central line shows that there is a surplus. On the left-hand side of the central line, it shows there is a shortage. Since many Chinese teachers use formulas in China to teach the Surplus and Shortage problems, so the following diagram should help students get a good grasp on the reason why 2 surpluses or 2 shortages distributions uses subtraction, and 1 surplus and 1 shortage use addition.

Model 1 (surplus, surplus) of two distributions

The two remainders difference = surplus1 – surplus2

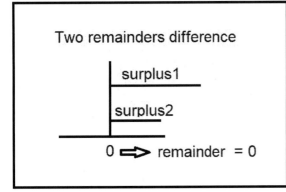

Model 2 (surplus, shortage) of two distributions

The two remainders difference = surplus + surplus

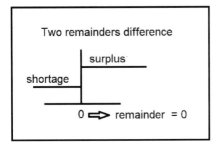

Model 3 (shortage, shortage) of two distributions

The two remainders difference = shortage1 − shortage2

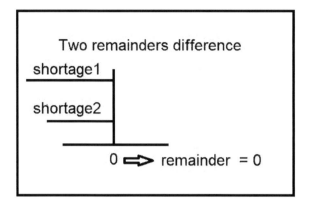

Model 4 (shortage, surplus) of two distributions

The same as Model 2.

Model 5 (surplus, 0) of two distributions

The two remainders difference = surplus

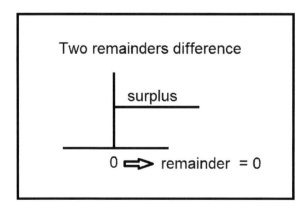

Model 6 (shortage, 0) of two distributions

The two remainders difference = shortage

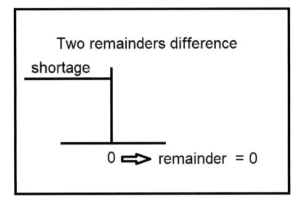

A quick way of drawing the Line Segment for the Surplus and Shortage problems

To draw the Line Segment Diagram for the Surplus and Shortage problem, we do not need to indicate the addition (surplus) or subtraction (shortage) on the Line Segment Diagram. The line segment Diagram can be drawn by using 3-line segments. One of them is the original number (dividend).

Example

If everyone pays $8, there will be $3 left. If everyone pays $7, then there will be a short of $4. How many people are there buying the goods and how much are the goods?

The dividend is the original number and is worked backwards by adding the remainder (surplus +)

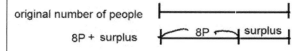

The shortage ($-$) always is to subtract a quantity to equal to the original number (opposite to the surplus), such as the follows. The dividend is worked backwards by subtracting the shortage.

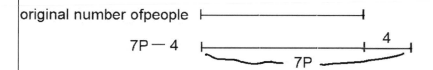

Advanced problem

If Max's class is divided into 3 groups, there will be 2 people left. If his class is divided into 5 groups, then there will be 4 people left. What will be the least number of students in Max's class?

Max's class size $= 3x + 2 = 5y + 4$, x and $y =$ the number of people in each group.
Use the equation of $3x + 2$, we know the class size could be $5, 8, 11, \mathbf{14}, 17, 20, 23, 26, \mathbf{29}$
Use the equation of $5y + 4$, we know the class size could be $9, \mathbf{14}, 19, 24, \mathbf{29}, 34$
There are 2 numbers satisfying both equations, so the answers could be 14, 29, ...
The answer must be the least, so is 14 the answer. 14 will satisfy both conditions even though the remaining 4 people could make 2 extra groups with 2 people in each group and in this case, there will be 7 groups. If this is not approved, then 29 will be the answer.

Student's name: _____ Assignment date: _____

Using multiple numbers method

A basket of apples is divided into many piles. If each pile has 8 apples, then there is a short of one apple, and if each pile has 7 apples, then there are 8 apples left. Find how many apples are there and how many piles are there?

Method 1, use multiples

Find the number of apples which satisfies the condition 1 with 8 apples in one pile short of one apple.
The number of apples could meet the above condition 1 are 7, 15, 23, 31, 39, 47, 55, 63, 71, …… (add 8 each time to get the next number.)

Find a number which satisfies the condition 2 with 7 apples in one pile, 8 apples left.
The number of apples that could meet the above condition is 15, 22, 29, 36, 43, 50, 57, 64, 71, …… (add 7 each time to get the next number.)

The 71 apples meet both conditions.

Method 2, use algebra

Let the number of piles $= x$

$8x - 1 = 7x + 8$

$x = $ **9 piles,**

$8x - 1$
$= 8 \times 9 - 1$
$= $ **71 apples.**

Model 1 盈盈 $ax + b = cx + d$, where all variables are natural numbers.

Every student gets 6 books, 4 books left. Every student gets 4 books, 8 books left. How many students are there?

Line Segment Diagram method	Algebraic method
The following shows how the Line Segment Diagram can be drawn.	$6S + 4 = 4S + 8$ $2S = 4$ $S = 2$

<table>
<tr>
<td>

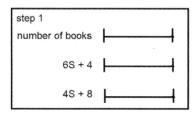

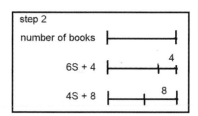

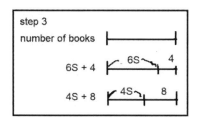

From the above last Line Segment Diagram, we can see that $6S - 4S = 8 - 4$
$2S = 4$.
$S = 2$ …… students

</td>
<td>

Formula

The reason for using the formula can be seen from the left-hand sideline Segment Diagram.

Number of receivers (x)

$$= \frac{large\ surplus - small\ surplus}{large\ share - small\ share}$$

$$= \frac{8-4}{6-4}$$

$$= \frac{4}{2}$$

$$= 2 \text{ students}$$

</td>
</tr>
</table>

Model 2 盈亏 $ax + b = cx - d$, where all variables are natural numbers.

Every student gets 4 books, 8 books left. Every student gets 6 books, 4 books short. How many students are there?

Line Segment Diagram method	Algebraic method
The following shows how the Line Segment Diagram can be drawn. 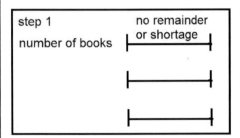 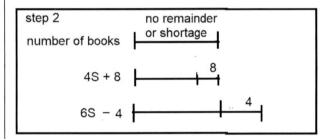 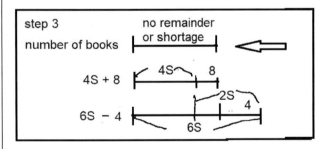 From the above last Line Segment Diagram, we can see that 2S = 12 S = 6	$6S - 4 = 4S + 8$ $2S = 12$ $S = 6$ **Formula** The reason for using the formula can be seen from the left-hand side Line Segment Diagram. Number of receivers (x) $= \dfrac{surplus + shortgage}{large\ share - small\ share}$ $= \dfrac{8+4}{6-4}$ $= \dfrac{12}{2}$ $= 6$ students The real difference between the two distributions is 8 + 4 =12. How to come with such a difference of 14 when each student gets 2 books for the book number difference? Each student's book number difference × total students = total difference between 2 remainders (see left-hand side diagram for visual understanding.)

Example 1

If Mrs. Ho awards 5 books to each student at the year-end award ceremony, there will be a **Surplus** of 20 books. If she awards each student 7 books, then there is a **shortage** of 30 books. How many students in her class and how many books does she have?

Comparison method using line segment diagram	**The arithmetic formula** for one surplus and one shortage 一盈一亏	**Algebraic method**
The numbers of books and students are fixed. Comparing the first distribution and the second distribution, we know the second distribution needs 50 more books than the first distribution. The reason is that, for the second distribution, each person gets 2 more books. In other words, if each person gets 2 more books, then we need 50 more books (For the reason, see the following Line Segment Diagram.), so the number of students = $\frac{50}{2}$ = 25 students. This explanation basically reflects the procedure of the algebraic calculation on the right-hand side.	The number of shares (The number of students) = $\frac{盈+亏}{每份的差}$ = $\frac{\text{The sum of surplus and shortage}}{\text{The difference between each personn's share}}$ # of students = $\frac{20+30}{7-5}$ = 25 # of apples = 5 × 25 + 20 = 145. The above formula can be derived from the equation on the right-hand side. How many grades 3 students really understand this formula method?	5S + 20 = 7S − 30 = the number of books 30 + 20 = 2S S = # of students = 25 # of apples = 5 × 25 + 20 = 145. **There are 25 students, 145 apples.** The algebraic method is recommended. If students do not understand algebra, then use the Line Segment Diagram.
Surplus = +, Shortage = − From the above Line Segment Diagram, we know that Number of books = 5S + 20 = 7S − 30. This becomes the algebraic equation method. We can also compare the 5S +20 and 7S −30 line segments, we know that 5S+20 +30 = 7S 2S = 50, 2= 25 students		

The drawing of the Line Segment Diagram requires some time, so we can try to use the double T-table and Comparison method to figure the answer.

T-table method for small numbers only

Example

If each student gets 2 balls, then there will be 1 ball left. If each student gets 3 balls, then there will be 2 balls short. How many balls are there?

7 balls

This problem has 2 equations, so we use 2 T-table to solve it.

Each student gets
2 balls with 1 ball left

Each student gets 3
3 balls with 2 balls short

student	ball
1	3
2	5
3	7

student	ball
1	1
2	4
3	7

From the above T-tables, we know that the student number is 3 and the number of balls is 7.

Student's name: _____ Assignment date: _____

Example

Problem	Use formula	Double T-table method
Every student gets 5 books, 22 books left. Every student gets 7 books, 18 short. How many students are there?	$5S + 22 = 7S - 18$ Students $= \frac{22+18}{7-5} = 20$ Number of books $= 20 \times 7 - 18 = 122$	The method would be too slow to get answer for large numbers.

Model 3 号号 $ax - b = cx - d$, where all variables are natural numbers.

Every student gets 6 books, 4 books short. Every student gets 9 books, 23 books short. How many students are there?

Line Segment Diagram method	Algebraic method
The following shows how the Line Segment Diagram can be drawn. 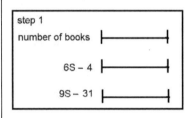 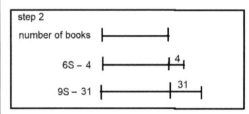 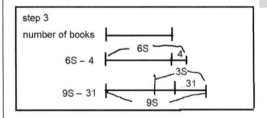 From the above last Line Segment Diagram, we can see that 3S = 27 S = 9	$6S - 4 = 9S - 31$ $3S = 27$ $S = 9$ **Formula** The reason for using the formula can be seen from the left-hand side Line Segment Diagram. Number of receivers (x) $= \dfrac{large\ shortgage - small\ shortgage}{large\ share - small\ share}$ $= \dfrac{31 - 4}{9 - 6}$ Every student gets 3 more, and then the total difference is 27. So, the total number of students = 27 ÷ 3 = 9 $= \dfrac{27}{3}$ $= 9$ students

Model 4亏盈 $ax - b = cx + d$, where all variables are natural numbers.

Every student gets 6 books, 4 books short. Every student gets 4 books, 8 books short. How many students are there?

Model model 4 has the same model and solution as Model 2.

Model 5 盈0 $ax + b = cx$, where all variables are natural numbers.

Every student gets 6 books, 5 books left. Every student gets 7 books, and there are no books left. How many students are there?

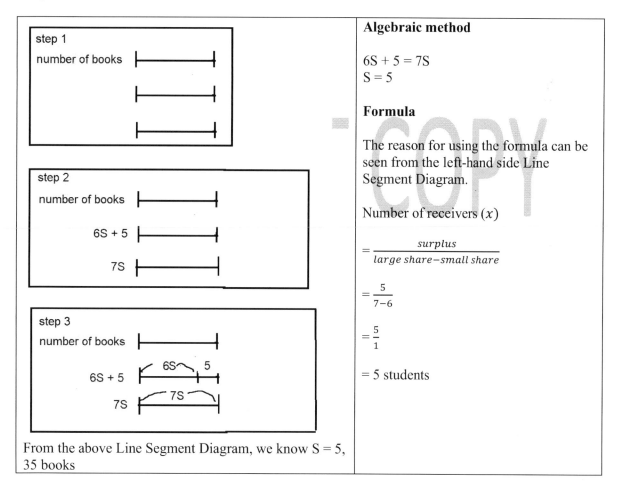

step 1
number of books

step 2
number of books
6S + 5
7S

step 3
number of books
6S + 5
7S

From the above Line Segment Diagram, we know S = 5, 35 books

Algebraic method

6S + 5 = 7S
S = 5

Formula

The reason for using the formula can be seen from the left-hand side Line Segment Diagram.

Number of receivers (x)

$$= \frac{surplus}{large\ share - small\ share}$$

$$= \frac{5}{7-6}$$

$$= \frac{5}{1}$$

= 5 students

Model 6 亏 0 (shortage, 0) $ax - b = cx$, where all variables are natural numbers.

Every student gets 8 books, 5 books short Every student gets 7 books, there are no books left. How many students are there?

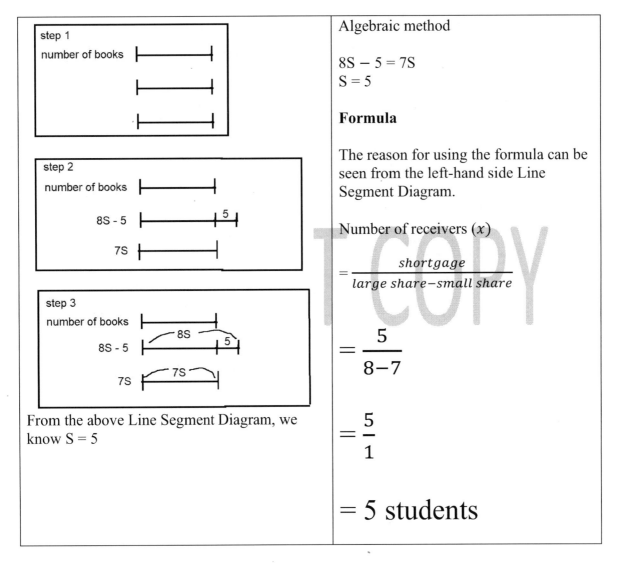

Algebraic method

$8S - 5 = 7S$
$S = 5$

Formula

The reason for using the formula can be seen from the left-hand side Line Segment Diagram.

Number of receivers (x)

$$= \frac{shortgage}{large\ share - small\ share}$$

$$= \frac{5}{8 - 7}$$

$$= \frac{5}{1}$$

$$= 5 \text{ students}$$

From the above Line Segment Diagram, we know S = 5

Summary

After going through the above 6 models, we perhaps can understand why we recommend using the algebraic method. The Line Segment Diagram is cumbersome and slow to get solutions when compared to the algebraic method.

The Chinese math contest books offer three formulas to teach students, but we have decided to offer an algebraic method by teaching students simple algebraic techniques to handle this problem in grade 4, which is the next higher edition of the series of our publications. Only the problems in surplus and shortage conditions are discussed in this edition.

Problem – one surplus and 1 shortage only 一盈一亏問題

Every student gets 14 books, 34 short. Every student gets 12 books, 4 books left.
How many students are there? How many books are there?

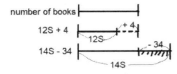

$12S + 4 = 14S - 34$ = number of students for the algebraic method
$12S + 4 + 34 = 14S$ for the Line Segment Diagram method.

$$\frac{4 + 34}{14 - 12} = 19 \; students$$

$19 \times 14 - 34 = 232$ books

Every room occupied by 12 students, 34 students left with no rooms. Every room occupied by 14 students, 4 rooms left empty (each room could be occupied by 14 students.). How many students are there? How many rooms are there?

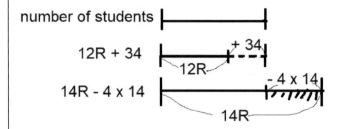

Units are different, convert rooms to students.

$$\frac{34+56}{14-12} = 45\ rooms,\ 574\ students$$

Every student gets 4 books, 3 left. Every student gets 5 books, 18 short.
How many students are there?

Students = $\frac{3+18}{5-4}$ =21
Number of books = 21 × 4+3 = 87

Every student gets 6 books, 3 left. Every student gets 8 books, 13 short.
How many students are there?

Students = $\frac{3+13}{8-6}$ =8
Number of books = 8 × 6 +3 = 51

Every student gets 7 books, 3 left. Every student gets 9 books, 15 short.
How many students are there?

Students = $\frac{3+15}{9-7}$ =9
Number of books = 9 × 7 +3 = 66

If Victoria adds one more bag, then she could put all the peanuts in bags with 6 peanuts in each bag. If she takes away one bag, then she needs to put 9 peanuts in one bag with no peanuts left. How many peanuts does she have?

The problem could be thought of as if Victoria put 6 peanuts in one bag, and then she will have 6 peanuts left. If she put 9 peanuts in each bag, then she will have a shortage of 9 peanuts.

The number of bags = $\frac{9+6}{9-6}$ = 5 bags.
The number of peanuts =5 × 6 +6 = 36

Hidden information in Sum and Difference

Sum

A + B = C, A, B, and C are three numbers. C is the sum of A + B.

Hidden differences
A = C - B, A is the difference between C and B.
B = C – A, B is the difference between C and A.

Example 1

Brenton has 139 pretzels, which are the difference between Charles' and Adam's. Adam has 23 pretzels. How many pretzels does Charlie have?

Charlie = 23 + 139 = 162.

Example 2

Adam has 23 pretzels, which are the difference between Charlie's and Breton's. Breton has 139 pretzels. How many pretzels does Charlie have?

Answer 1 Charlie = 139 – 23 = 116 = Breton - Charlie
Answer 2 Charlie = 139 + 23 = 162 = Charlie – Breton

Problem

13 + ? = 48
? = 48 – 13 = 35

? + 49 = 159
? = 159 – 49 = 110

Student's name: _____ Assignment date: _____

Difference

A – B = C, A, B and C are three numbers. C is the difference between a large number subtracting a small number.

Hidden sum

A = C + B

Hidden differences

B = A – C
C = A – B

Example 1

Brendon has $45 and has $29 less than Adam. How much do they have altogether?

Adam = 45 + 29 = 74
Together 74 + 45 = 119

Example 2

Brendon has $45, which is the difference between Adam and Charlie. Charlie has $39. How much does Adam have?
Difference 1, A – C = B, Adam = 45 + 39 = 84
Difference 2, C – A = 45 not posible

Example 3

Brendon has $45, which is the difference between Adm and Charlie. Charlie has $139. How much does Adam have?

Answer 1, 45 = C – A = 139 – A, A = 139 – 45 = 94
Answer 2, 45 = A – C = A – 139, A = 139 + 45 = 184

Problem

67 - ? = 43
? = 67 – 43 = 24

? – 69 = 139
? = 139 + 69 = 208

Student's name: _____ Assignment date: _____

Sum and Difference problem 和差問題

Adam and Bob have 5 apples. Adam and Bob decide to share the apples, but Bob agrees to give Adam one extra apple. How do you divide the apples?

The numbers in the above problem are very small, so many students could "see" the answers without using any methods. Change the above numbers to large numbers and then ask students to find the answers. Can they still use mental math to find the answer? If not, this is the chance that they learn a method to solve it.

Many math contest books teach students to use formulas to solve the Sum and Difference problems. We do not recommend using the formulas method without going through the reasoning.

Once the student master the Sum and Difference method, the skills learned can be transferred to Sum and Multiplier, Difference and Multiplier problems.

	Sum	Difference	Multiplier
Sum	x	Do addition or subtraction to adjust all values to Base Value.	Do addition or subtraction before division.
Difference	x	x	Do subtraction before division.
Multiplier	x	x	x

Student's name: _____ Assignment date: _____

Base value 基本值

The method of solving the Sum and Difference problem is to convert one of the large or the small number to a Base Value. There are a few ways that we can find the Base Value. The following shows how we can find the Base Value. For 2-variable Sum and difference problems, the Base Value is either the large or the small number. For the 3-variable Sum and Difference problems, the Base Value could be one of the 3 values.

Method 1, Use a story (recommended method)

Transferring Sum and Difference problem into a story 转化和差問题为情景問题

I change the Sum and Difference problem to a story to reflect the real situation on how two kids might divide their apples

Since Adam wants to have one extra apple, so he suggests to Bob, "why not. I just take one apple from the total and put it into my pocket first?"
Bob agrees,
Now there are 5 – 1 = 4 left.
Adam then says to Bob, "We then can divide the 4 apples equally, so you have 2, and I have 2.".
Adan finally gets 2 + 1 (in his pocket) = 3.

The above computation procedure is the opposite of the BEDMAS (bracket, exponent, multiplication, addition, subtraction). This problem requires working on addition (adding the number which is short of) or subtraction (taking off the extra quantity) first before division.

If we think deeply, this Sum and Difference problem is also a variation of Sum and Multiplier or Difference and Multiplier problem.

Method 2, Use the Line Segment Diagram (must learn)

We can also use the Line Segment Diagram to give a visual effect, so students could see it on how to solve this kind of problems. The Line Segment Diagram is a generalized method for students to solve word problems before they learn algebra, and even after they learned algebra, there are some problems much easier to be solved by using work backwards with the help of the Line Segment Diagram, for example, the kind of problems of finding the original amount from the remaining fractions.

We have discussed the Line Segment Diagram method in great detail in the *Math Contest Preparation, Problem Solving Strategies, and Math IQ Puzzles for Grades 2 and 3*.

From the various methods we teach in our *Math Contest Preparation, Problem Solving Strategies, and Math IQ Puzzles* series workbooks, we can see that there is a systematic introduction of concepts and problem- solving methods introduced gradually in different grades. Different problems also require different solving methods in different grades. With the above in mind, we know that the math contest preparation has a different set of teaching materials which are different from the regular school teaching materials.

The following gives a few examples of how our math contest learning workbook series is different from the regular day school curriculum.

1. For Chickens and Rabbits problems, grade 1 students may use the drawing diagram method and use the Assumption method when going to higher grades.
2. Students learn the Line Segment diagram in grade 2 or 3 to solve the word problems.
3. Students start to learn algebra in grade 4.
4. Students learn the idea of using *Quantity divided by its fractional number* to get the original number. Students learn what is the **fractional number,** and how is it different from a **fraction**?
5. Students learn how a problem can be solved by arithmetic and why some problems are easy to solve by using arithmetic.
6. Students learn some basic model word problems and use them in more complicated word problems in math contests.
7. Students learn the difficulty level of the math contest problems and how they are different from regular math word problems.
8. Students learn why only doing routine math computations is not enough when it comes to math contests.
9. Students learn lots of number theory than regular day school students, such as digit computations.

Method 3, Use the Systems of Equations

We can use the Systems of Equations to solve the problem.

Method 4, Use formulas

$$\text{Large number} = \frac{\text{sum} + \text{difference}}{2} \text{ and the smaller number is } \frac{\text{sum} - \text{difference}}{2}.$$

If the students are taught the Line Segment Diagram method and did some problems by using it, then the formulas will come to them naturally.

Sum and Difference expressed in Systems of Equations 联立方程解和差問题

Given	Then
$\spadesuit + \heartsuit = 45 \dots (1)$ $\spadesuit - \heartsuit = 15 \dots (2)$ (1) +(2) (equation property of addition) $2\spadesuit = 60$ $\spadesuit = 30$ $\heartsuit = 45 - 30$ $= 15$	$\spadesuit = 30$ $\heartsuit = 15$
Given $\spadesuit + \heartsuit = 30$ $\spadesuit - \heartsuit = 20$	**Then** $\spadesuit = 25$ $\heartsuit = 5$
Given $\spadesuit + \heartsuit = 50$ $\spadesuit - \heartsuit = 20$	**Then** $\spadesuit = 35$ $\heartsuit = 15$

Student's name: _____ Assignment date: _____

Sum and Difference problems using formulas 用公式解和差问题

Many problems involving Sum and Difference could be solved by the system of equations, for example, if the sum of two numbers x and y is s and the difference between x and y is d :

$$x + y = s$$
$$x - y = d$$

From the above, we know the larger number =
$\dfrac{\text{sum} + \text{difference}}{2}$ and the smaller number is $\dfrac{\text{sum} - \text{difference}}{2}$.

The above 2 larger and smaller numbers of formulas can be used as a shortcut to get an answer quickly instead of using the System of Equations. This type of problem can also be solved by using the line diagram. The more complicated problem can also be solved by the algebraic equation, which is a more generalized approach to solve problems and does not require any memorization of any formulas.

Example 1

The sum of two consecutive even numbers is 126, find these two numbers.

The difference between the two even numbers is 2, so the larger number is $\dfrac{126 + 2}{2} = 64$. The smaller number is $\dfrac{126 - 2}{2} = 62$.

Example 2

The average score of Andrew's science and math is 90, but his science is 5 points better than math, what are the scores of Andrew's science and math?

Science $= \dfrac{180 + 5}{2} = 92.5$

Math $= \dfrac{180 - 5}{2} = 87.5$

The Sum and Difference problem such as the following could be called a typical Sum and Difference problem, many times they appear in math contests or school enrichment program, but the numbers used are small, so many Canadian teachers use Guess and Check method. The Line Segment Method could be used to solve this kind of problem for lower grades students, and in higher grades, the concept of Systems of Equations could be introduced.

Changing Sum and Difference to two Base Values 转化和差问题为二个标准值

One method to solve the Sum and Difference problem is to decrease the large number to the small number (The small number is viewed as the Base Value) or to increase the small number to the large number (The large number is viewed as the Base Value.). This changing to Base Value method can be applied to the condition when there are more than two variables.

Example 1

Adam and Bob have 67 apples. Adam and Bob decide to share the apples, but Bob agrees to give Adam 43 extra apples. How do you divide the apples?

Since Adam wants to have 43 extra apples, so he suggests to Bob, "why not. I just take 43 apples from the total and put it into my pocket first?"
Bob agrees.
Now there are 67 – 43 = 24 left.
Adam then says to Bob, "We then can divide the 24 apples equally, so you have 12, and I have 12.".
Adan finally gets 12 + 43 (in his pocket) = 55.

Adam has 55 apples, and Bob has 12 apples.

Example 2

Andy has 23 more apples than Bob. Bob has 14 more apples than Cathy. Andy, Bob, and Cathy altogether have 213 apples. How many apples does each one of them have?

There are 3 variables, so how to use the formula, which is for two variables?

Convert Andy to Cathy.   Convert Bob to Cathy
Andy - 23 - 14 = Cathy   Bob - 14 = Cathy

Andy has 23 more apples than Bob. Bob has 14 more apples than Cathy. Andy, Bob, and Cathy altogether have 213 apples. How many apples does each one of them have?

A student can use three line segments to solve this problem.

213
$-23 - 14 - 14 = 162$ .... Cathy's apples
Cathy $= \dfrac{162}{3} = 54$
Bob $= 54 + 14 = 68$
Andy $= 68 + 23 = 91$

Student's name: _____ Assignment date: _____

Non-standard Sum and Difference problems

Normally, the Sum and Difference are two known factors for the Sum and Difference problems, but what happens if one of them is not obvious given? The following discusses the non-standard Su and Difference problems.

Standard Sum and Difference problem	There are 156 students in Steven`s grade 6 class. There are 16 more boys than girls. How many boys and girls are there, respectively? G=70, B=**86**
The difference is not given but can be calculated. The difference is twice the amount given. We have discussed this concept in lower grades *Ultimate Math Contest, Problem Solving Strategies, Math IQ problems* series. Example If Adam gives 7 apples to Bob, Adam still has 17 apples more than Bob. The difference is $7 \times 2 + 17 = 31$. When Adam gives Bob 7 and ends up with 17 more, so we know the real difference before 17 is to double 7.	**Case 1** Adam and Bob have 64 apples together. If Adam gives 8 apples to Bob, then they have the same number of apples. How many apples does each of them have originally? The difference is 16. Bob $= \frac{64-16}{2} = 24$ Adam $= \frac{64+16}{2} = 40$ Case 2 **Case 2** Adam and Bob have 493 apples altogether, and if Adam gives 7 apples to Bob, then Adam still has 17 apples more than Bob. How many apples does each one of them have in the beginning? The difference $= 7 \times 2 + 17 = 31$ **Bob** $= \dfrac{493-31}{2} = \mathbf{231}$ **Adam** $= 493 - 231 = \mathbf{262}$

Student's name: _____ Assignment date: _____

This difference is the opposite case of the above condition.	**Case 3** Adam and Bob have 493 apples altogether, and if Adam gives 17 apples to Bob, then Adam has 7 apples less than Bob. How many apples does each one of them have in the beginning?

Case 3

Adam and Bob have 493 apples altogether, and if Adam gives 17 apples to Bob, then Adam has 7 apples less than Bob. How many apples does each one of them have in the beginning?

The difference = $17 \times 2 - 7 = 27$
The difference must be 2 times the amount given = 17 $17 \times 2 = 34$ to make Adam and Bob have an equal number of apples. But since Adam has 7 less than Bob after giving, so the difference must subtract 7 to make the "less" happen.

If the student can not figure the above difference calculations, then we can use the following diagram to work backwards,

If =, then the difference will be 34.

Adam	Bob
17	= 17
34	0

But since the result is 10 < 17, so we must subtract 7 from 34. 34 — 7 = 27.

$$\text{Bob} = \frac{493 - 27}{2} = \mathbf{233}$$

$$\text{Adam} = 493 - 233 = \mathbf{260}$$

Sum and Difference problem connecting to Sum and Multiplier problem

Problem 1

Adam and Bob have 59 apples. After Adam gives 17 apples to Bob, then they have an equal number of apples. How many apples does each person have in the beginning?

Problem 2

Adam and Bob have 59 apples. Adam has 34 apples more than Bob. How many apples does each person have?

There is no real difference between problem 1 and problem 2. Problem 2 can also be viewed as a Sum and Multiplier problem after we perform addition or subtraction.

For problem 2, if we remove the 34 from the total 59, then Adam will have as many apples as Bob, so the multiplier is 1.

Problem

Adam, Bob, and Cathy have 73 books together. Adam has 5 books more than Bob, and Bob has 7 more books than Cathy. How many books are there for each person?	
Addition method to adjust all people to the highest number (Adam's books)	Subtraction method to adjust all people to the lowest value (Cathy's books).
$73 + 5 + 5 + 7 = 90$ which is 3 times of Adam's books $\frac{90}{3} = 30$ ...... Adam's books $30 - 5 = 25$ ..... Bob's books $25 - 7 = 18$ ..... Cathy's books The addition method follows the direct meaning of English sentences. The subtraction follows the reverse order of the English sentence. Which method do you like?	$73 - 5 - 7 - 7 = 54$ which is 3 times of Cathy's books $\frac{54}{3} = 18$ $18 + 7 = 25$ .... Bob's books $25 + 5 = 30$ ..... Adam's books

More than 2 variables Sum and Difference problem

Lots of parents would use the concept of solving this kind of 3 variables using Systems of Equations, but

See how beautiful it is to use the idea of Sum and Difference to solve the 3-variable System of Equations problems.

Bob and Cathy have 43 books together. Adam has 5 books more than Bob and 12 more books than Cathy. How many books are there for each person?

Arithmetic Sum and Difference method	Algebraic method
From the following diagram, we know that Bob has 7 more books than Cathy. 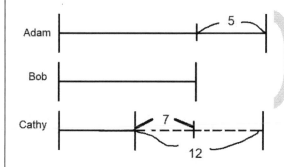 The above problem becomes a standard Bob and Cathy's Sum and Difference problem. $$\text{Bob} = \frac{43+7}{2} = 25$$ Cathy = 43- 25 = 18 Adam = 25 + 5 = 30	$B + C = 43$ ……….… ..(1) $A - B = 5$ …………………(2) $A - C = 12$ …………………(3) The normal way is to reduce 3 variables to 2 variables. From (2), B can be replaced by A. From (3) C can be replaced by A. $A - 5 + A - 12 = 43$ $2A = 43 + 12 + 5$ $ = 60$ $A = 30$

Adam, Bob, and Cathy have 847 books together. Adam has 175 books more than Bob. Bob has 150 books more than Cathy. How many books are there for each person?

Arithmetic Sum and Difference method	Algebraic method
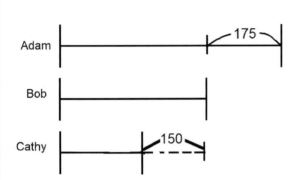 Look at the above diagram, to find Bob's books first is much easier. So how to find the Base Value depends on each individual problem. Bob $= \frac{847+150-175}{3} = 274$ Cathy $= 274 - 150 = 124$ Adam $= 274 + 175 = 449$	$A + B + C = 850 \ldots\ldots\ldots\ldots\ldots$(1) $A - B = 175 \ldots\ldots\ldots\ldots\ldots\ldots$(2) $B - C = 150 \ldots\ldots\ldots\ldots\ldots\ldots$(3) The left-hand side diagram shows to convert the sum to a sum of three Base Values is much easier.

Sum and Difference applications 和差問題举一反三

The concept of the Sum and Difference model problem can be applied to different types of other problems such as geometry and age etc. Sometimes, the Sum and Difference technique is one step in solving a multi-step math contest problem.

Perimeter and area problem

The perimeter of a garden is 92 m. The length is 12 m longer than the width. How long are the length and width each?

l=29m, w = 17 m

L+W=46
L-W=12

Age problem

The sum of Adam's age and Bob's age is 36. Five years ago, Adam was 6 years older than Bob. How old are Adam and Bob each, respectively?

Adam = 21, Bob = **15**

A + B=36
A − B=6

Work problem

Adam and Bob can make 56 Lego® cars in 4 hours. If Adam and Bob each work 5 hours separately, Adam can make 27 more than Bob. How many cars can each of them make in one hour?

This problem has Sum (Adam and Bob can make 56 Lego® cars in 4 hours.) and Difference (If Adam and Bob each works 3 hours separately, Adam can make 24 more than Bob.), but the time units are different.

Sum: $56 \div 4 = 16$ cars/hour
Difference: $24 \div 3 = 8$ cars/hour
Adam $= \frac{16+8}{2} = \mathbf{12}$
Bob $= \frac{16-8}{2} = \mathbf{4}$

Distance and speed problem

Adam and Bob cycled from the opposite ends of a road, which is 48 miles, and they met in 6 hours. If they started from the same end of the road towards the other end of the road, Adam would be 8 miles ahead of Bob in 4 hours. Find each person's speed in miles per hour.

The sum of Adam's speed and Bob's speed per hour is $48 \div 6 = 8$ miles / per hour
The difference between Adam's speed and Bob's speed per hour is $8 \div 4 = 2$ miles / per hour

$$\text{Adam} = \frac{8+2}{2} = 5 \text{ miles per hour}$$

$$\text{Bob} = \frac{8-2}{2} = 3 \text{ or } 8 - 5 = 3 \text{ miles per hour}$$

Student's name: _____ Assignment date: _____

Problem

Judy and Dominic have 20 pencils altogether, but Judy has 6 more pencils than Dominic, how many pencils does each one of them have?

Judy: 13 pencils, Dominic: 7 pencils

The sum of Angela and her brother's age is 28. Angela is 6 years younger than her brother. What is the age of Angela and her brother?

Angela's age 11, Her brother is 17

Angela is 14 years old, and her father is 50 years old. How many years back when Angela's father's age is exactly 4 times of Angela's?

2

If Kelsey and Allison paint the interior of their house together, it will take 6 days. If the entire house is painted by one person alone, it will take 5 more days for Kelsey to finish painting than Allison. How long will it take to finish painting the house by each person alone?

This problem is for advanced students only.
Allison: 10 days, Kelsey: 15 days.
Allison: x days, Kelsey: $x + 5$
$$1 \div \left(\frac{1}{x} + \frac{1}{x+5} \right) = 6$$

Student's name: _____ Assignment date: _____

With the current, a boat travels 65 km per hour. When against the current, its speed is 63 km per hour. What is the speed of the current?

The sum of the boat's speed and the current speed is 65.
The difference of the boat's speed minus the current speed is 63.

The current speed = $\frac{65-63}{2}$ = 1 km per hour

With the wind, a runner runs 90 m in 10 seconds. At the same running speed, when runs against the wind, the runner runs 70 m in 10 seconds. How long will it take for the runner to run 120 m with no wind?

The sum of the runner's speed and the current speed is 9 m.
The difference of the runner's speed minus the wind speed is 7m.

The runner's speed = $\frac{9+7}{2}$ = **8 m per second**

$\frac{120}{8}$ = **15 seconds**

If the perimeter of a rectangle is 68 m and its length is 8 m longer than its width. What is the width in metres?

Half of the perimeter is Length + width = 34.
Length – width = 8.
Width = $\frac{34-8}{2}$ = **13 metres**

The difference between the two people's ages is 22, and their sum of ages is 62. What are their ages?

Older person = $\frac{62+22}{2}$ = **42**
Younger person = 62 – 42 = **20**

Student's name: _____ Assignment date: _____

Sum and Difference in different data types 不同数性的和差問題

The Sum and Difference problem involves the concept of System of Equations, but elementary students who do not understand the System of Equations can solve it by using the line segment method.

The following fraction, percentage, and ratio are for advanced students only.

Comments	whole number	fractions	percentage	ratio
1. From the Whole Number word problems, we know that the concept of Sum and Difference model problem can be applied to different types of problems such as geometry and age etc.	There are 156 students in Steven's grade 6 class. There are 16 more boys than girls. How many boys and girls are there, respectively? G=70, B=86	There were some apples in the basket. Adam took $\frac{2}{3}$ of apples from the basket and Bob took $\frac{2}{5}$ from the same basket. If Adam gives Bob 30 apples, then Bob and Adam will have an equal number of apples. How many apples did Adam and Bob each take from the basket?	Adam took 80% apples from a basket, and Bob took the rest. If Adam gives Bob 90 apples, then Adam and Bob have an equal number of apples. How many apples did Adam and Bob have in the beginning? $180 \div (0.8 - 0.2) = 300$ Adam: $300 \times 0.8 = 240$ Bob $= 300-240=60$	Adam and Bob took some apples from a basket, and the ratio of the number of Adam's apples to Bob's apples is 5:3. **(a)** The difference between Adam's apples and Bob's apples is 240.
2. The difference can be expressed in different ways. For example, If Adam gives 7 apples to Bob, Adam still has 17 apples more than Bob. The difference is $7 \times 2 + 17 = 31$. When Adam gives Bob 7 and ends up with 17 more so we know the real difference before 17 is to double 7.	Adam and Bob have 493 apples altogether, and if Adam gives 7 apples to Bob, then Adam still has 17 apples more than Bob. How many apples does each one of them have in the beginning? Adam = 262, Bob = 231	The difference is 64. $60 \div \left(\frac{2}{3} - \frac{2}{5}\right) = 225$ $225 \times \frac{2}{3} = 150$... Adam $225 \times \frac{2}{5} = 90$ Bob **The perimeter of a rectangular garden is $196\frac{1}{4}$ m and its difference between length and width is $\frac{3}{4}$ m. Find length and width, respectively.**	Adam had 20% more apples than Bob, and this means Adam has 40 more apples than Bob. How many apples did Adam have in the beginning? $40 \div 0.2 = 400 \div 2 = 200$ ....Adam	How many apples did Adam and Both each have in the beginning? The difference in the number of apples corresponds to the ratio difference, which is $5 - 3 = 2$. So, each unit $=240 \div 2 = 120$ Adam $= 120 \times 5 = 600$ Bob $= 120 \times 3 = 360$ The above example shows that we do not even need to know the sum.
3. For fractions and percentage problems, there is always a sum of 1 hidden concept, so to get the original amount, we use the concept of *partial ÷ (% or fraction)* to get the whole idea. This backward work method to get the original amount is very different from the whole number Sum and Difference method.	The perimeter of a garden is 92 m. The length is 12 m longer than the width. What are the length and width? l=29m, w = 17 m The sum of Adam's age and Bob's age is 36. Five years ago, Adam was 6 years older than Bob. How old are Adam and Bob each, respectively? Adam = 21, Bob = 15	$196\frac{1}{4} \times \frac{1}{2} = 98\frac{1}{8}$ $\frac{98\frac{1}{8} - \frac{3}{4}}{2} = 48\frac{11}{16}$ width $48\frac{11}{16} + \frac{3}{4} = 49\frac{7}{16}$ length **The perimeter of a garden is 136 m, and its width is $\frac{3}{4}$ of its length. Find length and width, respectively.** $136 \times \frac{1}{2} = 68$ $\frac{68 - \frac{3}{4}}{2} = 33\frac{1}{2}$ width $\frac{3}{4} + 33\frac{1}{2} = 34\frac{1}{4}$ length		**(b)** Adam and Bob have apples 240. How many apples did Adam and Both each have in the beginning? The sum corresponds to the sum of ratio 5. $240 \div 5 = 48$ Adam $= 48 \times 5 = 240$ Bob $= 48 \times 3 = 144$

Sum and Multiplier 和倍问题

If 6 = 2 *times of* 3, then the "2" means a multiplier. Given the sum of two numbers $x + y$ and a multiplier (k), we can find these two numbers x and y if $y = kx$. Often we can convert the multiplier to a "box" or "bag" idea for countable objects to find out how many items in a bag to solve the problem.

The strategy is to correspond the sum to its sum of multipliers. Often the sum is corresponding to the multiplier plus 1, i.e.,

***smaller number* = sum ÷ (multiplier +1)**

1 份数或小数 = 和÷(倍数+1)

The reason is most of the problems dealing with two numbers, and one number is a multiple of another number. This formula will not work if five times of A is three times of B. In this case, the denominator for the formula will be **large multiplier + small multiplier = 5 + 3**. The ratio of A : B = 5 : 3.

Using the Line Segment Diagram method

Example 1

The Sum and Multiplier problems are really a special case when the ratio has a denominator of 1. The variables may not restrict to only two variables, so the Line Segment Diagram is the recommended method, instead of using formula.

Example

Adam and Bob had some money saved in a bank. Two times of Adam's money is three times of Bob's money. If Adam withdraws $240 and Bob withdraws $40, then their savings are equal. How much does each of them have in the bank originally?

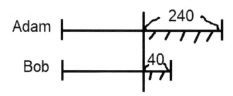

The difference is 240 − 40 = 200
$\frac{200}{3-2} = 200$ ......one share value of the ratio
Bob = 3 × 200 = 600
Adam = 2 3 × 200 = 400

Example 2

The perimeter of a rectangular garden is 72 m. The length is 2 m less than three times of width. What is the area of this garden?

It could be quadratic equation if use algebra $x(3x - 2) = 36$

Always gets only L+ W= $\frac{72}{2} = 36$

Width = $\frac{36+2}{4} = 9.5$

Length =$9.5 \times 3 - 2 = 26.5$

Area = $9.5 \times 26.5 = 251.75$

Student's name: _____ Assignment date: _____

Using the Box method for countable objects

Example 1

Adam and Bob made 350 parts working together, and Adam made 50 more than two times the number of parts made by Bob. Find the number of parts made by each of them.

Do the addition or subtraction first then do the division for the Sum and Multiplier problems.

Think to have all the parts placed in boxes. Bob has one box, and Adam has 2 boxes plus 50 more parts.

$350 - 50 = 300$
$300 \div (2+1) = 100$ …….. Bob
Adam $= 100 \times 2 + 50 = 250$

Example 2

The second angle of a triangle is four times as large as the first angle. The third angle is 60^0 greater than the first one. How large are three angles?

$180 - 60 = 120$, which is the sum of all 3 angles.
$120 \div 6 = 20$ …….. the first angle
$4 \times 20 = 80$ ….. the second angle
$100 - 80 - 20 = 80$ ….. the third angle

Difference and Multiplier 差倍问题

If $6 = 2$ *times of* 3, then the "2" means a multiplier. Given the sum of two numbers $x + y$ and a multiplier (k), we can find these two numbers x and y if $y = kx$. Often we can convert the multiplier to a "box" or "bag" idea for countable objects to find out how many items in a bag to solve the problem.

The strategy is to correspond the difference to its difference of multipliers. Often the difference is corresponding to the **multiplier minus 1**, i.e.,

smaller number = difference ÷ (multiplier −1)

1 份数或小数 = 差÷(倍数−1)

The reason is most of the problems dealing with two numbers, and one number is a multiple of another number. This formula will not work if five times of A is three times of B. In this case, the denominator for the formula will be **large multiplier − small multiplier = 5 − 3**. The ratio of A : B = 5 : 3.

Using the Line Segment Diagram method

The Sum and Multiplier problems are really a special case when the ratio has a denominator of 1. The variables may not restrict to only two variables, so the Line Segment Diagram is the recommended method, instead of using formula.

Example 1

Adam and Bob had some money saved in a bank. Two times of Adam's money is three times of Bob's money. If Adam withdraws $240 and Bob withdraws $40, then their savings are equal. How much does each of them have in the bank originally?

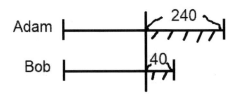

The difference is 240 − 40 = 200
$\frac{200}{3-2} = 200$ ......one share value of the ratio
Bob = 3 × 200 = 600
Adam = 2 3 × 200 = 400

Student's name: _____ Assignment date: _____

Example 2

The second angle of a triangle is four times as large as the first angle. The second angle is 60^0 greater than the first one. How large are three angles?

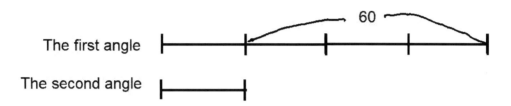

$\frac{60}{4-1} = 20$ ……. First angle

$20 \times 4 = 80$ …… second angle

$180 - 20 - 80 = 100$ …..third angle

Example 3

Three variables

Adam has $40 more than Bob and four times as much as Cathy. Bob has $8 more than Cathy. How much does each one of them have?

The line segment length may not reflect the actual length proportionally.

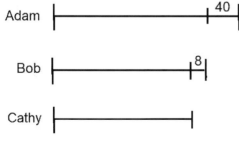

Adam has $48 more than Cathy.
$\frac{48}{4-1} = \$16$ ……Cathy
Bob = 16 + 8 = 24
Cathy = 24 − 8 = 16

Using the Box method for countable objects

Example 1

Adam and Bob made parts working together, and Adam made 350 more than two times the number of parts made by Bob. Find the number of parts made by each of them.

Do the addition or subtraction first then do the division for the Sum and Multiplier problems.

Think to have all the parts placed in boxes. Bob has one box, and Adam has 2 boxes plus 350 more parts.

$350 - 50 = 300$
$300 \div (2 - 1) = 300$ …….. Bob
Adam $= 300 \times 2 + 50 = 650$

Example 2

Adam has 200 more apples than Bob and Adam's apples are three times as many as Bob. How many apples does each one of them have?

Place apples into the box so that Bob has one box, and Adam has 3 boxes.
$200 \div 2 = 100$
Adam. $100 \times 3 = 300$
Bob 100

Student's name: _____ Assignment date: _____

Sum, Difference, and Multiplier

Example of Difference and Multiplier

Adam has 90 more apples than Bob. Adam has three times as many as Bob's apples. How many apples does each one of them have?

90 (difference) is corresponding to 2 times (2 units), and we assume Bob is multiple of 1.
So, each unit is 45.
Adam: $45 \times 3 = $ **135**, **Bob** = 135 - 90 = **45**.

Example of Sum, Difference and Multiplier combined

After Adam gives 200 apples to Bob, then Bob's apples are 3 times as many as Adam's. Together they have 2000 apples.

Hint: Since 200 apples are moved from Adam to Bob, and their total does not change, so the problem becomes the Sum and Difference problem.

2000 apples correspond to 4 equal units (3 +1). So, each unit is 500 apples.
500 + 200 = 700 Adam.
2000 – 700 = 1300... Bob

Sum and Difference word problems 和差文字問題

Calculate 1+2+3+4+5+6+7+8+9 = _____ 45	Calculate 18+12+13+14+5+6+7+8+2 = ____ 85
Calculate 1+3+5+7+3+5+7+9 = _____ 40	Calculate 11+13+15+17+3+5+7+9 = _____ 80
Calculate 2+4+6+8+2+4+6+8 = _____ 40	Calculate 21+24+26+28+2+4+6+8 = _____ 119

After Johnny gave 5 cookies to Joyce, Johnny had the same number of cookies as Joyce. Together they had 50 cookies. How many cookies did Johnny have before he gave some to Joyce? J(Johnny) − O(Joyce) = 10 J + O =50 J = **20**, O = 30	Tony has 2 more marbles than Michelle, and their total is 24. How many marbles does each one of them have in the beginning? T+M = 24 T- M = 2 T = 13, M = 11

何数棋谜算独 Frankho ChessDoku™

Rule: All the digits 1 to 3 must appear exactly once in every row and column. The number appears in the bottom right-hand corner is the result calculated according to the arithmetic operator(s) and chess move(s) as indicated by the darker arrow(s).

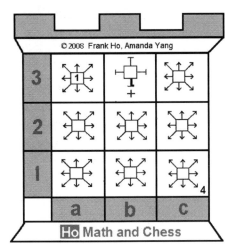

132, 213, 321

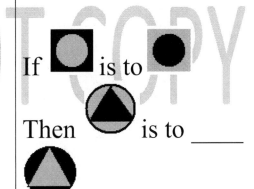

If ⬛⚪ is to ⬛⚫

Then ◯▲ is to ____

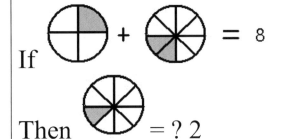

Sum and Difference, sum and product, remaining quantity 和差, 和绩, 餘数

$2 - 1 = $ ____ 1 $3 - 2 = $ ____ 1 $2 - 1 + 4 - 3 + 6 - 5 + 8 - 7 + 10 - 9 = $ ____ 5 $12 - 1 + 14 - 3 + 16 - 5 + 18 - 7 + 20 - 9 = $ ____ 55	Steven spent \$30 after saving one half of his money and he had \$20 left. How much did he have originally? \$100
Ho数棋谜算独 Frankho ChessDoku™ Frankho Puzzle™ is solved by using addition, subtraction, multiplication or division by following chess moves and logic. Rule: All the digits 1 to 3 must appear in every row and column. The number appears in the bottom right-hand corner is the result calculated according to the operator(s) and chess move(s). 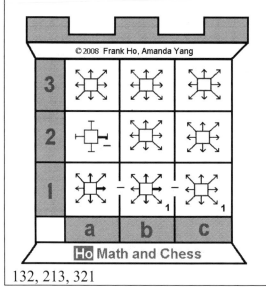 132, 213, 321	Mrs. Wang has some candies in each of 2 baskets with a total of 20 candies in total. She knows the difference between the numbers of candies between 2 baskets is the biggest. Can you find out how many candies in each basket? 19, 1 Mrs. Wang has some candies in each of 2 baskets with a total of 20 candies in total. She knows the product of the numbers of candies between 2 baskets is the biggest. Can you find out how many candies in each basket? 10, 10 Mrs. Wang has some candies in each of 2 baskets with a total of 20 candies in total. She knows the difference of candies between 2 baskets is 6. Can you find out how many candies in each basket? 7, 13, by drawing a line diagram.

Student's name: _____ Assignment date: _____

Transferrable Sum, Difference, and Multiplier

Many word problems of Sum and Difference, Sum and Multiplier, and Difference and Multiplier can be each other transferred into different problems. Once you know how to solve one type of problem, then the knowledge learned can be transferred to another type of problem.

Difference and Multiplier of Age problem

Jim is 28 younger than his father, and now his father is five times as old as Jim. How old are Jim and his father now?

Use LSD to explain the following.
$\frac{28}{4} = 7$ … Jim
28+7=35 ….. father

The above Age problem can be easily transferred into a Difference and Multiplier of Perimeter problem.

A rectangular width is 16 cm shorter than its length. The length is five times as long as its width. What is the length and width of the rectangle?

$16 \div 4 = $ **4 cm** … width
$4 + 16 = $ **20 cm** …. Length

Work problem of Sum and Difference

Adam and Bob can make 56 Lego® cars in 4 hours. If Adam and Bob each works 5 hours separately, Adam can make 27 more than Bob. How many cars can each of them make in one hour?

This problem has Sum (Adam and Bob can make 56 Lego® cars in 4 hours.) and Difference (If Adam and Bob each works 3 hours separately, Adam can make 24 more than Bob.), but the time units are different.

Sum: $56 \div 4 = 16$ cars/hour
Difference: $24 \div 3 = 8$ cars/hour
Adam $= \frac{16+8}{2} = $ **12**
Bob $= \frac{16 - 8}{2} = $ **4**

Student's name: _____ Assignment date: _____

Difference and Multiplier of Work problem

We can turn the above **Sum and Difference Work problem** into a Difference and Multiplier Work problem as follows:

Adam makes 56 more Lego® cars in 4 hours than Bob. Adam works three times as fast as Bob. Find the number of Lego® cars made by each in 3 hours.

Each hour Adam makes 16 (56 ÷ 4) more than Bob. The reason is Adam works faster with multiplier 2 (3 - 1). You can think of the 2 as 2 boxes.
16 ÷ 2 = 8 cars …….. Bob makes each hour, so for 3 hours, Bob makes 8 × 3 = **24 cars**.

Adam makes 8 × 3 × 3 = **72 cars**.

Sum and Multiplier of Age problem

The sum of the ages of Adam and Bob is 32. Bob is 7 years older than four times Adam's age. How old are they now?

Handle the addition or subtraction first before division.

$32 - 7 = 25$
$25 \div 5 = (4 + 1) = 5 \ldots\ldots \textbf{Adam's age}$
$32 - 5 = 27 \ldots$ Bob's age

Difference and Multiplier Age problem

We can turn the above problem into a Difference and Multiplier problem as follows.
Bob is 6 years older than four times Adam's age. Their age difference is 42. How old are they each?

The difference between the above two problems is the Sum problem adds the multiplier by 1, and the Difference subtracts the multiplier by 1. Handle the addition or subtraction first before division.

$42 - 6 = 36$
$36 \div 3 (4 - 1) = \textbf{12} \ldots\ldots \textbf{Adam's age}$
$42 + 12 = \textbf{54} \ldots$ **Bob's age**

Sum and Difference Distance and Speed problem

Adam ├──────────✕──┤ Bob

Adam and Bob cycled from the opposite ends of a road, which is 48 miles, and they met in 6 hours. If they started from the same end of the road towards the other end of the road, Adam would be 8 miles ahead of Bob in 4 hours. Find each person's speed in miles per hour.

Use the sum of 2 average speeds and the difference of the 2 average speeds to find each speed.

The sum of Adam's speed and Bob's speed per hour is $48 \div 6 = 8$ miles / per hour (sum of 2 average speed)
The difference between Adam's speed and Bob's speed per hour is $8 \div 4 = 2$ miles / per hour (difference of 2 average speed)

Adam $= \frac{8+2}{2} = 5$ miles per hour

Bob $= \frac{8-2}{2} = 3$ or $8 - 5 = 3$ miles per hour

Sum and Multiplier Distance and Speed problem

Adam ├──────────✕──┤ Bob

You can transfer the above problem to a Sum and Multiplier Distance and speed problem.

Adam and Bob cycled from the opposite ends of a road, which is 48 miles, and they met in 6 hours. Adam's speed is three times of Bob's speed. Find the distance travelled by each person.

The average speed travelled per hour by Adam and Bob is $48 \div 6 = 8$ miles per hour. This is the sum of average speed they travelled together, but Adam's speed is 3 times of Bob's. (Assume Bob = 1, then Adam = 3 (multiplier), together it is 4.)

Bob's speed $= \frac{8}{3+1} = 2$ miles per hour. In 6 hours, **Bob travelled $2 \times 6 = 12$ miles**

Adam's speed $= 2 \times 3 = 6$ miles per hour. In 6 hours, **Adam travelled $6 \times 6 = 36$ miles**

Difference and Multiplier Distance and Speed problem

You can transfer the above Sum and Multiplier problem to a Difference and Multiplier Distance and speed problem.

The original **Sum and Multiplier** problem was as follows:

Adam and Bob cycled from the opposite ends of a road, which is 48 miles, and they met in 6 hours. Adam's speed is three times of Bob's speed. Find the distance travelled by each person.

The new **Difference and Multiplier** problem is as follows.

Adam and Bob cycled from the same end of a road in the same direction. After 6 hours of cycling, Adam is 48 miles ahead of Bob. Adam's speed is three times of Bob's speed. Find their speeds and the distance travelled by each person.

Arithmetic method	Algebraic method
The difference and multiplier must have the same measuring unit. Adam travelled 48 miles ahead of Bob in 6 hours, which means average 8 miles ahead (difference) per hour. Adam's speed is three times of Bob's speed means the multiplier is 3. The 8 miles difference was created because of the speed of Adam to Bob = 3 to 1 (For every 1 mile of Bob travelled, Adam would have travelled 3 miles). The answer is the Base Value, which is Bob's average speed.	Let Bob's speed = B Adam's speed = 3B $6(3B - B) = 48$ $3B - B = 8$ $B(3 - 1) = 8$ $B = \frac{8}{3-1} = 4$ ......Bob's speed
Bob's speed $= \frac{8}{3-1} = $ **4 miles per hour**. In 6 hours, **Bob travelled** $4 \times 6 = $ **24 miles** **Adam's speed is 12 miles per hour**. **Adam travelled** $48 + 24 = $ **72 miles**	

Student's name: _____ Assignment date: _____

Mixed Sum, Difference, and Multiplier

The sum of the ages of Adam, Bob, and Cathy is 77. Bob is 7 years older than four times Adam's age and three years younger than Cathy's age. How old is each one of them?

It is easier to sort out the addition or subtraction by drawing the Line Segment Diagram.

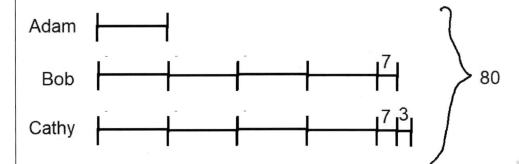

To find the Base Value first.
$80 - 7 - 10 = 63$
63 is the multiple of 9, so **Adam = 7**.
Bob $= 4 \times 7 + 7 = $ **35**
Cathy $= 35 + 3 = $ **38**

Examples

The following problems appear in Ultimate Math Contest Preparation, Problem Solving strategies, Math IQ Puzzles Grades 2 and 3. However, our experience shows that many lower grades students were not able to do all the problems, so we include that section again here to give one more chance to review and learn.

Whole numbers Arithmetic using the line segment
Give and take (Building foundation of learning equation) 取捨問題

Caroline has 185 pogs, and Thomas has 79 pogs. How many pogs must Carolina give to Thomas so that both have the same number of pogs?

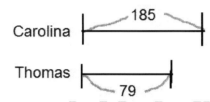

53

Caroline has 185 pogs, and Thomas has 79 pogs. How many pogs must Carolina give to Thomas so that he would have 40 more pogs than her?

73 (53+20)

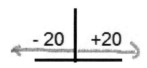

+ 20 and - 20, the difference is 40.

Caroline is 48 years old, and Thomas is 11 years old. In how many years will Caroline be twice as old as Thomas?

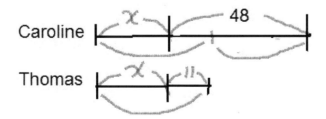

48-11=37 ($37 = x + 11$)which will be Thomas' age in the future., 37-11=26 in 26 years.

.

Line segment Diagram

Whole numbers Arithmetic using the line segment

Sum/Difference and Multiplier 和差倍問题

Caroline has five times as many muffins as Thomas. Caroline has 120 more muffins than Thomas. How many muffins must Carolina give to Thomas so that Caroline has three times as many muffins as Thomas? How many muffins does each have after Caroline gives some to Thomas?
Hint: This problem is for advanced students only. We can transfer the muffins (objects) to boxes.

Line Segment Diagram method	Box Method
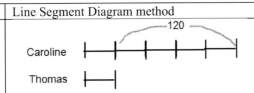 $\frac{120}{5-1} = 30 \ per \ box$ or per part of the line segment diagram. The new boxes ratio for Thomas to Caroline is 1 to 3. $\frac{180}{1+3} = 45$ ......Thomas has. $45 - 30 = 15$ .... **Thomas should get 15 more.** Caroline will have 150 – 15 = **135**. .... **Caroline has.**	We can transfer the "times" (multiplier) to "boxes" without drawing the line segment diagram. The "times" is just another way of expressing the concept of the ratio of a reduced form. In this case, the "times" is the reduced number of muffins. $\frac{120}{5-1} = 30 \ per \ box$ or per part of the line segment diagram. The new boxes ratio for Thomas to Caroline is 1 to 3. $\frac{180}{1+3} = 45$ ......Thomas has. $45 - 30 = 15$ .... **Thomas should get 15 more.** Caroline will have 150 – 15 = **135**. .... **Caroline has.**

There are 145 students in Class A, B, and C. There are 7 more students in Class B than in Class A. There are four times as many students in Class C as in Class A. How many students are there in Class A?

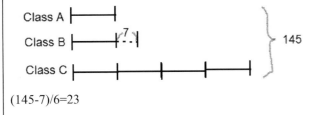

(145-7)/6=23

Student's name: _____ Assignment date: _____

Line segment Diagram

Whole numbers Arithmetic using the line segment

Sum and Difference 和差問題

Caroline and Thomas had 174 apples altogether. If Caroline gave 23 apples to Thomas, then both would have an equal number of apples. How many apples did each one of them have in the beginning?

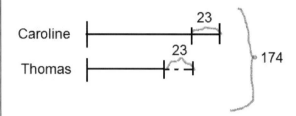

174/2=87, 87+23=**110. Caroline**, 174-110 = **64 Thomas**

Caroline had 220 beads, and Thomas had 120 beads. How many beads did Caroline have to give to Thomas so that Thomas would have 44 more beads than Caroline?

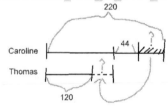

220-120=100, 100 + 22 = **72.**

Word problems using Line Segment Diagrams

Some problems are for advanced students only. Skip those problems which appear too difficult for students to comprehend after teaching them. algebra is out of the question until grade 7 or 8. So the Line Segment Diagram is a very good strategy used to substitute the operation of algebra. Many word problems such as age, weight, numbers, sum and difference could be solved using Line Segment Diagrams.

Using Line Segment Diagram – Age Problems 年齡問題

Many word problems could be easily solved using algebra but for elementary students in Canada, using

Equation	Line segment	Word problems	Solutions
Addition 和 $x + 4 = 20$	4 ... 20	In four years, I will be twenty years old. How old am I?	? $20 - 4 = 16$
Addition 和 $x - 6 = 5$ $x = 11$	? 6 5 ?	Six years ago, I was five. How old am I?	? $5+6 = 11$
Addition 和 $x = 7 + 3$	No need to draw.	I am three years older than Ling, who is 7. How old am I?	? $7+3 = 10$
Subtraction 差 $x = 16 - 6$ $x = 10$	No need to draw. Age difference will never change.	My sister is 16 years. I am six years younger than my sister. How old am I?	? $16 - 6 = 10$
One half 二分之一 $6 = \frac{1}{2}$ of my age	6 12	My six years old is one half of my age. How old am I?	? $6 \times 2 = 12$
Sum Multiplier 和倍 $3x = 30$ $x = 10$	Amanda Andrew X 30	I am as old as Andrew. Andrew and Amanda have the same age. Together we are 30 years old. How old am I?	? $30 \div 3 = 10$

Using Line Segment Diagram – Age Problems

Equation	Line segment	Problems	Solutions
Sum and Multiplier 和倍 ? $10 + x = 3x$ **x = 5**	? now answer	Adding 10 to my age, I will be three times as old as I am now. How old am I?	? The increase of 10 years is 2 times of age now, so 10 divided by 2 = 5.
Sum and Multiplier 和倍 $x + 11 = 2x$ **x = 11**	? answer	In 11 years, I will be twice as old as I am now. How old am I?	? The increase of 11 is a one-time increase of age now, so my age now is 11.
Sum and Multiplier 和倍 ? $x = 15 - 0.5$ **x = 14.5**	No need to draw.	I am as old as Melody, who turned 15, six months ago, how old am I?	? For advanced students only. 14 years 6 months 14.5 years
Sum and Multiplier 和倍 $x + 2x + \dfrac{x}{2} = 3.5$ **x = 10**	2 units 4 units Carmen Mary 1 unit	Carmen is twice as old as I am, and Mary is half as old as I am. The sum of all our age is 35. How old am I?	? For advanced students only. We can think of ages as marbles. I have 2 bags. Carmen has 2 bags. Mary has 1 bag. Total marbles are 35. $\dfrac{35}{2+4+1} = 5$ $5 \times 2 = 10$
Sum and Multiplier 和倍 ? $(x+4)4 = 76 + 4$ **x = 16**	No need to draw.	My grandfather is 76 years old, who will be four times my age, then in 4 years. How old am I?	? $\dfrac{76 + 4}{4} - 4 = 16$

Student's name: _____ Assignment date: _____

Using Line Segment Diagram – Weight Problems 重量問題

Equation	Line segment	Problems	Solutions
Sum Difference Multiplier 和差倍 ? $6x - 3 = 5x + 2$		Andy's' weight is 3 kg less than six times of his brother's weight and 2 kg more than 5 times of his brother's weight. How much does each one of them weigh?	? Andy's weight = 6 times of his brother's weight + 3 = 5 times of his brother's weight – 2 The weight difference is 5 kg (3 +2), corresponding to the one-time difference. Andy weighs 5 kg. Andy 27 kg Brother 5 kg
Sum Difference Multiplier 和差倍 $2x + x - 5$ $= 55$	From unequal quantities to equal quantities by adding or subtracting any quantities which are not part of multiples.	Celina, Arthur, and Eldon altogether weigh 85 kg. Celia and Arthur have the same weight. Eldon weighs 5 kg less than Arthur. What is the weight of each person?	? Adding 5 kg to 85 kg means all three people weigh the same, which is 30kg. Arthur 30 kg Celia 30 kg Eldon 25 kg
Sum Fraction 和 分数 ? $\dfrac{x}{2} + 40 = 55$ $\dfrac{x}{2} = 15$ $x = 30$		Forty kilograms added to half of Amy's weight is her mother's weight, which is 55 kg. How much does Amy weigh?	? 30 kg

Student's name: _____ Assignment date: _____

Using Line Segment Diagram – Mixed problems 混合题

Equation	Line segment	Problems	Solutions
Fraction 分数 $\dfrac{x}{3} = 10$	No need to draw. One part (top number) of 3 parts (bottom number) is 10.	One-third of Angela's weight is 10 kg, how much does Angela weigh?	? 30kg
Sum Multiplier 和倍 $x + 15 + x + 25 + x = 400$	From unequal quantities to equal quantities by adding or subtracting any quantities.	There are 3 beanbags. The total number of beans is 400. The second has 15 beans more than the first bag. The third has 10 more than the second bag. How many beans are in each bag?	? $1^{st} = 120$ $2^{nd} = 135$ $3^{rd} = 145$
Sum Difference Multiplier Work backwards 和差倍倒算 $x = \dfrac{33}{3} = 11$	From equal quantities to unequal quantities by adding or subtracting any quantities to get back to the original numbers.	Stephanie gave 3 oranges to Kimberley. Frank gave 2 oranges to Stephanie and was given 5 oranges by Kimberley. After these oranges exchange, each one of them has an equal number of oranges, and their total number of oranges is 33. How many oranges does each one have at first?	? $33 \div 3 = 11$ $S = 11 + 3 - 2 = 12$ $K = 11 - 3 + 5 = 13$ $F = 11 + 2 - 5 = 8$
Sum and Difference 和差 2-digit is $\overline{TU}$. $T = U - 4$ $Y + U = 14$ $U = 9$		A number has 2 digits. The unit's digit is 4 more than the tens digit. The sum of 2 digits is 14. What is the number?	? 59

Student's name: _____ Assignment date: _____

Using the Line Segment Diagram – Mixed problems

Equation	Line segment	Problems	Solutions
Sum and Difference 和差 R+M=321 R−M=51	answer R ⊢————————⊣51⊣ M ⊢————————⊣ } 321	Altogether Rosalind and Michelle have 321 marbles. Michelle has 51 marbles less than Rosalind. How many marbles does Rosalind have?	? $321 - 51 = 270$ $270 \div 2 = 135$ Michelle has 135. $135 + 51 = 186$ Rosalind has 186.
Average 平均数 $x - 1 + x$ $+ x + 1$ $= 471$	The average of consecutive numbers is also the median (The middle number of the 3 consecutive numbers.).	Meghan bought 3 tickets for a school dance party. When Meghan added all three consecutive numbers, she got 471. What were the numbers on the tickets?	? 156, 157, 158
Difference and Multiplier 差倍 I = 3D I−D = 20 2D=20	Dick ⊢—⊣ I ⊢—⌒20⌒—⊣	I have as much as three times of Derrick's money. If I have $20 more than he does, how much does Derrick have?	? $10
Sum and Difference 和差 $x + y = 47$ $x - y = 17$	X ⊢————————⊣17⊣ Y ⊢————————⊣ } 47	The sum of the two numbers is 47, and their difference is 17. What are these two numbers?	? 15, 32

Sum and Difference, Sum and Multiplier, Difference and Multiplier link to Math Contests

One thing is they often appear in various math contests. Further, they could be one step of a complicated multi-step math contest problems. The following problem appeared in the 2016 Canadian Math Contest Grade 7 and 8.

9.   After a party, Jane washed half of the glasses, Alex washed half of the rest and then Sasha washed half of the remaining glasses. There were only three glasses left for David to wash. Half of the guests used one glass each and the other half of the guests used two glasses each. How many people were there at the party?

(A) 8   (B) 16   (C) 18   (D) 24   (E) 36

The first step is to find the number of guests in the party, and we use the idea of *Quantity divided by its corresponding fractional number*.

$3 \div \frac{1}{2} \div \frac{1}{2} \div \frac{1}{2} = 24$ glasses (This is Sum)

The glasses are divided into 1 glass group and two glasses group, so it means one group used glasses is 2 times of the other group. (This is Multiplier)

$\frac{24}{2+1} = 8$ glasses ..... 8 guests

$\frac{24 - 8}{2} = 8$ guests

Total guests are 8 + 8 = 16 guests.

Travelling problem 行程問題

Introduction

The travelling problem is for advanced students only. In China, this type of problem appears in as early as grade 3, and in Canada, they appear in grade 9. The difference is students could use algebra to solve the travelling problem in grade 9 and what can students do in grade 3? The grade 3 students must understand the concept of using the formulas which show the relationships between Distance, Time and Speed. This is the way how a grade-9 student in Canada would solve the t travelling problem, so there is really no difference. Most grade-9 students could not solve some of the advanced t travelling problems appeared in Chinese grade 3 math contest books, and this really puzzled me on why the authors gave such difficult travelling problems at grade 3? I would suggest we move those more advanced problems to a higher grade and have students use algebra to solve them.

The following grade 3 problem appears in China.

Problem	arithmetic	algebra
Adam and Bob drove separately from city A and B towards each other, and they met 5 hours later. The distance from city A to city B is 240 km. Bob drove slower than Adam. Adam and Bob met after 15 hours at the distance of 240 km if Adam and Bob started to drive toward the same direction. What was Adam's speed, and what was Bob's speed? If the student has the training in Sum and Difference problem, then this problem could be viewed as the Sum and Difference problem. When Adam and Bob drove towards each other, the total speed is the SUM. When they drove towards the same direction, the catch-up speed is the DIFFERENCE.	The sum of the speed of Adam and Bob = $\frac{240}{5}$ = 48 It takes 15 hours for Adam to catch up to Bob, so the difference is $\frac{240}{15}$ = 16. $\frac{48-16}{2}$ = 16 … Bob's speed 48 − 16 = 32 … Adam's speed	Let Adam's speed = A and Bob's speed = B $\frac{240}{A+B}$ = 5 $\frac{240}{A-B}$ = 15 If we use algebra, the problems become a Systems of Equations. A = 16, B = 32

The above problem demonstrates, sometimes. that students need to know more about how to solve a problem using arithmetic than using an algebra because by using algebra, the equation becomes a routine procedure.

One variable problem

The travelling problem uses a very simple triangle relationship that is $Time = \frac{Distance}{Speed}$. The problem becomes complicated for grade 3 students because it involves the calculations of cross multiplication and the concept of a fraction such as

$$Speed = \frac{Distance}{Time}$$
$$Distance = Time \times Speed.$$
$$Time = \frac{Distance}{Speed}$$

Example

A car needs 1 minute 45 seconds to travel 2 km. At this rate, how many km will the car travel in 1 hour?

1 minute 45 seconds = 105 seconds
$\frac{2}{105} \times 60 \times 60 = \textbf{68.57 km}$

A car travels 180 km in 4 hours. What is its speed per hour?

Speed = 45 km/hr.

Student's name: _____ Assignment date: _____

Two-variable problems

	Example	Diagram	Solution
When to meet when walking towards each other?	The distance between the school and the library is 5 km. Adam walks from school towards the library at a speed of 2 km per hour, and his mom walks from the library towards school at 3 km per hour. When will they meet each other?	2 km per hour → ← 3 km per hour; 5 km	$Time = \dfrac{Distance}{Speed\ 1 + Speed\ 2}$. They both walk together at 5 km per hour. $\dfrac{5}{2+3} = 1$ hour
When to catch up when one walks first?	Adam's walking speed from school to the library was at 2 km per hour. After Adam walked for 1 hour, his mom started to walk at the speed of 3 km per hour form school towards the library. When can Mom catch up with Adam?	2 km; Adam ● 2 km per hour; Mom ● 3 km per hour	The distance is 1×2 km = 2 km, which mom must try to catch up to. $Time = \dfrac{Distance}{Speed\ 1 - Speed\ 2}$ Mom catch up 1 km per hour, $3 - 2 = 1$. $\dfrac{2}{3-2} = 1$ hour

Student's name: _____ Assignment date: _____

	Example	Diagram	Solution
What is the distance given two walkings at different speeds?	Adam and his mom walk from home in the opposite direction. Adam's speed is 2 km per hour, and mom's speed is 3 km per hour. After 3 hours, how far are they?	distance after 3 hours? Mom 3 km per hour ← ● → Adam 2 km per hour	Distance = time × (speed 1 + speed 2) $3 \times (3 + 2) = 15$ km

Example

Isaac starts to deliver the morning newspaper at 7:30 a.m. and comes back to his home at 8:15 a.m. He drives 5 km in 9 minutes. What is the distance of his morning paper route in one way?

$8:15 - 7:30 = 45$

$\frac{45}{9} \times 5 = 25$ km

Student's name: _____ Assignment date: _____

Problem

The distance from Vancouver to Beijing is about 8500 km. The speed of a Boeing 777 is 900 km/hr. About how long will the plane in the air if it goes from Vancouver to Beijing?

9 hr. 27 min

A car travels from Vancouver to Banff. It took Andy 4.5 hours for the first 250 miles and 5.5 hours for the rest of 280 miles. What is his average speed?

The average speed is calculated for the physics view. $Speed = \frac{distance}{time\ 1+time\ 2}$

$Speed = \frac{250+280}{4.5+5.5} =$ **53 miles/hour**

The distance between Toronto and Ottawa is about 428 km. A car travels from Toronto to Ottawa at a speed of 80 km/h. Another car travels from Ottawa to Toronto at a speed of 100 km/h. If they both start at 8:00 a.m., at what time will they meet?

$Time = \frac{428}{100+80} = 2.38$ hour

0.38×60 minutes/per hour= 23 minutes. The answer is **10:23 a.m**.

Two buses start from the same bus station at the same time. The eastbound bus travels at 20 km/h, and the westbound bus travels at 25 km/h. How long will it take them to be 9 km apart?

$Time = \frac{9}{20+25} = \frac{1}{5}$ hour, the answer is **12 minutes**.

Kathleen drove to downtown at 30 km/h. How fast does she have to go back to average 40 km/h?

The average speed is in the meaning of physics such that $Time = \frac{Distance}{Speed\ 1+Speed\ 2}$

We assume the one-way trip distance is 1.

$Time = \frac{2}{\frac{1}{30}+\frac{1}{x}} = 60$ km/ h

At 8:00 a.m., the Carters left for Portland 525 km away. They drove the first part at 65 km/hr. At 10:30 a.m., they stopped for one hour. Then they complete the rest of the trip at 70 km/hr. Find its average speed and the time they arrive in Portland.

$65 \times 2 = 130$

Time $= 2+ \frac{525-132}{70} = 7.61$ hour taken $60 \times 0.61 = 37$ minutes, times takes 7:37

$Time = \frac{525}{2+\frac{525-130}{70}} = 68.69$

Arrived at 16:37 (8+7:37+1) 68.69 km/h

Student's name: _____ Assignment date: _____

Give and Take 取捨問題

"Give and Take" problem appeared in SSAT®, so understand it and perhaps use it as a Model Problem to solve other problems is important. The methods and skills used in solving some whole model problems can be used in solving fractions, percentages, or ratios. The following demonstrates the idea.

"Give and Take" problem uses the idea of $a - x = b + x$. The equation is more complicated than a simple model of a $x = a - b$. At this point only one variable (x) is involved.

	the whole number
Give and take	Adam has 14 apples, and Bob has 6 apples. How many apples does Adam have to give to Bob so that they each have an equal number of apples? 4 David has 128 marbles, and Amanda has 96 marbles. How many marbles should David give to Amanda so that both have the same number of marbles? 16

Student's name: _____ Assignment date: _____

Give and Take in different data types 不同数型的取捨問題

The methods and skills used in solving some whole model problems can be used in solving fractions, percentages, or ratios. The following demonstrates the idea.

"Give and Take" problem uses the idea of $a - x = b + x$. The equation is more complicated than a simple the model of a $x = a - b$. At this point only one variable (x) is involved. Fraction, percentage, and ratio are for advanced students only.

	the whole number	fractions	percentage	the
Give and take	Adam has 20 apples, and Bob has 6 apples. How many apples does Adam have to give to Bob so that they each have an equal number of apples? 7	Adam took $\frac{1}{3}$ of apples from a basket and Bob took $\frac{1}{7}$ of apples from the same basket. How many apples in fraction does Adam have to give to Bob so that they each have an equal number of apples? $\left(\frac{7}{21} - \frac{3}{21}\right) \div 2 = \frac{2}{21}$	Adam took 34 apples out of a basket of 170 apples, and Bob took 10 apples from the same basket. How many percentages of Adam's apples must be given to Bob so that they each have the same number of apples? $\frac{34}{170} = 20\%$ $\frac{10}{170} = 6\%$ $\frac{20\% - 6\%}{2} = 7\%$	Adam and Bob have 144 apples in total. The ratio of Adam's apples to Bob's apples is 3:1. How many apples does Adam have to give to Bob so that they each have an equal number of apples? Adam: $144 \times \frac{3}{4} = 108$ Bob: $144 \times \frac{1}{4} = 36$ $\frac{108 - 36}{2} = 36$

Some students do not do well in math grade 5 or in higher grades. The reason is they have not mastered the basic skills of whole number operations, especially they have very little mental math ability. When students do not have a good grasp of basic computing skills, then it hurts their ability to solve problems, including word problems.

A few important math skills needed to be good at math; some of them are discussed as follows.

Complementary numbers 互補数

When two numbers add up to a number ending with lots of zeros, then these two numbers are called complementary numbers. For example, 1 and 9, 2 and 8, 53 and 47.

Arithmetic factoring 算術共因子

Many teachers or students would think the concept of factoring is taught at high schools but because the pattern problems often involve so
e calculation and it is important for students to have the arithmetic factoring concept, so they can get the sum of math contest digits problems answers much quicker.

There are also other problems that often use the idea of factoring and students will be at a disadvantage if they do not understand arithmetic factoring.

Arithmetic factoring is the reverse procedure concept of Distributive Law.

Distributive Law 分配律

Arithmetic	Factoring	Algebra Factoring
$6 \left(\frac{1}{2} + \frac{1}{3} \right)$	$6 \times \frac{1}{2} + 6 \times \frac{1}{3}$	$x \times \frac{1}{2} + x \times \frac{1}{3}$
$\frac{2}{3} \left(\frac{6}{7} - \frac{1}{2} \right)$	$0.3 \times \frac{1}{2} + 0.7 \times \frac{1}{2}$	$0.3(x + y) + 0.2(x + y)$

Example 1

$2 \times 4 + 8 \times 4 + 4 \times 4 + 4 \times 6$
=
=
=

Example 2

Factor the following problem.

$$1 \times 6 \times 100 + 2 \times 6 \times 100 + 2 \times 6 \times 100 + 2 \times 6 \times 100$$

$$= 6 \times 100 \, (1 + 2 + 3 + 4)$$
$$=$$
$$=$$

Example 3

Factor the following problem.

$$1 \times 1000 + 2 \times 100 + 3 \times 10 + 4 \times 1 + 1 \times 1000 + 2 \times 100 + 3 \times 10 + 4 \times 1 + 1 \times 1000 + 2 \times 100 + 3 \times 10 + 4 \times 1$$

$$=$$

Example 4

Factor the following problem.

$$1 \times 1000 + 2 \times 1000 + 3 \times 1000 + 4 \times 1000 + 1 \times 100 + 2 \times 100 + 3 \times 100 + 4 \times 100 + 1 \times 10 + 2 \times 10 + 3 \times 10 + 4 \times 10 + 1 \times 1 + 2 \times 1 + 3 \times 1 + 4 \times 1$$

Student's name: _____ Assignment date: _____

Number pattern and distributive law 数的规律及分配律

Subtracting reverse digits

Observe the following pattern and relation. Fill in ☐with a number.

Equation	Pattern	Comment
$21 - 12 = 9$	$= 9 \times (2 - 1)$	Do not use a calculator. Can you see the pattern?
$32 - 23 = 9$	$= 9 \times (3 - 2)$	
$43 - 34 = 9$	$= 9 \times (4 - 3)$	
$75 - 57 = ☐\ 18$	$= 9 \times (☐ - ☐)\ 7 - 5$	
$95 - 59 = ☐\ 45$	$= 9 \times (☐ - ☐)\ 9 - 5$	

Student's name: _____ Assignment date: _____

Number pattern and distributive law

Adding reverse digits

Observe the following pattern and relation. Fill in □ with a number.

Equation	Pattern	Comment
21 + 12 = 33	= 11 × (2 + 1)	Do not use calculator. Can you see the pattern?
32 + 23 = 55	= 11 × (3 + 2)	
43 + 34 = 77	= 11 × (4 + 3)	
75 + 57 = □ **132**	= 11 × (□ + □) 5 + 7	
95 + 59 = □ **154**	= 11 × (□ + □) 5 + 9	

Add 27272727 to 25252525 = _____ **52525252**

Number pattern and distributive law

Number multiplying by 101

Observe the following pattern and relation. Fill in _____ with a number.

		Comments
27×101	$27 \times (100 + 1)$ $= 2700 + 27$ $= 2727$	Are you writing 27 twice in a row as the answer?
29×101	$29 \times (100 + 1)$ $=$ 　　**2929**	
55×101	$55 \times (100 + 1)$ $=$ 　　**5555**	
35×101	$35 \times (100 + 1)$ $=$	
49×101	$49 \times (100 + 1)$ $=$ 　　**4949**	
359×101	$359 \times (100 + 1)$ $=$ 　　**36259**	Can you write 359 twice in a row as the answer?

Order of operations 先乘除後加减

The order of operation is to tell students how to perform an arithmetic expression from left to right in the order of BEDMAS (Bracket, Exponent, Division, Multiplication, Addition, Subtraction). It is also called PEMDAS (Parenthesis, Exponent, Multiplication, Division, Addition, Subtraction).

One of the reasons to ask students to follow the order of operations in elementary school is because the Order of operations is in line with the evaluation order of algebraic operations. It can be clearly seen by studying the following comparison table.

Arithmetic order of operation	Algebraic order of operation
$3 + 2 \div 5$ is not equal to 1 because this is a fraction of $3\frac{2}{5}$. $3 + 2 \times 2$ is not equal to 10 because this is an exponential number. $3 + 2^2 = 7$.	$3 + 2 \div x = 3 + \frac{2}{x} \neq \frac{5}{x}$ $3 + 2 \times x = 3 + 2x \neq 5 \times x$
$10 + 8 \times 7 - 6 \div 2 \times 7$ 45	$10 + 8 \times x - 6 \div 2 \times x$ When working on the above algebraic expression, you cannot do $10 + 8$ first, then $\times x$. $8 \times x$ cannot be separated. This meaning is translated to multiplication or division must be done first in an arithmetic operation.
$(10 + 8) \times 7 - 6 \div 2 \times 7$ 105	$(10 + 8) \times x - 6 \div 2 \times x$ You cannot do $18x - 6$ first then $\div 2$ because $6 \div 2 \times x = \frac{6x}{2}$.
$10 + 8 \times (7 - 2) \div 2$ 30	
$10 \div 2 + 18 \div 3$ 11	
$10 + 2 \div 4 - 5 \div 10$ 10	

Student's name: _____ Assignment date: _____

Order of operations 先乘除後加減

The concept of Order of operations is good for the basic principle of computing, but it shall not be viewed as the only way of doing the basic computation. The following will demonstrate that in some examples, it may not be a good idea of working from left to right and follow the rule of "order of operations".

	Commutative law		Associative law	
Addition	Yes	$a + b = b + a$	Yes	$(a + b) + c = a + (b + c)$
Subtraction	No	$a \times b \neq b \times a$	No	$(a - b) - c = a - (b - c)$
Multiplication	Yes	$a \times b = b \times a$	Yes	$(a \times b) \times c = a \times (b \times c)$
Division	No	$a \div b \neq b \div a$	No	$(a \div b) \div c = a \div (b \div c)$

Distributive law

$(a + b) \times c = a \times c + b \times c$
$(a - b) \times c = a \times c - b \times c$
$(a + b) \div c = a \div c + b \div c$
$(a - b) \div c = a \div c - b \div c$

Student's name: _____ Assignment date: _____

Order of operations

$a + b + c = a + c + b$
$a - b + c = a + c - b$
$a - b - c = a - c - b$
$a \times b \times c = a \times c \times b$
$a \div b \times c = a \times c \div b$
$a \times b \div c = a \div c \times b$

$a \times (b \div c) = (a \times b) \div c = (a \div c) \times b$

Sometimes, it is easier to change the operation format to a fraction so that numbers can be reduced in vertical format.

$$a \times (b \div c) = \frac{a \times b}{c}$$

$$a \times b = (a \times m) \times (b \div m) = (a \div m) \times (b \times m)$$

The mixed operations of division and multiplication with parentheses sometimes confuse students.
It would not make sense for students to memorize the above relationship, so what would be an easier way to work on these kinds of problems? The answer is to convert them to fractions, instead of following "order of operations".

Problem 1
$84 \times (1000000 \div 7) = 12000000$

Problem 2
$75 \div 12 \times 144 \div 4$
$=225$

Problem 3
$814 \div 36 \div 7 \times 18$
$= \frac{407}{7}$

Student's name: _____ Assignment date: _____

Problem 4

$3720 \div 201 \times 3$

$= \frac{3720 \times 3}{201} = \frac{3720}{67}$

Problem 5

$2144 \div 58 \times 29$

$= 1072$

Problem 6

$2144 \times 29 \div 58$

$= 1072$

Problem 7

Convert the following into a fraction
$87 \div 11 + 13 \div 11$

$= \frac{100}{11}$

Problem 8

Convert the following result into a product of prime. (For advanced students only)
$103 \times 15 + 130 \times 15$
$= 3 \times 5 \times 233$

Problem 9

Factorize the following into a product of primes. (For advanced students only)
$615 \times 17 + 1582 \times 17$
$= 17 \times 2197$
$= 17 \times 13^3$

Ho Math Chess   何数棋谜   英文奥数, 解题策略, 及 IQ 思唯训练宝典
Frank Ho, Amanda Ho © 2020   All rights reserved.

Student's name: _____ Assignment date: _____

Fill in operators or parentheses 填充運算符号或括号

These kinds of problems are very good at training the skills of reversing thinking and work backwards. Work backwards is normally the way to figure out the problems of ``filling in operators and parentheses`` but other methods such as work forward, guess and check, an estimate can also be used.

Fill in operators $+ - \times \div$ or parentheses in the following equation such that the left side is equal to the right side.
$1\ 2\ 3\ 4\ 5\ 6\ 7\ 8\ 9 = 1$

Solution 1
$1\ 2\ 3\ 4\ 5\ 6\ 7\ 8\ 9 = 1$

$1 \times 2 + 3 + 4 + 5 - 6 - 7 + 8 \div 9 = 1$

Solution 2
$1\ 2\ 3\ 4\ 5\ 6\ 7\ 8\ 9 = 1$

$1+2+3+4+5-6-7+8-9=1$ (note 10 -9=1 by working backwards.)

Solution 3
$1\ 2\ 3\ 4\ 5\ 6\ 7\ 8\ 9 = 1$

$(1 \times 2 + 3 + 4 - 5 + 6 + 7) + (8 + 9) = 1$

Solution 4
$1\ 23\ 4\ 5\ 6\ 7\ 8\ 9 = 1$

$1 \times 23 - 4 \times 5 + 6 - 7 + 8 - 9 = 1$

Solution 5
$1\ 23\ 4\ 5\ 6\ 7\ 8\ 9 = 1$

$1 + 23 - (4 + 5 + 6 + 7) + 8 - 9 = 1$

Solution 6
$1\ 2\ 3\ 45\ 6\ 7\ 8\ 9 = 1$

$(1 + 2) \div 3 \times 45 \div (6 + 7 - 8) \div 9 = 1$

Insert an operator + or − between digits in the following such that the left side of the equation is equal to the right side.
1 2 3 4 5 6 7 8 9 = 100

$1 + 2 + 34 - 5 + 67 - 8 + 9 = 100$

Insert an operator + or − between digits in the following such that the left side of the equation is equal to the right side.
1 2 3 4 5 6 7 8 9 = 100

$123 - 45 - 67 + 89 = 100$

Insert one digit from 0, 1, 2, 3, 4, 5, 6,7, 8, or 9 in each box ☐ such that the right-hand side is 100.

☐☐ + ☐☐ + ☐ + ☐ + ☐ + ☐ − ☐ − ☐ = 100

$50 + 43 + 1 + 2 + 8 + 9 - 6 - 7 = 100$

Insert one digit from 0, 1, 2, 3, 4, 5, 6,7, 8, or 9 in each box ☐ such that the right-hand side is 100.

☐☐ + ☐☐ + ☐☐ + ☐☐ − ☐☐ = 100

$12 + 30 + 45 + 89 - 76 = 100$

Insert one digit from 1, 2, 3, 4, 5, 6,7, 8, or 9 in each box ☐ such that the right-hand side is 100.

☐☐☐ − ☐☐ − ☐☐ + ☐☐ = 100

$123 + 89 - 45 - 67 = 100$

Geometry 几何

Bar graph 柱狀图

After the Nature Park trip, 6 students recorded the time they spent birdwatching. Draw a bar graph showing the data and label the graph completely.

Student	Amount of time
1	180 minutes
2	115 minutes
3	1.25 hours
4	2 hours 30 minutes
5	2 and one-third hours
6	25 minutes less than 2 hours

Convert all time to minutes 75, 150, 140, 95.

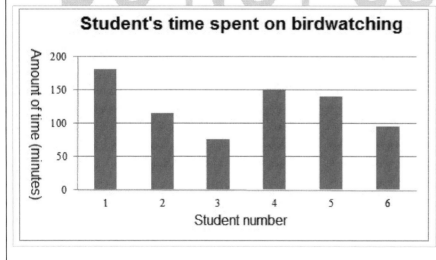

answer

Bar graph

Study the following bar graph and then answer the questions.

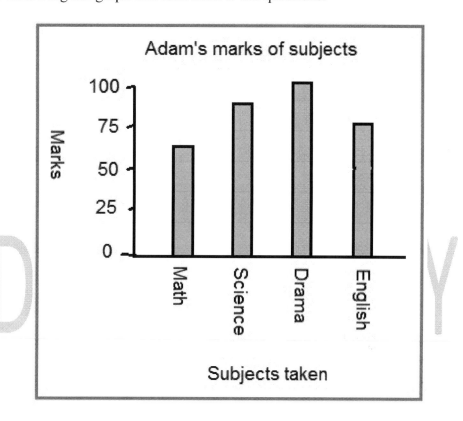

(1) What mark did Adam score $\frac{4}{5}$ of the highest possible marks?

English

(2) What is the difference between Adam's highest and lowest marks?

37.5

Student's name: _____ Assignment date: _____

Dividing shapes 分割图形

Can you divide each of the following shapes into three equal pieces?

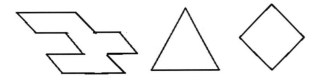

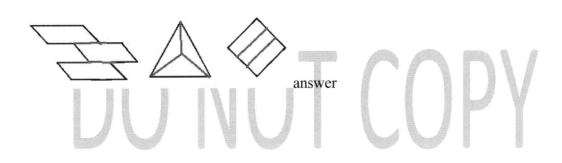

answer

Student's name: _____ Assignment date: _____

Solid Nets 立体图平面分解

Draw the net of a triangular prism.	Draw the net of a square-based prism (cube)
answer	answer
Draw the net of a rectangular prism.	Draw the net of a hexagonal prism.
answer	answer
Draw the net of a tetrahedron (triangle-based pyramid).	Draw the net of a square-based pyramid.
answer	answer
Draw the net of a rectangle-based pyramid.	Draw the net of a pentagonal prism.
answer	answer

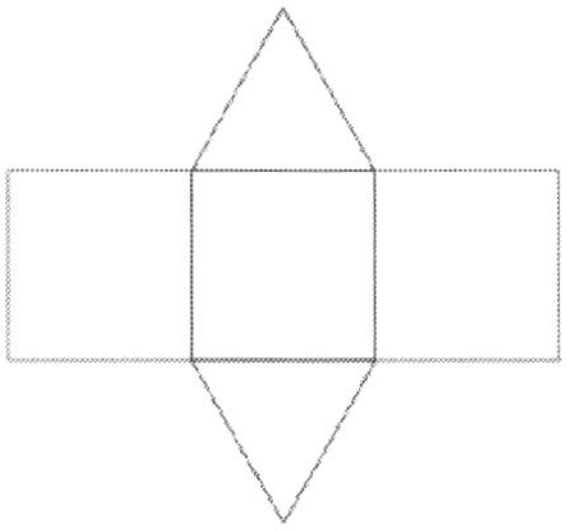

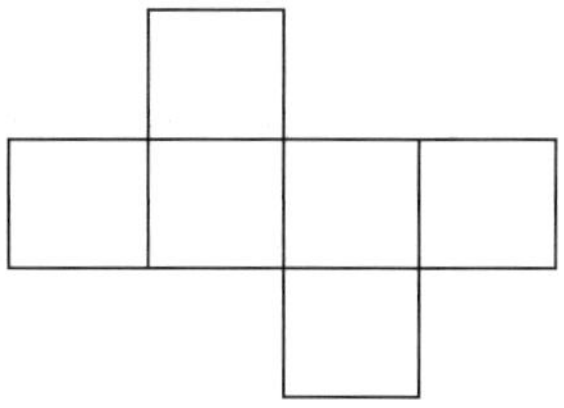

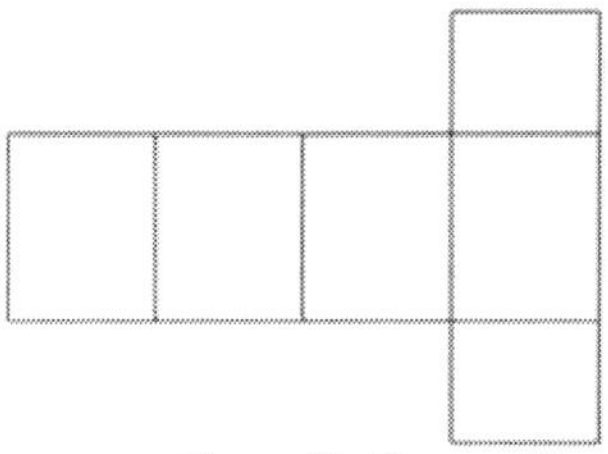

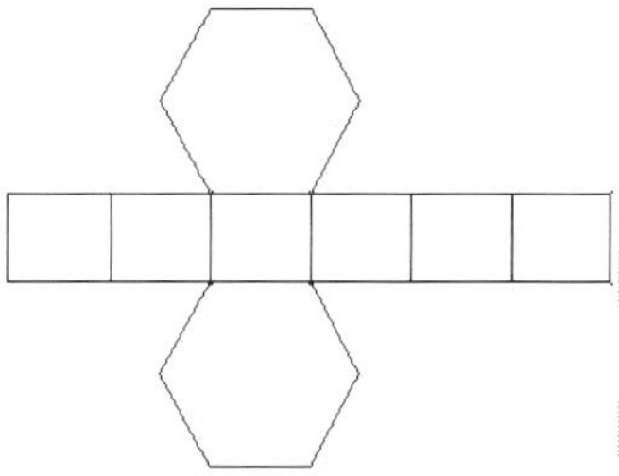

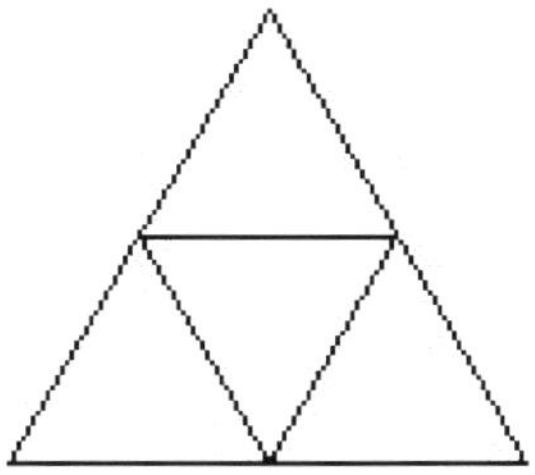

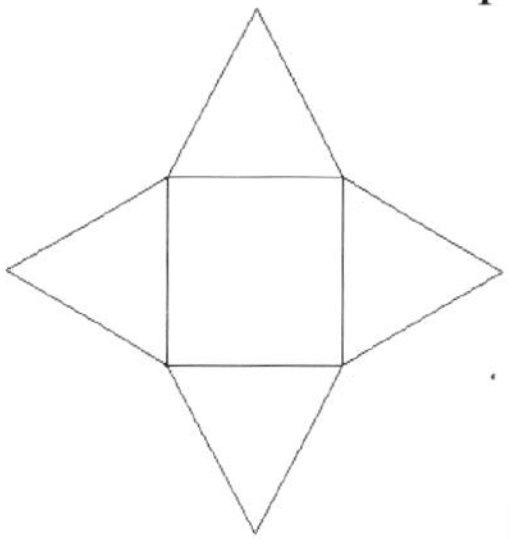

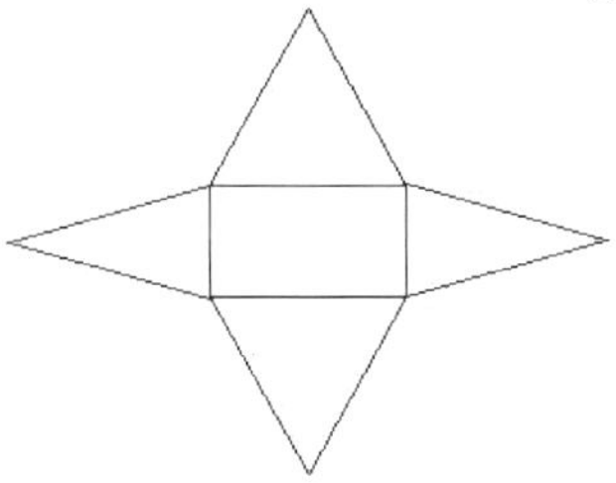

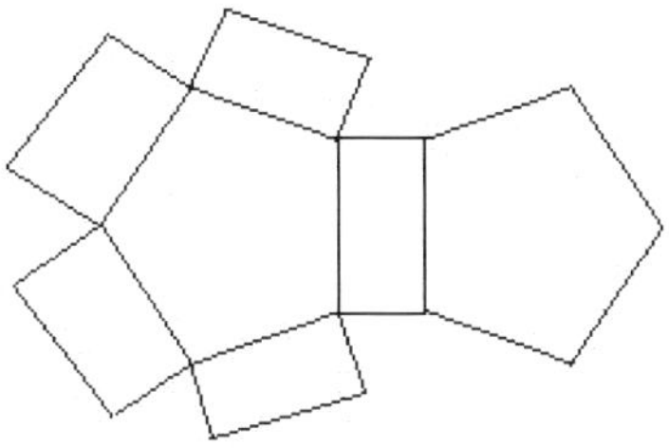

Parallel line 平行线

Circle the following parallel line(s).　**The first one.**

What is the property of a rhombus?

A rhombus is a quadrilateral whose four sides have the same length. Opposite angles are equal. The two diagonals are perpendicular. Its diagonals bisect opposite angles.

What is the property of a rectangle?

A rectangle is any quadrilateral with four right angles. Its opposite sides are parallel and congruent, the diagonals are congruent and bisect each other. All angles are right angles.

Quadrilateral Attributes 四边形特质

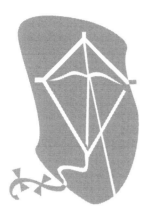

Quadrilaterals	Pairs of Parallel sides	Pairs of Equal sides	Equal angles or pairs of equal angle
Trapezoid	1 pair	0 (except equilateral trapezoid)	0 (except equilateral trapezoid)
Rectangle	2 pairs	2 pairs	4
Square	2 pairs	4	4
Rhombus	2 pairs	4	2 pairs
Kite	0	2 pairs	1 pair

Student's name: _____ Assignment date: _____

Counting digits 数数字

Melissa wants to number the pages of a box of lined papers with 100 pages. How many times will you need to print a "7"?

20

Melissa wants to number the pages of a box of lined papers with 100 pages. How many times will you need to print a "2"?

20

Melissa wants to number the pages of a box of lined papers with 100 pages. How many times will you need to print a "1"?

20

Can you draw a conclusion by observing the above results?

Each digit appears 20 times from 00 to 99.

Melissa wants to number the pages of a box of lined papers with 250 pages. How many times will you need to print a "7"?

45

Counting line segments, shapes 数形状

Many counting problems involve pattern rules and keen observations.

Counting line segments

Line segments	Line segments with 2 points	Line segments with 3 points	Line segments with 4 points
A B C D E	10 AB, AC, AD, AE BC, BD, BE CD, CE DE **Add natural numbers from 1 to 4 = 1+ 2 + 3 + 4 = 10**	8 ABC, ABD, ABE ACD, ACE BCD, BCE, CDE	4 ABCD, ABCE ACDE, BCDE

Counting angles

Angles	
	How many acute angles are there? 1
	How many acute angles are there? 12, 23, 123 3
	How many acute angles are there? 12, 13, 23, 24, 34 123, 124, 134, 234 1234 10
1 2 3 4 5	How many acute angles are there? 12, 13, 23, 24, 34 123, 124, 134, 234 1234 15, 25, 35, 45 125, 135, 235, 345 1235, 2345, 12345 **21**

Counting triangles

Line segments	Use every 2 points as a base to draw a triangle through point p. How many triangles are there?	Use every 3 points as a base to draw a triangle through point p. How many triangles are there?	Use every 4 points as a base to draw a triangle through point p. How many triangles are there?
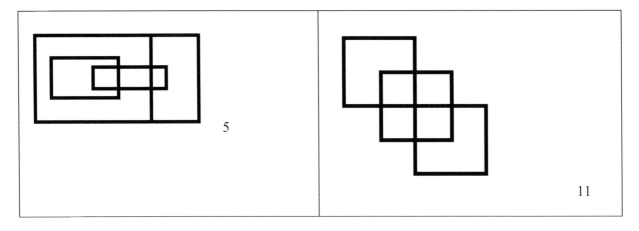	10 Same answer as the previous line segment problem.	8 ABC, ABD, ABE ACD, ACE BCD, BCE, CDE Same answer as the previous line segment problem.	4 ABCD, ABCE ACDE, BCDE Same answer as the previous line segment problem.

Compare these results to the results of the above "number of line segments" problem, can you draw a conclusion? _____

If all requested points are used on one baseline, then the number of triangles will be the same as the number of line segments.

Counting rectangles

How many rectangles are in the following figures?

5

11

Mixed Counting problems 混合数夨, 线, 形

Count the number of the following dots and write down the number counted. _____ **15** 	The following problems are all handshake problems. Count the number of the following line segments. _____ **15**  6 people shake hands with each other. How many handshakes will there be? 5+4+3+2+1=15 or $_6C_2 = 15$. How many lines can be connected between each dot in the following figure?  Each dot connects to 5 lines, so there are total 5 lines × 6 = 30 lines but each line is counted twice, so the answer is 30 ÷2 = **15**	Count the number of the following triangles. **15 = 5+4+3+2+1**  Connect the points A, B, or C to point D or E to create as many triangles as possible. How many triangles can you create?　**9** Each letter is used as a vertex. 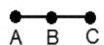 Count the following number of acute angles. Answer _____ **9** 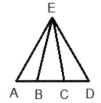

Student's name: _____ Assignment date: _____

Counting diagonals 数对角线

	How many diagonals are there for each shape?	
	Lower grade	High grades
	0	$_3C_2 - 3 = 0$
	2	
	5	Method 1 $_5C_2 - 5 = 5$ Method 2 $\dfrac{5 \times 2}{2} = 5$
	9	Method 1 $_6C_2 - 6 = 9$ Method 2 $\dfrac{6 \times 3}{2} = 9$
Heptagon 	14	
Octagon 	20	Method 1 $_8C_2 - 8 = 20$ Method 2 $\dfrac{8 \times 5}{2} = 20$

Tetromino 四连方

How many different figures can you create if you connect four identical squares? Each square can connect to one or more of other squares, but the connected sides must be all in full length. Each 4-square connected figure is called a Tetromino.

The following connections are not correct.

The following connection is correct.

Draw as many different tetrominoes as you can find. The figure will be considered the same one if the figure itself can be turned and then becomes the original one.

answer

Tetris 俄罗斯方块

Tetris is a tile-matching puzzle video game originally designed and programmed by Alexey Pajitnov in Russia. Tetris game is a popular use of tetrominoes.

If flipping is allowed, then there are seven tetrominoes in Tetris.

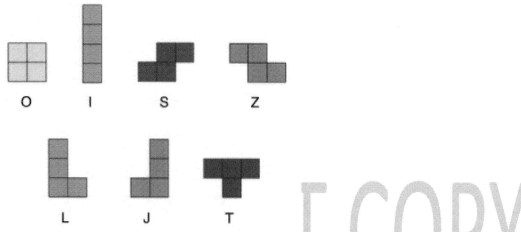

Many Tetris shapes or Tetris-like shapes problems appear in the past Kangaroo Math Contests.

The following figure can be composed by using the 3-square figures ⌐ or 4-square figures ∟.

To slide, flip, and rotate each of the 4-square figures, or the 3-square figures are allowed.

What is the largest number of three-square figures that can be placed in the following figure? Answer _____

answer 7

Student's name: _____ Assignment date: _____

How many of this shape can be used to cover the following square? The shape used may be rotated or flipped over. Show them by drawing.

4

How many of this shape can be used to cover the following square? The shape used may be rotated or flipped over. Show them by drawing.

4

Show how you can use the following three tetrominoes to cover the 4 by 4 square? Each tetromino used may be rotated or flipped over.

answer

Show how you can use the following three tetrominoes to cover the 4 by 4 square? Each tetromino used may be rotated or flipped over.

Show how you can use some of the following tetrominoes to cover the 3 by 4 square in 5 ways. Each tetromino used may be rotated or flipped over.

answer*

A traceable graph without lifting the pencil 一筆画

How can you tell whether a graph can be drawn (or traced) with one continuous stroke? For example, the following graph (figure) can be traced with one stroke without lifting the pencil.

The followiing graph has 2 vertices of odd path and 2 vertices of even path.

← a vertex (point)

← edge (line)

A path is a list of lines which a vertex can visit adjacent vertices.

- A graph can be drawn in one stroke if there are 0 or 2 points of the odd path,
- A graph with 0 odd points of the odd path (i.e., all points have even path), then it can be drawn in one stroke.
- A graph with 2 points of the odd path can be drawn with one stroke but must start and end at a vertex. For example, the following graph cannot be drawn in one stroke even it only has 2 points of the odd path.
- The number of lines needs to be traced to draw the graph =
$$\left\lceil \frac{number\ of\ points\ with\ odd\ path}{2} \right\rceil$$

Student's name: ______________________________ Assignment date: __________________

Find out if you can use a pencil to trace the following figures without lifting your pencil. Each line can be traced once only.

Figure	Number of even paths	Number of odd paths	Comments	Traceable or not.
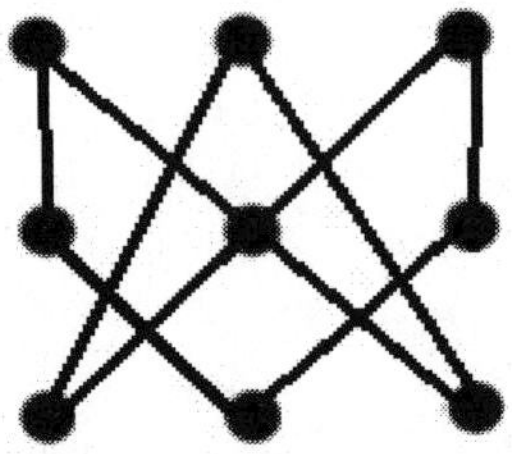	9	0	All even paths, no odd paths	yes
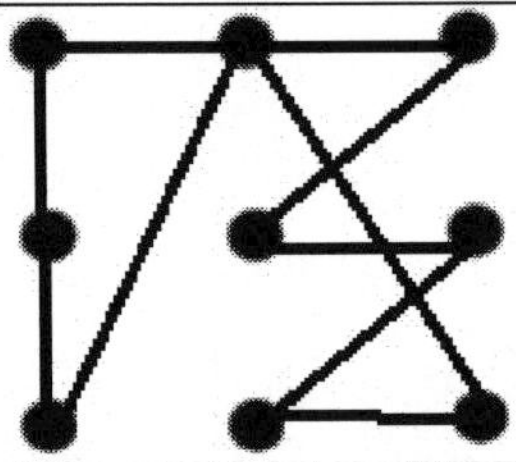				
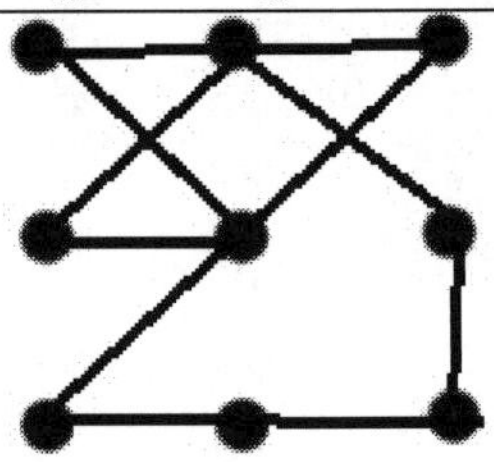				
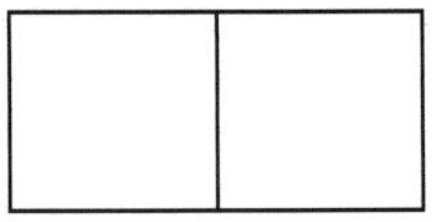				
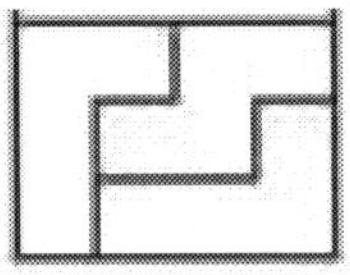				

Traceable figure without lifting the pencil

Find out if you can use a pencil to trace the following figures without lifting your pencil. Each line can be traced once only.

Figure	Number of even paths	Number of odd paths	Comments	Traceable or not.
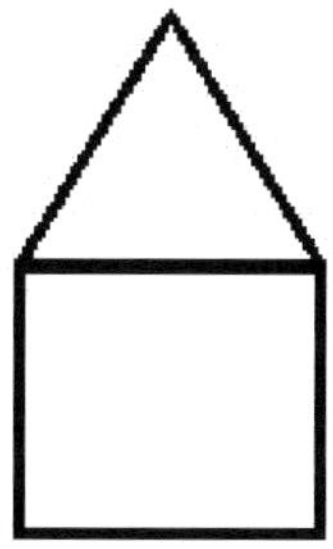	3	2		yes
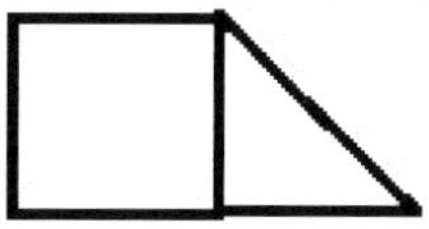	3	2		yes
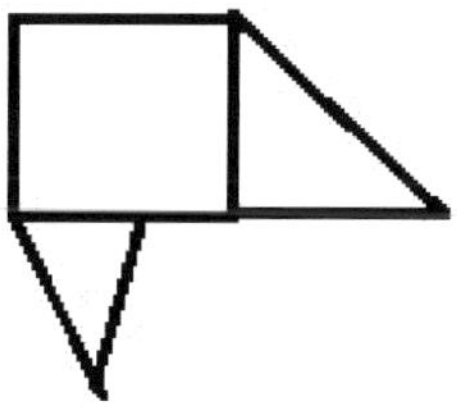	3	3		no
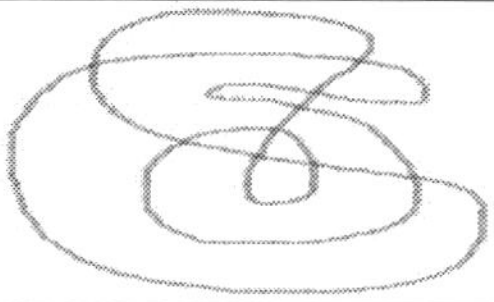	8	1		yes
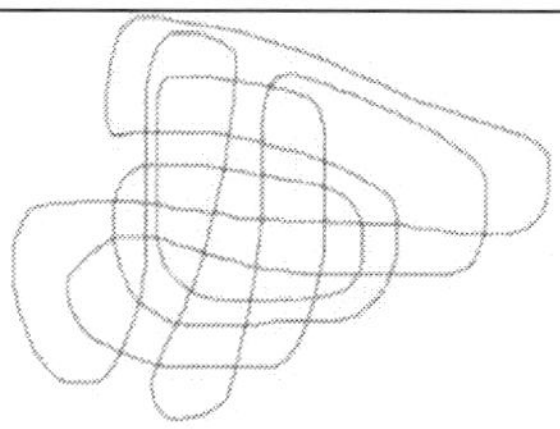				yes

Student's name: _____ Assignment date: _____

Some perimeter problems 周長問题

What is the value of ? in the following equation? $(4.01+ ?) \times 4 = 22.48$ **1.61**
When 5.09 is added to a number, and the sum is multiplied by 3, the product is 23.34. What is the number? **2.69**
Wailed used 7 kg 600 g of water to fill 4 identical containers completely, how much water can each container hold? Answer in _____ kg _____ g. **1kg 900 g**
Amanda built a rectangular fence in her backyard garden measuring 10 m long and 8 m wide. Posts used for the fence were placed 2 m apart. How many posts did she use for her garden? **18 posts**
Square A's perimeter is twice the perimeter of rectangle B. Find the area of square A.   (18+14)2=32 x 2 = 64 $\frac{64}{2} = 32$ $32^2 = 1024$ cm^2
The perimeter of the following figure is 62 cm. The figure is made of a square and a triangle. Find the perimeter of the triangle. $18 + 14 + 10 =$ **42 cm**

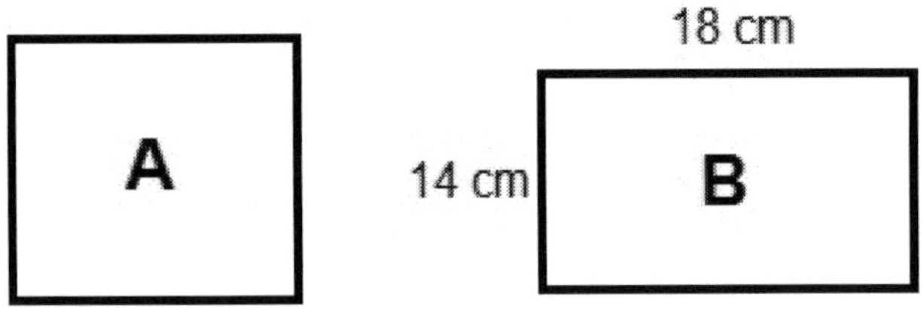

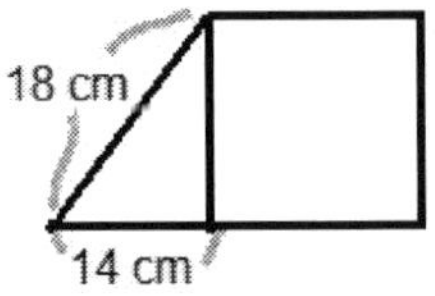

Student's name: _____ Assignment date: _____

Find the perimeter of the following shape. All measurements are approximate.

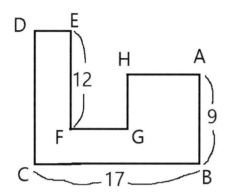 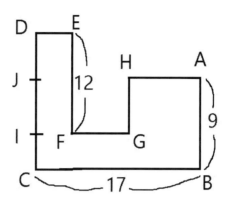

answer

Method 1	Method 2	Method 3
AB + HG + EF + DC = 9 + HG + 12 + DC (Note HG + IC = 9) = 9 + HG + 12 + CI + IJ + JD = 9 + IJ + 12 + CI + IJ + JD (IJ+CI=9, IJ+JD=12) = 9 + 12 + 9 + 9 + 12 = 42 The perimeter = 42 + 17 × 2 = 76	Moving line segment method DC + HG = DJ + JI + IC + HG = 12 + 9 (HG replaces JI) = 21 The perimeter = 21 + 12 + 9 + 17 × 2 = 76	Intersection method DC + HG = 12 + 9 = 21 = 17 × 2 + 21 + 12 + 9 = 76

Find the perimeter of the following shape. All measurements are approximate.

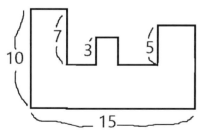 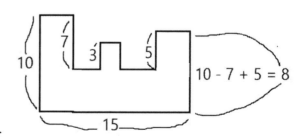

answer

$10 + 7 + 3 + 3 + 5 + 8 + 15 + 15 = 66$

Student's name: _____ Assignment date: _____

Transformation 图形的转换

Slide (translate) 移, 平行移

Horizontal slide	Vertical slide	Diagonal slide

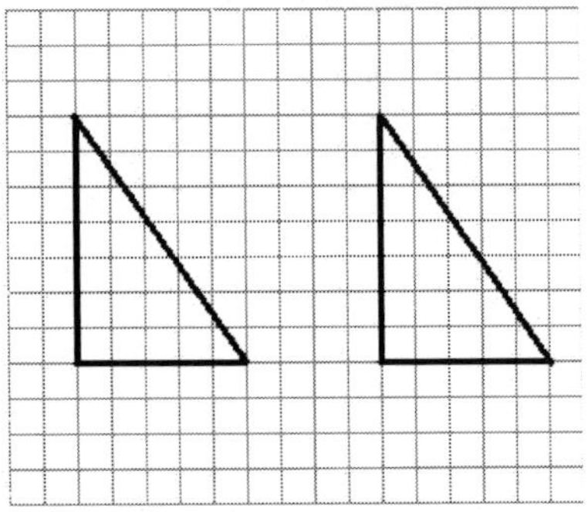

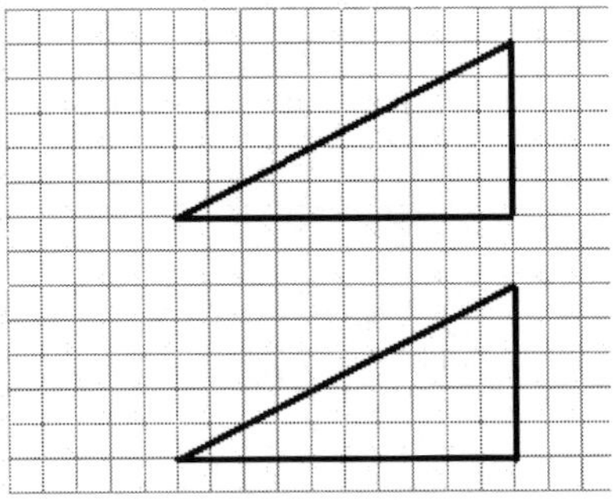

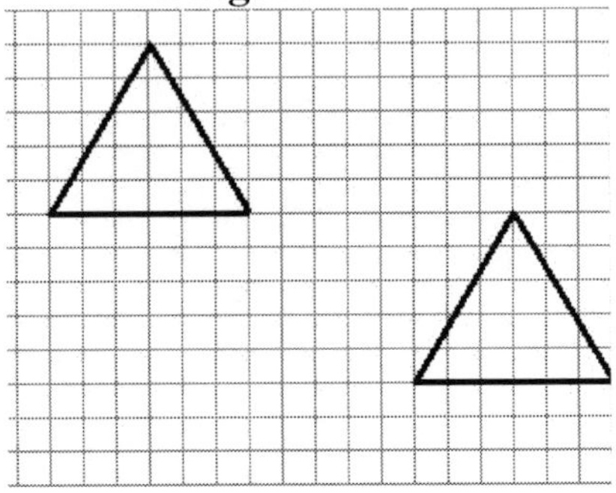

Indicate whether each slide a horizontal, a vertical, or a diagonal slide.

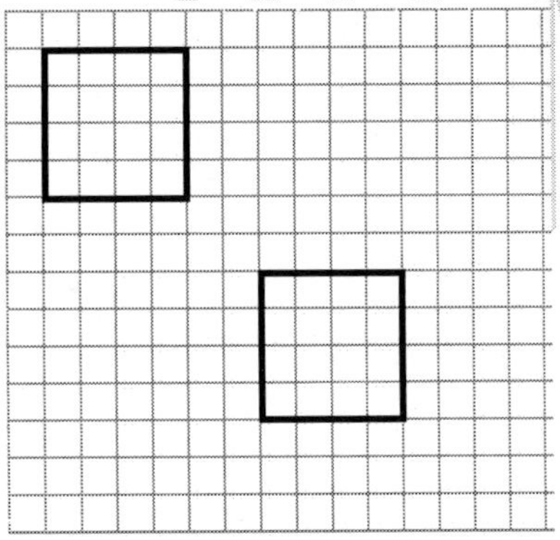

diagonal	vertical	horizontal

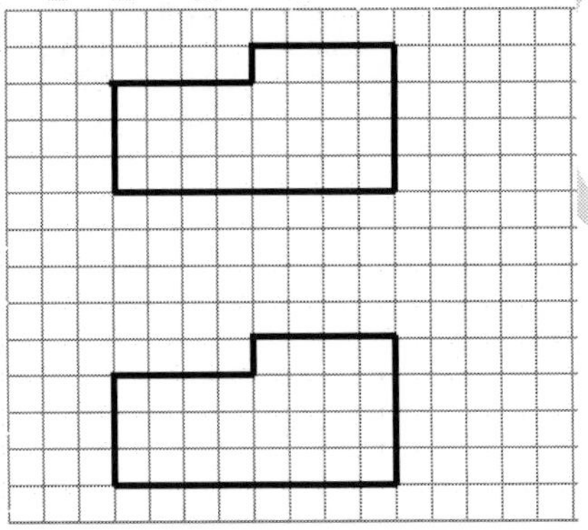

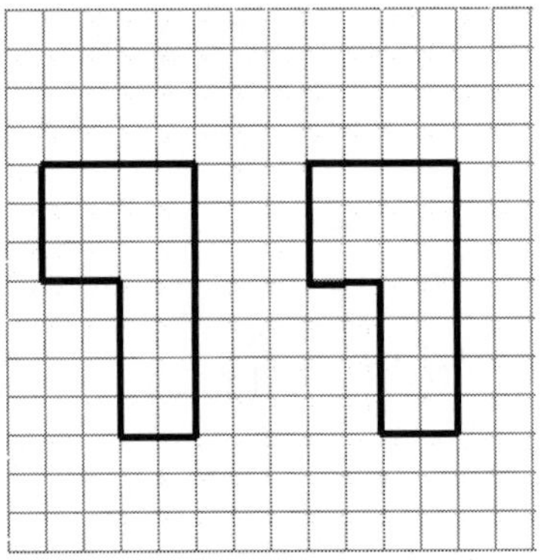

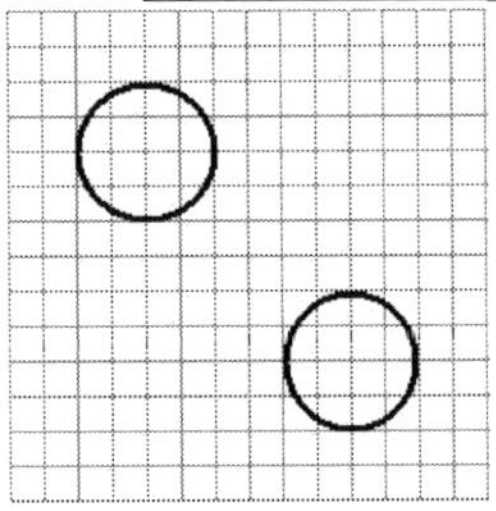

Diagonal	horizontal	vertical

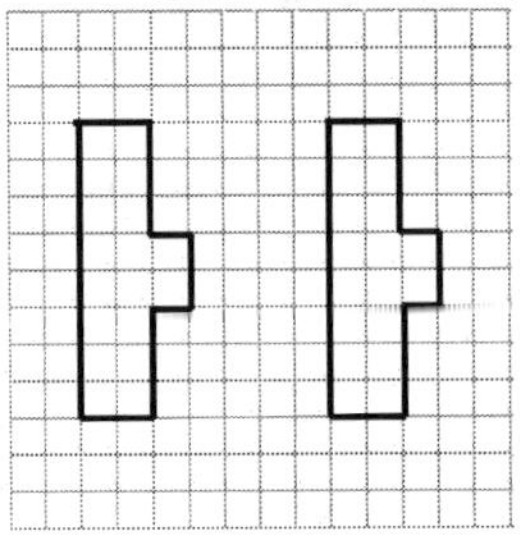

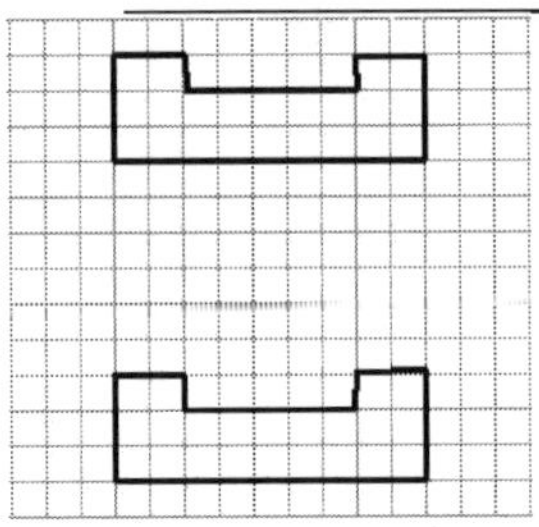

Turn (rotate) 旋转, 定桌顺时針或反时針旋转

Point C is the turn centre, figure A is turned from A to B,

| A quarter-turn clockwise or a three-quarter turn counterclockwise | Half turn | Three-quarter turn clockwise or a quarter-turn counterclockwise |

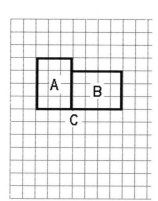 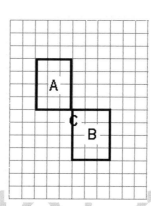 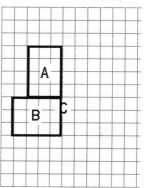

Each figure turned from A to B, indicate whether each turn is a quarter-turn clockwise, half turn or a three quarter turn clockwise about point O.

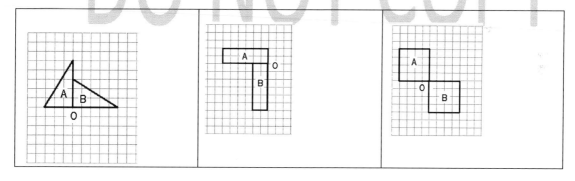

$\dfrac{1}{4}$ $\dfrac{3}{4}$ $\dfrac{1}{2}$

Student's name: _____ Assignment date: _____

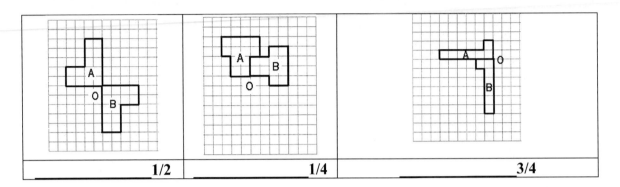

| 1/2 | 1/4 | 3/4 |

Flip (reflect) 翻, 反射

Finish the symmetric shapes below using the straight-line (mirror line) as lines of symmetry. Each vertex (corner) of the original figure flips to the opposite side with the same distance from the line to form an image.

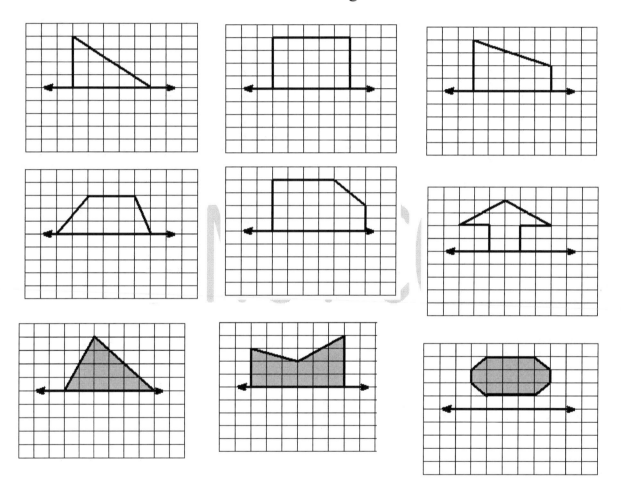

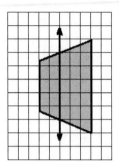
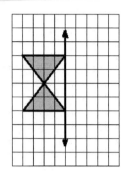
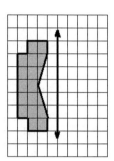

Flip along the symmetry line with equal distance to the symmetry line.

Symmetry line 对称线

Find the lines of symmetry for these drawings

Symmetry line 对称线

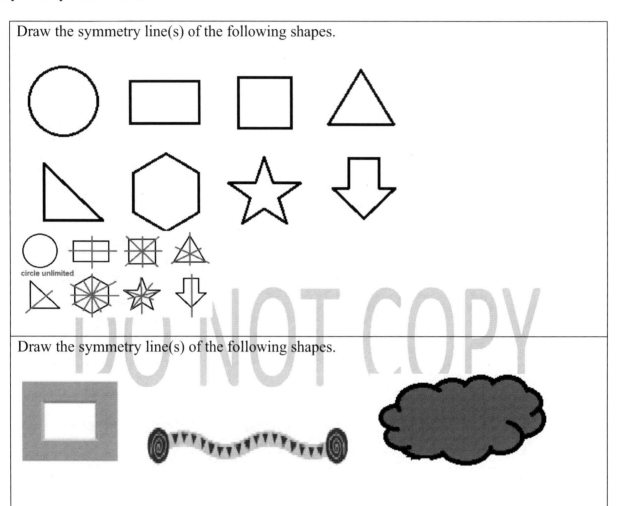

Student's name: _____ Assignment date: _____

Draw symmetry lines of the following figures.

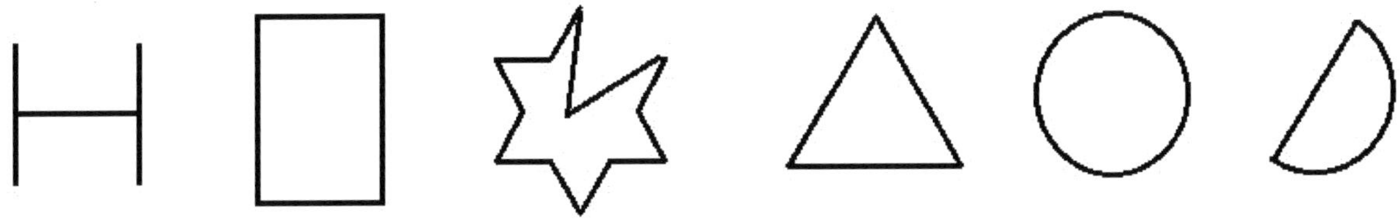

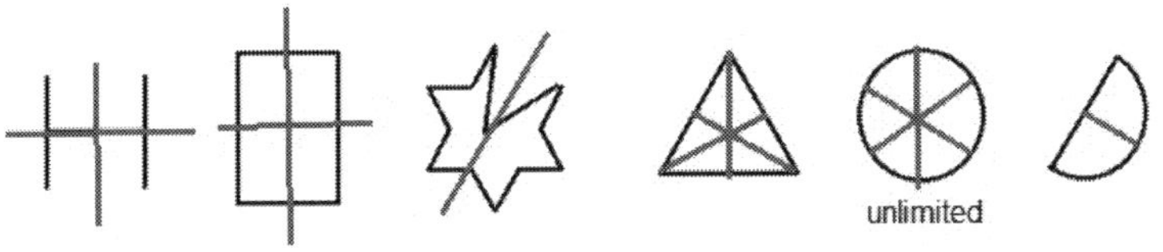

unlimited

answer

Problem

Decide whether each figure is a slide, a turn or a reflection of figure A.

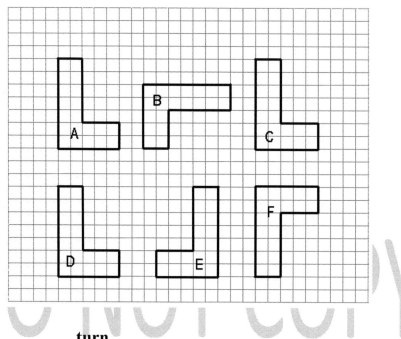

1. Figure B is a **turn** _____ of figure A.

2. Figure C is a **slide** _____ of figure A.

3. Figure D is a **slide** _____ of figure A.

4. Figure E is a **reflection** _____ of figure A.

5. Figure F is a **turn** _____ of figure A.

Student's name: _____ Assignment date: _____

Which transformation has been performed on the following?

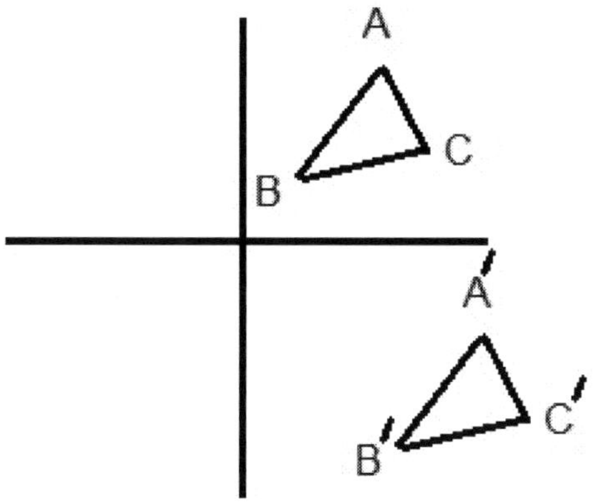

slide

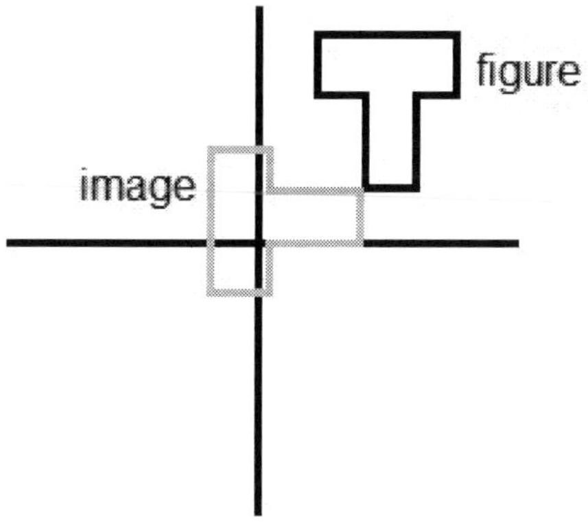

rotation

Student's name: _____ Assignment date: _____

Congruent Figures (figures with the same size and shape) 等樣形

If figures have the same size and same shape, then these figures are congruent.
Example:

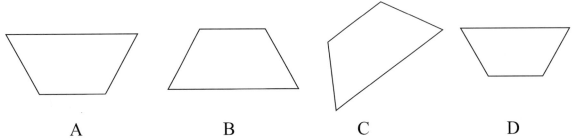

A　　　　　　　　B　　　　　　　　C　　　　　　　　D

Figures A, B, and C are congruent because they have the same size and same shape.
Figure D is not congruent to A, B, or C, because they have different sizes.

Connect all the pairs of congruent figures.

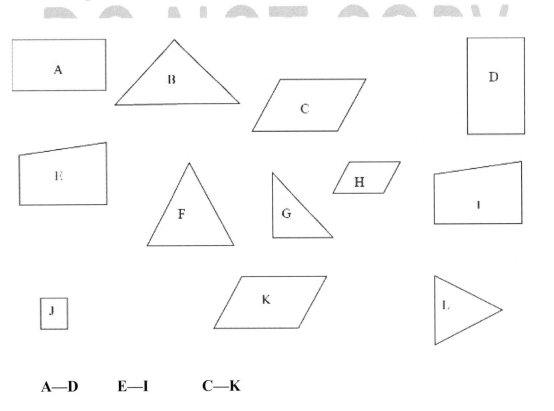

A—D　　　E—I　　　C—K

Student's name: _____ Assignment date: _____

Geometry with arithmetic 几何计算题

Anne has a 24 cm² rectangular sheet. What could be her sizes of rectangles?

4 ways:
4 by 6, 3 by 8, 2 by 12, 1by 24

Anne has a 36 cm² rectangular sheet. What could be her sizes of rectangles?
5 ways:
1 by 36, 2 by 18, 3 by 12, 4 by 9, 6 by 6

Anne has a rectangular sheet with a 36 cm perimeter. What could be her sizes of rectangles?

9 ways:
1 by 17, 2 by 16, 3 by 15, 4 by 14, 5 by 13, 6 by 12, 7 by 11 8 by 10, 9 by 9

Anne has a rectangular sheet with a 24 cm perimeter. What could be her sizes of rectangles?
6 ways:
1 by 11, 2 by 10, 3 by 9, 4 by 8, 5 by 7, 6 by 6

Find the volume of the following solid, which is made up of 1-cm cubes.

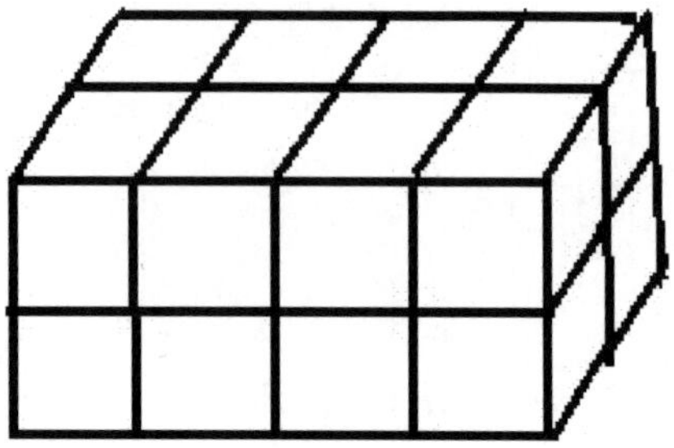

16

What fraction of the figure below is shaded out of the square ABCD? _____

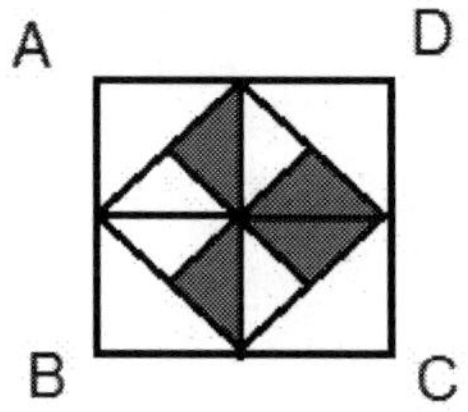

$$\frac{1}{4}$$

Fernando is standing at point X and facing point H. Which point would he be facing if he makes a $\frac{3}{4}$ turn? Which point would he be facing if he makes a 1 and $\frac{1}{4}$ turns to start at X?

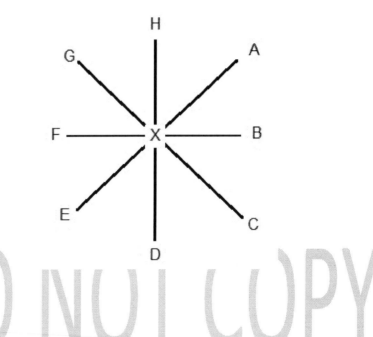

1 turn: H
$\frac{1}{4}$ turns: B, F

Circle the following isosceles triangle(s) (graph may not draw in scale).

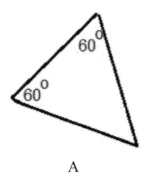

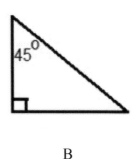

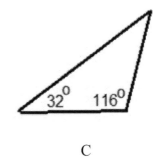

A　　　　　　　　　　　　B　　　　　　　　　　　　C

A, B, C are all isosceles triangle.

Two identical rectangles are each 13 cm long and 7 cm wide. There are overlapped to make the following shape. What is the perimeter of the overlapped shape?
The size may not be exact.

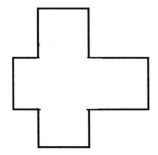

Method 1
4(13 - 7) = 24 For length wiithout counting th emiddle.
24 + 7 x 4 = 52 cm (the length of 4 widths)

Method 2, To move the identical width into the middle square, then the question becomes, what is the length of 4 lengths of the rectangle?
13 x 4 = 52 cm

Student's name: _____ Assignment date: _____

3 Dimensional perspective drawings

Identical cubes were glued together to build a structure. The following figures show the structure views from the front, from the side, and from the top. How many cubes did each structure have?

How to find it?

Step 1, Examine the top view first because the top view reflects the foundation of the structure.
Step 2, Build cubes up from the top view according to the front view by writing numbers.
Step 3, Build cubes up from the top view according to the right-side view.

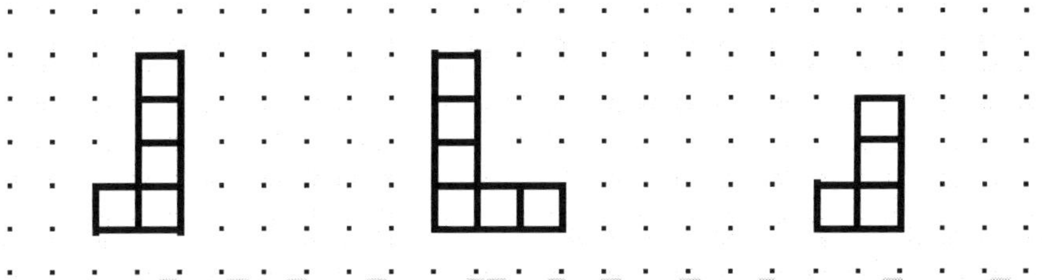

Front view   Right-side view   Top view

How many cubes?

7

Perspective view

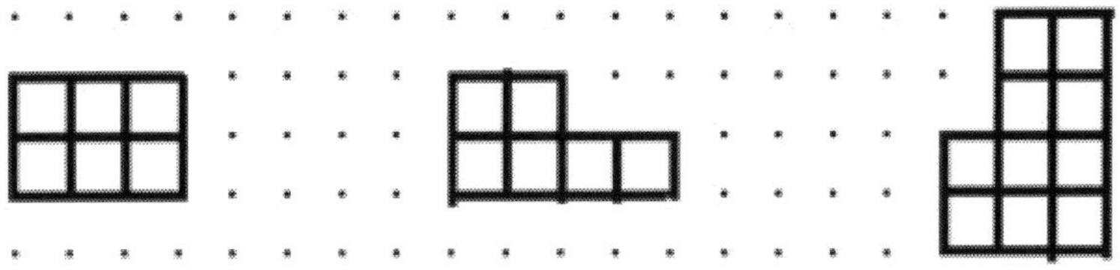

Step 2 and 3, Write the numbers of cubes needed to build up from the top view.

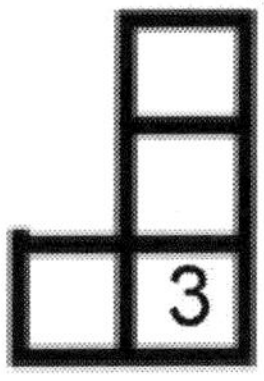

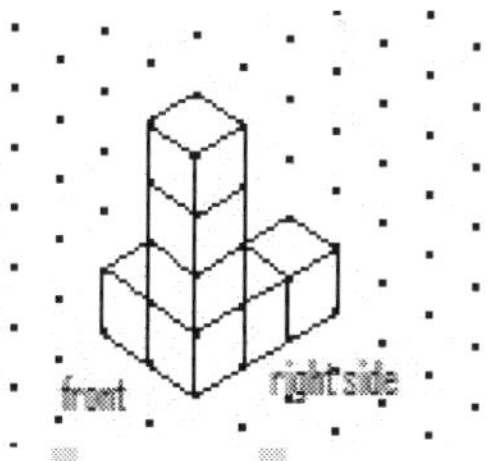

3

$4 + 3 = 7$

Front view   Right-side view   Top view

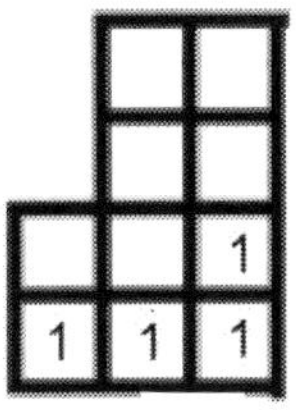

How many cubes?

14

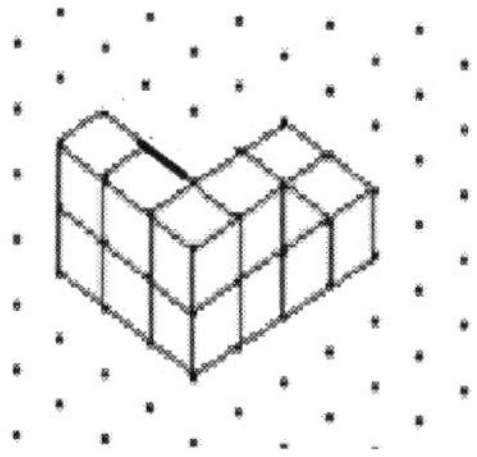

Perspective view

1
1 1 1

Student's name: ______________________ Assignment date: ______________

3 Dimensional perspective drawings

Identical cubes were glued together to build a structure. The following figures show the structure views from the front, from the side, and from the top. How many cubes did each structure have?

How to find it?

Step 1, Examine the top view first because the top view reflects the foundation of the structure.
Step 2, Build cubes up from the top view according to the front view.
Step 3, Build cubes up from the top view according to the right-side view.

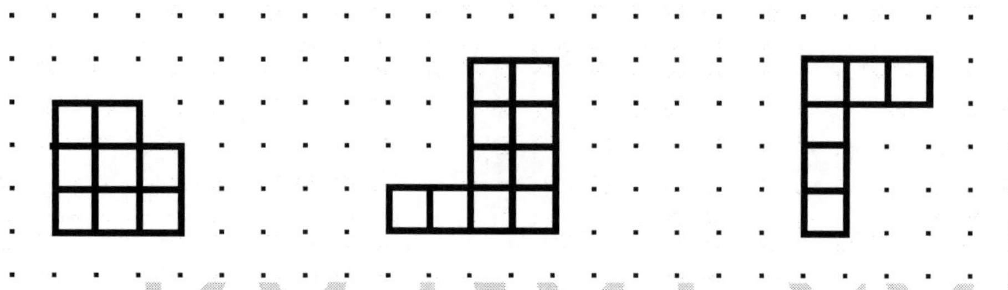

Front view Right-side view Top view

How many cubes?

13

Perspective view

Front view Right-side View Top view

How many cubes?

12

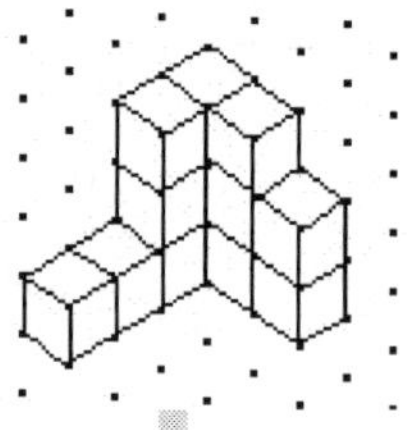

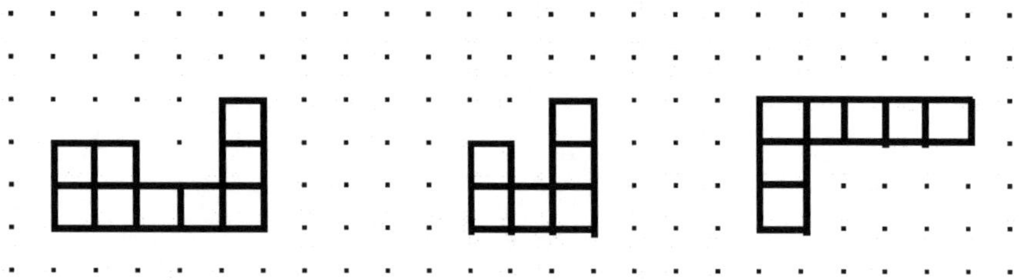

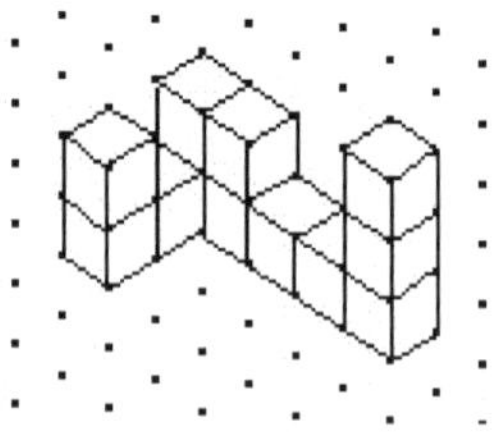

Perspective view

Student's name: _____ Assignment date: _____

3 Dimensional perspective drawings

Identical cubes were glued together to build a structure. The following figures show the structure views from the front, from the side, and from the top. How many cubes did each structure have?

How to find it?

Step 1, Examine the top view first because the top view reflects the foundation of the structure.
Step 2, Build cubes up from the top view according to the front view.
Step 3, Build cubes up from the top view according to the right-side view.

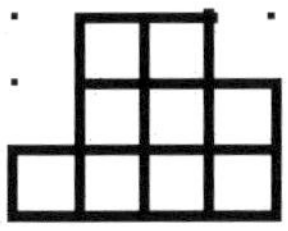

Front view　　Right-hand side view　　Top view

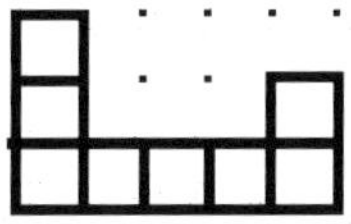

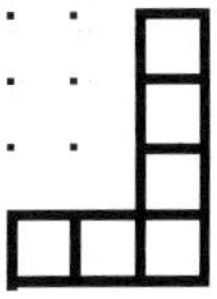

How many cubes?

14

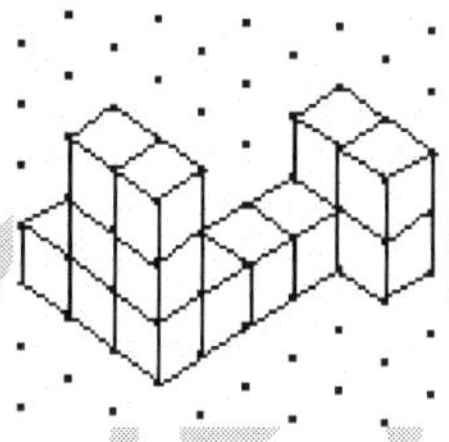

Perspective view

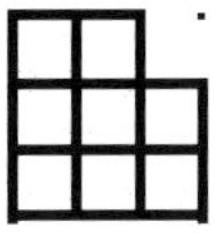

Front view　　Right-hand side view　　Top view

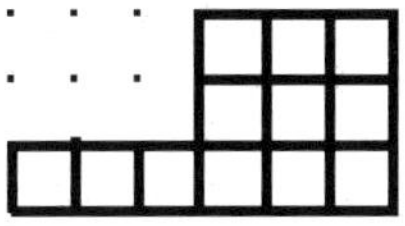

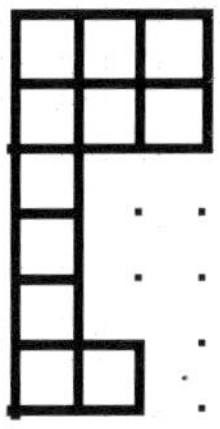

How many cubes?

21

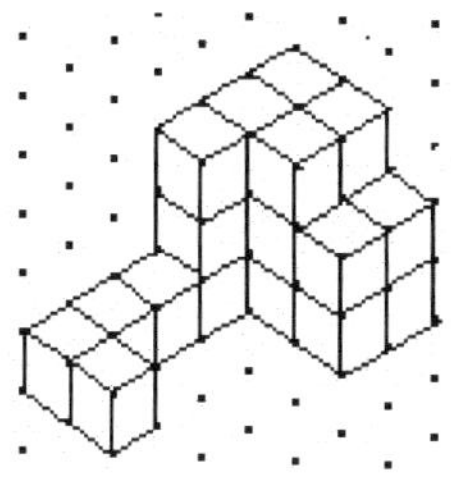

Perspective view

Venn diagram 思維图

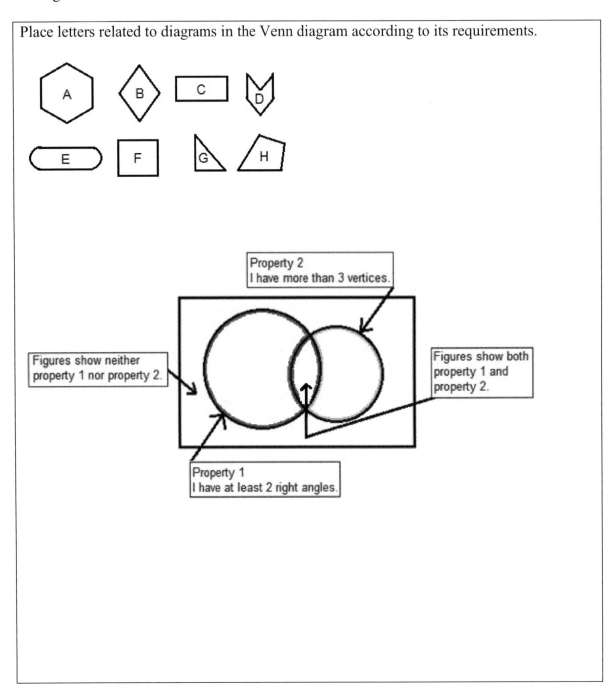

Answer to the previous problem

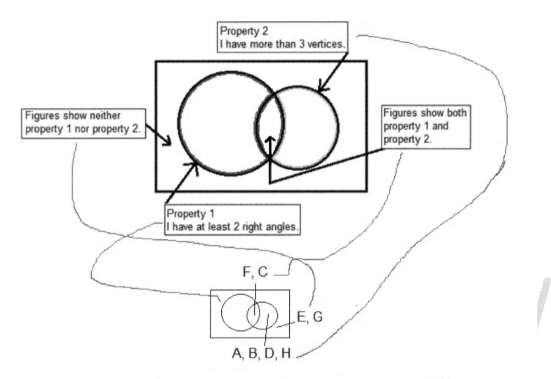

Answer

Problem

900, 176, 531, 384, 413, 679, 325, 424

Describe the attributes of the following Venn diagrams by observing how the data are sorted and then placed in each circle.

Separate circles	Overlapping circles	One circle inside another circle
Separate circles Describe the attribute of each circle.	**Overlapping circles** Describe the attribute of each circle and the common area.	**One circle is inside another circle.** Describe the attribute of each circle and the common area.
Answer The left circle has even numbers, and the right circle has odd numbers.	Answer The intersection has numbers over 500 and are even. The left-side circle has odd numbers, and the right-side circle has even numbers.	Answer The large circle has numbers under 1000. The small circle has even numbers under 500.

Sort and place each of the following numbers according to the requirements of the following Venn diagram into each region.

23, 32, 45, 54, 67, 76, 50, 55, 56, 65

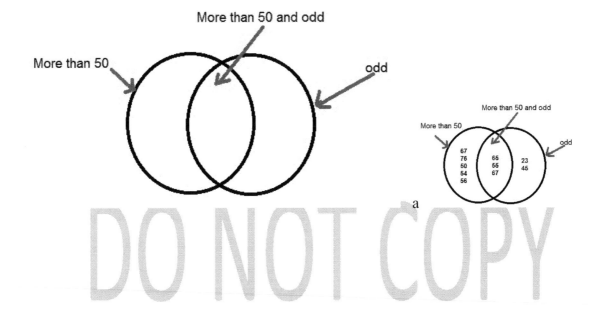

diagram vs. Venn diagram 卡罗尔图及维思图

Use the Carroll diagram and the Venn diagram to solve the following problem.

Find out what are the common factors (公因数) of 12 and 15.

Venn diagram   Carroll diagram

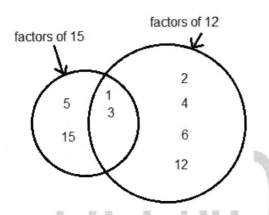

	12	15
Common factors of both 12 and 15	1, 3	
Non-common factors of 12 and 15	2, 4, 6, 12	5, 15

Which method is better for you to find the answer and why?

Venn diagram only gives you two separate information, but the Carroll diagram gives you 4 separate information. The Venn diagram is clear on the common factor because of its interaction. The common factor in the Carroll diagram is not as clear as the Venn diagram.

Use the following Carroll diagram to sort out the following numbers.

16, 15, 23, 25, 21, 30, 43, 45, 18, 60

	Even	Odd
Multiples of 5	**30, 60**	**15, 25, 45**
Not multiples of 5	**16, 18**	**21, 23, 43**

Student's name: _____ Assignment date: _____

Metric Measurement 度量衡公制

Circle the better estimate of the following.

1. Milk carton: 1000 *ml* or 1000 *l* **1000 ml**

2. Car gas tank 40 *ml* or 4 *l* **4 l**

3. small orange juice box: 200 *ml* or 900 *ml* **200 ml**

4. grade 4 boy: 30 *kg* or 100 *kg* **30 kg**

5. watch: 2 *kg* or 100 *g* **100 g**

6. lunch sandwich: 150 *g* or 950 *g* **950 g**

7. 3 *kg* = _____ **3000** *g*

8. 2000 *g* = _____ **2** *kg*

9. 5000 *g* = _____ **5** *kg*

10. 10 *kg* = _____ **10000** *g*

11. 50 *dm* = _____ **500** *cm*

12. 90 *cm* = _____ **9** *dm*

13. 2400 *dm* = _____ **240** *m*

14. 210 *cm* = _____ **21** *dm* = _____ **2.1** *m*

15. 0.5 *m* = _____ **50** *cm*

16. 2 *mm* = _____ **0.2** *cm*

Student's name: _____ Assignment date: _____

Likelihood 可能性

Circle the quarter part of the spinner for which it is certain to land on the most triangles?

answer

The jar is tipped, and a shape falls out. What is the likelihood it will be a shaded triangle?

(A) certain
(B) equally likely
(C) impossible
(D) less likely
D

Student's name: _____ Assignment date: _____

Probability 机率

Jessica spins the following spinner. Show what colour is the spin most likely to land on and at what fraction?

$red\frac{3}{8}$

Two colours are chosen from white, green, black, blue, and red. Colours can be repeated. How many possible ways of colours can be chosen?

11 22 33 44 55 12 23 34 45 13 24 35 14 25 15 **15**	You can code each colour to a digit, then arrange two digits. Work area

Five people are shaking hands from each other. How many possible handshakes are there?

10

Frank Ho, Amanda Ho © 2020

Student's name: _____ Assignment date: _____

Standard and expanded forms 标准数及展開式

Use each of these digits 0, 2, 4, 7 once to make a 4-digit number.

(1) The greatest possible number _____ .7420

(2) The least possible number _____ .2047

(3) The greatest number with 7 tens _____ .4270

(4) The least number with 0 hundreds _____ 2047

(5) How many 4-digit numbers can you make? List them all.
18 ways
2047, 2074, 2407, 2470, 2704, 2740, 4027, 4072, 4207, 4270,
4702, 4720, 7024, 7042, 7204, 7240, 7402, 7420

Standard from	English words	Expanded from	Block form
2345.12	**Two thousand three hundred forty-five and twelve hundredths**	**2000 + 300 + 40 + 5 + 0.1 + 0.02**	
1331	One thousand three hundred thirty-one	**1000 + 300 + 30 + 1**	

Number formats 数的表示法

Standard	Words	Expanded	Place value	Factors	Prime Factors	3 Multiples
12	twelve	10+2	1 ten 2 ones	1, 12 2, 6 3, 4	2, 3	12, 24, 36
24	**Twenty-four**	**20 + 4**	**2 tens 4 ones**	**1, 2, 3, 4, 6, 8, 12, 24**	**2, 3**	**24, 48, 72**
48	**Forty-eight**	**40 + 8**	**4 tens 8 ones**	**1, 2, 3, 4, 6, 8, 12, 16, 24, 48**	**2, 3**	**48, 96, 144**
36	**Thirty-six**	**30 + 6**	**3 tens 6 ones**	**1, 2, 3, 4, 6, 9, 12, 18, 36**	**2, 3**	**36, 72, 108**
52	**Fifty-two**	**50 + 2**	**5 tens 2 ones**	**1, 2, 4, 13, 26, 52**	**2, 13**	**52, 104, 156**
164	**One hundred sixty-four**	**100 + 60 + 4**	**1 hundred 6 tens 4 ones**	**1, 2, 4, 41, 82, 164**	**2, 41**	**164, 328, 492**

Number formats

Standard	Words	Expanded	Place value			
			Thousands	Hundreds	Tens	Ones
100		100		1		
2349		2000 + 300 + 40 + 9	2	3	4	9
195		100 + 90 + 5		1	9	5
1999		1000 + 900 + 90 + 9	1	9	9	9
2193		2000+100+90+3	2	1	9	3
222	Two hundred twenty-two	200 + 20 + 2		2	2	2
319		300 + 10 + 9		3	1	9
215		200 + 10 + 5		2	1	5

Two million twenty-five thousand nine hundred fifteen − eight hundred thirty-seven thousand nine hundred ninety-nine.

2025915 - 837999 = 1187916

Write an expanded form for each of the following numbers.

$$4 \times 1\,000\,000 + 3 \times 1\,000 + 2 \times 100 + 7 \times 10 + 8$$

4003278 = _____

$$5 \times 10\,000\,000 + 3 \times 100\,000 + 2 \times 100 + 7 \times 10$$

50300270 = _____

Write a numeral for the following number words.

Nineteen million eight hundred ninety thousand nine hundred nineteen.

19890919

What is the greatest number you can add to 987893 without having to regroup?

12106

What is the greatest number you can deduct from 13497072 without having to borrow?

13497072

Estimating 估算

1. Estimate 6 × 399. _____ **2400**

2. Estimate 10 × 1999. _____ **20000**

3. Estimate 399 × 399. _____ **160000**

4. Estimate 699 ÷7 = _____ **100**

5. Estimate 199 + 91 = _____ **290**

6. Estimate 395 − 197 = _____ **200**

7. Estimate 19.98 + 2.01 = _____ **22**

8. Estimate 29.85 ÷ 2.96 = _____ **10**

9. Estimate 19.20 −9.03= _____ **10**

10. Estimate 16.70 × 9.69 = _____ **170**

11. What is the sum of 199 + 897? **1096**

12. What is the difference between 982 and 793? **189**

13. What is product 199 and 897? **178503**

14. What is the quotient of 897 and 3? **299**

Rounding 四捨五入

What place value describes the rounding 385690 to 390000? **Ten thousand**
What place value describes rounding 2312545 to 2313000? **thousand**
What place value describes the rounding 9900.091 to 9900.1? **tenth**
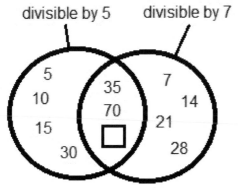 Which numbers belong in ☐ ? (A). 15 and 14 (B) 30 and 35 (C) 45 and 105 (D) 105 and 140 **D**
15 ¢ = $ _____ **0.15** $ 0.55 = _____ ¢ **55**

How many numbers between 100 and 900 would round to 1000 when rounded to the nearest hundred? **501**

Standard form	Round to the nearest tens	Round to the nearest hundreds	Round to the nearest thousands
1999	**2000**	**2000**	**2000**
2222	**2220**	**2200**	**2000**
5555	**5560**	**5600**	**6000**
7857	**7860**	**7900**	**8000**
6111	**6110**	**6100**	**6000**
1973	**1970**	**2000**	**2000**
7065	**7070**	**7100**	**7000**

Rounding

A number is represented by 6 B C D . E.
Replace each letter with a digit such that the result is true when rounding to the following required places.

The result is 7000 numbers when it is rounded to the nearest ones place.

The numbers could be _____.

6999.9,　6999.8,　6999.7,　6999.6,　6999.5

The piano in Fernando's house weighs 300 kg and his sofa weighs 135 kg. How much more does the piano weigh than a sofa? Is the following answer correct?

300 - 135 = 165

It weighs 165 more

Yes

Empire Stadium can hold 21785 people, Roger's Arena can hold 18650 people, and BC Place can hold 48215 people. Estimate how many people will fit in both Empire and Roger's Arena?

40000 people using front-end estimate 20000 + 20000 = 400000

Circle the following mass, which is closest to 1 kg.

641 g

1100 g

992.75 g *

875.5 g

Circle 992.75 g

There are 16 rabbits, gerbils, and hamsters in the pet store. There is the same number of rabbits as gerbils. How many of each animal could there be? Make a list.

# of rabbits	1	2	3	4	5	6	7
# of gerbils	1	2	3	4	5	6	7
# of hamsters	14	12	10	8	6	4	2

Student's name: _____   Assignment date: _____

Athens feeds lettuce, pellets, carrots and seeds to her hamsters but only two kinds each day. Show how many ways she could feed the hamsters?

6 ways

Rank the following time from the shortest to the longest.

Sue: 65 minutes   **3**

Lee: 30 minutes less than 2 hours **90 minutes**   **4**

Emily:40 minutes   **2**

Ryan:150 minutes   **5**

Anne: half an hour **30 minutes**   **1**

Anne, Emily, Sue, Lee, Ryan
How much was more time spent by Ryan than by Sue?
85 minutes

How many ways that you can make a 3-digit number using 3 digits 1, 3, 5. No repeating digits are allowed.

6 ways: 135, 153, 315, 351, 513, 531

Is $\frac{1}{2} = \frac{4}{8}$?

The reason for your answer is
_____**yes**

$88 \div 8$ **11**

$8848 \div 8 =$ **1106**

$8808 \div 8 =$ **1101**

$4020036007200000 \div 6 =$ **670 006 001 200 000**

A train started to travel 5 a.m. from city A to city B at the planned speed of 120 km and should have arrived at the city B at 3 p.m., but the train arrived at 5 p.m. What was the train's speed from city A to city B?

100 km/hr 120x10/12 = 100 km

A train started to travel at 8 a.m. from city A to city B at the planned speed of 60 km and should have arrived at the city B at 4 p.m., but the train arrived at 6 p.m. What was the train's speed from city A to city B?

48 km/hr, 60 x 8 / 10 = 48 km

Adam, Bob, and Charlie bought some pencils. Adam bought 18 pencils, and Bob bought 15 pencils and Charlie did not buy any. Adam paid the total cost of $1.65 and then divided the pencils evenly. How much should Charlie pay to Adam, and how much should Bob pay Adam?

1.65/33=0.05 … cost of each pencil
Bob: 15 x 0.05 = $0.75
Charlie: 9 x 0.05 = $0.45

Bob: $0.75
Charlie: $0.45

What is the product if the factors are 7 and 12?

84

The following problems require thinking skills to solve because even a student could do $+ - \div \times$ does not mean he/she can solve the following problems without thinking.

Thinking 1

The student could use an estimating method to get a ballpark figure first, for example, convert 180 to 200, 270 to 300, 310 to 300, and 450 to 500 to do estimates.

Thinking 2

The number 400 in the second problem below has 2 zeros, so it should provide some hints on how to get answer 00 from just 2-digit numbers 80, 70, 10, and 50 by dropping the hundreds of digits first.

Place 3 numbers out of 180, 270, 310, 450 into 3 boxes on the left side such that the equation is true.

$$\bigcirc = + \text{ or } -$$

$$\square \ \bigcirc \ \square \ \bigcirc \ \square = \boxed{2\,2\,0}$$

$$\square \ \bigcirc \ \square \ \bigcirc \ \square = \boxed{4\,0\,0}$$

$$\square \ \bigcirc \ \square \ \bigcirc \ \square = \boxed{9\,0\,0}$$

$$\square \ \bigcirc \ \square \ \bigcirc \ \square = \boxed{1\,4\,0}$$

310+180-270=220
270-180+310=400
180+270+450=900
180+270-310=140

After Alex spent one half of his money and one dollar, He had $18 left. How much did he have originally?

38

Find a number to replace the ?.

100, 3, 98, 6, 96, 9, ? **94**

Pages and sheets 頁数及纸张数

The following table illustrates the relationships between pages and sheets of a book.

	The page number on the left side	The page number on the right side	How many missing sheets between pages
A book has some missing pages between the left and the right pages.	1	4	$1=\frac{4-1-1}{2}$
	24	45	**10**
	39	56	$8=\frac{56-39-1}{2}$

Sarah was 10 years old when her brother was born. Today she blew out 19 candles on her birthday cake. What is the difference between Sarah's age and her brother's age today?

10

Sarah was 10 years old when her brother was 7 years old. Today she blew out 19 candles on her birthday cake. What is her brother's age today?

16

Sarah was 12 years old when her brother was 9 years old. Today she blew out 20 candles on her birthday cake. What is the difference between Sarah's age and her brother's age today?

17

About how tall is a door in a classroom? _____

2 metres, about 8 feet

Rachel counted 40 squirrels in the park. Three out of every 4 squirrels were grey. How many squirrels were not grey?

$40 \times \frac{3}{4} = 30$ *grey squirrels*
$40 - 30 = $ **10**

Scale problems 秤量问题

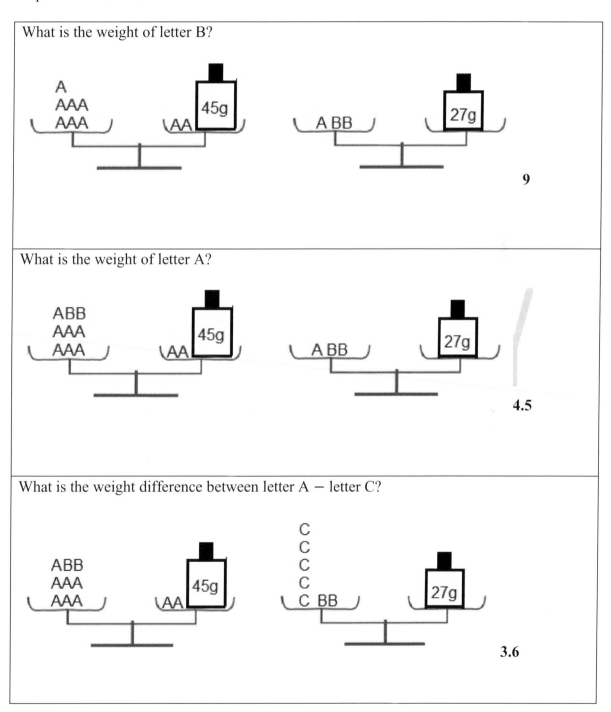

What is the weight of letter B?

9

What is the weight of letter A?

4.5

What is the weight difference between letter A − letter C?

3.6

Clock problems 时鐘问题

`Here are 4 clocks on the wall. Only one of them is correct. One is 30 minutes ahead, another is 30 minutes late, and the other is stopped. What is the correct time?

6:10 (5:40, 6:00, 6:10, 6:40)

Here are 4 clocks on the wall. Only one of them is correct. One is 30 minutes ahead, another is 30 minutes late, and the other is stopped. What is the correct time?

1:45 (2:15, 1:15, 1:45, 1:00)

Here are 4 clocks on the wall. Only one of them is correct. One is 30 minutes ahead, another is 30 minutes late, and the other is stopped. What is the correct time?

9:40 (9:10, 10:10, 9:40, 8:40)

Time 时间问题

Express 11:11 p.m. in 24-hour clock. _____ 23:11	
The clock shows 8:29 p.m. What time (in 24-hour clock) will be after 240 minutes? _____ 0:29	
The clock shows at 12 midnight. What time will be after 3600 seconds, express the time in a 12-hour clock? _____ 10 a.m.	
1.25 hours = _____ hours _____ minutes　　　1, 15	
$1\frac{7}{15}$ hours = _____ hours _____ minutes　　　1, 28	
1.75 hours + 3 hours 333 minutes = _____ hours _____ minutes　10 hours 18 minutes	

12-hour clock	The 24-hour clock
11 a.m.	11:00
11 p.m.	23:00
10 a.m.	10:00
10 p.m.	22:00
1:05 p.m.	13:05
10:30 p.m.	22:30
7: 15 p.m.	19:15
4 a.m.	4:00
12 noon	12:00
12 midnight	0:00
12:12 pm	12:12
10:30 am	10:30
1:11 am	1:11

Ho Math Chess　　　　何数棋谜　　　英文奥数, 解题策略, 及 IQ 思唯训练宝典
Frank Ho, Amanda Ho © 2020　　　　　　All rights reserved.

Student's name: _____ Assignment date: _____

Time

12-hour	24-hour
2:45 p.m.	14.45
9:15 a.m.	9.15
6:51 a.m.	6:51
6:13 p.m.	18:13
11:30 p.m.	23:30
3:15 p.m.	15:15
5:12 p.m. + 15 minutes	17:27
1:55 p.m.	50 minutes before 14:45
45 minutes + 12 midnight	0:45

3 days 14 hours 120 minutes subtracts 2 days 28 hours 225 minutes

= __**0**__ days __**8**__ hours __**15**__ minutes

7 of (2 days 10 hours 15 minutes) = __**16**__ days __**23**__ hours __**45**__ minutes

4 days 9 a.m. subtracts 2 days 3 p.m. = __**1**__ days __**18**__ hours

Find the average of (10 hours 145 minutes + 8 hours 30 seconds + 23 hours 170 minutes)

= __**14**__ hours __**45**__ minutes __**10**__ seconds

Total is 30 seconds 315 minutes 41 hours
Average is 10 seconds 105 minutes 13 hours remainder is 2 when divided by 3 then it is converted to the final answer 13 h 105 m 10 s -> 13 h 225 m 10 s -> 16 h 45 m 10 s .

Student's name: _____ Assignment date: _____

Metric time (Y, M, D) 公制的时间

Dates	Dates in metric notation
May 5, 2014	2014, May 5
25th May 2015	**2015, May 25**
July 1, 1997	**1997, July 1**
October 1st, 2020	**2020, October 1**
2017 12 1	**2017, December 1**
2020 03 06	**2020, March 6**
2013 11 17	**2013, November 17**
2025 02 23	**2025, February 23**

Student's name: _____ Assignment date: _____

Write 8 names of the 8 directions of the following chess queen symbol to which each arrow is pointing to.

north

	North
Northwest	Norheast
West	East
Southwest	Southeast
	South

answer

Cher has two hats: a cap and a toque; two blouses: long sleeves and short sleeves; three skirts: black, green, and white. Find all the different combinations she could have? Show all your work.

12

Student's name: _____ Assignment date: _____

Bag, Rag, and Tag rabbits eat daily carrots as follows:

- Bag eats 2 carrots.
- Rag eats one more than Bag.
- Tag eats one more than twice as many as Rag does.

For how many days can all the rabbits be fed from a crate of 7 dozen carrots?

7 days

We are finding a solution from multiple choices.

Fernando had $2.23 with 103 coins in nickels and pennies in his pocket. How many nickels and pennies did he have?

(A) 66 nickels and 37 pennies.
(B) 73 pennies and 30 nickels.
(C) 70 nickels and 43 pennies
(D) 63 pennies and 40 nickels.

B

Fernando had $1.13 with 33 coins in nickels and pennies in his pocket. How many nickels and pennies did he have?

(A) 15 nickels and18 pennies.
(B) 3 pennies and 30 nickels.
(C) 10 nickels and 23 pennies
(D) 13 pennies and 20 nickels.

D

Spinner problems 旋转器

Jaden spun one spinner. Show all possible scores that he could get.

1, 2, 3, 4

What is the chance that he could get number 2?

½

Jaden spun two spinners once. Show all the possible scores that he could get.

16

Student's name: _____　Assignment date: _____

Sum partition with no restrictions 没限制和的分解

Andy has 50 cents in his pocket with no pennies. How many different combinations of coins could he have had?

10 WAYS

5 ¢	10	8	6	4	2	0	5	0	3	1
10 ¢	0	1	2	3	4	5	0	0	1	2
25 ¢	0	0	0	0	0	0	1	2	1	1
TOTAL	50	50	50	50	50	50	50	50	50	50

Kelly has a fish tank that can hold 5 fish. Kelly wants to buy some goldfish, guppies, and catfish. She wants to buy at least one of each kind of fish. Show all the combinations of fish Kelly can buy.

Goldfish	3	2	2	1	1	1
Guppies	1	2	1	3	2	1
Catfish	1	1	2	1	2	3

Sum partition with restrictions 有限制和的分解

Sarah has 48 fruits with 3 kinds of apples, oranges, and bananas. Sarah wants to set out these fruits at a food stand with the following conditions:

- For every 3 apples, she sets out one orange.
- The rest are bananas.

How many of each kind of fruit can she set out? 11 ways

Apples	3	6	9	12	15	18	21	24	27	30	33
Oranges	1	2	3	4	5	6	7	8	9	10	11
Bananas	44	40	36	32	28	24	20	16	12	8	4

Sarah sold $40 all in bills at the food stand. The bills received were all in $5, $10, $20 with no one-dollar or two-dollar bills. Find all the different combinations of bills to make $40.

$20	2	1	1	1	0	0	0	0	0
$10	0	2	1	0	4	3	2	1	0
$5	0	0	2	4	0	2	4	6	8

Sarah had 38 cents in her pocket. She had 10 coins with no quarter. What were the coins did she have in her pocket?

7 nickels 3 pennies

There is a 3-digit number and the sum of its hundreds digit and the tens digit is 9. Its sum of tens digit and ones digit is 13. Its hundreds digit and one digit is 10. What is this number?

367

Logic and reasoning 邏輯思唯

When Adam, Bob, and Charles, as a group, left a party, each of them wore the cap that belonged to someone else and the gloves that belonged to yet another person in that group. Adam wore Bob's gloves. Whose cap and whose gloves did each boy wear?

Gloves	Cap
A	B C
B	C A
C	A B

answer

Four people Adam, Bob, Charles, and David meet at a party. They are from Vancouver, Richmond, Surrey, and Burnaby. David is from Burnaby and Bob is not from Richmond. Adam is from Vancouver. Where are Bob and Charles from?
Charles from Richmond, Bob from Surrey

Four people Adam, Bob, Charles, and David played in a chess tournament with two rounds. David lost to Charles. Adam played Charles in the second round. Adam won one game and lost one game. Who won the tournament?
Charles won by using a tree diagram.

Four people Adam, Bob, Charles, and David had a track race. Charles won the first, and Adam is not the second. If Bob is the fourth, where is David ranked?
2nd

David is between Kitty and Kathy. Kitty is on the east side of David. Ricky is between Kitty and Michael. Who is the farthest west?
Kathy

In a movie theatre, Adam, Bob, Charlie, David, and Ethan all sit in one row. Bob sits first, and David sits last. Adam sits in the middle. Ethan sits before David. Who sits next to Bob?
Charlie

At a party, Nancy wore a green dress and Mabel wore a black one. Emily sat beside the girl who wore blue. What colour did Joyce wear at the party?
Blue

Logic and reasoning

Alvin wrote numbers 1, 2, 3, and 4 on a sheet of paper and the order of numbers are written according to the following clues:

- The 3 was between 2 numbers.
- The 1 had no numbers on its right.
- A number is 2 times of its adjacent number on the right.

4231 or 4321

Adam, Bruce, Cathy, David like math, science, writing, and music. Use the following clues to find out who likes which subject.
- Adam likes the subject that calculates a lot.
- Boys won prizes in music and writing contests.
- David's favourite subject is writing.

Adam likes math, and Bruce likes music, Cathy likes science, David likes writing

In the bird park, all birds are on one path. The peacocks are between parrots and flamingoes. The parrots are between crows and peacocks. The last birds on the path are flamingoes. Which birds are the first on the path?

Crows

Student's name: _____ Assignment date: _____

Consecutive numbers 连續数

Five consecutive numbers add to 20. What are these numbers?

2+3+4+5+6

Five consecutive numbers add to 215. What are these numbers?

41+42+43+44+45

Five consecutive numbers add to 105. What are these numbers?

19+20+21+22+23

Cindy tries to memorize 207 English vocabularies, and her strategy is to memorize 15 vocabularies during the day, but each night Cindy tends to forget 3 words. At this rate, on what day will she memorize all her 207 English vocabularies?

17 days

Inequality 不等式

Fill in the following ☐ with an inequality sign.

$15 - 8 \boxed{>} 6$	$15 - 7 \boxed{>} 6$
$13 - 8 \boxed{<} 6$	$13 - 7 \boxed{>} 4$
$14 - 8 \boxed{<} 7$	$14 - 7 \boxed{<} 8$
$8 + 7 \boxed{<} 8 + 8$	$42 \div 6 \boxed{>} 42 \div 7$
$7 + 7 \boxed{<} 7 + 8$	$56 \div 7 \boxed{>} 56 \div 8$
$3 \times 3 \boxed{<} 3 \times 4$	$72 \div 8 \boxed{>} 72 \div 9$
$5 \times 5 \boxed{>} 4 \times 4$	$36 \div 6 \boxed{=} 36 \div 6$
$6 \times 5 \boxed{>} 5 \times 5$	$25 \div 5 \boxed{>} 25 \div 25$
$8 \times 9 \boxed{=} 9 \times 8$	$40 \div 5 \boxed{>} 40 \div 8$
$11 \times 9 \boxed{>} 11 \times 8$	$64 \div 4 \boxed{>} 64 \div 8$
$12 \times 9 \boxed{<} 10 \times 13$	$75 \div 5 \boxed{<} 63 \div 3$
$13 \times 8 \boxed{<} 12 \times 9$	$82 \div 2 \boxed{>} 96 \div 3$

Student's name: _____ Assignment date: _____

Inequality 不等式

Find the answer(s) to replace the question mark(s).

$3 ♠ 0 \geq 1$

$3 ♠ 1 \geq 2$

$3 ♠ 1 \geq 3$

$3 ♠ 2 \geq 4$

$3 ♠ 2 \geq 5$

$3 ♠ 2 \geq 6$

$3 ♠ 2 \geq 7$

$3 ♠ 2 \geq 8$

$3 ♠ ? 2 \geq 9$

$3 ♠ 3 \geq 10$

$3 ♠ ? 3 \geq 11$

Inequality 不等式

1. $\square$ is a whole number. What is the value of $\square$?

$$\square + 10 < \square + \square$$

$$\square + \square - 13 = \square - 2 \quad \textbf{11}$$

2.

$$3 \times \square = 4 \times \triangle$$

$$20 < \square + \triangle < 30 \quad \square = \textbf{16}, \triangle = \textbf{12}$$

Systems of equations 联立方程 - 二元一次方程

Find all possible answers to the following equation.

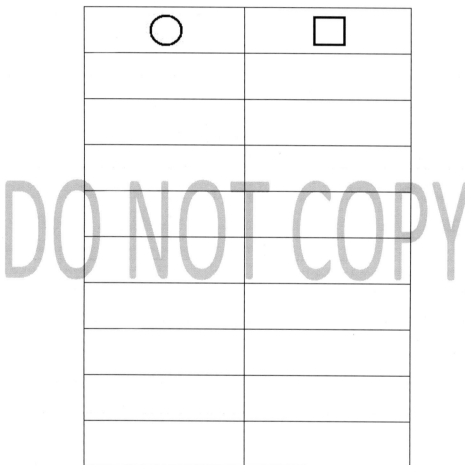

$$\bigcirc \times_4 + \square \times_2 = 32$$

$\bigcirc$	$\square$

0, 16; 1,14; 2,12; 3,10; 4,8; 5,6; 6,4; 7,2; 8,0

Student's name: _____ Assignment date: _____

Mr. Ho's class was observing birds in the trees. On each tree, there were 3 cardinals and 2 mockingbirds in each tree. The class counted 35 birds altogether. How many of each bird did they see, respectively?

21 mockingbirds and 14 cardinals.

Student's name: _____ Assignment date: _____

$$\square + \triangle = 30$$

$$\square + \square + \triangle = 50 \qquad \square = 20, \triangle = 10$$

Three friends went shopping. Together, Adam and Bob spent $32. Bob and Cathy spent $16. Cathy and Adam spent $26. How much did each friend spend?

$$A = 21, B = 11, C = 5$$

Part 4 School math mixed English word problems 学校数学混合文字应用题

Students learn math is not always centred around math contests, and there are many word problems that do not require any skilful computation skills or book strategies or any model problems but an understanding of the problem itself and the willingness of deep thinking mind.

This section contains a variety of diversified word problems. Students who are interested in improving school math problem-solving ability should work on these problems first before studying other model math contest problems.

Ho Math Chess   何数棋谜   英文奥数, 解题策略, 及 IQ 思唯训练宝典
Frank Ho, Amanda Ho © 2020   All rights reserved.

Student's name: _____ Assignment date: _____

Basic facts word problems 四则基本计算应用题

Andy has 17 apples. Bob has 9 apples more than Andy. How many do they have altogether?

$17 + 17 + 9 =$**43**

Andy has 26 apples. Bob has 9 apples less than Andy. How many do they have altogether?

$26 + 26 - 9 = 43$

Andy has 49 apples. Bob has 9 apples more than Andy. How many do they have altogether?

$49+9+49=$**107**

Bob has twice as many apples as Andy. Altogether, they have 81 apples. How many apples does Bob have?

$81 \div 3 = 27$ ……. Andy
$27 \times 2 = 54$ ……. Bob

Andy has one third as fewer apples as Bob. Bob has 42 apples. How many apples does Andy have?

$42 \times \frac{2}{3} =$ **28 using Line Segment Diagram**

,

Student's name: _____ Assignment date: _____

DIY word problems 自己动手文字题, 答案因人而異

We have produced Intelligent Computation worksheets that allow students to select numbers to input into problems. Here we demonstrate that students can also choose numbers to feed into word problems.

Example

Adam is 5 years older than Bob. Cathy is _____ (Fill in your number here.) years younger than Bob. How many years older is Adam than Cathy?

$5 + x$, x is the number which you fill in. Answers may vary depending on the value of x.

The problem (Answers may vary.)

A telephone company charges $1 for the first minute and _____ cents (Fill in your number here.) for each additional minute. If a phone call lasts 5 minutes, find its total cost.
Sandy bought one pen, two pencils. If each pen is $1 more than a pencil, how much did she spend if a pencil was bought at _____ cents (Fill in your number here.)?
Cindy spent $15 less than twice of Ashley. Ashley spent $_____ which is more than $10 (Fill in your number here.). How much did they spend in total?

Sum and Multiplier or Partition of Sum 和倍的分项

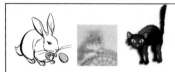

There are rabbits, gerbils, and cats in a pet store.

- There are 13 animals in total.
- There is the same number of rabbits as cats.

How many of each animal could there be?

Numbers appear in the order of cats, gerbils, and rabbits. 4 ways
2, 9, 2; 3, 7, 3; 4, 5, 4; 5, 3, 5

The pet store sold 25 pets and sold three times as many rabbits as gerbils. The rest were cats. What combinations are possible? Note there is more than one animal of each kind.
4 combinations as follows
R G C
18 6 1 no
15 5 5
12 4 9
9 3 13
6 2 17
3 1 21 no

If you pick two digits from 1 to 4 to make a 2-digit number, how many different numbers can you make?

12 ($4 \times 3 = 12$)

If you choose two kinds of fruits from the following fruits to make a fruit plate, then how many kinds of fruit plates can you have?

3 ways

Student's name: ______________________ Assignment date: ______________

Mixed word problems 混合文字题

Four people played in a chess tournament. Each played the other person once. How many games were played in total at the tournament?

$\mathbf{3 + 2 + 1 = 6}$

If the problem is changed to play the other person twice, then how many games were played?

$6 \times 2 = 12$ games

Find the next three numbers.

6, 10, 15, ____, _____, _____ **21, 28, 36**

Show Andy what the all possible 3-digit numbers you can make from the 3 digits 3, 5, and 8 are.
No digits can be repeated.

6 numbers

How many different sums of digits of 2-digit numbers can you get by choosing two digits from 3, 5, 7, and 9?

5 different sums
35 (8), 37(10), 39 (12), 57 (12), 59 (14), 79 (16)

How many rectangles are in the following diagram?

15

Student's name: _____ Assignment date: _____

James is 5 years older than his cousin Louise. In three years, Louise will be 16. How old is James now?

18

Each box carries 8 cans. You have 57 cans. How many boxes do you need to carry all these cans?

8 boxes

What is the positive difference between 14.8 and 3.09?

11.71

What is the sum of 4 tenths and 2 hundredths?

0.42

Student's name: _____ Assignment date: _____

Is $\frac{3}{4}$ closer to 0 or 1? Draw a number line to show.

1

Is 50 closer to 0 or 100? Draw a number line to show.

the same

Is 0.51 closer to 0 or 1.5? Draw a number line to show.

1.5

We know the answer by taking the difference $1.5 - 0.51 = 0.99$.

Student's name: _____ Assignment date: _____

Find the area of the following shaded rectangle when ABCD is a square.

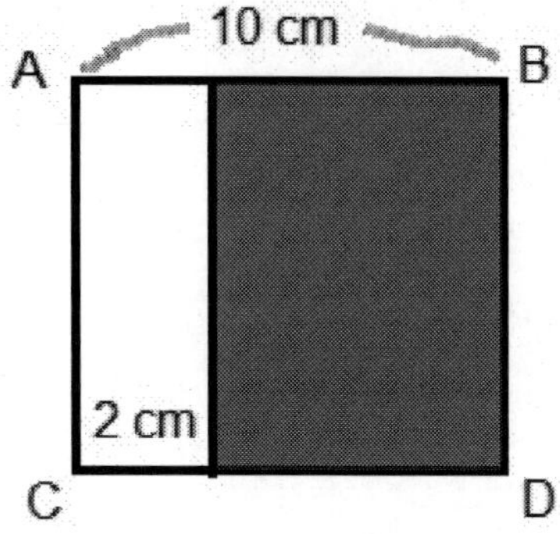

80 cm²

Use all the digits 9, 7, 0, 8, and 5 to form the greatest 5-digit odd number.

98705

Pattern

Find the answers for the missing numbers by using pattern rule.

A	B
3	120
7	280
9	360
13	? **520**

What is the pattern rule of getting B from A? _____ **B=A × 40**

What should be the next number for the following number sequence?

1, 4, 9, 16, _____ **25**

$\frac{5}{8}$ of guests at the party are boys and $\frac{1}{4}$ of the guests are girls, and the rest guests are adults. What fraction of the guests are adults?

The correct answer is 1/8

Fernando used the following diagrams and figured out the answer was $\frac{3}{6}$. Was he right?

_____ **No**

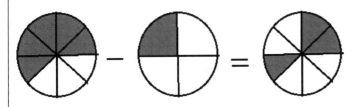

What is 4 tens, 17 tenths and 7 thousandths in decimal numbers?

This problem is for advanced students.

4 x 10 + 17 x 0.1 + 7 x 0.001 = 41.707

The measurements of a water tank are 35 cm long, 15 cm wide, and 25 cm high. Ten litres (L) of water are poured into this empty tank. How much is more water needed to fill the tank to its brim in L^3? (1 L = 1000 cm^3)

$\frac{35 \times 15 \times 25}{1000} - 10 = 13.125\,L - 10 = 3.125\,L$

Fernando paid a total of $74 for a pair of earrings, a dress and a bracelet for his mom. The bracelet costs $6.60 more than the earrings. The dress cost was triple as much as the bracelet. Find the cost of the dress.

$$\frac{74+6.6}{5} \times 3 = \$48.36$$

The number of girls at the party was $\frac{4}{10}$ the number of boys. There were 48 more boys than girls at the party. How many boys were at the party? How many girls were at the party?

80 boys, 32 girls

Assume boys had 10 groups and girls had 4 groups (Translate the concept of numbers into groups to get the reduced fraction.).

$\frac{48}{10-4}$=8 .... # of boys in each group
8 x 10 = 80 .... # of boys
8 x 4 =32 ...... # of girls

After some girls left the party, the number of boys was 4 times the number of remaining girls at the party. How many girls left in the party?

Since there were no boys left the party, use the answers to the previous question w know the number of girls remaining in the party is $\frac{80}{4} = 20$
32 – 20 = **12 girls left**

Aaron gets paid $2 per car wash and an additional $3 per hour. He worked three hours last week doing 15 car washes. How much did he earn?

$39

Rank the following number from lowest to greatest.

$1.3, \dfrac{1}{2}, 0.32, \dfrac{4}{10}$

$0.32, \dfrac{4}{10}, \dfrac{1}{2}, 1.3$ answer

Write 3 dimes (each dime = 10 cents) and a nickel (each nickel = 5 cents) in decimal with a dollar sign. _____ **$0.35**

Write 3 dimes and a nickel in whole number _____ **35¢**

There are 6 soldiers in $\dfrac{1}{5}$ of a set of plastic army commandos. How many plastic army commando soldiers are there is a complete set?

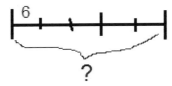

30

There are 6 soldiers in $\dfrac{2}{5}$ of a set of plastic army commandos. How many plastic army commando soldiers are there is a complete set?

15

Student's name: _____ Assignment date: _____

Fernando studied at 8:30 a.m. and finished at 3:15 p.m. with a one-hour lunch break. Melissa studied at 12:45 and finished at 20:55 with a one-hour dinner break. Who studied longer and by how much time?

$$(20:55 - 12:45) = (15:15 - 8:30) = 8:10 - 6:45 = 1:25$$
Melissa by 1 hour and 25 minutes

A rectangular pool deck has a width of 4 m and a length of 6 m. It costs $4 to buy a meter fence. How much does it cost to install a fence around the pool deck?

$80

A rectangular pool deck has a width of 5 m and a length of 7 m. It costs $4 to buy a 120 cm of the fence. How much does it cost to install a fence around the pool deck?

$$(5 + 7) \times 2 = 240\,m = 2400\,cm$$
$$\frac{2400}{120} \times 4 = \$80$$

Is $\frac{1}{4}$ closer to 0 or 1? Draw a number line to show.

0

One car is needed to give a ride for every 4 students to Fun Fair. How many cars are needed for 27 students?

7

Michael is about to cross a bridge, and we know the following information:

- The bridge is 7 m.
- Michael's one-foot step is about 45 cm.

About how many full steps are needed for Michael to cross the bridge?

16

There are 5 cedar trees for every 2 oak trees at the Nature Park. How many cedar trees are there if there are 8 oak trees?

20

It takes 12 seconds for the elevator from the first floor to the fourth floor, how many seconds does it take for the elevator to go from the first floor to the eighth floor?

28

At the Pre-Loved Skates shop, the price of a pair of skates is reduced by half each day if not sold yesterday. If on the first day, a pair of skates cost $4, then how much will it cost to buy on the fourth day if they are not sold in 3 days?

50 cents

There are three whole numbers ranked from the smallest to the largest and the difference between each number is 3. The total of the three numbers is 21. What are these three numbers?

4, 7, 10

A basket of apples is divided into many piles. If each pile has 8 apples, then there is a short of one apple, and if each pile has 7 apples, then there are 8 apples left. Find how many apples are there and how many piles are there?

Method 1

Find the number of apples which satisfies the condition 1 with 8 apples in one pile short of one apple.

The number of apples could meet the above condition 1 are 7, 15, 23, 31, 39, 47, 55, 63, 71, ……

Find a number which satisfies the condition 2 with 7 apples in one pile, 8 apples left.

The number of apples could meet the above condition are 15, 22, 29, 36, 43, 50, 57, 64, 71, ……

The 71 apples meet both conditions.

Method 2

Let the number of piles = x

$8x - 1 = 7x + 8$

$x = $ **9 piles**, $9 \times 8 - 1 =$ **71 apples.**

Eric has 105 marbles, and Alex has 25 marbles. How many marbles does Eric have to give to Alex such that each of them has an equal number of marbles?

40

Ho Math Chess   何数棋谜   英文奥数, 解题策略, 及 IQ 思唯训练宝典
Frank Ho, Amanda Ho © 2020   All rights reserved.

Student's name: _____ Assignment date: _____

Isaac wants to build a rectangular pen for his cat. He has 16 m of fencing. He wants the sides to be whole numbers. What are all the different rectangular areas he could possibly get?

7, 12, 15, 16
1 by 7 =7, 2 by 6 = 12, 3 by 5 =15, 4 by 4 = 16

Isaac wants to build a rectangular pen for his cat. He has 22 m of fencing. He wants the sides to be whole numbers. What are all the different rectangular areas he could possibly get?

10, 18, 24, 28, 30

The pattern rule is to start the first number with 9 and adds 7 to the previous number. If the pattern continues, what is the fifth number? What is the total up and including the fifth number?

9, 16, 23, 30, 37

If 4.2 m roll of paper is cut into 3 equal pieces and each piece is 1.3 m long. How much paper in cm will be left in the roll?

30 =4.2 – 3 x 1.3 =0.3 m = 30 cm

Write 1111 in English words. _____. **One thousand one hundred eleven**

Write 11.11 in English words. _____. **Eleven and eleven hundredth**

What is the next shape? hexagon

 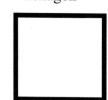 

? answer

I am a 3-digit number. My tens digit is 4 times my ones digit, and the sum of my digits is 12. What number am I?

741 or 282

In the following expression, find the value of the ?.

 is to + ◯ as is ? is to 31 and 1.

32

Compare the following numbers using >, =, or <.

1. $\dfrac{0.1}{2}$ $\dfrac{0.1}{2}$. =

2. $\dfrac{0.01}{2}$ $\dfrac{0.1}{0.02}$. <

168
1 week = _____ hours

$\dfrac{1}{168}$
1 hour = _____ week

Jordan has 13 more than as many as four times of Jocelyn's apples. Jordan has 81 apples. How many apples does Jocelyn have?

Line Segment Method	Assumption Pattern method	Pre-algebra using symbol
Jocelyn ⊢——⊣ Jordan ⊢——⊢——⊢——⊢—¹³⌐ ⌣———81———⌣ $\dfrac{81-13}{4} = 17$	<table><tr><td>Jocelyn</td><td>Jordan</td></tr><tr><td>10</td><td>40+13 =53</td></tr><tr><td>11</td><td>57</td></tr><tr><td>15</td><td>73</td></tr><tr><td>16</td><td>77</td></tr><tr><td>17</td><td>81</td></tr></table>	$4 \times \square + 13 = 81$

17

The Spring fair director planned the daily sale of 2.5 tons of hot dogs, but the actual daily sale on average was 1 ton more than planned. The stock lasted for 7 days. How many days did the fair director originally plan to finish selling the hot dogs?

$$9 = \frac{3.5 \times 7}{2.5}$$

Compute $2.09 - 1.999 = ?$

0.091

$2.64 - 1.999 =$

0.641

Two and one tenths + one hundred and one hundred two thousandths

102.202

Add the face values of the underlined digits.

5623<u>6</u> + <u>1</u>876453 + 623<u>5</u>21 + 478<u>20</u> + 45<u>3</u>=?

1003029

Make a 3-digit number such that

- The hundreds place digit is 3 times of the ones place digit.
- The number is greater than 600.
- The number is divisible by 9.

963

Use the digits 1, 2, 3, 4, 5, 6, 7, and 8 once each to make the following sum greatest. What is the sum?

$$\begin{array}{c}\square\ \square\ \square\ \square\\ +\quad \square\ \square\ \square\ \square\\ \hline \square\ \square\ \square\ \square\ \square\end{array}$$

8641+7532=16173

Use the digits 1, 2, 3, 4, 5, 6, 7, and 8 once each to make the following difference greatest. What is the difference?

$$\begin{array}{c}\square\ \square\ \square\ \square\\ -\quad \square\ \square\ \square\ \square\\ \hline \square\ \square\ \square\ \square\ \square\end{array}$$

8765 - 1234 = 7531

Student's name: _____ Assignment date: _____

There are 36 children in Shelby's class. For every 2 girls, there is a boy. How many boys are in Shelby's class?

12

There are 36 birds in the Nature Park. For every heron , there are 3 ducks. For every heron, there are two geese. How many of each bird are in the Nature Park?

6 herons
18 ducks
12 geese

4000 < A × 8 <5000 but closet to 4000. What is the natural number A?

501

What fraction of the letters in the word "Vancouver" are consonants?

$$\frac{5}{9}$$

What is the rounded result to the nearest hundreds after 2968 is added by 150?

3100

What is the area of the following triangle within a square with a side length of 15 cm?

112.5

Student's name: _____ Assignment date: _____

A box of a dozen bags of biscuits along with a box altogether weighs 5000 g. Seven bags along with a box were sold, and they all weigh 3550 g. How much does each bag weigh, and how much does the box weigh?

Method 1, Think logically using a mental diagram without using an equation.

5000-3550=1450, 1450/5=**290 g weight of each bag**.
3550 – 290 x 7 = **1520g weight of box**

Method 2, Use an algebra.

12B + X = 5000
7B + X =3550

Alex's house is 1.5 km from school and Eric's house is 2 km from the school. How far is the distance from Alex's house to Eric's house?

Assume Alex's house, Eric's house and school are all on a straight line. Show two answers by drawing two diagrams.

Show two answers by drawing two diagrams.

0.5 and 3.5 km

On the first day, Justin read half his book and 15 more pages. The second day he read half of what was left and 5 more pages, there were 30 pages left. How many pages are there in the book?

 170

35x2+15=85, 85x2=170

It takes 10 people 6 days to build one road. Now, if adding 5 more people, how long will it take to build one road?

4   6x10/(10+5)=4

$+ - \times \div$

The following two-word problems are for advanced students.

Calculate	Calculate
$27.25 + 18.45 \times 0.45 + 18.45 \times 0.55$ Hint: Factor out 18.45 first. $ab + ac = a(b+c)$ **45.7**	$1.7 + 4.6 + 7.7 + 8.3 + 5.4 + 2.3$ Hint: Pair two numbers to make the sum ending with 0. **30**

A rectangular box is designed to hold exactly 5 balls lined up, as shown below. What fraction of the space in the box do they occupy?

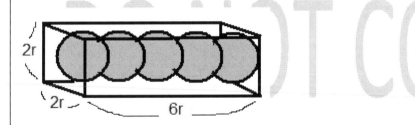

The student must know how to calculate the volume of a sphere and rectangular prism. The volume of a sphere is $\frac{4\pi\gamma^3}{3}$. The volume of a rectangular prism is $l \times w \times h$.

The width is 2r, and the length is 6r. Sphere volume = $\frac{4\pi\gamma^3}{3} \times 5 \text{ (balls)} = \frac{20\pi\gamma^3}{3}$

The ratio = $\frac{20\pi\gamma^3}{3} \div 24r^3 = \frac{20\pi\gamma^3}{3} \times \frac{1}{24r^3} = \frac{5\pi}{18}$

Part 5 Mixed computations and number puzzles 混合计算技巧及数迷

This part includes some basic number facts training and number puzzles. It does not include word problems.

Shortcuts for number computations

There are some shortcuts that can be used to do computation mentally, these shortcuts allow students to do the computation in a more efficient way, and they also improve computation skills.

It is multiplied by 5.

Try to find a matching 2 so that $2 \times 5 = 10$.

Example

$5 \times 16 = \underline{5} \times \underline{2} \times 8 = 10 \times 8 = 80$

$124 \times 5 = 62 \times \underline{2} \times \underline{5} = 62 \times 10 = 620$

1. $5 \times 46 =$ **230**

2. $5 \times 58 =$ **290**

3. $64 \times 5 =$ **320**

4. $78 \times 5 =$ **390**

5. $102 \times 5 =$ **510**

6. $372 \times 5 =$ **1860**

7. $5 \times 612 =$ **3060**

8. $5 \times 406 =$ **2030**

9. $306 \times 5 =$ **1530**

10. $1004 \times 5 =$ **5020**

11 $92 \times 5 =$ **460**

12. $5 \times 3040 =$ **15200**

Student's name: _____ Assignment date: _____

Multiplied by 25

Try to find a matching 4 so that $4 \times 25 = 100$

Example:

$25 \times 8 = \underline{25 \times 4} \times 2 = 100 \times 2 = 200$
$132 \times 25 = 33 \times \underline{4 \times 25} = 33 \times 100 = 3300$

1. $28 \times 25 = $ **700**

2. $44 \times 25 = $ **1100**

3. $25 \times 36 = $ **900**

4. $25 \times 72 = $ **1800**

5. $25 \times 124 = $ **3100**

6. $84 \times 25 = $ **2100**

7. $172 \times 25 = $ **4300**

8. $452 \times 25 = $ **11300**

9. $208 \times 25 = $ **5200**

10. $356 \times 25 = $ **8900**

11 $25 \times 332 = $ **8300**

12. $704 \times 25 = $ **17600**

Student's name: _____ Assignment date: _____

Multiplied by 125

Try to find a matching 8 so that $8 \times 125 = 1000$

Example

$125 \times 48 = \underline{125} \times \underline{8} \times 6 = 1000 \times 6 = 6000$
$168 \times 125 = 21 \times \underline{8} \times \underline{125} = 21 \times 1000 = 21000$

1. $125 \times 16 =$ **2000**

2. $125 \times 48 =$ **6000**

3. $88 \times 125 =$ **11000**

4. $72 \times 125 =$ **9000**

5. $96 \times 125 =$ **12000**

6. $125 \times 56 =$ **7000**

7. $125 \times 24 =$ **3000**

8. $64 \times 125 =$ **8000**

9. $80 \times 125 =$ **10000**

10. $125 \times 160 =$ **20000**

11 $32 \times 125 =$ **4000**

12. $125 \times 720 =$ **90000**

Ho Math Chess　　　何数棋谜　　　英文奥数, 解题策略, 及 IQ 思唯训练宝典

Student's name: _____ Assignment date: _____

Multiplying an even number by a number ending with 5

Example

$26 \times 35 = 13 \times \underline{2} \times \underline{35} = 13 \times 70 = 910$

$45 \times 38 = \underline{45} \times \underline{2} \times 19 = 90 \times 19 = 1710$

1. $15 \times 28 =$ **420**

2. $35 \times 74 =$ **2590**

3. $15 \times 34 =$ **510**

4. $25 \times 52 =$ **1300**

5. $36 \times 45 =$ **1620**

6. $66 \times 35 =$ **2310**

7. $128 \times 35 =$ **4480**

8. $14 \times 85 =$ **1190**

9. $75 \times 12 =$ **900**

10. $135 \times 16 =$ **2160**

11. $325 \times 6 =$ **1950**

12. $715 \times 4 =$ **2860**

Multiplying two numbers with the same tens or hundreds digit and the sum of ones digits is 10.

The numbers of higher than 3 digits lose the appealing of speedy calculations.

Example

$$15 \times 15 = \underline{1 \times (1+1)}\, 25 = 225$$

$$35 \times 35 = \underline{3 \times (3+1)}\, 25 = 1225$$

$$107 \times 103 = 11021$$

$$118 \times 112 = 13216$$

$25 \times 25 =$ **625**	$45 \times 45 =$ **2025**
$35 \times 35 =$ **1225**	$65 \times 65 =$ **4225**
$55 \times 55 =$ **3025**	$75 \times 75 =$ **5625**
$85 \times 85 =$ **7225**	$195 \times 195 =$ **38025**
$15 \times 15 =$ **225**	$205 \times 205 =$ **42025**
$105 \times 105 =$ **11025**	$125 \times 125 =$ **15625**
$26 \times 24 =$ **624**	$21 \times 29 =$ **681**
$35 \times 37 =$ **1235**	$304 \times 306 =$ **93024**
$54 \times 56 =$ **3024**	$225 \times 225 =$ **50625**
$83 \times 87 =$ **7221**	$177 \times 173 =$ **30621**
$13 \times 17 =$ **221**	$208 \times 202 =$ **42016**
$125 \times 125 =$ **15625**	$222 \times 228 =$ **50616**

Multiplied by 11

Example

16 × 11 = 1(1 + 6) 6 = 176

11 × 37 = 3 (3 + 7) 7 = 3 (10) 7 = 407

1. 24 × 11 = **264**

2. 11 × 18 = **198**

3. 32 × 11 = **352**

4. 11 × 27 = **297**

5. 61 × 11 = **671**

6. 11 × 81 = **891**

7. 56 × 11 = **716**

8. 78 × 11 = **858**

9. 11 × 77 = **847**

10. 11 × 84 = **924**

11. 11 × 123 = **1353**

12. 458 × 11 = **5838**

Shortcut for adding numbers ending with 0's

This shortcut can also be used for subtraction.

Thousands adding thousands

1. $4000 + 9000 = 1300$
2. $5000 + 9000 = 14000$
3. $5000 + 3000 = $ **8000**
4. $7000 + 4000 = $ **11000**
5. $3000 + 2000 = $ **5000**
6. $6000 + 800 = $ **6800**
7. $8000 + 5000 = $ **13000**
8. $7000 + 3000 = 10000$
9. $7000 + 7000 = 14000$
10. $6000 + 3000 = $ **9000**
11. $5000 + 4000 = $ **9000**
12. $3000 + 7000 = 10000$
13. $8000 + 4000 = $ **12000**
14. $9000 + 7000 = 16000$
15. $9000 + 8000 = 17000$

Fill in each blank to add up to thousands or ten thousand.

1. $5000 + $ **5000** $ = 10000$
2. $3000 + $ **7000** $ = 10000$
3. $6700 + $ **3300** $ = 10000$
4. $5200 + $ **4800** $ = 10000$
5. $7420 + $ **2580** $ = 10000$
6. $3810 + $ **6190** $ = 10000$
7. $8409 + $ **1591** $ = 10000$
8. $3617 + $ **6383** $ = 10000$
9. $2509 + $ **2491** $ = 5000$
10. $2175 + $ **825** $ = 3000$
11. $3096 + $ **3904** $ = 7000$
12. $3289 + $ **2711** $ = 6000$
13. $2078 + $ **1922** $ = 4000$
14. $2843 + $ **2157** $ = 5000$
15. $1745 + $ **6255** $ = 8000$
16. $2004 + $ **4996** $ = 7000$

Student's name: _____ Assignment date: _____

The following does the subtraction to get nice numbers ending with 0 first.

$25 + \underline{36 - 16}$
$= 25 + 20$
$= 45$

$31 - 17 + 47$
$= 31 + \underline{47 - 17}$
$= 31 + 30$
$= 61$

1. $42 + 37 - 17$ $= \mathbf{62}$

2. $23 - 16 + 36$ $= \mathbf{43}$

3. $41 - 28 + 38$ $= \mathbf{51}$

4. $63 - 35 + 45$ $= \mathbf{73}$

5. $72 - 38 + 58$ $= \mathbf{92}$

6. $57 + 21 - 47$ $= \mathbf{31}$

7. $53 - 24 + 44$ $= \mathbf{73}$

8. $56 + 33 - 46$ $= \mathbf{43}$

9. $39 + 41 - 29$ $= \mathbf{51}$

10. $37 - 29 + 49$ $= \mathbf{57}$

multiplied or divided by 10, 100, or 1000

It is multiplied by the power of multiples of 10. Add the sum of ending zeros two factors to the end of the non-zero product. $2 \times 5 = 10$ $4 \times 25 = 100$, $5 \times 20 = 100$ $8 \times 125 = 1000$	Divided by the power of multiples of 10. Cross out the same number of ending zeros of both dividend and divisor. $3120000 \div 300 = 10400$
$10 \times 10 = 24100$	$10 \div 10 = 1$
$100 \times 10 = 1000$	$100 \div 10 = 10$
$200 \times 2 \times 5 = 1000$	$200 \div 2 \div 50 = 2$
$7200 \times 900 = 6480000$	$7200 \div 900 = 8$
$300 \times 570000 = 171000000$	$570000 \div 300 = 1900$
$40000 \times 1560000 = 62400000000$	$1560000 \div 40000 = 39$
$8005 \times 76000 = 608,380,000$	$576000 \div 800 = 720$
$6500 \times 4 \times 25 = 650,000$	$6500 \div 8 \div 125 = 6.5$
$105000 \times 700 = 73,500,000$	$105000 \div 700 = 150$
$472000 \times 400 = 188,800,000$	$472000 \div 400 = 1180$
$50000 \times 2000 = 100,000,000$	$50000 \div 2000 = 25$
$640000 \times 40010 = 254,06,400,000$	$640000 \div 40010 = 16$
$10 \times 8 \times 125 = 10,000$	$100 \div 10 = 10$
$100 \times 4 \times 25 = 10,000$	$1000 \div 4 \div 25 = 10$
$200 \times 5 \times 20 = 2,000,000$	$2000 \div 10 = 200$
$7200 \times 9000 = 64,800,000$	$72000 \div 900 = 80$
$570000 \times 3000 = 1,710,000,000$	$5700000 \div 300 = 19000$
$1560000 \times 400000 = 624,000,000,000$	$15600000 \div 40000 = 390$
$576000 \times 8000 = 4,608,000,000$	$5760000 \div 800 = 7200$
$6500 \times 500 = 3,250,000$	$65000 \div 50 = 1300$
$105000 \times 7000 = 735,000,000$	$1050000 \div 700 = 1500$
$472000 \times 4000 = 18,888,000,000$	$4720000 \div 400 = 11800$
$50000 \times 20000 = 1,000,000,000$	$500000 \div 2000 = 250$

,

Shortcuts for mixed operation

The following expressions can be thought of as vertical formats so that the top and the bottom number can be reduced by a common factor first.

$28 \times \dfrac{36 \div 9}{}$

$= 28 \times 4$

$= 112$

$57 \div 3 \times 6$

$= 57 \times \dfrac{6 \div 3}{}$

$= 57 \times 2$

$= 114$

1. $56 \times 12 \div 4 \quad = \mathbf{168}$

2. $64 \div 4 \times 8 \quad = \mathbf{128}$

3. $81 \div 3 \times 9 \quad = \mathbf{243}$

4. $51 \times 26 \div 13 \quad = \mathbf{102}$

5. $84 \div 7 \times 21 \quad = \mathbf{252}$

6. $75 \times 15 \div 5 \quad = \mathbf{225}$

7. $53 \times 36 \div 12 \quad = \mathbf{159}$

8. $84 \div 6 \times 48 \quad = \mathbf{672}$

Numbers, digits, place values 数, 数字, 位数值

Without understanding patterns in math, students cannot do Kangaroo Math Contest well. Patterns can be described in numbers, tables, figures, or words etc. Students must understand the concept of number patterns, figure patterns, or patterns described in words. In the Math Kangaroo Contest, to understand the pattern only means students possess the qualification to be trained because many contest problems involve using patterns and other math concepts to solve problems.

One type of problem for higher grades students requires students to use patterns or combinations to find numbers by using digits, then find the sum of all numbers. There are a few hurdles that prevent students from solving this kind of problem. The problems facing students could be as follows:

1. How to create a set of numbers according to some conditions. Often, the set of data involves patterns.
2. How to calculate based on the data sets created.

The above problems could be classified into a few categories as follows. Lower grade students will work on simple problems, and higher grade students work on more difficult problems.

There are a few methods listed below, but for the lower grade students, the List Method or Box Method can be used.

For the higher grades students, the Box Method or factorial method can be used.

Basics concepts review 基本计算观念複習

GCF and LCM 最大公約数及最小公倍数

GCF and LCM form the backbone of calculating fractions, and this concept is used all the way to high school.

Example 1

Find the GCF and LCM of the following pairs of numbers.

Problems	GCF	LCM
40, 210	10	840
130, 390	130	390
240, 320	80	160
550, 880	110	1400

Bradley gives $\frac{1}{3}$ of his sticks to Elise, who gives $\frac{1}{4}$ of what he receives to Cindy, who gives $\frac{1}{5}$ of what she receives to Mabel. If each of them receives a whole number of sticks, what is the fewest number of sticks that Bradley could have started with?

60

Divisibility 約数

Divisibility rules

"Divisible by" means a number can be evenly divided by another number without a remainder.

The followings are divisible rules:

A number is divisible by 2 if and only if the last digit is divisible by 2.

A number is divisible by 3 if and only if the sum of all digits is divisible by 3.

A number is divisible by 4 if and only if the last 2-digit number is divisible by 4.

A number is divisible by 5 if and only if the last digit is 0 or 5.

A number is divisible by 6 if and only if the number can be divisible by 2 and 3.

Divisibility Rule of 7
The last digit is multiplied by 2 and subtracted its product from the rest of the digits. The result is either 0 or divisible by 7. For example, Is **3416** divisible by 7? The steps are as follows:

Last digit multiply by 2, $6 \times 2 = 12$
Subtracted 12 from the rest of digits 341, $341 - 12 = 329$ ($341 - 6 \times 2 = 329$)
Last digit multiplied by 2, $9 \times 2 = 18$
Subtracted 18 from the rest of digits $32 - 18 = 14$ ($32 - 9 \times 2 = 14$)
The result 14 is a multiple of 7.
The number 3416 is divisible by 7.

A number is divisible by 8 if and only if the last 3-digit number is divisible by 8.
A number is divisible by 9 if and only if the sum of all digits is divisible by 9 (same rule as 3).
A number is divisible by 10 if and only if the last digit is 0.
A number is divisible by 11 if and only if the difference between the sum of odd-numbered digits and the sum of even-numbered digits) is 0 or divisible by 11.
A number is divisible by 12 if and only if the number can be divisible by 3 and 4.
A number is divisible by 14 if and only if the number can be divisible by 2 and 7.
A number is divisible by 15 if and only if the number can be divisible by 3 and 5.
A number is divisible by 25 if and only if the number ends with 00, 25, 50, and 75.

Student's name: ______________________________ Assignment date: __________________

Example 1

How do you know 4 is a factor of a number if 8 is a factor of that number?

Example 2

Is 8 a factor of a number which has a factor of 4?

Sometimes it is true.

16, yes, but 12 is not. The number 12 is a counterexample

At the Fun Fair, students can guess the number of jelly beans in the jar with the following clues:

- is less than 230
- is greater than 105
- can be divisible by 8
- can be divisible by 3

How many jelly beans are in the jar?

A. 116
B. 204
C. 216
D. 163
C

At the Fun Fair, students can guess the number of jelly beans in the jar with the following clues:

- is less than 1000
- is greater than 100
- can be divisible by 4
- can be divisible by 5

How many jelly beans are in the jar?

A. 316
B. 504
C. 916
D. 860
D

Student's name: _____ Assignment date: _____

Multiplication and divisions facts 乘除恒等式

Place each number in □.

6, 5, 30	$6 \times 5 = 30$ $5 \times 6 = 30$ $30 \div 5 = 6$ $30 \div 6 = 5$	$\square \times \square = \square$ $\square \times \square = \square$ $\square \div \square = \square$ $\square \div \square = \square$
8, 6, 48	$8 \times 6 = 48$ $6 \times 8 = 48$ $48 \div 6 = 8$ $48 \div 5 = 6$	$\square \times \square = \square$ $\square \times \square = \square$ $\square \div \square = \square$ $\square \div \square = \square$
7, 4, 28	$7 \times 4 = 28$ $4 \times 7 = 28$ $28 \div 4 = 7$ $28 \div 7 = 4$	$\square \times \square = \square$ $\square \times \square = \square$ $\square \div \square = \square$ $\square \div \square = \square$

Ho Math Chess 何数棋谜　英文奥数, 解题策略, 及 IQ 思唯训练宝典
Frank Ho, Amanda Ho © 2020

Student's name: _____ Assignment date: _____

Multiplication review 乘法複習

$$\begin{array}{r} 123456789 \\ \times \qquad 4 \\ \hline 493827156 \end{array}$$

$$\begin{array}{r} 987654321 \\ \times \qquad 4 \\ \hline 3950617284 \end{array}$$

393827156, 3950617284

Student's name: _____ Assignment date: _____

Multiplication review

$$
\begin{array}{r}
123456789 \\
\times \qquad 5 \\
\hline
617283945
\end{array}
$$

$$
\begin{array}{r}
987654321 \\
\times \qquad 5 \\
\hline
4938271605
\end{array}
$$

617283945, 4938271605

Student's name: _____ Assignment date: _____

Multiplication review

$$
\begin{array}{r}
123456789 \\
\times \quad\quad 6 \\
\hline
740740734
\end{array}
$$

$$
\begin{array}{r}
987654321 \\
\times \quad\quad 6 \\
\hline
5925925926
\end{array}
$$

740740734, 5925925926

Student's name: _____ Assignment date: _____

Multiplication review

$$
\begin{array}{r}
123456789 \\
\times \qquad 7 \\
\hline
864197523
\end{array}
$$

$$
\begin{array}{r}
987654321 \\
\times \qquad 7 \\
\hline
6913580247
\end{array}
$$

864197523, 6913580247

Student's name: _____ Assignment date: _____

Multiplication review

$$123456789 \times 8$$

987654312

$$987654321 \times 8$$

7901234568

987654312, 7901234568

Student's name: _____ Assignment date: _____

Multiplication review

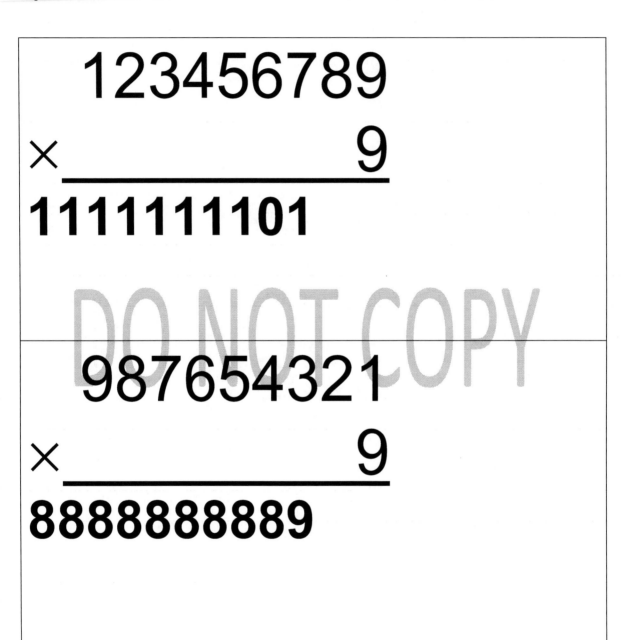

$$123456789 \times 9$$

1111111101

$$987654321 \times 9$$

8888888889

1111111101, 8888888889

Student's name: _____ Assignment date: _____

Multiplication review

$$\begin{array}{r} 123456789 \\ \times 3 \\ \hline 370370367 \end{array}$$

$$\begin{array}{r} 987654321 \\ \times 3 \\ \hline 296292963 \end{array}$$

370370367, 296292963

Multiplying numbers ending in 9 尾数是 9 的乘法

1. $6 \times 99 = 6 \times (100 - 1) = 600 - 6 = \mathbf{594}$

2. $6 \times 4.99 = 6 \times (5 - 0.01) = 30 - 0.06 = \mathbf{29.94}$

3. $9 \times 99 = 9 \times (100 - 1) = 900 - 9 = \mathbf{891}$

4. $5 \times 99 = \mathbf{495}$

5. $7 \times 99 = \mathbf{693}$

6. $8 \times 99 = \mathbf{792}$

Student's name: _____ Assignment date: _____

Mixed computations

Problems

1.　　$(11 + 22) - (16 + 17)$

0

2.　　$(13 + 23) - (13 + 15)$

8

3.　　$(14 + 19) - (10 + 11)$

12

4.　　$(3 \times 18) - (3 \times 17)$

3

5.　　$(4 \times + 19) - (4 \times 18)$

4

6.　　$(5 \times 18) - (5 \times 17)$

5

7.　　$(6 \times 19) - (6 \times 18)$

6

Student's name: _____ Assignment date: _____

Cross multiplication 交义相乘

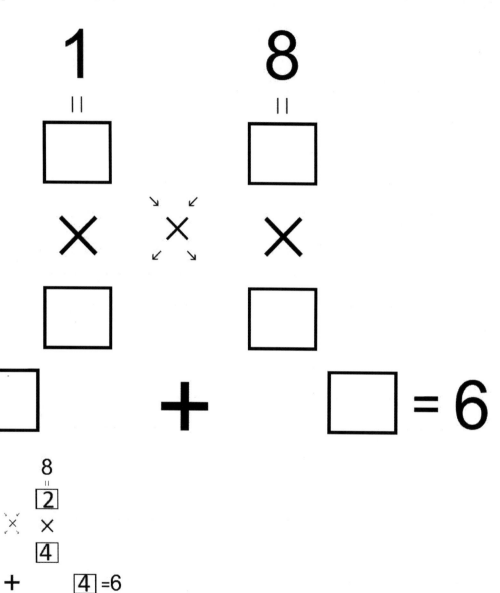

Cross multiplication

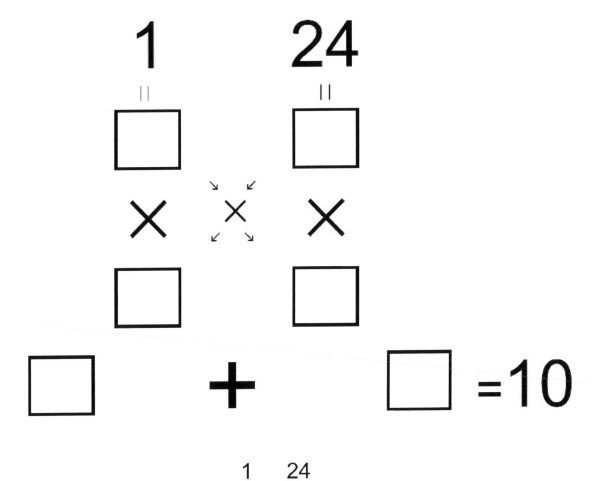

Student's name: _____ Assignment date: _____

Cross multiplication

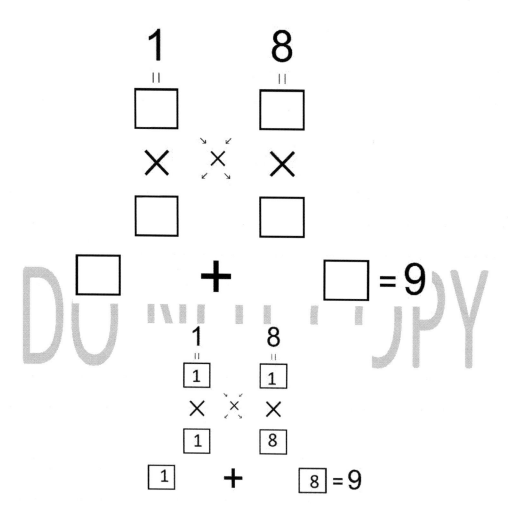

Student's name: _____ Assignment date: _____

Cross multiplication

1   35

=
□   □

×      ×

□   □

□   +   □ = 36

1   35

=
1   35

×      ×

1   1

35   +   1 = 36

Cross multiplication

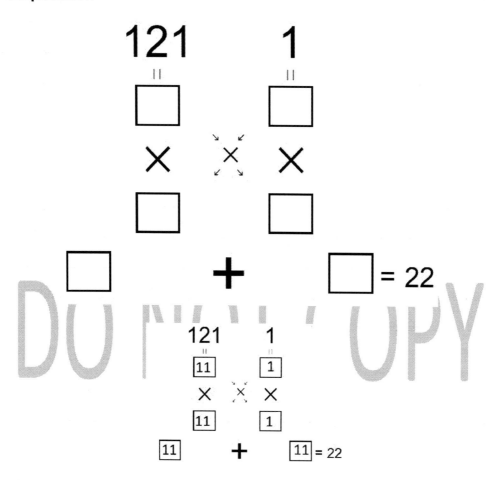

Cross multiplication

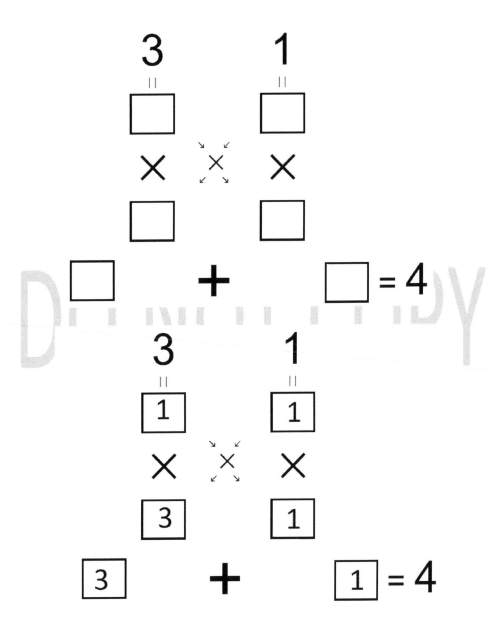

Student's name: ______________________ Assignment date: ______________

Cross multiplication

28 1

= =

□ □

× × ×

□ □

□ + □ = 11

28 1

= =

7 1

× × ×

4 1

4 + 7 = 11

Cross multiplication

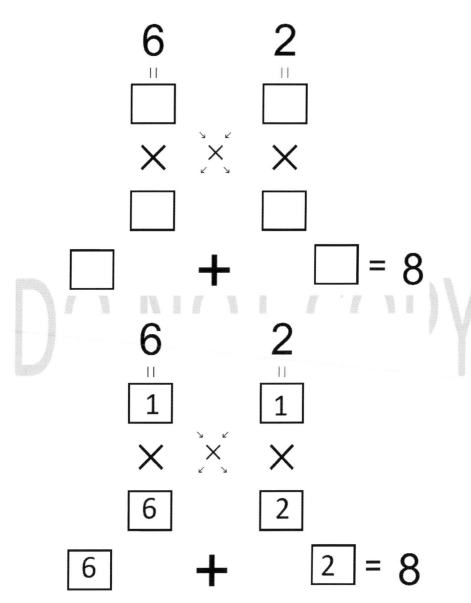

Ho Math Chess 何数棋谜　英文奥数, 解题策略, 及 IQ 思唯训练宝典
Frank Ho, Amanda Ho © 2020　　　All rights reserved.
Student's name: _____ Assignment date: _____

Cross multiplication

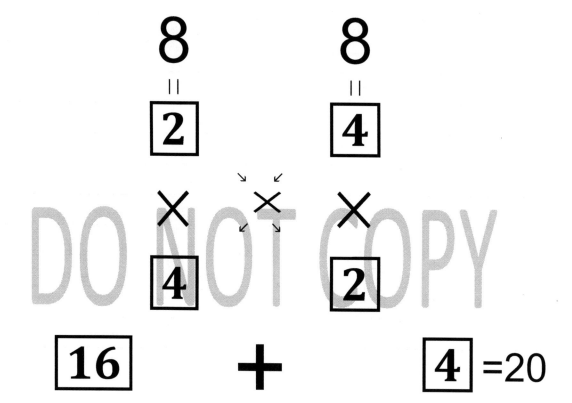

Cross multiplication

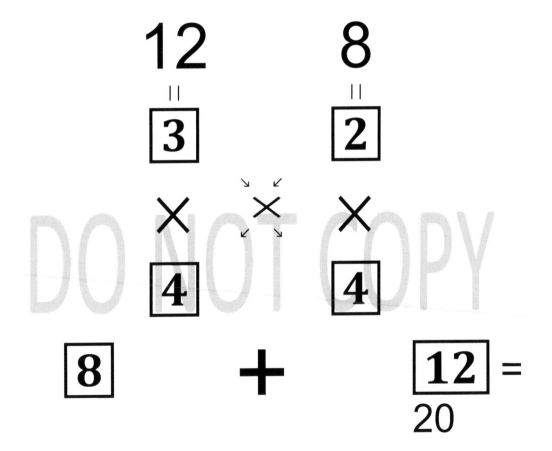

Student's name: ______________________________ Assignment date: __________________

Cross multiplication

9		4
||		||
3		4
×	×	×
3		1

12 + 3 = 15

Cross multiplication

$$16 \qquad\qquad 8$$

$$= \qquad\qquad\qquad =$$

$$\boxed{4} \qquad\qquad\qquad \boxed{4}$$

$$\times \qquad \times \qquad \times$$

$$\boxed{4} \qquad\qquad\qquad \boxed{2}$$

$$\boxed{16} \qquad + \qquad \boxed{8} = 24$$

DO NOT COPY

Student's name: _____ Assignment date: _____

Cross multiplication

$$16$$ $$12$$

$$=$$ $$=$$

$$\boxed{2}$$ $$\boxed{6}$$

$$\times \quad \times \quad \times$$

$$\boxed{8}$$ $$\boxed{2}$$

$$\boxed{48} \quad + \quad \boxed{4} = 52$$

Cross multiplication

24　　　　　12

||　　　　　||

6　　　　　6

×　　×　　×

4　　　　　2

24　　　　**+**　　　　12　=36

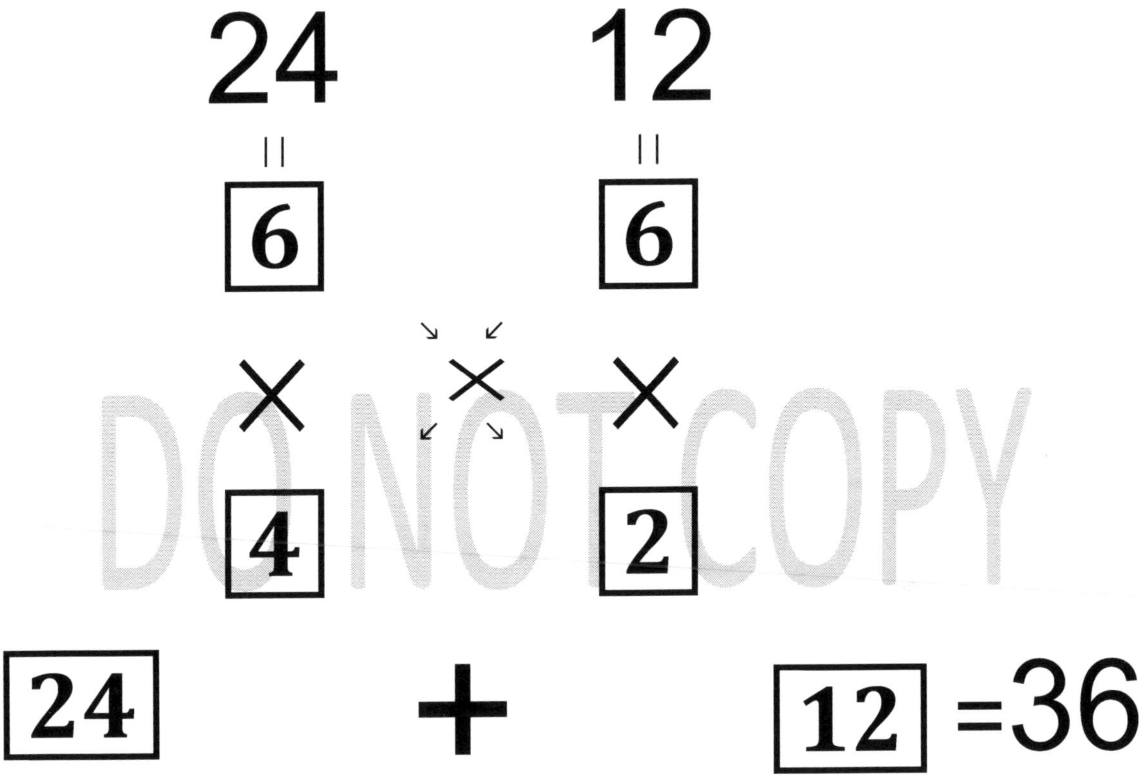

Cross multiplication

7 = 1   30 = 5

× × ×

7   6

+ 6 = 41

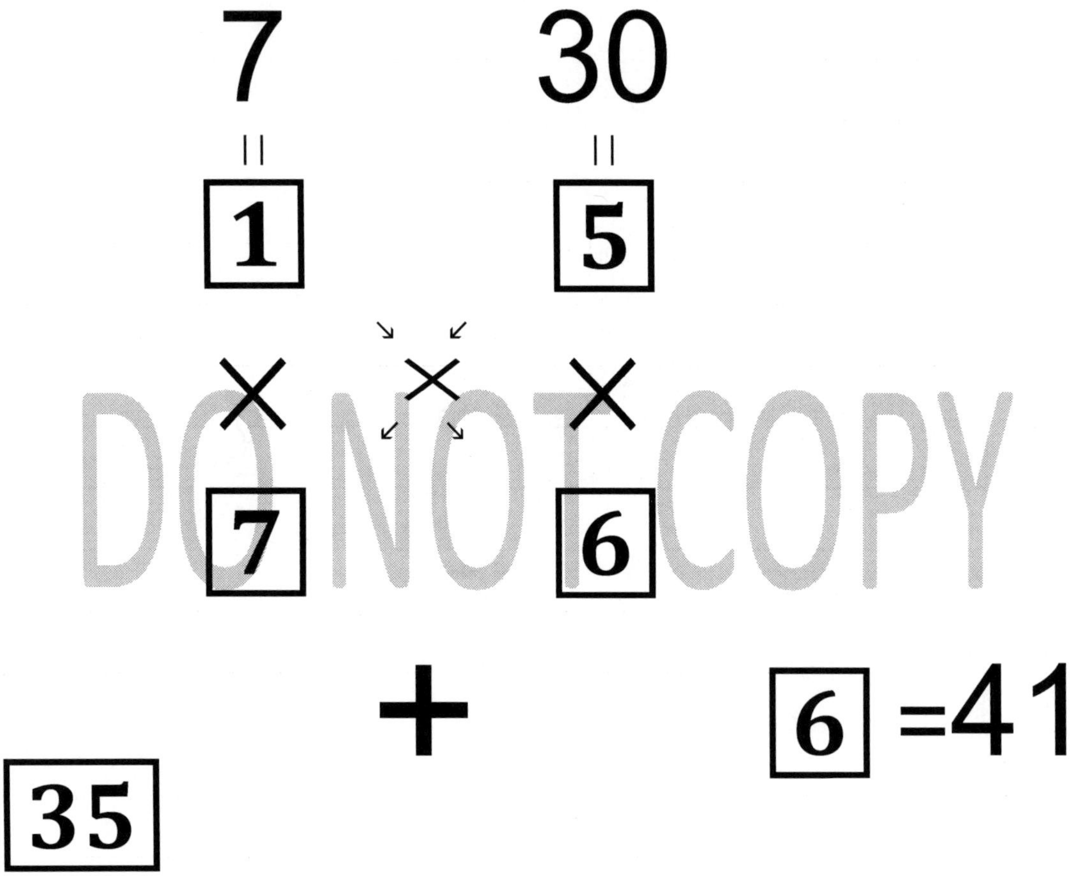

35

Cross multiplication

$$5 = \boxed{1}$$

$$6 = \boxed{2}$$

$$\times \quad \times \quad \times$$

$$\boxed{5} \qquad \boxed{3}$$

$$\boxed{10} \quad + \quad \boxed{3} = 13$$

Cross multiplication

$$11$$ $$24$$

$$=$$ $$=$$

$$\boxed{1}$$ $$\boxed{2}$$

$$\times$$ $$\times$$

$$\boxed{11}$$ $$\boxed{12}$$

$$\boxed{22}$$ $$+$$ $$\boxed{12}$$

$$=34$$

Cross multiplication

$$12 \qquad 6$$

$$\boxed{3} \qquad \boxed{3}$$

$$\times \qquad \times$$

$$\boxed{4} \qquad \boxed{2}$$

$$\boxed{12} \quad + \quad \boxed{6} = 18$$

Cross multiplication

$$18 \qquad\qquad 8$$
$$\| \qquad\qquad\qquad \|$$
$$\boxed{2} \qquad\qquad \boxed{4}$$
$$\times \qquad \times \qquad \times$$
$$\boxed{9} \qquad\qquad \boxed{2}$$
$$\boxed{36} \qquad + \qquad \boxed{8} = 40$$

Cross multiplication

$$6 \quad 7$$

$$\| \quad \|$$

$$\boxed{2} \quad \boxed{7}$$

$$\times \quad \times \times \quad \times$$

$$\boxed{3} \quad \boxed{1}$$

$$\boxed{21} \quad + \quad \boxed{2} = 23$$

Cross multiplication

$$28$$　　$$12$$

$$=$$　　$$=$$

$$\boxed{14}$$　　$$\boxed{6}$$

$$\times \qquad \times \qquad \times$$

$$\boxed{2}$$　　$$\boxed{2}$$

$$\boxed{12} \qquad + \qquad \boxed{28} = 40$$

Cross multiplication

$$8 = \boxed{1} \qquad 18 = \boxed{3}$$

$$\times \quad \times \quad \times$$

$$\boxed{8} \qquad \boxed{6}$$

$$\boxed{24} \quad + \quad \boxed{6} = 30$$

Student's name: _____ Assignment date: _____

Cross multiplication

$$5 \qquad\qquad 15$$

$$\| \qquad\qquad\qquad \|$$

$$\boxed{1} \qquad\qquad\qquad \boxed{5}$$

$$\times \qquad \times \qquad \times$$

$$\boxed{5} \qquad\qquad\qquad \boxed{3}$$

$$\boxed{25} \qquad + \qquad\qquad \boxed{3} = 28$$

Smallest and largest products 最小及最大乘积

Take any 2 numbers from the numbers: 1, 2, 3, 4, 5, 6, 7, 8, and 9 to come up with the sum of 10.

Sum	Difference	Product	Comment
9 + 1 = 10	9 − 1 = 8	9 × 1 = 9	
8 + 2 = 10	8 − 2 = 6	8 × 2 = 16	
7 + 3 = 10	7 − 3 = 4	7 × 3 = 21	
6 + 4 = 10	6 − 4 = 2	6 × 4 = 24	
5 + 5 = 10	5 − 5 = 0	5 × 5 = 25	When the parameter is fixed, the square gives the largest area.

Observe the above table, when the difference of 2 numbers is smaller, their product is

_____. *greater*

When the difference of the 2 numbers is larger, their product is
_____. *smaller*

The largest product is ____**25**____ and their difference is ____**0**____.

Smallest and largest products

Take 4 numbers out of 1, 2, 3, 4, 5, 6, 7, 8, and 9 such that the following product is the largest.

There could be 2 choices for answers and list them all as follows:

$$97 \times 86 = 8342 \qquad 96 \times 87 = 8352$$

The choices of answers are: _____ × _____ or _____ × _____.
Which one is correct?

Because 96 – 87 = _____**9** which is < 97 – 86 = _____**11**, so
the largest product is _____ × _____. **96 × 87 = 8352**

Take 4 numbers out of 1, 2, 3, 4, 5, 6, 7, 8, and 9 such that the following product is the smallest.

There could be 2 choices for answers and list them all as follows:

$$13 \times 24 = 312 \qquad 14 \times 23 = 322$$

The choices of answers are: _____ × _____ or _____ × _____.
Which one is correct?

Because 24 – 13 = _____**11** which is > 23 – 14 = _____**9**, so
the smallest product is _____ × _____. **13 × 24 = 312**

Student's name: _____ Assignment date: _____

Smallest and largest products

Take 6 numbers out of 1, 2, 3, 4, 5, 6, 7, 8, and 9 such that the following product is the largest.
There could be 6 choices and list them all as follows:

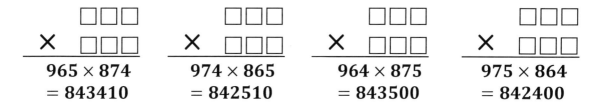

965×874 974×865 964×875 975×864
$= 843410$ $= 842510$ $= 843500$ $= 842400$

The choices for answer could be: $965 \times 874, 974 \times 865, 964 \times 875, 975 \times 864$.

Note that the sum of the above 2 numbers is all 1839.

The differences are:

$$
\begin{array}{cccc}
965 & 974 & 964 & 975 \\
-\,874 & -\,865 & -\,875 & -\,864 \\
\hline
91 & 109 & 89 & 111
\end{array}
$$

$964 - 875 = 89$ $964 \times 875 = 843500$

Since _____ has the least difference, so _____ × _____ is the largest.

Smallest and largest products

Take 6 numbers out of 1, 2, 3, 4, 5, 6, 7, 8, and 9 such that the following product is the smallest.

There could be 6 choices and list them all as follows:

$$235 \times 145 \qquad 245 \times 136 \qquad 235 \times 146 \qquad 246 \times 135$$
$$= 34075 \qquad = 33320 \qquad = 34310 \qquad = 33210$$

The choices for answer could be: 236×145, 245×136, 235×146, 246×135.

Note that the sum of the above 2 numbers is all 481.

The differences are:

236	245	235	246
− 145	− 136	− 146	− 135
91	**109**	**89**	**111**

$$246 - 135 = 111 \qquad\qquad 246 \times 135 = 33210$$

Since _____ has the largest difference, so _____ × _____ is the smallest.

Ho Math Chess   何数棋谜   英文奥数, 解题策略, 及 IQ 思唯训练宝典

Frank Ho, Amanda Ho © 2020   All rights reserved.

Student's name: _____ Assignment date: _____

Finding missing digits – multiplication 乘的数字迷

Fill in each □○ with a number.

$$○□ × 6 = 45□$$

76 × 6 = 456

Fill in each □△○ with a number.

$$□△ × 9 = 38○$$

43 × 9 = 387

Fill in each □ with a number.

$$72 × □ = □$$

72 × 0 = 0

Fill in each □△○ with a number.

$$□△ × ○ = 235$$

47 × 5 = 235

Fill in each □○△ with a number.

$$□○ × 9 = △68$$

52 × 4 = 268

Fill in each □△○ with a number.

$$□○ × ○ = △59$$

53 × 3 = 159

76, 6; 0, 0; 52, 4

Student's name: _____ Assignment date: _____

Finding missing digits - multiplication

Fill in each □ with a number.

$$\begin{array}{r} \square\triangle \\ \times\quad \bigcirc \\ \hline 1\ 4\ 2 \end{array}$$

71 × 2 = 142

Use the same number to fill in each of the following □.

$$\begin{array}{r} 4\square \\ \times\quad 5\square \\ \hline 2\square\square\square \end{array}$$

40 × 50 = 2000

Fill in each □ with a number.

$$\begin{array}{r} \square\triangle \\ \times\quad \bigcirc \\ \hline 3\ 6\ 9 \end{array}$$

41 × 9 = 369

Use one number to fill in each of the following □ ○ △.

$$\begin{array}{r} \square 6 \\ \times\quad \triangle \\ \hline \bigcirc\ \triangle\ \triangle \end{array}$$

36 × 4 = 144

Fill in each □ with a number.

$$\begin{array}{r} \square\triangle \\ \times\quad \bigcirc \\ \hline 2\ 4\ 6 \end{array}$$

82 × 3 = 246

Use one number to fill in each of the following □ ○ △.

$$\begin{array}{r} \square 7 \\ \times\quad \square \\ \hline \bigcirc\ \triangle\ \triangle \end{array}$$

47 × 4 = 188

71, 2; 41, 9; 82

Student's name: _____ Assignment date: _____

Finding missing digits - multiplication

Use one number to fill in each of the following □△○.

$$2\ 4$$
$$\times\ \ \ \ \triangle$$
$$\overline{}$$
$$\square\ \bigcirc\ \bigcirc$$

$$24 \times 6 = 144$$

Use one number to fill in each of the following □△○.

$$\bigcirc\ 7$$
$$\times\ \ \ \ \triangle$$
$$\overline{}$$
$$\square\ \square\ \square$$

$$37 \times 6 = 222$$

Use one number to fill in each of the following □○.

$$\square\ 7$$
$$\times\ \ \ \ \square$$
$$\overline{}$$
$$\bigcirc\ \bigcirc\ \bigcirc$$

$$37 \times 3 = 111$$

Use 1, 2, or 3 to fill in each of the following □○△.

$$\square\ \bigcirc\ \triangle\ 4$$
$$\times\ \ \ \ \ \ \ \ \ \square$$
$$\overline{}$$
$$\square\ \bigcirc\ \triangle\ 4$$

$$1234 \times 1 = 1234 \text{ or}$$
$$1234 \times 1 = 1324$$

Student's name: _____ Assignment date: _____

Finding missing digits – multiplication

Fill in each □△ with a number.

$$\begin{array}{r} \square\triangle \\ \times\ 1\ 1 \\ \hline \square\triangle \\ \square\triangle \\ \hline 1\ 6\ \triangle \end{array}$$

$15 \times 11 = 165$

Fill in each □△ with a number.

$$\begin{array}{r} \square\triangle \\ \times\ 1\ 1 \\ \hline \square\triangle \\ \square\triangle \\ \hline 8\ \square\ 5 \end{array}$$

$75 \times 11 = 825$

Fill in each □△○ with a number.

$$\begin{array}{r} \square\triangle \\ \times\ 1\ 1 \\ \hline \square\triangle \\ \square\triangle \\ \hline 2\ \bigcirc\ 7 \end{array}$$

$27 \times 11 = 297$

Fill in each □△ with a number.

$$\begin{array}{r} 1\ 1\ 1 \\ \times\ \ \triangle\ \square \\ \hline \square\ \square\ \square \\ \triangle\ \triangle\ \triangle \\ \hline \square\ 4\ 3\ \square \end{array}$$

$111 \times 67 = 7437$

15, 15, 15, 5; 27, 27, 27, 9 (17, 17, 17, 8) 75, 75, 75, 2, 67, 777, 666, 77 (49, 999, 444, 59)

Finding missing digits – multiplication

Use one number of 2, 3, 4 and 9 to fill in each of the following □.

A B
× C D
————

1 6 3 8

$39 \times 42 = 1638$

Finding missing numbers - multiplication

□ □ □
× 1 0 0 1
————

5 □ 6 □ 7 □

$576 \times 1001 = 576576$

Finding missing numbers - multiplication

□ □ □
× 1 0 1
————

3 1 □ □ 5

$315 \times 101 = 31815$

Finding missing numbers - multiplication

□ □ □ □
× 1 0 0 1
————

2 □ 4 □ 3 □ 5

$2345 \times 1001 = 2344355$

39, 42, 78, 156; 4, 4, 188

Ho Math Chess   何数棋谜   英文奥数, 解题策略, 及 IQ 思唯训练宝典
Frank Ho, Amanda Ho © 2020   All rights reserved.

Student's name: _____ Assignment date: _____

Finding missing digits - multiplication

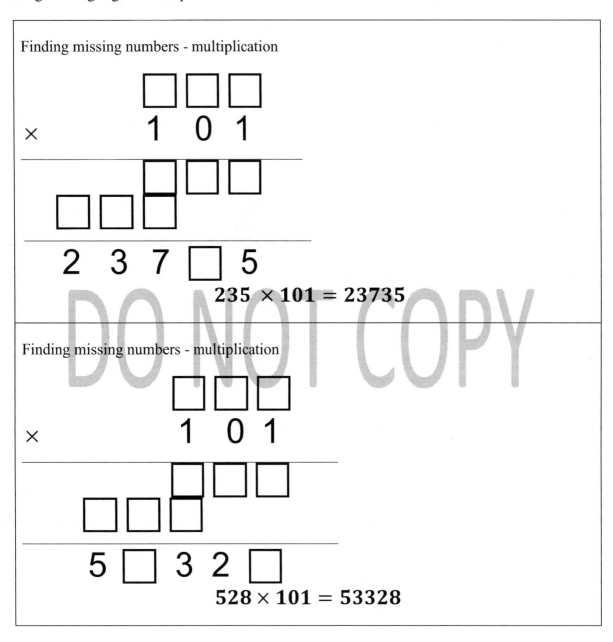

Finding missing numbers - multiplication

$$235 \times 101 = 23735$$

Finding missing numbers - multiplication

$$528 \times 101 = 53328$$

Ho Math Chess　　何数棋谜　　英文奥数, 解题策略, 及 IQ 思唯训练宝典

Frank Ho, Amanda Ho © 2020　　　　　　All rights reserved.

Student's name: _____　Assignment date: _____

$$\begin{array}{r} 3\ \square \\ \times\qquad 3 \\ \hline 1\ 1\ \square \end{array}$$

$37 \times 3 = 111$

$$\begin{array}{r} 4\ \square\ \square \\ \times\qquad 8 \\ \hline 3\ 8\ 5\ 6 \end{array}$$

$482 \times 8 = 3856$

$$\begin{array}{r} \square\ \square \\ \times\quad 7\ \square \\ \hline \square\ \square\ \square \\ \square\ \square \\ \hline \square\ \square\ 9\ \square \end{array}$$

$14 \times 78 = 1092$

$$\begin{array}{r} 3\ 7\ 5 \\ \times\quad \square\ \square \\ \hline 1\ \square\ 7\ \square \\ \square\ \square\ \square \\ \hline \square\ 6\ 8\ \square\ \square \end{array}$$

$375 \times 45 = 16875$

$394 \div 9 = 41R7$

$591 \div 7 = 84R3$

Division review 除法複習

Dividing by 0 除以 0

Example

How do you know you can calculate $0 \div 4$ but not $4 \div 0$?

Let $\frac{0}{4} = x$, x is a real number.

Then $0 = 4 \times x$

x must be 0 to make the above equation true.

Let $\frac{4}{0} = x$, x is a real number.

$4 = 0 \times x = 0$

The above statement is not true, so it proves the original statement "Let $\frac{4}{0} = x$, x is a real number".
is not definable.

Student's name: _____ Assignment date: _____

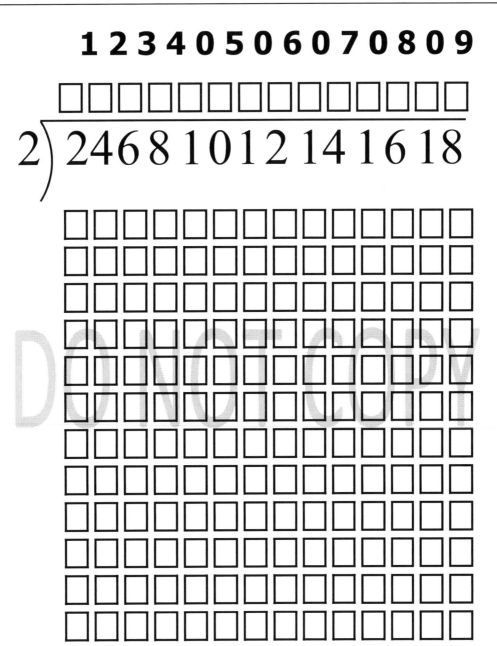

Student's name: _____ Assignment date: _____

Division

$$\begin{array}{r} 1\,2\,3\,0\,4\,0\,5\,0\,6\,0\,7\,0\,8\,0\,9 \\ 3\overline{)\,3\,6\,9\,1\,2\,1\,5\,1\,8\,2\,1\,2\,4\,2\,7} \end{array}$$

Division

$$12\,03\,04\,05\,06\,07\,08\,09$$
$$4\,\overline{)48121620242832 36}$$

Division

$$\begin{array}{r} 1\,0\,2\,0\,3\,0\,4\,0\,5\,0\,6\,0\,7\,0\,8\,0\,9 \\ 5\,\overline{)\,5\,1\,0\,1\,5\,2\,0\,2\,5\,3\,0\,3\,5\,4\,0\,4\,5} \end{array}$$

Division

$$\overline{6)\,6121824303642485 4}$$

with quotients: 10 20 30 40 50 60 70 80 9

Division

$$1\ 0\ 2\ 0\ 3\ 0\ 4\ 0\ 5\ 0\ 6\ 0\ 7\ 0\ 8\ 0\ 9$$
$$7\overline{)714212835424495663}$$

Division

$$\overset{\displaystyle 1\,0\,2\,0\,3\,0\,4\,0\,5\,0\,6\,0\,7\,0\,8\,0\,9}{8\,)\,\overline{8\,1\,6\,2\,4\,3\,2\,4\,0\,4\,8\,5\,6\,6\,4\,7\,2}}$$

Division

$$\begin{array}{r} 10\ 20\ 30\ 40\ 50\ 60\ 70\ 80\ 9 \\ 9{\overline{\smash{\big)}\,9182736455463728 1}} \end{array}$$

Finding missing digits – Division 除的数字迷

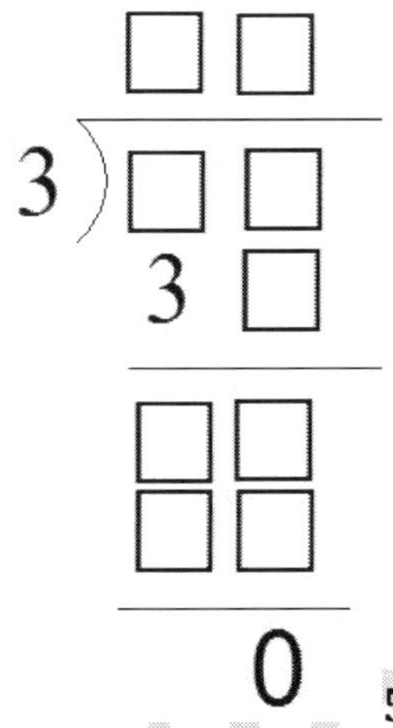

$57 \div 3 = 19$

$607 \div 9 = 67$

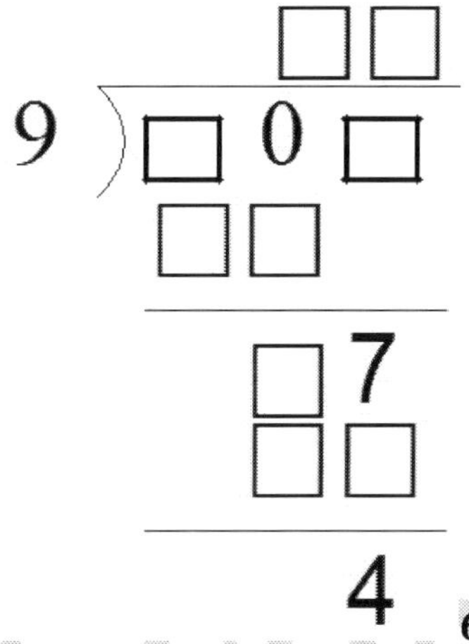

$69 \div 3 = 2$

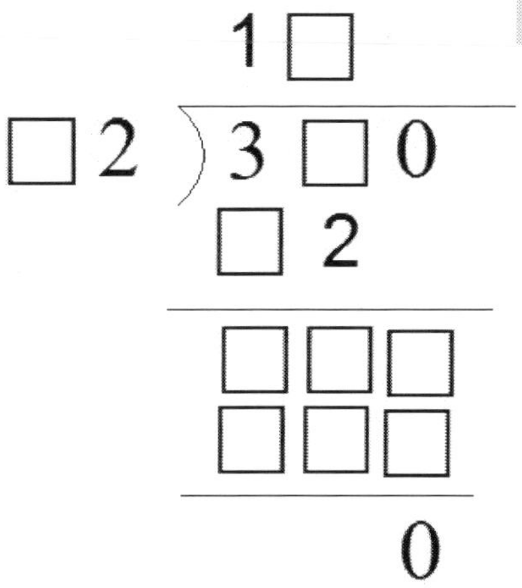

$330 \div 22 = 15$

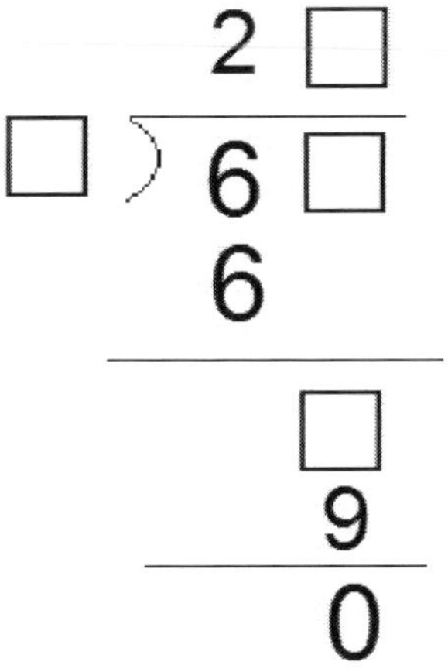

19, 57, 27, 2; 3, 9, 6, 9

Finding missing digits – Division

The different number can be used in each □.

$$352 \div 6 = 58R4$$

Use numbers 1, 2, 3, 4, and 8 such that the following is true.

$$5796 \div \square\square\square = \square\square$$
$$5796 \div 138 = 42$$

The different number can be used in each □.

$$5901 \div 7 = 843$$

The different number can be used in each □.

$$462 \div 2 = 231$$

Student's name: _____ Assignment date: _____

Using operators to make math sentences 用+, −, ×, ÷ 或 小括号造数学等式

Using +, −, ×, $\div$ or ( ) to make mathematical sentences. The following explanation (credit to Henry Leung) is mainly for the instructor's use.

A general formula is listed below for a and a can be 1, 2, 3, 4, 5, 6, 7, 8, and 9.

$a + a - a - a = 0$
$(a + a) \div (a + a) = 1$
$(a \div a) + (a \div a) = 2$
$(a + a + a) \div a = 3$
$a - (a + a) \div = a - 2$
$(a \times a - a) \div a = a - 1$
$(a - a) \times a + a = 2a$
$(a \times a + a) \div a = a + 1$
$a + (a + a) \div a = a + 2$
$(a + a) - (a \div a) = 2a - 1$
$(a + a) \times a \div a = 2a$
$(a + a) + (a \div a) = 2a + 1$
$a \times a - a - a = a^2 - 2a$
$a \times (a - a \div a) = a^2 - a$
$a \times (a + a - a) = a^2$
$a \times (a + a \div a) = a^2 + a$
$a \times a + a + a = a^2 + 2a$
$a \times a + a \times a = 2a^2$
$(a + a) \times (a + a) = 4a^2$
$a \times a - a \div = a^2 - 1$
$a \times a + a \div a = a^2 + 1$
$a \times a \div (a + a) = \dfrac{a}{2}$

Student's name: _____ Assignment date: _____

Note that the above 5, 6, 7, 8, 9 are consecutive integers, 10, 11, 12 are consecutive integers. 20, 15, 21 are consecutive integers. Only 3 or 4 can have answers from 0 to 9.

The reason is to obtain the longest consecutive numbers, we may assume equation 9 + 1 = equation 10 such that $a + 2 + 1 = 2a - 1 \Rightarrow a = 4$. For the same reason we assume equation 12 + 1 = equation 20 $\Rightarrow a = 3$.

Equations	Value obtained ($a = 2$)	Equations	Value obtained ($a = 3$)
1	0	1	0
2	1	2	1
3	2	3	2
4	3	4	3
9	4	8	4
12	5	9	5
16	6	11	6
17	8	12	7
		20	8
		15	9

Equations	Value obtained ($a = 4$)	Equations	Value obtained ($a = 5$)
1	0	1	0
2	1	2	1
3	2	3	2
4	3	4	3
7	4	6	4
8	5	7	5
9	6	8	6
10	7	9	7
11	8	10	9
12	9		

Equation	Value obtained $a = 6$	Equation	Value obtained $a = 7$	Equation	Value obtained $a = 8$	Equation	Value obtained $a = 9$
1	0	1	0	1	0	1	0
2	1	2	1	2	1	2	1
3	2	3	2	3	2	3	2
4	3	4	3	4	3	4	3
5	4	5	5	22	4		
6	5	6	6	5	6		
7	6	7	7	6	7		
8	7	8	8	7	8		
9	8	9	9	8	9		

Student's name: _____ Assignment date: _____

Using operators to create an equation 造算式

Use $+, -, \times, \div$ or ( ) to make the following mathematical sentences equal.

$2\ 2\ 2\ 2\ =\ 0$ $2+2-2-2$	$3\ 3\ 3\ 3\ =\ 0$ $3+3-3-3$	$4\ 4\ 4\ 4\ =\ 0$ $4+4-4-4$	$5\ 5\ 5\ 5\ =\ 0$ $5+5-5-5$
$2\ 2\ 2\ 2\ =\ 1$ $2\div2\times2\div2$	$3\ 3\ 3\ 3\ =\ 1$ $3\times3\div3\div3$	$4\ 4\ 4\ 4\ =\ 1$ $4\times4\div4\div4$	$5\ 5\ 5\ 5\ =\ 1$ $5\times5\div5\div5$
$2\ 2\ 2\ 2\ =\ 2$ $(2+2+2)\div2$	$3\ 3\ 3\ 3\ =\ 2$ $3\div3+3\div3$	$4\ 4\ 4\ 4\ =\ 2$ $4\div4+4\div4$	$5\ 5\ 5\ 5\ =\ 2$ $5\div5+5\div5$
$2\ 2\ 2\ 2\ =\ 3$ $2\div2\times2+2$	$3\ 3\ 3\ 3\ =\ 3$ $3\times3-3-3$	$4\ 4\ 4\ 4\ =\ 3$ $(4+4+4)\div4$	$5\ 5\ 5\ 5\ =\ 3$ $(5+5+5)\div5$
$2\ 2\ 2\ 2\ =\ 4$ $2\div2\times2\times2$	$3\ 3\ 3\ 3\ =\ 4$ $(3\times3+3)\div3$	$4\ 4\ 4\ 4\ =\ 4$ $(4-4)\div4+4$	$5\ 5\ 5\ 5\ =\ 4$ $(5\times5-5)\div5$
$2\ 2\ 2\ 2\ =\ 5$ $2\div2+2\times2$	$3\ 3\ 3\ 3\ =\ 5$ $3+3-3\div3$	$4\ 4\ 4\ 4\ =\ 5$ $(4\times4+4)\div4$	$5\ 5\ 5\ 5\ =\ 5$ $(5-5)\div5+5$
$2\ 2\ 2\ 2\ =\ 6$ $2\times2\times2-2$	$3\ 3\ 3\ 3\ =\ 6$ $3+3+3-3$	$4\ 4\ 4\ 4\ =\ 6$ $(4+4)\div4+4$	$5\ 5\ 5\ 5\ =\ 6$ $(5\times5+5)\div6$
$2\ 2\ 2\ 2\ =\ 7$ n/a	$3\ 3\ 3\ 3\ =\ 7$ $3+3+3\div3$	$4\ 4\ 4\ 4\ =\ 7$ $4+4-4\div4$	$5\ 5\ 5\ 5\ =\ 7$ $(5+5)\div5+5$
$2\ 2\ 2\ 2\ =\ 8$ $2\times2+2\times2$	$3\ 3\ 3\ 3\ =\ 8$ $3\times3+3-3$	$4\ 4\ 4\ 4\ =\ 8$ $4\times4\div4+4$	$5\ 5\ 5\ 5\ =\ 9$ $5+5-5\div5$
	$3\ 3\ 3\ 3\ =\ 9$ $3\times3+3-3$	$4\ 4\ 4\ 4\ =\ 9$ $4+4+4\div4$	

Student's name: _____ Assignment date: _____

Use +, −, ×, ÷ or ( ) to make the following mathematical sentences equal.

$6\ 6\ 6\ 6 = 0$ $6+6-6-6$	$7\ 7\ 7\ 7 = 0$ $7+7-7-7$	$8\ 8\ 8\ 8 = 0$ $8+8-8-8$	$9\ 9\ 9\ 9 = 0$ $9+9-9-9$
$6\ 6\ 6\ 6 = 1$ $6\times6\div6\div6$	$7\ 7\ 7\ 7 = 1$ $7\times7\div7\div7$	$8\ 8\ 8\ 8 = 1$ $8\times8\div8\div8$	$9\ 9\ 9\ 9 = 1$ $9\times9\div9\div9$
$6\ 6\ 6\ 6 = 2$ $6\div6+6\div6$	$7\ 7\ 7\ 7 = 2$ $7\div7+7\div7$	$8\ 8\ 8\ 8 = 2$ $8\div8+8\div8$	$9\ 9\ 9\ 9 = 2$ $9\div9+9\div9$
$6\ 6\ 6\ 6 = 3$ $(6+6+6)\div6$	$7\ 7\ 7\ 7 = 3$ $(7+7+7)\div7$	$8\ 8\ 8\ 8 = 3$ $(8+8+8)\div8$	$9\ 9\ 9\ 9 = 3$ $(9+9+9)\div9$
$6\ 6\ 6\ 6 = 4$ $6-(6+6)\div6$	$7\ 7\ 7\ 7 = 5$ $7-(7+7)\div7$	$8\ 8\ 8\ 8 = 4$ $8-(8+8)\div8$	$9\ 9\ 9\ 9 = 7$ $9-(9+9)\div7$
$6\ 6\ 6\ 6 = 5$ $(6\times6-6)\div6$	$7\ 7\ 7\ 7 = 6$ $(7\times7-7)\div7$	$8\ 8\ 8\ 8 = 6$ $8-(8+8)\div8$	$9\ 9\ 9\ 9 = 8$ $(9\times9-9)\div9$
$6\ 6\ 6\ 6 = 6$ $(6-6)\div6+6$	$7\ 7\ 7\ 7 = 7$ $(7-7)\div7+7$	$8\ 8\ 8\ 8 = 7$ $(8\times8-8)\div8$	$9\ 9\ 9\ 9 = 9$ $(9-9)\div9+9$
$6\ 6\ 6\ 6 = 7$ $(6\times6+6)\div6$	$7\ 7\ 7\ 7 = 8$ $(7\times7+7)\div7$	$8\ 8\ 8\ 8 = 8$ $(8-8)\div8+8$	
$6\ 6\ 6\ 6 = 8$ $6+(6+6)\div6$	$7\ 7\ 7\ 7 = 9$ $7+(7+7)\div7$	$8\ 8\ 8\ 8 = 9$ $(8\times8+8)\div9$	

Use seven 1's and +, −, ×, ÷ or ( ) to make the result to be 100.

$$111 - 11 + 1 - 1 = 100$$

Use seven 2's and +, −, ×, ÷ or ( ) to make the result to be 100.

$$222 \div 2 - 22 \div 2 = 100$$

Use seven 3's and +, −, ×, ÷ or ( ) to make the result to be 100.

$$333 \div 3 - 33 \div 3 = 100$$

Use seven 4's and +, −, ×, ÷ or ( ) to make the result to be 100.

$$444 \div 4 - 44 \div 4 = 100$$

Use seven 5's and +, −, ×, ÷ or ( ) to make the result to be 100.

$$555 \div 5 - 55 \div 5 = 100$$

Use seven 6's and +, −, ×, ÷ or ( ) to make the result to be 100.

$$666 \div 6 - 66 \div 6 = 100$$

Use seven 7's and +, −, ×, ÷ or ( ) to make the result to be 100.

$$777 \div 7 - 77 \div 7 = 100$$

Use seven 8's and +, −, ×, ÷ or ( ) to make the result to be 100.

$$888 \div 8 - 88 \div 8 = 100$$

Use seven 9's and +, −, ×, ÷ or ( ) to make the result to be 100.

$$999 \div 9 - 99 \div 9 = 100$$

Use 1, 2, 3, 4, 5 or +, −, ×, ÷ or ( ) to make the result to be 1.

$$1 \times 2 \times 4 \div (3 + 5) = 1$$

Use 1, 2, 3, 4, 5 or +, −, ×, ÷ or ( ) to make the result to be 2.

$$(4 + 5) \div 3 - 2 + 1 = 2$$

Use 1, 2, 3, 4, 5 or +, −, ×, ÷ or ( ) to make the result to be 3.

$$(4 + 5) \div 3 \times (2 - 1) = 3$$

Use 1, 2, 3, 4, 5 or +, −, ×, ÷ or ( ) to make the result to be 4.

$$(4 + 5) \div 3 + 2 - 1 = 4$$

Use 1, 2, 3, 4, 5 or +, −, ×, ÷ or ( ) to make the result to be 5.

$$(4 + 5) \div 3 - 2 \times 1 = 5$$

Use 1, 2, 3, 4, 5 or +, −, ×, ÷ or ( ) to make the result to be 6.

$$(4 + 5) \div 3 + 2 + 1 = 6$$

Use 1, 2, 3, 4, 5 or +, −, ×, ÷ or ( ) to make the result to be 7.

$$(4 + 5) \div 3 \times 2 + 1 = 7$$

Use 1, 2, 3, 4, 5 or +, −, ×, ÷ or ( ) to make the result to be 8.

$$(4 + 5) - 3 + 2 \times 1 = 8$$

Use 1, 2, 3, 4, 5 or +, −, ×, ÷ or ( ) to make the result to be 9.

$$(4 + 5) - 3 + 2 + 1 = 9$$

Use 1, 2, 3, 4, 5 or +, −, ×, ÷ or ( ) to make the result to be 10.

$$(4 + 5) + 3 - 2 \times 1 = 10$$

Roman Numerals 罗馬数符

1. A symbol is not repeated more than four times.
2. I is subtracted only from V and X.
3. X is subtracted only from L and C.
4. C is subtracted only from D and M.
5. V, L, and D are not subtracted at all.

Standard number	Roman Numeral	Comments
1	I	
2	II	
3	III	
4	IV	The small number on the left means subtraction.
5	V	
6	VI	
7	VII	
8	VIII	
9	VIIII	
10	X	
19	**XIX**	
21	**XXI**	
40	XL	
41	**XLI**	
45	**XLV**	
50	L	
60	LX	
70	LXX	
66	**LXV**	
80	LXXX	
100	C	
400	**CD**	
500	D	
1000	M	

XIX, XXI, XLI, XLV, LXVI,CD

Decimals 小数

Decimal multiplications 小数乘法

$87 \times 123 =$

10701

$8.7 \times 0.123 =$

10701

$8.7 \times 1.23 =$

10.701

$0.87 \times 0.0123 =$

0.010701

Student's name: _____ Assignment date: _____

Decimal divisions 小数除法

Evaluate the following divisions up to 2- decimal places.
$421 \div 70$ 6.01
$492 \div 70$ 7.029
$15400 \div 0.3$ 51333.33
$212.44 \div 0.040$ 5311
$181.404 \div 20$ 9.0702
$402005 \div 0.05$ 8040100

Find the quotient when 800.32 is divided by 8. _____   100.04
Express $1\frac{2}{5}$ as a decimal.   1.4
Express $1\frac{1}{2}$ as a decimal.   1.5
Express 8.75 as an improper fraction in its lowest term. $\frac{35}{4}$

List the following nine decimals in descending order of their values: 1.1, 1.01, 1.11, 1.10, 1.0, 1.001, 1.111, 1.010, 1.101 1.111, 1.11, 1.101, 1.1 = 1,10, 1.01,-1.010, 1.001, 1.0
The tens place value of 96.15 + the tenth place value of 46.89 = _____ 90 + 0.8 = 90.8
The hundreds place value after 5152.56 is rounded at the hundreds place is _____. 2

Student's name: _____ Assignment date: _____

Mixed decimal data type calculations 混合小数型的计算

1.9090 − one and 9 hundredths =

$$0.819$$

2.09 − 1.9 =

$$0.19$$

$2.64 − 99 ¢ =

$$\$1.65 = 3.64 = 0.99$$

$7.2 − $1.68 − 300 ¢ =

$$\$2.52$$

$\frac{1}{2} + 4.6 − 0.75 =$

$$4.35$$

Student's name: _____ Assignment date: _____

Decimal word problems 小数文字题

$350¢ + \frac{1}{2}¢ = \$$ _____

$3.505

Two and twenty hundredths + one hundred and nine-tenths

$103.1

Frank is building a rectangularly shaped fence around his garden with a perimeter of 14 meters. He uses 1-metre fence sections. What could be the sizes of his garden?

1 by 6 or 2 by 5 or 3 by 4

The coach wants to buy one pair of shorts and one tee shirt for each of his 47-member track team, and he wants the least amount of clothing leftover. If shorts are sold as 3 pairs in a package and the tee shirt is sold as 5 in a package. How many packages of each item does he buy?

16 packages of shorts and 10 packages of tee shirts

How many can complete uniforms (one pair of shorts and one tee shirt as a complete uniform) be made from the leftover clothing?

1

What two 4-digit numbers added together is 4589?

ABCC + AACD = 4589
2344+2245=4589

Decimal word problems and calculations 小数文字应用题

Jonathan bought the following items at the Nature Store:

- Chip $0.85
- Milk $1.25
- Chocolate bar $0.90
- Gum $0.70
- Candy $0.55
- Peanuts $0.65

Jonathan paid $10. Show all the ways he could get his changes if he received as fewer coins or bills as possible, and his changes could include 1 cent, 5 cents, 10 cents, 25 cents, 50 cents and $1, or $5.

One $5 bill and one 10¢
$10 – $4.9 = $5.10

　　　　　　　　0.99
$40.1 \div 5$ is _____ less than 9.01.

　　　　　　0.32
$19.05 \div 5$ is _____ less than 4.13,

$4.13 - 3,81 = 0.32$

Decimal 小数文字应用题

Athens ordered three different items and paid $4.25. What are the three items he ordered?

Menu

Meals		Drinks	
Hot Dog	$1.50	Small milk	$1.00
Pizza	$2.50	Large milk	$1.25
Hamburg	$2.25	Orange juice	$0.50

7 ways.
Large milk+ 2 dogs, P+LM+J, H + D+J, LM+ D+J, 3 LM+J, 3 SM+ 1 LM, 2 SM+H

If she bought a hot dog and one small milk and paid three dollars, show all the ways she could get her to change if she received no pennies.

10 WAYS

5 ¢	10	8	6	4	2	0	5	0	3	1
10 ¢	0	1	2	3	4	5	0	0	1	2
25 ¢	0	0	0	0	0	0	1	2	1	1
TOTAL	50	50	50	50	50	50	50	50	50	50

Carmen has $3.00, and she wants to buy two different items from the menu. Find all the combinations of food she can buy and how much she would spend?
8 WAYS

Hot Dog + Small Milk	$2.50	**Hamburg + Orange Juice**	$2.75
Hot Dog + Large Milk	$2.75	**Small Milk + Large Milk**	$2.25
Hot Dog + Orange Juice	$2.00	**Small Milk + Orange Juice**	$1.50
Pizza + Orange Juice	$3.00	**Large Milk + Orange Juice**	$1.75

Decimal word problems 小数文字题

Nicholas bought 2 game tickets, 3 drink tickets, and 15 food tickets. He paid two $5 bills. How much change should he have received?

Fun Fair

Game $0.25/per ticket

Drink $0.50/per ticket

Food $0.25/per ticket

$4.25

Nicholas' family went to the Fun Fair. This family included 9-year old Nicholas, a 4-year-girl, a 13-year-girl, his father, and his grandmother. How much did it cost the family to get into the Fun Fair?

Fun Fair

18+ years $5.50
12+ to 18 years $3.50
5+ to 12 years $2.75
Under 5 years   Free

$17.25

Mixed decimal problems 小数混合题

$1 + 20 ¢ = _____ ¢	120

List the following nine decimals in descending order of their values:

65455, 64565, 64655, 65554, 56554

65554, 65455, 64655, 64565, 56554

The one place value of 96.15 + the tenth place value of 46.89 = _____

6 + 9 = 15

The hundredths place value after 5152.67956 is rounded at the hundredths place is _____.

8

$100.29 − $89.092 = _____	11.198
$11.89 + $201.798 = _____	213.688
1234.56 × 1000 ÷ 0.01 =	123456000
1234.56 × 10000 ÷ 0.001 =	12345600000
0.1234 × 10000 ÷ 0.001 =	1234000
12.3456 × 10000 ÷ 0.001 =	123456000
123.456 × 0.0001 ÷ 0.001 =	12.3456

Student's name: _____ Assignment date: _____

Fractions 分数
Pie chart and fractions 圆形图及分数

Shaded pies	fractions
answer	$\frac{9}{4}$
answer	$\frac{14}{4}$

Shaded pies	fractions
	?$2\frac{3}{4}$
	?$2\frac{5}{8}$
	$3\frac{5}{6}$
	? $\frac{2}{8}$answer
	? $\frac{3}{8}$answer
	? $\frac{2}{6}$answer
	? $\frac{3}{8}$answer

Shaded figures and fractions 阴影图及分数

fractions	Shaded figure
$\dfrac{3}{4}$	
$\dfrac{5}{8}$	
$\dfrac{3}{4}$	
$\dfrac{2}{3}$	
$\dfrac{2}{6}$	
$\dfrac{5}{12}$	

Student's name: _____ Assignment date: _____

Fraction drawings 画分数图

Draw and shade a rectangle to show $\frac{4}{6}$.

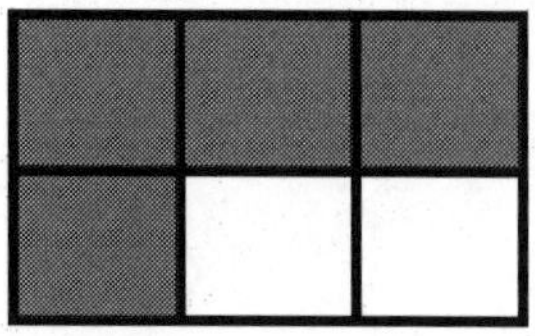

Draw and shade a square to show $\frac{5}{9}$.

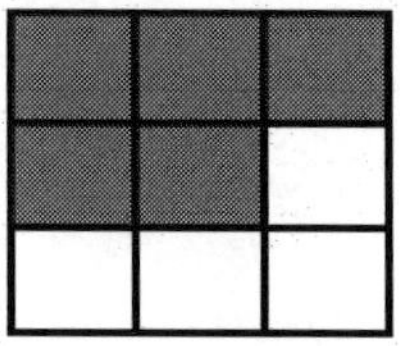

Compare which one is larger Draw and shade a rectangle to show $\frac{7}{8}$ or $\frac{5}{6}$?

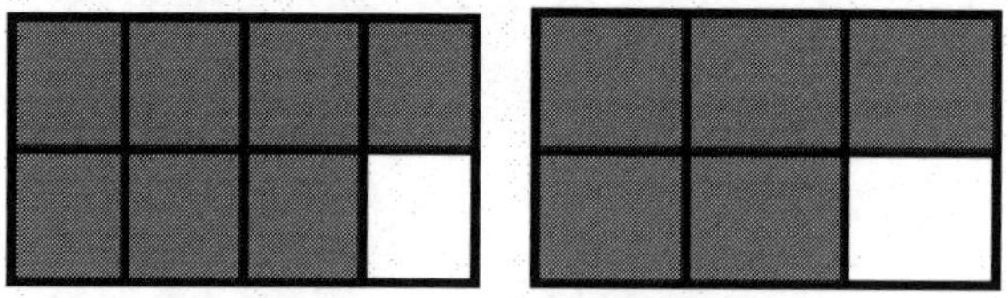

Which one of the following is larger? Circle the larger one.

the same

Daniel ate 12 crackers out of 36 crackers. What fraction did he eat?

$\frac{12}{36} = \frac{1}{3}$ **answer**

Fractions represented by figures 以图形代表分数

How many white squares in the following diagram need to be shaded so that the number of shaded squares equals to $\frac{4}{5}$ of the total?

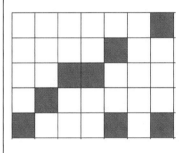

$\frac{4}{5} = \frac{28}{35}, 28 - 8 = \mathbf{20}$

How many white squares in the following diagram need to be shaded so that the number of shaded squares equals to $\frac{4}{7}$ of the number remaining white squares?

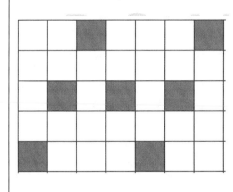

$\frac{4}{7} = \frac{20}{35}, 20 - 7 = 13$

How many white squares in the following diagram need to be shaded so that the number of shaded squares equals to $\frac{6}{7}$ of the total?

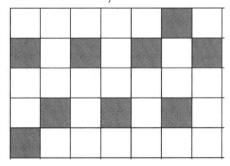

$\frac{6}{7} = \frac{30}{35}, 30 - 9 = \mathbf{21}$

Student's name: _____ Assignment date: _____

Equivalent fractions 等值分数

 Amanda has 12 thin rice crackers; how many are $\frac{2}{3}$ of them?

8

Find the number from the length A to B?

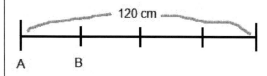

A   B

30

Circle the two equivalent fractions.

$\frac{7}{8} = \frac{14}{15}$

$\frac{7}{9} = \frac{14}{18}$

$\frac{7}{8} = \frac{14}{15}$

$\frac{14}{26} = \frac{7}{13}$

$\frac{24}{36} = \frac{7}{13}$

$\frac{24}{36} = \frac{12}{12}$

$\frac{3}{8} = \frac{3}{4}$

From the top, the second and the fourth one

Student's name: _____   Assignment date: _____

Order fractions from least to greatest 分数小到大的排列

$\frac{7}{8}$, $\frac{14}{8}$, $\frac{3}{8}$ $\frac{3}{8}, \frac{7}{8}, \frac{14}{8}$ **answer**
$4\frac{3}{7}$, $2\frac{6}{7}$, $4\frac{4}{7}$ $2\frac{6}{7}, 4\frac{3}{7}, 4\frac{4}{7}$ **answer**
$4\frac{3}{7}$, $4\frac{6}{8}$, $4\frac{4}{5}$ $4\frac{3}{7}, 4\frac{6}{8}, 4\frac{4}{5}$ **answer**
0.9, $\frac{4}{10}$, $\frac{3}{5}$ $\frac{4}{10}, \frac{3}{5}, 0.9$ **answer**
$19.9, 19.09, 19.90$ $19.09, 19.9 = 19.90$ **answer**
$4.31, 3.14, 3.41$ $3.14, 3.41, 4.31$ **answer**

Student's name: _____ Assignment date: _____

Fraction 3-model problems 三个分数模式的计算

What is $\frac{3}{4}$ of 120?

90

What is $\frac{2}{3}$ of 99?

66

Is $1\frac{3}{4}$ closer to 2 or 1?

2

Converting figures to fractions 由图转分数

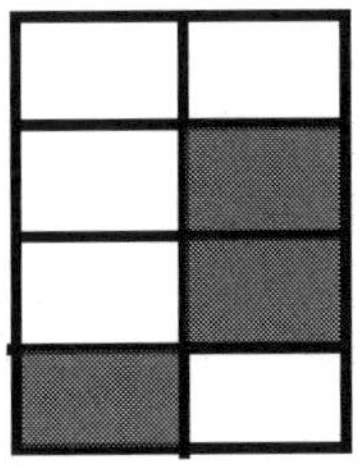

$\dfrac{3}{8}$

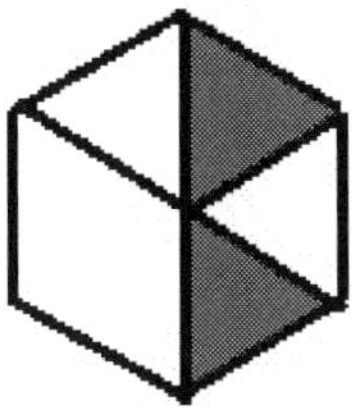

$\dfrac{2}{6}$

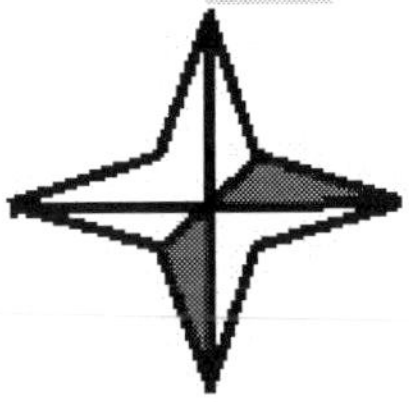

$\dfrac{2}{8}$

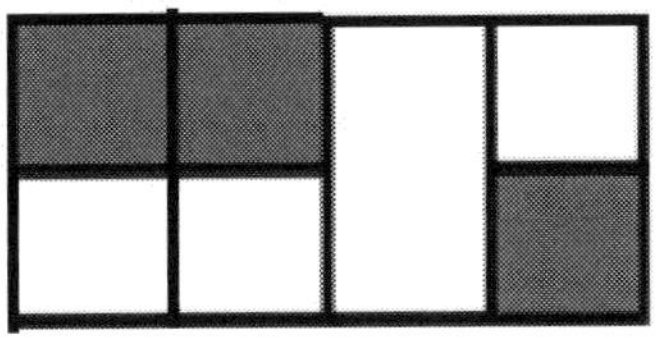

$\dfrac{3}{8}$

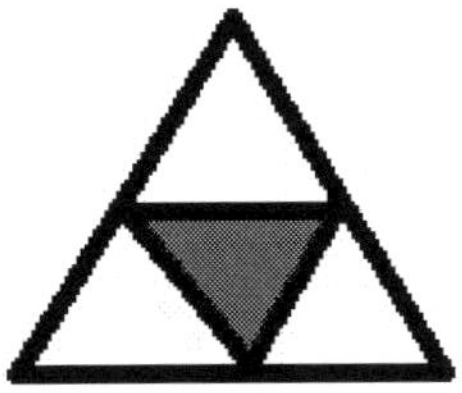

$\dfrac{1}{4}$

Student's name: _____ Assignment date: _____

Converting figures to fractions 由分数转图

Use the figure(s) to chart the following fractions.	Figures
$\dfrac{3}{2}$	or
$\dfrac{1}{6}$	
$\dfrac{1}{2} + \dfrac{1}{4}$	
$\dfrac{1}{9} + \dfrac{1}{3}$	
$\dfrac{2}{9}$	
$\dfrac{1}{3} + \dfrac{2}{3}$	
$1\dfrac{1}{5}$	

Fractions represented by figures 以图形代表分数

What is a fraction of the shaded circles?

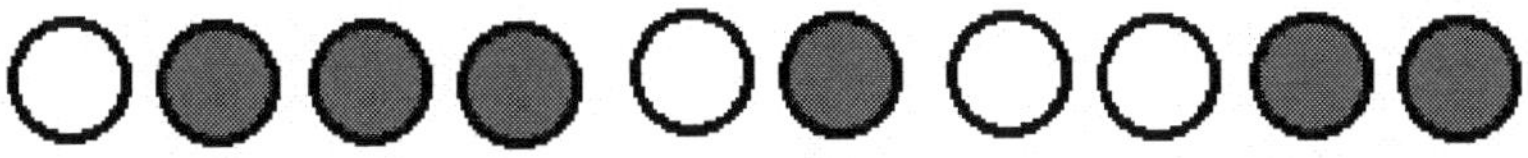

(A) 0.06
(B) 6.00
(C) 0.04
(D) 0.6 　　　　　　　**D**

What fraction of the circles is not shaded?

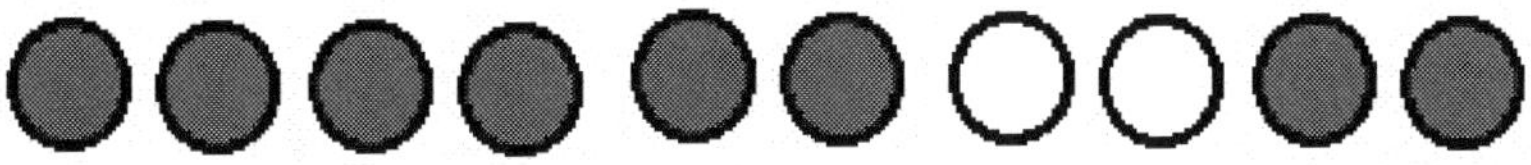

(A) $\frac{1}{4}$
(B) $\frac{3}{4}$
(C) $\frac{2}{10}$
(D) $\frac{2}{4}$ 　　　　　**C**

What fraction of the letters in the word **Columbia** are consonants?
1/2

What fraction of the letters in the word **Columbia** are vowels?
½

What number is as much greater than 37 as it is less than 95?
　66

The midpoint = (37+95)/2=66.　　95 - 66 = 29　66 – 37 = 29

Student's name: _____ Assignment date: _____

Picking the largest fraction 选最大的分数值

Jeff should have added \$3 to his original amount; instead, he subtracted \$3 and got an incorrect amount. What is the difference between the correct amount and the incorrect amount? **6**
Circle the largest fraction. $$\frac{1}{2}, \frac{1}{3}, \frac{1}{4} \quad \mathbf{\frac{1}{2}}$$
Circle the largest fraction. $$\frac{100}{12}, \frac{100}{23}, \frac{100}{34} \quad \mathbf{\frac{100}{12}}$$
Circle the largest fraction. $$\frac{120}{32}, \frac{130}{23}, \frac{140}{14} \quad \mathbf{\frac{140}{14}}$$
Circle the largest fraction. $$\frac{12}{5}, \frac{13}{5}, \frac{14}{5} \quad \mathbf{\frac{14}{5}}$$
Circle the largest fraction. $$\frac{112}{11}, \frac{113}{11}, \frac{114}{11} \quad \mathbf{\frac{114}{11}}$$
Circle the largest fraction. $$\frac{112}{14}, \frac{113}{13}, \frac{114}{12} \quad\quad \mathbf{\frac{114}{12}}$$
Out of a group of 5 children, $\frac{4}{5}$ are boys. $\frac{2}{5}$ of the group have brown eyes, $\frac{1}{5}$ have black eyes, and $\frac{1}{5}$ have blue eyes. (1) Could the girl child have brown eyes? **yes** (2) Could the girl child have black eyes? **yes** (3) Could the girl child have blue eyes? **yes** (4) Could the girl child have green eyes? **Yes, since one person does not know the eye colour. All 4 persons could be boys.**

Student's name: _____ Assignment date: _____

Splitting unit circle into equal pieces 分数單位园的等分

Split each slice into 3 new equal pieces by drawing 2 diagrams (before and after) to show that $\dfrac{2}{3} = \dfrac{?}{9}$. Replace each ? with a number.   6

 =

Split each slice into 3 new equal pieces by drawing 2 diagrams (before and after) to show that $\dfrac{1}{2} = \dfrac{?}{4}$. Replace each ? with a number.

 =   answer

Split each slice into 3 new equal pieces by drawing 2 diagrams (before and after) to show that $1\dfrac{1}{4} = 1\dfrac{?}{8}$. Replace each ? with a number.   2

 =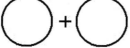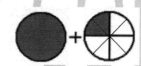

Connect those fractions that show the same amount. Write the value of each fraction besides its diagram.

 $\dfrac{1}{2}$  $\dfrac{2}{3}$

 $\dfrac{6}{9}$ $\dfrac{2}{4}$

Show how to split each of $\dfrac{3}{8}$ into three equal pieces and write its equivalent fraction.

answer

Fraction calculation for advanced students 学霸分数计算

Regrouping

Evaluate $\frac{1}{2} + \frac{1}{3} - \frac{1}{4} + \frac{1}{5} - \frac{1}{6} + \frac{1}{12}$

$= \frac{1}{3} - \frac{1}{4} + \frac{1}{12} - \frac{1}{6} + \frac{1}{2} + \frac{1}{5} - \frac{1}{6}$

$= \frac{1}{12} + \frac{1}{12} - \frac{1}{6} + \frac{1}{2} + \frac{1}{5}$

$= \frac{1}{2} + \frac{1}{5}$

$= \frac{7}{10}$

Factoring out the common factor

Evaluate $1\frac{13}{17} \times \left(3\frac{2}{5} - 1\frac{1}{3}\right) + 1\frac{21}{15} \div \frac{17}{30}$

$= \frac{30}{17} \times 2\frac{1}{15} + \frac{36}{15} \times \frac{30}{17}$

$= \frac{30}{17}\left(\frac{31}{15} + \frac{36}{15}\right)$

$= \frac{30}{17} \times \frac{67}{15}$

$= \frac{134}{17}$

$= 7\frac{15}{17}$

Keeping in fractional numbers

$9 \times 32 \div 7 \div 13 \times 7 \times 11 \div 2 \div 48 \times 13 \div 33$

$= \frac{9 \times 32 \times 7 \times 11 \times 13}{7 \times 13 \times 2 \times 48 \times 33}$

$= 1$

Converting decimal to fractions when there are chances for reducing
Do not convert a fraction to a decimal when its result is a non-terminating decimal.

Memorize $\frac{1}{4} = 0.25, \frac{1}{2} = 0.5, \frac{1}{8} = 0.125, \frac{3}{4} = 0.75$

Evaluate $(2.25 \div 0.125 \times \frac{2}{3}) - \frac{2}{3} \times 0.3$

$= \frac{9}{4} \div \frac{1}{8} \times \frac{2}{3} - \frac{2}{3} \times \frac{1}{3}$

$= 11\frac{7}{9}$

Fraction word problems 分数文字应用题

Students like the word problems with whole numbers only. We did an experiment that is to replace the whole numbers with fraction or percent, and then students get confused. Also, when small numbers are replaced by large numbers, then students easily get confused without knowing how to solve the same word problem. So, the trick is to replace the fraction or percent with a whole number and let the student think about the problem from the whole number's point of view.

For example, the student may not know how to solve the following problem.

What % of 25 is 150?

If we replace the above problem as

How many of 3 is 6? Students will know it is 2. Ask students how they solve this problem. The step is $\frac{6}{3} = 2$. So the answer for the problem "What % of 25 is 150?" is $\frac{150}{325} = 6 = 600\%$.

Jenny scored 220, which was 25% more than Mabel. How much were Mabel's points?   176
Jenny scored 220 which was $\frac{1}{4}$ more than Mabel. How much were Mabel's points?   176
Jenny scored 220 which was $1\frac{1}{4}$ more than Mabel. How much were Mabel's points?   176
Jenny scored 220, which was as many as 2 times of Mabel's. How much were Mabel's points?   110
At a party, there were 48 guests. $\frac{1}{4}$ of guests were adults. How many were children?   36
At a party, there were 225 fewer children than adults. $\frac{1}{5}$ of guests were children. How many were adults?   300 (225 divided by three fifths = 375 total)
At a party, there were 321 more children than adults. $\frac{3}{5}$ of guests were children. How many were adults?   642 (total = 1605)

Fraction word problems 分数文字应用题

Annabelle ate $\frac{1}{4}$ of her pie. How much pie did she have left in a fraction, in decimal, and in percent? $\frac{3}{4}$, 0.75, 75%
Annabelle ate some portion of her pie and had $\frac{2}{5}$ of her pie left. How much pie did she eat in a fraction, in decimal, and in percent? $\frac{3}{5}$, 0.6, 60%
Do multiplication first then do division. $\frac{60}{5} \times 4$ 48
Do division first then do multiplication. $\frac{60}{5} \times 4$ 48
Do multiplication first then do division. $\frac{15}{6} \times 12$ 30
Do division first then do multiplication. $\frac{15}{6} \times 12$ 30
The \$100 stock is increased by \$$1\frac{2}{5}$. What is the new price? 101.4
The \$100 stock is increased by $1\frac{2}{5}$ of its price. What is the new price? 240
You had \$100. You spent $\frac{1}{4}$ of it to buy a pair of jeans and \$$\frac{1}{4}$ to buy a pair of buttons. How much did you have spent? 50

Student's name: _____ Assignment date: _____

Fraction word problems 分数文字应用题

Marcus has 12 coins. One-quarter of his coins are quarters, one-third of his coins are dimes, and one-half of his coins are nickels. What is the value of Marcus' coins?

$1.45

There are 16 players in a chess tournament, and the way they decide the final winner is to let only winners continue to play - that is, the winner plays with a winner. How many games will be played to find the champion of the tournament?

15

Forty fence posts were used to build a square garden with an equal number of posts on each side. How many posts were on each side?

11

Road markers were placed on a highway from 1 to 12, with 25 km between each marker. If you start at marker 1, how far will you have travelled when you stop at marker 12?

25 x 11 = 275

Student's name: _____ Assignment date: _____

Fraction word problems 分数文字应用题

Cher had 20 pieces of cut apples, and she ate 4 pieces, what fraction did she not eat?

$$\frac{4}{5}$$

Jessica had 2 dozen eggs, and she cooked half a dozen eggs. What fraction of total eggs did she cook?

$$\frac{1}{4}$$

What fraction of total eggs did she not cook?

$$\frac{3}{4}$$

Twenty children out of a group of 50 students in the class went to the outside field to play balls, and the rest stayed in class. What fraction of children stayed in class?

$$\frac{30}{50} = \frac{3}{5}$$

Decimals, fractions match 小数分分数配对

Match left to right by connecting a straight line.

left	Right
0.2	$\frac{1}{9}$
0.666....	$\frac{2}{3}$
0.111...	$\frac{2}{4}$
0.5	$\frac{3}{4}$
0.875	$\frac{1}{5}$
0.75	0.125
$\frac{6}{16}$	0.025
0.1	0.25
0.05	$\frac{1}{10}$
$\frac{1}{8}$	$\frac{1}{20}$
0.3333...	$\frac{8}{24}$
$\frac{1}{40}$	$\frac{7}{8}$
$\frac{2}{8}$	0.375

Student's name: _____ Assignment date: _____

Answer to the previous problem

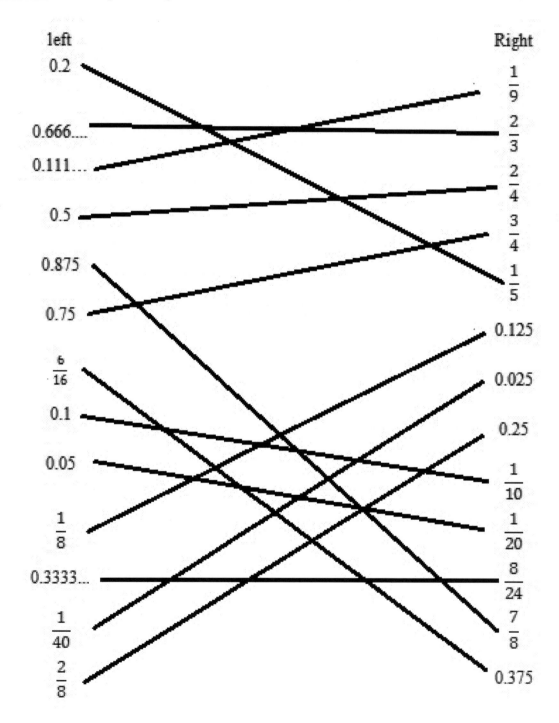

Fraction, decimal, percent 分数, 小数, 百分比

At a party, there were 48 guests. $\frac{1}{4}$ of guests were adults. How many were children?
36
At a party, there were 120 guests. $\frac{2}{3}$ of guests were children. How many were children?
20

Student's name: _____ Assignment date: _____

Decimal and fraction conversion 小数及分数的转换

decimal	fraction
Two tenths + 67 hundredths	$\dfrac{87}{100}$
0.01	$\dfrac{1}{100}$
0.1	$\dfrac{1}{10}$
0.700	$\dfrac{7}{10}$
3 and 8 hundredths	$3\dfrac{2}{25}$
1.5	$\dfrac{3}{2}$
1.15	$1\dfrac{3}{20}$
$0.\overline{3}$	$\dfrac{3}{9}$

Student's name: _____　Assignment date: _____

Ratio 比

Marcus reads 32 pages in 8 minutes. How many pages will he read in 48 minutes if he reads at the same rate each page?

192.

Frank and Amanda were picking apples in an apple farm. Frank picked 7 bushels of apples a day, and Amanda picked 9 bushels a day. How many bushels will Frank have picked when Amanda has picked 108 bushels?

84

Jocelyn lost her cat in an apartment, so she started to look for her cat in the middle floor of the apartment. She went up 3 floors to look around. Then she heard a cat meowing, so she went down 6 floors, but the cat was not there. She then went up 7 floors to look but nowhere to be found. Finally, she went up 6 floors to the top floor of the apartment and found her cat. How many floors were there in the apartment?

23

One ratio problem 3 methods 一比例题 3 解

Alex is 18 years younger than Oscar. After 5 years, their ages will be in the ratio of 2:3. Find their present ages.

Method 1, use ratio method

The ratio is to compare the ages of Alex to Oscar and simplified their ages to lowest term (no common terms other than 1.), so 2 and 3 are not their real ages. For example, 4 to 6 can be reduced to 2 to 3. The age difference will not change over time, so in 5 years, the age difference will still be 18.

From the Line Segment Diagram, we know that each ratio unit is $18 = \frac{18}{3-2} = 1$.
In 5 years, Alex will be _____ and Oscar will be ___. $36 \, (2 \times 18), 54 \, (3 \times 18)$
Now Alex is _____ and Oscar is _____.   31, 49

Method 2, Use algebra

$$\frac{x + 15}{(x + 18) + 15} = \frac{2}{3}$$

$x = 31$ Alex, 5 years later $31 + 5 = 36$
31+18=49 …Oscar, 5 years later $49 + 5 = 54$

Method 3, use ratio pattern

Alex	Oscar	difference	comment
2	3	1	
4	6	2	
6	9	3	
8	12	4	
10	15	5	
36	54	18	now
41	159	18	In 5 years

Student's name: _____ Assignment date: _____

Ratio problems for advanced students

1	The number of Jenny's baseboard cards is $\frac{3}{7}$ the numbers of Vera's cards. If Jenny gives $\frac{2}{3}$ of her cards to Vera, what will be the ratio of Jenny's cards to Vera's cards? Jenny : Vera = 3 : 7 To consider using the fraction of $\frac{3}{7}$, we can use the equivalent ratio of Jenny : Vera = 3 : 7 = 30:70 Because the answer asks for ratio, so the real quantity is not important to solve the ratio problem. $\frac{2}{3}$ of Jenny's cards to Vera means Jenny will have 10 cards left, and Vera will have 90 cards. The ratio of Jenny's cards to Vera's cards = 10 : 90 = **1 : 9**
2	The ratio of Justin's blue marbles to his green marbles is 7 : 4. There are 12 more blue marbles than green marbles. If 4 more green marbles are added to his collection, what will be the new ratio of the blue marbles to the green marbles? B : G = 7 : 4 $\frac{12}{3} = 4$ ... each unit (or box) is 4. B : G = 28 : 16 After 4 more green marbles are added, the ratio = 28 : 20 = **7 : 5**
3	The ratio of before and after There were 392 apples. After 117 oranges were given away, there were twice as many apples as oranges left. What is the ratio of the original number of oranges to the original number of apples? Half of the apples = $\frac{392}{2}$ = 196 = the number of oranges left. The original number of oranges = 117 + 196 = 313 The ratio of the original number of oranges to the original number of apples = **313 : 392**

Mixed computations ＋－×÷混合式计算

$100 + 2 \times 2 \times 2 \times 2 =$ _____**116**

$100 - (2 + 2 + 2 + 2) = 100 - 4 \times$____ = _____**92**

$100 + 3 \times 3 \times 3 \times 3 =$ _____**181**

$100 - 3 \times 3 \times 3 \times 3 =$ _____**19**

$100 + 4 + 4 + 4 + 4 = 100 + 4 \times$ __ = _____**116**

$4 \times 4 \times 4 \times 4 - 100 =$ _____**156**

$700 - (5 + 5 + 5 + 5) = 700 - 5 \times$ __ = _____ **4, 680**

Student's name: _____ Assignment date: _____

Mixed multiplication and division 乘除混合计算

1.	$3 \times 2 = \boxed{}$ **6**, $6 \div 2 = \dfrac{\square}{2} = 6 \times \dfrac{1}{2} = \dfrac{\square}{\square} \times 6 = \square$ **3**
2.	$4 \times 2 = \boxed{}$ **8**, $8 \div 2 = \dfrac{\square}{2} = 8 \times \dfrac{1}{2} = \dfrac{\square}{\square} \times 8 = \square$ **4**
3.	$5 \times 2 = \boxed{}$ **10**, $10 \div 2 = \dfrac{\square}{2} = 10 \times \dfrac{1}{2} = \dfrac{\square}{\square} \times 10 = \square$ **5**
4.	$6 \times 2 = \boxed{}$ **112**, $12 \div 2 = \dfrac{\square}{2} = 12 \times \dfrac{1}{2} = \dfrac{\square}{\square} \times 12 = \square$ **6**
5.	$8 \times 2 = \boxed{}$ **16**, $16 \div 2 = \dfrac{\square}{2} = 16 \times \dfrac{1}{2} = \dfrac{\square}{\square} \times 16 = \square$ **8**
6.	$9 \times 2 = \boxed{}$ **18**, $18 \div 2 = \dfrac{\square}{2} = 18 \times \dfrac{1}{2} = \dfrac{\square}{\square} \times 18 = \square$ **9**
7.	$10 \times 2 = \boxed{}$ **20**, $20 \div 2 = \dfrac{\square}{2} = 20 \times \dfrac{1}{2} = \dfrac{\square}{\square} \times 20 = \square$ **10**
8.	$11 \times 2 = \boxed{}$ **22**, $22 \div 2 = \dfrac{\square}{2} = 22 \times \dfrac{1}{2} = \dfrac{\square}{\square} \times 22 = \square$ **11**
9.	$12 \times 2 = \boxed{}$ **24**, $24 \div 2 = \dfrac{\square}{2} = 24 \times \dfrac{1}{2} = \dfrac{\square}{\square} \times 24 = \square$ **12**
10.	$13 \times 2 = \boxed{}$ **26**, $26 \div 2 = \dfrac{\square}{2} = 26 \times \dfrac{1}{2} = \dfrac{\square}{\square} \times 26 = \square$ **13**

Mixed puzzles operations 数字迷混合计算

$5 \times 3 + \bigcirc 4 = 19$

$\times \qquad \times$

$4 \times 5 + \bigcirc 9 = 29$

$+ \qquad +$

$5 \times 3 + \ 3 = 18$

$\| \qquad \qquad \|$

$\bigcirc 25 \quad + \quad \bigcirc 39 = \bigcirc 64$

$4 \times 3 + \bigcirc 5 = 17$

$\times \qquad \times$

$6 \times 5 + \bigcirc 3 = 33$

$+ \qquad +$

$5 \times 3 + \ 4 = 19$

$\| \qquad \qquad \|$

$\bigcirc 29 \quad + \quad \bigcirc 19 = \bigcirc 48$

$8 \times 3 + \bigcirc 6 = 30$

$\times \qquad \times$

$5 \times 5 + \bigcirc 5 = 30$

$+ \qquad +$

$7 \times 3 + \ 5 = 26$

$\| \qquad \qquad \|$

$\bigcirc 47 \quad + \quad \bigcirc 35 = \bigcirc 82$

$7 \times 3 + \bigcirc 6 = 27$

$\times \qquad \times$

$8 \times 5 + \bigcirc 9 = 49$

$+ \qquad +$

$8 \times 3 + \ 6 = 30$

$\| \qquad \qquad \|$

$\bigcirc 64 \quad + \quad \bigcirc 60 = \bigcirc 124$

Student's name: _____ Assignment date: _____

Mixed puzzles operations 数字迷混合计算

$7 \times 4 - \bigcirc 8 = 20$

$\times \quad \times$

$4 \times 6 - \bigcirc 4 = 20$

$- \quad -$

$2 \times 4 + 12 = 20$

$\| \quad \|$

$\bigcirc 20 \quad \bigcirc 20$

$5 \times 6 - \bigcirc 5 = 25$

$\times \quad \times$

$7 \times 6 - \bigcirc 17 = 25$

$- \quad -$

$12 \times 5 - \bigcirc 35 = 25$

$\| \quad \|$

$31 \quad \bigcirc 50$

$9 \times 4 - \bigcirc 11 = 25$

$\times \quad \times$

$4 \times 7 - \bigcirc 3 = 25$

$- \quad -$

$2 \times 9 + 7 = 25$

$\| \quad \|$

$\bigcirc 19 \quad \bigcirc 26$

$8 \times 4 - \bigcirc 12 = 20$

$\times \quad \times$

$4 \times 6 - \bigcirc 4 = 20$

$- \quad -$

$2 \times 4 + \bigcirc 28 = \bigcirc 36$

$\| \quad \|$

$\bigcirc 20 \quad 20$

Mixed puzzles operations 数字迷混合计算

$8 \div 4 - \bigcirc 1 = 1$
$\times \quad \times$
$9 \div 3 - \bigcirc 2 = 1$
$- \quad +$
$2 \times 4 + 2 = \bigcirc 10$
$\| \quad \|$
$\bigcirc 8 \quad \bigcirc 4$

$8 \div 4 - \bigcirc 0 = 2$
$\times \quad \times$
$9 \div 3 - \bigcirc 1 = 2$
$- \quad +$
$2 \times 5 + 2 = \bigcirc 12$
$\| \quad \|$
$\bigcirc 7 \quad \bigcirc 2$

$8 \div 4 + \bigcirc 1 = 3$
$\times \quad \times$
$12 \div 3 - \bigcirc 1 = 3$
$- \quad +$
$4 \times 4 + 2 = \bigcirc 18$
$\| \quad \|$
$\bigcirc 8 \quad \bigcirc 3$

$16 \div 4 - \bigcirc 2 = 2$
$\times \quad \times$
$15 \div 3 - \bigcirc 2 = 3$
$- \quad -$
$4 \times 7 + 2 = \bigcirc 30$
$\| \quad \|$
$\bigcirc 5 \quad \bigcirc 2$

Ho Math Chess   何数棋谜   英文奥数, 解题策略, 及 IQ 思唯训练宝典

Frank Ho, Amanda Ho © 2020

Student's name: _____ Assignment date: _____

Mixed operations 混合题计算

$$\boxed{21} - 17 \quad = 4 = \quad 81 - \boxed{77}$$

$$\frac{24}{\Box \times} = 4 = \boxed{27} - 3 \qquad \boxed{30} \div 5 = 6 \qquad \frac{24}{\Box \times} = 6 = 67 - \boxed{61}$$

$$2 \times \boxed{12} = 4 \times \boxed{6} \qquad = \boxed{24} = \qquad 6 \times \boxed{4} = 3 \times \boxed{8}$$

$$\begin{array}{r} \times \boxed{6} \\ 4\overline{)\,24} \end{array} \qquad \begin{array}{c} 6 \\ \times \\ \boxed{4} \\ || \end{array} \qquad \begin{array}{r} \times \boxed{4} \\ 6\overline{)\,24} \end{array}$$

$$\begin{array}{r} 4\,)\,24 \\ \times \boxed{6} \end{array} \qquad \boxed{72} \div 3 = 24 = 32 - \boxed{8} \qquad \begin{array}{r} 6\,)\,24 \\ \times \boxed{4} \end{array}$$

$$\begin{array}{c} 8 \\ + \\ \boxed{16} \end{array}$$

$$
\begin{array}{ccccc}
17 & + & 16 & = & \boxed{33} \\
+ & & + & & + \\
18 & + & 15 & = & \boxed{33} \\
|| & & || & & || \\
\boxed{35} & + & \boxed{31} & = & \boxed{66}
\end{array}
$$

Student's name: _____ Assignment date: _____

Mixed Operations

$$\boxed{27} - 21 \qquad = 6 = \qquad 85 - \boxed{79}$$

$$\frac{48}{\square \times} = 3 = \boxed{28} - 25 \qquad \boxed{40} \div 5 = 8 \qquad \frac{48}{\square \times} = 4 = 67 - \boxed{63}$$

$$2 \times \boxed{24} = 4 \times \boxed{12} \qquad = \boxed{48} = \qquad 6 \times \boxed{8} = 3 \times \boxed{16}$$

$$16 \overline{)48}^{\times \boxed{3}} \qquad \begin{array}{c} 6 \\ \times \\ \boxed{8} \\ \| \end{array} \qquad 4 \overline{)48}^{\times \boxed{12}}$$

$$2 \overline{)48} \quad \boxed{144} \div 3 = 48 = 56 - \boxed{8} \quad 6 \overline{)48}$$
$$\times \boxed{24} \qquad\qquad \| \qquad\qquad \times \boxed{8}$$
$$\qquad\qquad\qquad 8$$
$$\qquad\qquad\qquad +$$
$$\qquad\qquad\qquad \boxed{40}$$

23	+	16	=	39
+		+		+
18	+	25	=	43
‖		‖		‖
41	+	41	=	82

Student's name: _____ Assignment date: _____

Mixed Operations

$$\boxed{21} - 13 = 9 = 69 - \boxed{60}$$

$$\frac{45}{\boxed{} \times} = 3 = \boxed{26} - 23 \qquad \boxed{75} \div 15 = 5 \qquad \frac{45}{\boxed{} \times} = 5 = 67 - \boxed{62}$$

$$3 \times \boxed{15} = 9 \times \boxed{5} \qquad\qquad = \boxed{45} = \qquad\qquad 15 \times \boxed{3} = 3 \times \boxed{15}$$

$$^{\times \boxed{15}}\; 3\overline{)45} \qquad\qquad \begin{array}{c} 9 \\ \times \\ \boxed{5} \\ || \end{array} \qquad\qquad ^{\times \boxed{3}}\; 15\overline{)45}$$

$$9\overline{)45}\;^{\times \boxed{5}} \qquad \boxed{135} \div 3 = 45 = 69 - \boxed{24} \qquad 5\overline{)45}\;^{\times \boxed{9}}$$

$$\begin{array}{c} || \\ 8 \\ + \\ \boxed{35} \end{array}$$

$$37 - 16 = \boxed{21}$$
$$- \qquad - \qquad -$$
$$18 - 15 = \boxed{3}$$
$$|| \qquad || \qquad ||$$
$$\boxed{19} - \boxed{1} = \boxed{18}$$

Mixed Operations

| $\boxed{28}$ -17 | $= 11 =$ | $81 - \boxed{70}$ |

$$\frac{66}{\boxed{} \times} = 3 = \boxed{26} - 23 \qquad \boxed{36} \div 6 = 6 \qquad \frac{66}{\boxed{} \times} = 11 = 67 - \boxed{56}$$

$$2 \times \boxed{33} = 3 \times \boxed{22} \qquad\qquad = \boxed{66} = \qquad\qquad 6 \times \boxed{11} = 3 \times \boxed{22}$$

$$\begin{array}{ccc}
\times \boxed{22} & 6 & \times \boxed{33} \\
33 \overline{)\, 66} & \times & 2 \overline{)\, 66} \\
& \boxed{11} & \\
& || & \\
11 \overline{)\, 66} \quad \boxed{198} & \div 3 = 66 = 82 - \boxed{16} & 6 \overline{)\, 66} \\
\times \boxed{6} & || & \times \boxed{11} \\
& 8 & \\
& + & \\
& \boxed{58} &
\end{array}$$

$$47 \quad - \quad 19 \quad = \quad \boxed{28}$$
$$- \qquad\quad - \qquad\quad -$$
$$28 \quad - \quad 11 \quad = \quad \boxed{17}$$
$$|| \qquad\quad || \qquad\quad ||$$
$$\boxed{19} \quad - \quad \boxed{8} \quad = \quad \boxed{11}$$

Student's name: _____ Assignment date: _____

Mixed Operations

| $\boxed{31}$ -17 | $= 14 =$ | $81 - \boxed{67}$ |

$$\frac{84}{\boxed{} \times} = 4 = \boxed{27} - 23$$

$$\boxed{12} \div 2 = 6$$

$$\frac{84}{\boxed{} \times} = 6 = 97$$
$$- \boxed{91}$$

$2 \times \boxed{42} = 4 \times \boxed{21}$ $= \boxed{84} =$ $6 \times \boxed{14} = 3 \times \boxed{28}$

$$\times \boxed{21}$$
$$4 \overline{)\, 84}$$

$$6$$
$$\times$$
$$\boxed{14}$$
$$||$$

$$\times \boxed{14}$$
$$6 \overline{)\, 84}$$

$$4 \overline{)\, 84}$$
$$\times \boxed{21}$$

$$\boxed{252} \div 3 = 84 = 132 - \boxed{48}$$
$$||$$
$$8$$
$$+$$
$$\boxed{76}$$

$$21 \overline{)\, 84}$$
$$\times \boxed{4}$$

52	$-$	28	$=$	$\boxed{24}$
$-$		$-$		$-$
27	$-$	9	$=$	$\boxed{18}$
$\|$		$\|$		$\|$
$\boxed{25}$	$-$	$\boxed{19}$	$=$	$\boxed{6}$

Student's name: _____ Assignment date: _____

Mixed Operations

$34 \times 6 = \boxed{2}\boxed{0}\boxed{4}$
$+ 24 \times 7 = \boxed{1}\boxed{6}\boxed{8}$
_____
$\boxed{3}\boxed{7}\boxed{2}$

$37 \times 2 + 38 \times 2$

= _____ + _____ **74+76**

= $\boxed{\ }\boxed{\ }\boxed{\ }$ **150**

$37 \times 6 = \boxed{2}\boxed{2}\boxed{2}$
$+ 34 \times 7 = \boxed{2}\boxed{3}\boxed{8}$
_____
$\boxed{4}\boxed{6}\boxed{0}$

$35 \times 3 + 33 \times 3$

= _____ + _____ **105+99**

= $\boxed{\ }\boxed{\ }\boxed{\ }$ **204**

$34 \times 6 = \boxed{2}\boxed{0}\boxed{4}$
$+ 24 \times 7 = \boxed{1}\boxed{6}\boxed{8}$
_____
$\boxed{3}\boxed{7}\boxed{2}$

$39 \times 8 + 36 \times 4$

= _____ + _____ **312+144**

= $\boxed{\ }\boxed{\ }\boxed{\ }$ **456**

$34 \times 6 = \boxed{2}\boxed{0}\boxed{4}$
$+ 39 \times 7 = \boxed{2}\boxed{7}\boxed{3}$
_____
$\boxed{4}\boxed{7}\boxed{7}$

$37 \times 7 + 35 \times 4$

= _____ + _____ **259+140**

= $\boxed{\ }\boxed{\ }\boxed{\ }$ **399**

372, 150, 460, 204, 372, 456, 477, 399

Mixed Operations

$44 \times 6 = \boxed{2}\boxed{6}\boxed{4}$
$+\ 45 \times 7 = \boxed{3}\boxed{1}\boxed{5}$
$\boxed{5}\boxed{7}\boxed{9}$

$47 \times 2 + 48 \times 2$
= _____ + _____ **94+96**
= $\boxed{1}\boxed{9}\boxed{0}$

$47 \times 6 = \boxed{2}\boxed{8}\boxed{2}$
$+\ 45 \times 7 = \boxed{3}\boxed{1}\boxed{5}$
$\boxed{5}\boxed{9}\boxed{7}$

$45 \times 3 + 46 \times 3$
= _____ + _____ **135+138**
= $\boxed{2}\boxed{7}\boxed{3}$

$49 \times 6 = \boxed{2}\boxed{9}\boxed{4}$
$+\ 41 \times 7 = \boxed{2}\boxed{8}\boxed{7}$
$\boxed{5}\boxed{8}\boxed{1}$

$49 \times 8 + 46 \times 4$
= _____ + _____ **392+184**
= $\boxed{5}\boxed{7}\boxed{6}$

$48 \times 6 = \boxed{2}\boxed{8}\boxed{8}$
$+\ 49 \times 7 = \boxed{3}\boxed{4}\boxed{3}$
$\boxed{6}\boxed{3}\boxed{1}$

$48 \times 7 + 42 \times 4$
= _____ + _____ **336+168**
= $\boxed{5}\boxed{0}\boxed{4}$

579, 190, 597, 273, 581, 576, 631, 504

Mixed Operations

$54 \times 6 = \boxed{3|2|4}$
$+ 54 \times 7 = \boxed{3|7|8}$
$\boxed{7|0|2}$

$57 \times 2 + 58 \times 2$
= _____ + _____ **114+116**
= $\boxed{2|3|0}$

$57 \times 6 = \boxed{3|4|2}$
$+ 54 \times 7 = \boxed{3|7|8}$
$\boxed{7|2|0}$

$55 \times 3 + 56 \times 3$
= _____ + _____ **165+168**
= $\boxed{3|3|3}$

$54 \times 6 = \boxed{3|2|4}$
$+ 53 \times 7 = \boxed{3|7|1}$
$\boxed{6|9|5}$

$59 \times 8 + 56 \times 4$
= _____ + _____ **472+224**
= $\boxed{6|9|6}$

$56 \times 6 = \boxed{3|3|6}$
$+ 59 \times 7 = \boxed{4|1|3}$
$\boxed{7|4|9}$

$55 \times 7 + 58 \times 4$
= _____ + _____ **385+232**
= $\boxed{6|1|7}$

702, 230, 720, 333, 695, 696, 749, 617

Student's name: _____ Assignment date: _____

Mixed Operations

$64 \times 6 = \boxed{3}\boxed{8}\boxed{4}$ $+ 67 \times 7 = \boxed{4}\boxed{6}\boxed{9}$ $\boxed{8}\boxed{5}\boxed{3}$	$67 \times 2 + 68 \times 2$ $= \underline{\hspace{2cm}} + \underline{\hspace{2cm}}$ **134+136** $= \boxed{2}\boxed{7}\boxed{0}$
$65 \times 6 = \boxed{3}\boxed{9}\boxed{0}$ $+ 64 \times 7 = \boxed{4}\boxed{4}\boxed{8}$ $\boxed{8}\boxed{3}\boxed{8}$	$65 \times 3 + 66 \times 3$ $= \underline{\hspace{2cm}} + \underline{\hspace{2cm}}$ **195+198** $= \boxed{3}\boxed{9}\boxed{3}$
$64 \times 6 = \boxed{3}\boxed{8}\boxed{4}$ $+ 69 \times 7 = \boxed{4}\boxed{8}\boxed{3}$ $\boxed{8}\boxed{6}\boxed{7}$	$69 \times 8 + 67 \times 4$ $= \underline{\hspace{2cm}} + \underline{\hspace{2cm}}$ **552+268** $= \boxed{8}\boxed{2}\boxed{0}$
$67 \times 6 = \boxed{4}\boxed{0}\boxed{2}$ $+ 69 \times 7 = \boxed{4}\boxed{8}\boxed{3}$ $\boxed{8}\boxed{8}\boxed{5}$	$67 \times 7 + 75 \times 4$ $= \underline{\hspace{2cm}} + \underline{\hspace{2cm}}$ **469+300** $= \boxed{7}\boxed{6}\boxed{9}$

852, 270, 838, 393, 867, 820, 885, 769

Student's name: _____ Assignment date: _____

Mixed Operations

$74 \times 6 = \boxed{4}\boxed{4}\boxed{4}$
$+ 76 \times 7 = \boxed{5}\boxed{3}\boxed{2}$

$\boxed{9}\boxed{7}\boxed{6}$

$77 \times 2 + 78 \times 2$

$= $ _____ $+$ _____ **154+156**

$= \boxed{3}\boxed{1}\boxed{0}$

$78 \times 6 = \boxed{4}\boxed{6}\boxed{8}$
$+ 75 \times 7 = \boxed{5}\boxed{2}\boxed{5}$

$\boxed{9}\boxed{9}\boxed{3}$

$75 \times 3 + 76 \times 3$

$= $ _____ $+$ _____ **225+228**

$= \boxed{4}\boxed{5}\boxed{3}$

$73 \times 6 = \boxed{4}\boxed{3}\boxed{8}$
$+ 74 \times 7 = \boxed{5}\boxed{1}\boxed{8}$

$\boxed{9}\boxed{5}\boxed{6}$

$79 \times 8 + 76 \times 4$

$= $ _____ $+$ _____ **632+304**

$= \boxed{9}\boxed{3}\boxed{6}$

$78 \times 6 = \boxed{4}\boxed{6}\boxed{8}$
$+ 79 \times 7 = \boxed{5}\boxed{5}\boxed{3}$

$\boxed{1}\boxed{0}\boxed{2}\boxed{1}$

$74 \times 7 + 75 \times 4$

$= $ _____ $+$ _____ **518+300**

$= \boxed{8}\boxed{1}\boxed{8}$

976, 310, 993, 453, 956, 936, 1021, 818

Student's name: _____ Assignment date: _____

Mixed operations

Evaluate the expressions.

1.	$20 \times 5 \div 4 = 25$
2.	$30 \times 2 \div 6 = 10$
3.	$17 \times 2 \div 2 = 17$
4.	$18 \times 2 \div 4 = 9$
5.	$18 \times 4 \div 9 = 8$
6.	$15 \times 2 \div 6 = 5$
7.	$16 \times 3 \div 8 = 6$
8.	$18 \times 4 \div 9 = 8$
9.	$20 \times 4 \div 8 = 10$
10.	$30 \times 4 \div 6 = 20$
11.	$12 \times 4 \div 8 = 6$
12.	$13 \times 5 \div 13 = 5$
13.	$14 \times 6 \div 7 = 12$
14.	$14 \times 5 \div 10 = 7$
15.	$16 \times 4 \div 8 = 8$
16.	$15 \times 8 \div 4 = 30$
17.	$16 \times 4 \div 8 = 8$
18.	$14 \times 7 \div 2 = 49$

Student's name: _____ Assignment date: _____

Mixed operations

Evaluate the expressions.

1.	$22 \times 5 \div 11 = \mathbf{10}$
2.	$30 \times 3 \div 9 = \mathbf{10}$
3.	$17 \times 3 \div 3 = \mathbf{17}$
4.	$12 \times 2 \div 3 = \mathbf{8}$
5.	$12 \times 5 \div 6 = \mathbf{10}$
6.	$12 \times 7 \div 4 = \mathbf{21}$
7.	$12 \times 8 \div 4 = \mathbf{24}$
8.	$13 \times 3 \div 13 = \mathbf{3}$
9.	$26 \times 4 \div 8 = \mathbf{13}$
10.	$13 \times 5 \div 13 = \mathbf{5}$
11.	$13 \times 6 \div 3 = \mathbf{26}$
12.	$13 \times 8 \div 4 = \mathbf{26}$
13.	$14 \times 3 \div 2 = \mathbf{21}$
14.	$14 \times 5 \div 2 = \mathbf{35}$
15.	$16 \times 2 \div 8 = \mathbf{4}$
16.	$17 \times 3 \div 17 = \mathbf{3}$
17.	$16 \times 4 \div 8 = \mathbf{8}$
18.	$14 \times 7 \div 2 = \mathbf{49}$

Mixed operations

Evaluate the expressions.

1.	$(3 + 2 - 1) \times 4 \div 2 = \mathbf{8}$
2.	$(5 + 2 - 2) \times 8 \div 4 = \mathbf{10}$
3.	$(6 + 2 - 4) \times 2 \div 2 = \mathbf{4}$
4.	$(7 + 2 - 1) \times 2 \div 4 = \mathbf{4}$
5.	$(9 + 2 - 1) \times 2 \div 5 = \mathbf{4}$
6.	$(11 + 2 - 3) \times 4 \div 2 = \mathbf{20}$
7.	$(12 + 4 - 1) \times 2 \div 5 = \mathbf{6}$
8.	$(8 + 2 - 1) \times 3 \div 9 = \mathbf{3}$
9.	$(6 + 5 - 1) \times 3 \div 6 = \mathbf{5}$
10.	$(8 + 4 - 2) \times 4 \div 5 = \mathbf{8}$
11.	$(3 + 12 - 1) \times 5 \div 7 = \mathbf{10}$

Student's name: _____ Assignment date: _____

Mixed operations

Evaluate the expressions.

$20 + 8 - 7 + 11$ **32**	$21 + 7 - 9 + 13$ **32**
$36 \div (2 + 2) - 4$ **5**	$169 \div (6 + 7) - 9$ **4**
$(9 \times 8) - (8 \times 9)$ **0**	$(72 \div 8) - (49 \div 7)$ **2**
$(24 + 12 - 8) \times (7 + 3 - 4)$ **168**	$(25 + 11 - 8) \times (8 + 3 - 5)$ **168**
$8 - 2 + 19 - 6 \times 2 \div 1$ **13**	$18 - 2 + 19 - 16 \times 2 \div 1$ **3**
$18 \div 3 \div 2 - 12 \div 3 \div 2$ **1**	$56 \div 4 \div 2 - 16 \div 4 \div 2$ **5**
$36 \times (12 \div 3) + 5$ **149**	$72 \times (18 \div 3) + 8$ **440**

Mixed 4 operations 混合四则计算

Evaluate the expressions.

$16 + 22 \div 2 - 5$ **22**	$18 + 24 \div 2 - 9$ **21**
$169 \div 13 \times 20$ **260**	$144 \div 12 \times 25$ **300**
$49 \div 7 + 56 \div 8$ **14**	$81 \div 9 + 49 \div 7$ **16**
$(45 + 10) \div (5 + 6)$ **5**	$(35 + 37) \div (5 + 4)$ **8**
$18 - 2 + 19 - 16 \times 2 \div 1$ **3**	$23 - 2 + 19 - 18 \times 2 \div 9$ **36**
$16 + 22 \div 2 - 5$ **22**	$30 + 24 \div 3 - 7$ **31**

Mixed 4 operations

Evaluate the expressions.

[(3×7)+3] ÷3 **8**	[(4×9)+12] ÷8 **6**
38 ÷[3+(32 ÷2)] **2**	64 ÷[20+(24 ÷2)] **2**
[3×(12+4)] ÷ 12 **4**	[4×(8+4)] ÷ 24 **2**
[12+(4 ÷2)] ÷2 **7**	[24–(8 ÷2)] ÷5 **4**
18–[2 + (16 ÷ 2)] **8**	20–[2 + (16 ÷ 2)] **10**
[(48 ÷8)+ (24 ÷ 6) – (8 ÷4)]+5 **13**	[(46 ÷2)+ (16 ÷ 2) – (8 ÷2)]+2 **29**

Ho **Math Chess**   何数棋谜   英文奥数, 解题策略, 及 IQ 思唯训练宝典

Frank Ho, Amanda Ho © 2020   All rights reserved.

Student's name: _____ Assignment date: _____

Mixed 4 operations

Evaluate the expressions.

$\dfrac{10+20+30}{4+5+6}$ **4**	$\dfrac{12+25+35}{4+2+6}$ **6**
$\dfrac{6\times4+5}{3\times3-4}$ $\dfrac{\mathbf{29}}{\mathbf{5}}$	$\dfrac{50\times4+5}{6\times3-13}$ **41**
$\dfrac{20+4-8}{12-3}$ $\dfrac{\mathbf{16}}{\mathbf{9}}$	$\dfrac{37-15+8}{12-3+1}$ $\dfrac{\mathbf{10}}{\mathbf{3}}$
$\dfrac{50\div2+15}{4+32\div2}$ $\dfrac{\mathbf{20}}{\mathbf{9}}$	$\dfrac{20\div4-1}{12-8\div2}$ **5**
$\dfrac{15-2\times3}{19-9}$ $\dfrac{\mathbf{39}}{\mathbf{10}}$	$\dfrac{23-3\times3}{19-2}$ $\dfrac{\mathbf{60}}{\mathbf{17}}$
$\dfrac{6\times8\times10}{3\times4\times5}$ **8**	$\dfrac{6\times8\times10}{5\times6\times7}$ $\dfrac{\mathbf{48}}{\mathbf{21}}$

Mixed 4 operations

Finding digits

Sum of 2 digits	Product of 2 digits	What are the 2 digits?
18	81	**9, 9**
12	35	**7, 5**
14	48	**8, 6**
12	32	**8, 4**
15	56	**7, 8**
16	64	**8, 8**
7	12	**4, 3**
11	30	**5, 6**
13	42	**6, 7**
9	45	**6, 9**
3	6	**2, 3**
10	24	**6, 4**
11	28	**7, 4**
14	49	**7, 7**
6	9	**3, 3**
4	4	**2, 2**
10	25	**5, 5**

Student's name: _____ Assignment date: _____

Mixed 4 operations

$(10 \times 22) - (6 \times 18)$ **112**	$(14 \times 19) - (13 \times 11)$ **123**
$(12 \times 23) - (3 \times 17)$ **225**	$(18 \times 21) - (15 \times 19)$ **93**
$(9 \times 19) - (3 \times 11)$ **138**	$(16 \times 17) - (11 \times 22)$ **30**
$(7 \times 20) - (4 \times 15)$ **80**	$(13 \times 23) - (13 \times 15)$ **104**
$(8 \times 21) - (5 \times 19)$ **73**	$(14 \times 19) - (10 \times 11)$ **156**
$(10 \times 22) - (6 \times 17)$ **118**	$(12 \times 23) - (3 \times 15)$ **231**
$(7 + 20) \div (4 - 1)$ **9**	$(5 + 21) \div (5 + 8)$ **2**
$(24 - 9) \div (6 - 1)$ **3**	$(10 + 22) \div (6 + 2)$ **4**

Mixed 4 operations

Mixed Computations

How many even numbers are there in 1 , 2 , 3 , 4 , ... , 98 , 99 , 100?
_____ **50**

How many odd numbers are there in 1 , 2 , 3 , 4 ,, ... , 98 , 99 , 100? _____
50

How many even numbers are there in 1 , 2, 3 , 4 , ... , 98 , 99 ? _____ **50**

How many odd numbers are there in 1 , 2 , 3 , 4 , ... , 98 , 99 ? _____ **49**

$8 \times 100 \div 100 =$ _____ **8**

$10 \times 100 \div 100 =$ _____ **10**

$82 \times 100 \div 100 =$ _____ **82**

$85 \div 100 \times 100 =$ _____ **85**

$10 \div 100 \times 100 =$ _____ **10**

$80 \div 100 \times 100 =$ _____ **80**

$7 \div 3 \times 3 =$ _____ **7**

$9 \div 5 \times 5 =$ _____ **9**

Student's name: _____ Assignment date: _____

Mixed 4 operations

8. $(11 + 22) - (16 + 17)$

0

9. $(13 + 23) - (13 + 15)$

8

10. $(14 + 19) - (10 + 11)$

12

11. $(3 \times 18) - (3 \times 17)$

3

12. $(4 \times + 19) - (4 \times 18)$

4

13. $(5 \times 18) - (5 \times 17)$

5

14. $(6 \times 19) - (6 \times 18)$

6

Student's name: _____ Assignment date: _____

Mixed 4 operations

(4 × 18) – (3 × 17)
21
(5 × 19) – (4 × 18)
23
(6 × 18) – (5 × 17)
23
(7 × 19) – (6 × 18)
25
(4 × 19) – (3 × 17)
25
(6 × 20) – (4 × 18)
48
(8 × 21) – (5 × 17)
83

Part 6 Ho Math Chess Puzzles for the Creative Minds 棋谜式智趣题

This part consists of many math, chess and puzzles integrated problems. The purpose of this part partly is to foster a student's creativity and perseverance. It also encourages a student's willingness to take on challenges.

Number puzzle 数字谜

```
  S E N D
+ M O R E
---------
M O N E Y
```

Analyze

1. M first. M must be 1. If M =1, then O must be 0. S can be 9 or 8. E + O = E + 0 = N. If S = 8 then there is 1 carrier from E + O., In this case, E must be 9 and N must be 0 since O is already 0 so E cannot be 9 and it concludes S cannot be 8. S = 9.

2. E + 0 = N so we know N = E+1
    N + R +(+1) = 10 + E
    (+1) means there could a 1 carrier over.
    Subtract the first equation from the second. We get R +(+1) = 9. But R cannot be 9 because S is already 9. So, **R must be 8.** 1 is carried over from D + E

3. Try to work on N+R and found it is more difficult than D+E since we must check if there is a carrier from D + E.

4. D + E must be at least 12 because 1 has been assigned to M. D + E could be 12, 13, 14, 15, 16, 17, 18 and only 12 (7 +5) and 13 (6+7) make sense because of all others including those digits which have been assigned. So only 3 digits 5, 6, and 7 are available. Use the following table to assign D and E first. The answer is D=6, E = 7, and N = 8.

D	E	N (E+1)	N+R (8) =E	N=E+1 ok?
5	7	8	8+8=16	no
7	**5**	**6**	6+8=14	N=5 yes
6	7	8	8+8=16	N=7 no
7	6	7	7+8=15	N=6 no

5. **9567 + 1085=10652**

Domino number puzzle 骨牌数字谜

Place 4 pairs of Domino pieces in the following square such that the sum of each side is 11. Circle each answer.

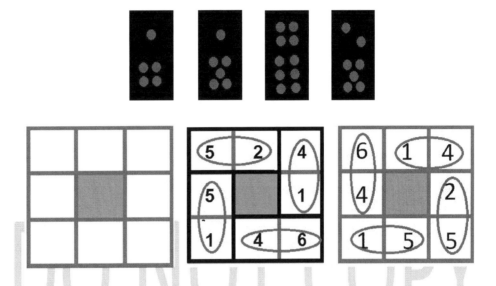

Find a number to replace each letter.

A B
+   B
‾‾‾‾‾
C 0 0

45+55=100

Student's name: _____ Assignment date: _____

Frankho Cube Math™ 何数棋谜 Frankho 方块数学

This is a classic exercise that combines a manipulative cube, puzzles, and arithmetic. It is created by Frank Ho.

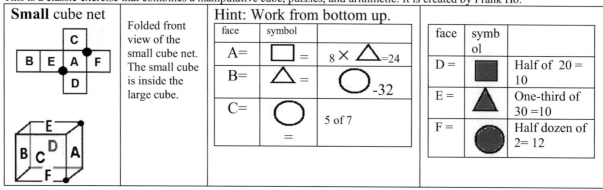

Note that the above face value is decided by symbol and the above outer large cube face value is obtained from the small inner cube with the same symbol. When two values of cubes are shown inside each other, add them up for the following problems.

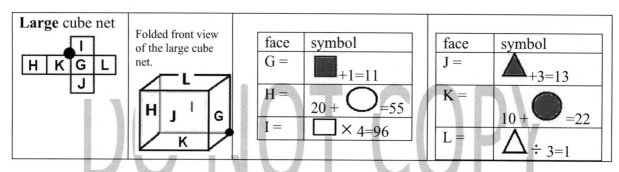

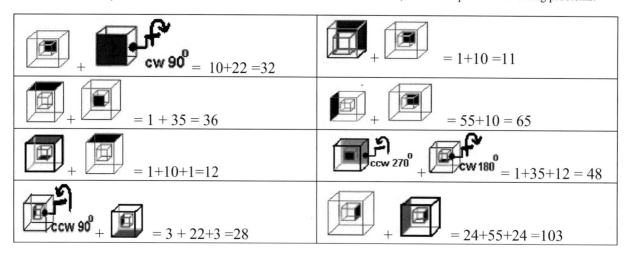

Student's name: _____ Assignment date: _____

Frankho Happy Math™ 何数棋谜 Frankho 快乐数学

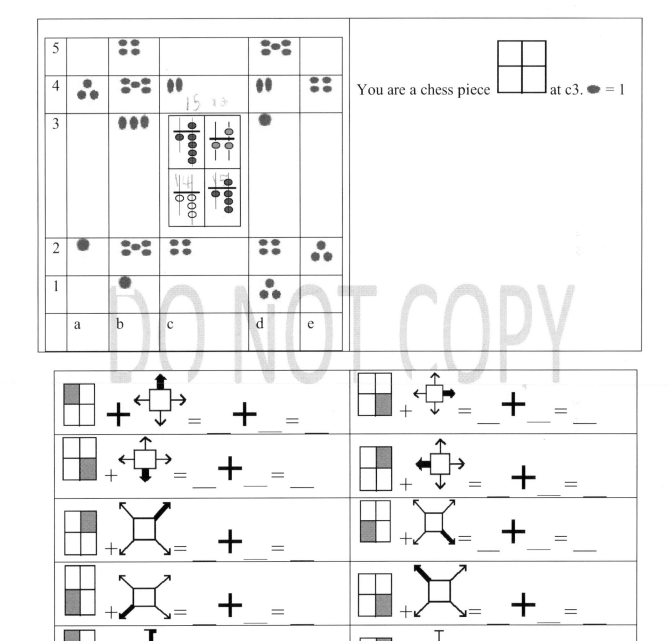

Student's name: _____ Assignment date: _____

1. Fill in each box with a number from 1 to 5, no repeats.

$\square \times \square + \square + \square + \square = 26$, **4x5 + 1 + 2 + 3**

$\square \times \square + \square + \square + \square = 22$, **3x5+1+2+4**

2. Fill in each box with a number from 1 to 9, no repeats..

$\square \times \square + \square + \square + \square + \square + \square + \square + \square =$

100, **9x8+1+2+3+4+5+6+7**

3. Fill in each box with a number. The same shape means the same number.

$25 + \square = \bigcirc \times \bigcirc$ **25+11=6x6**

$5 + \square = \triangle \times \triangle$ **5+11=4x4**

4. Fill in each box with a number.

$3 + \square + 2 = 12$, **7**

2 quarters + $\square$ dimes = $1.20, **7**

5. How many small △ does it take to cover the following entire area?

8

6. Fill in each blank with a symbol.

☦ , ♞ , ⤬ , ♝ , ___   ✳ , ♚ , ❋ , ___ ♛

7. How many times does the number 7 appear from 1 to 50?
5 (7,17,27,37,47)

1. Evaluate and show your work. Fill in a number in each symbol. The same symbol represents the same number.

$$\square - 3 = 6, \ \mathbf{9}$$

$$\triangle + 5 = \square, \ \mathbf{4}$$

$$\triangle + \square = \underline{\hspace{2cm}} \quad \mathbf{4, 9, 13}$$

2. Evaluate.

$$11 + 12 - 2 + 13 - 1 - 3 - 4 + 14 + 15 - 5 = \underline{\hspace{1cm}} \quad \mathbf{50}$$

3.
$$\square + \Leftrightarrow = 10 + \nwarrow\!\!\searrow$$

$$21 - \square = \underline{\hspace{2cm}} \quad \mathbf{13}$$

4. In 10 years, Melody will be half of Amanda's age. Amanda now is 44. How old is Melody now?
44 + 10 = 54
54 / 2 = 27
27 − 10 = **17**

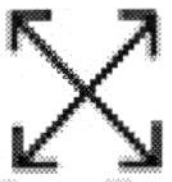

5. A triangle is called an isosceles triangle when it has two sides equal. Find out how many isosceles triangles in each of the following figures.

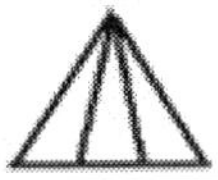 2	 4	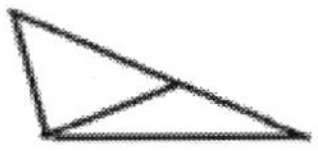 2

Student's name: _____ Assignment date: _____

---

1. Evaluate and show your work. Fill in a number in each symbol. The same symbol represents the same number.

   $\square - 4 = 7$, **11**

   $\triangle + 5 = \square$, **6**

   $\triangle + \square = $ _____ **17**

---

2. Evaluate and show your work.

   $8 \times 9 = 72 \times$ ____ **1**

   $4 \times \square = 20$, **10** $\times \square = $ ____

   50

---

3. Complete the following pattern.

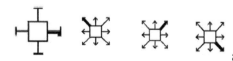

   answer

Number puzzles using figures 图形数字迷

1. Place one of the numbers 1, 2, 3, 4 into each circle such that no two consecutive numbers are connected by the same line.

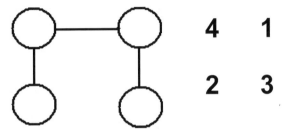

4 1

2 3

2. Place one number in each square box such that the number in each circle is the product of two numbers inside 2 connected squares adjacent to each circle.

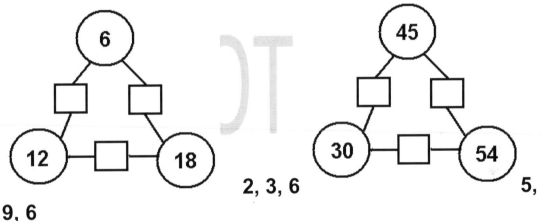

2, 3, 6

9, 6

5,

3. Place one number in each square box such that the number in each circle is the product of two numbers inside 2 connected squares adjacent to each circle.

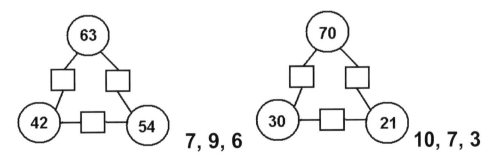

7, 9, 6

10, 7, 3

Evaluate and show your work.

$2 \times 8 \times 3 \times 7 \times 1 \times 9 \times 6 \times 4 \times 0 =$ _____ **0**

Evaluate and show your work.

$10 - 2 + 2 - 3 + 3 - 4 + 4 - 5 + 5 - 6 =$ _____ **4**

When I am added by a knight, subtracted by 4, taken away by 4, added one more bishop, now I am 33, what number am I?

_____ $+ 3 - 4 - 4 + 3 = 33$

$33 - 3 + 4 + 4 - 3 =$ **35**

Replace each ? with a number.

24, 12, 24, 36 72, 60, 47, 59 12, ?, 25, ?	24-12=12 36-12=24 72-12 60 59-12=47 12-12= **0** 25+12=**37**

English and math 英文数学

1. Twenty less 2, plus 6 = _____. **24**

2. 6 less than twenty, plus 6 = _____. **20**

3. The sum of 12 and 6, divided by 2 = _____. **9**

4. The sum of 12 and 6 divided by 2 = _____. 15

5. The number 5 is multiplied by itself, minus 3 = _____. **22**

6. The number 5 is multiplied by itself minus 3 = _____. **10**

Evaluate and show your work.
$8 + 89 + 899 + 8999 + 89999$

$= 9 - 1 + 90 - 1 + 900 - 1 + 9000 - 1 + 90000 - 1 = 99999 - 5 = $ **99994**

Evaluate and show your work.

$500 - 54 - 21 - 96 - 46 - 4 - 79 = 500 - 100 - 100 - 100 = $ **200**

Destine went to U-Pick yourself and picked some apples and pears. She placed 7 apples in each apple basket and 4 pears in each pear basket. She picked a total of apples and pears in the number of between 40 to 60, and the total number of apples is the same as the total number of pears. How many apples and how many pears did she pick?
Since the number of total apples is the same as the total number of pears so the total must be the LCM of 4 and 7 between 40 and 60.
$40 < 7A + 4P < 60$, $7A = 4P = 28$ So the total must be 56. Apples = pears = 28

Replace each ? with a number.

2, 3	6
3, 4	12
4, 5	20
3, 6	? 18

Student's name: _____ Assignment date: _____

Fill in each box with a number.

1.
$\square \div \bigcirc = 9$, $\square = 72$, $\bigcirc = 8$

$\square - \bigcirc = 64$

2.
$\square \times \bigcirc = 27$, $\square = \underline{\ 9}$, $\bigcirc = \underline{\ 3}$

$\square \div \bigcirc = 3$

3.
$\square + \bigcirc = 50$, $\square = \underline{\ 32}$, $\bigcirc = \underline{\ 18}$

$\square - \bigcirc = 14$

4.
$\square + \bigcirc = 24$, $\square = \underline{\ 19}$, $\bigcirc = \underline{\ 5}$

$\square = \bigcirc + 14$

5.
$\square + \square = 18$, $\square = \underline{\ 9}$, $\bigcirc = \underline{\ 30}$

$\square + \bigcirc = 39$

Student's name: _____ Assignment date: _____

Fill in each box with a number.

1.

□ × ○ = 48
□ + ○ = 14   □ = 6,   ○ = 8

2.

□ × ○ = 36
□ − ○ = 5   □ = 9,   ○ = 4

3.

□ ÷ ○ = 7
□ + ○ = 24   □ = 21,   ○ = 3

4.

□ ÷ ○ = 4,
□ − ○ = 48,   □ = 64,   ○ = 16

5.

□ − ○ = 34,
□ + ○ = 48   □ = 41,   ○ = 7

Student's name: _____ Assignment date: _____

$1 + 9 + 9 + 2 + 18 + 1 = 40$

What is twenty-three more than forty-two?

23+22=45

$10 + 11 + 12 + 13 + 14 + 15$
$= 11 + 12 + 13 + 14 + 15 + $ _____ 10

$0 = 5$ _____ $5 = 5 \times$ ___ $=$ ___ $\div 5$
-, 0, 0

$1 + 11 + 111 + 1111 = $ _____ 1234

$1000 - 3 + 1000 - 2 + 1000 - 1$
$= $ _____ $3000 - 6$
$= $ _____ 2994

$(21 \times 100) + (21 \times 10) + (21 \times 1000)$
$= $ _____ 23310

Fill in each ? by a number. Each circle has a sum of 19.

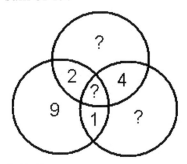

6, 7, 7

Fill in each ? by a number. Each circle has a sum of 25.

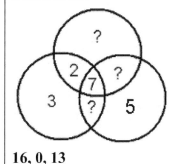

16, 0, 13

Christine has no more than half as many marbles as Celine. Celine has 16 marbles. How many marbles could Christine have?

7, 6, 5, 4, 3, 2, or 1

The number N = $2 \times 2 \times 3 \times 3 \times 5 \times 11$. Is 4 a factor of N? Explain reason.

Yes

Factorize 1870 to produce a product of primes.

$2 \times 5 \times 11 \times 17$

Test if 167 a prime. Write the answer in steps.

Yes

Find GCF and LCM of 41 and 2.

GCF=1, LCM=82

Find GCF and LCM of 13, 39, 2.

GCF=1, LCM=78

Find GCF and LCM of $2^2 \times 3^2 \times 5$, $2^2 \times 3^3 \times 5^2$, $2 \times 3^2 \times 5$.

GCF=$2 \times 3^2 \times 5$ =90, LCM=$2^2 \times 3^3 \times 5^2$ =27000

Student's name: ______________________ Assignment date: ______________

□□3 - □□ 9 $103 - 94 = 9$	□□5 - □□ 7 $105 - 98 = 7$
□□3 - 19□ 8 $203 - 195 = 8$	□□□ - 245 7 $352 - 245 = 7$
□□□□ - 3393 1088 $4481 - 3393 = 1088$	□□□□ - 379 2734 $3113 - 379 = 2734$
3□7 × □ 3□93 $377 \times 9 = 3393$	□□7 × □ □588 $647 \times 4 = 2588;$ $397 \times 7 = 1588$

Student's name: _____ Assignment date: _____

只见棋谜不见题 劝君迷路不哭涕 数学象棋加谜题 健脑思维眞神奇

2 (No calculator, show all your work on empty space.)

Robot Math 机器人数学

There are three number robots: Andy, Bob, and Cindy; they work as a team to communicate with each other through figure or number patterns, magic squares, number puzzles, and balance scales. Now they all have unsolved math problems, and your job is to solve for them so that they can communicate with each other logically again. The following control panel will guide you on the directions on how to solve them.

b2	Replace ? by a number on the arm.
b3	Replace ? by a number on the leg and pelvis.
b4	Find out how many O's to replace ? in Cindy's unbalanced scale tray.
c2	Complete robot Cindy's antenna magic square* for numbers of 1, 3, 5, 7, ..., 15, and 17.
c4	Complete robot Andy's antenna magic square* from 1 to 9.
d2	Replace each letter by a digit on all robot chests. The same letter means the same digit for the same robot.
d3	Complete robot Bob's antenna magic square* from 0 to 8.
d4	Replace ? by a number on the antenna

Antenna Magic square*

Place a number in each square box so that each row, column, and main diagonal has the same sum.

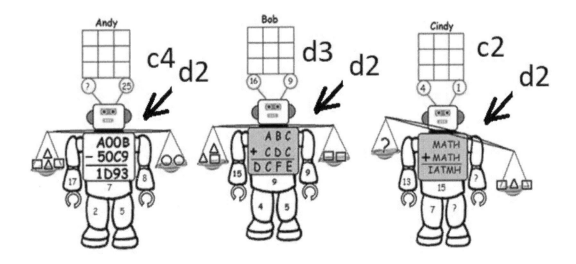

Antenna Magic square answer

Partition technique can also be used in solving magic square fractions. For example, Place numbers from 1 to 9 in each square box of a 3 by 3 square so that the sum of each row, column, and major diagonal is equal.

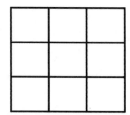

Partition 15 into 1 to 9 as follows:

$15 = 9 + 5 + 1, 9 + 4 + 2$
$15 = 8 + 6 + 1, 8 + 5 + 2, 8 + 4 + 3$
$15 = 7 + 6 + 2, 7 + 5 + 3,$
$15 = 6 + 5 + 4$

5 is used 4 times, so it must be in the centre. The corner number used 3 times, and the number appears 3 times are 8, 6, 4, and 2

Once you solve Andy's magic square. then Bob can use 1 to 1 corresponding to get an answer from Andy, its sum of each line is 12 ($\frac{0+8}{2} \times 9 \div 3 = 12$).

Cindy's magic square can solve using the template of Andy's magic square. For example, 1- 1, 2 – 3, 3 – 5, …,9 – 17. Its row sum is $\frac{1+17}{2} \times 9 \div 3 = 27$.

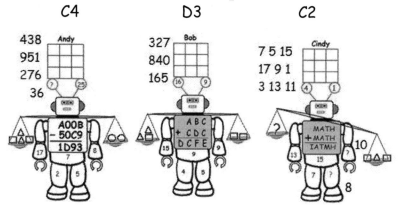

Ho Math Chess   何数棋谜   英文奥数, 解题策略, 及 IQ 思唯训练宝典

Frank Ho, Amanda Ho © 2020

Student's name: _____ Assignment date: _____

Antenna pattern (d4) answer

Each number is a square number, so 36 is 6 squared.

Arm pattern (b2) answer

17, 5, 13 and the other pattern is 8, 9, 10.

Leg and pelvic pattern (b3) answer

2 + 5 = 7, 4 + 5 = 9, 7 + 8 = 15.

Number puzzles on chests (d2) answer

Andy	Bob (Two answers)	Cindy
7002 − 5009 1993	986 987 + 616 + 717 1602 1704 ABC + CDC DCFE D must be 1 for two-digit addition. If D = 1 then B = 8.	8740 + 8740 17470

Balancing scale (b4) answer

□△△□ = ○○
□△△ = □□
□ = △△
△△△△△△ = ○○

$6\triangle = 2\bigcirc$

$\triangle = \dfrac{\bigcirc}{3}$

$5\triangle = \dfrac{5\bigcirc}{3}$

+ − × ÷

Observe the pattern and find a number to replace the ?

2, 3, 5, 9, 17, ____, _____

2, 2x2-1, 2x3-1, 2x5-1, 2x9-1, 2x17-1, 2x the previous number – 1

□ + △ + ○ =210

□ = △ = ○ 70

□ = ○ − 17 53

◎ = □ + 4 53

What is the final value of ◎ ?_57_

Evaluate

$20082009 \times 2009 - 20092009 \times 2008$

20082009(2008+1)-(20082009+10000)2008
=20082009x2008+20082009-20082009x2008-20080000
= 20082009-20080000
=**2009**

何数棋谜算独 Frankho ChessDoku™

Rule: All the digits 1 to 4 must appear exactly once in every row and column. The number appears in the bottom right-hand corner is the result calculated according to the arithmetic operator(s) and chess move(s) as indicated by the darker arrow(s).

© 2008 Frank Ho, Amanda Yang

Ho Math and Chess

3214, 1432, 4321, 2143

Magic square 幻方

Introduction

A 3 by 3 magic square is shown below. We normally do not deal with the higher order of magic squares in the lower grades or elementary school.

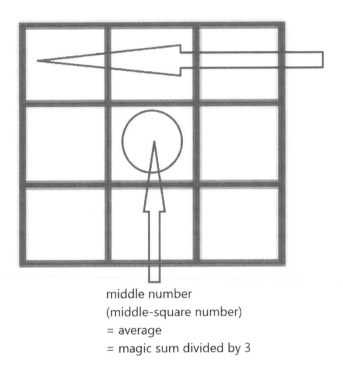

magic sum

The sum of numbers in each row, column, or diagonal is equal.

middle number
(middle-square number)
= average
= magic sum divided by 3

Example

Arrange the whole numbers 1, 2, 3, 4, 5, 6, 7, 8, 9 in the following 3 by 3 squares so that the sum of the numbers in each row, column, and diagonal is the same.

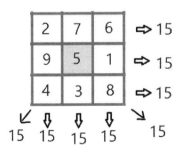

Student's name: _____ Assignment date: _____

An n by n square with numbers filled all squares in is called a magic square if the sums of each row, each column, and two main diagonals are all equal. The sum is called the **magic sum** (幻和).
The number in the middle of the magic square is the **middle-square number** or **middle number**.

Magic squares	Numbers are consecutive whole numbers	Numbers are not consecutive numbers **The way to do the non-consecutive whole numbers magic square is the same as the consecutive numbers because they all follow a number pattern.**
3 by 3	• The **magic sum** (幻和) is *is the sum of nine numbers divided by* Magic sum = $\frac{the\ sum\ of\ 9\ numbers}{3}$. • The **middle-square number** = average of the 9 numbers = **median** = $\frac{magic\ sum}{3}$. • The 4 corners of a magic square are the numbers of 2nd, 4th, 6th, 8th of ordered numbers. **Example** Arrange 3, 4, 5, 6, 7, 8, 9, 10, 11 in 3 by 3 squares so that the sum of each row, column, and diagonal is the same. The average is 7 (median). So, you do not need to calculate the average in this consecutive number example. The magic sum is $7 \times 3 = 21$.	• The **magic sum** (幻和) is *is the sum of nine numbers divided by* Magic sum = $\frac{the\ sum\ of\ 9\ numbers}{3}$. • The **middle-square number** = average of the 9 numbers = **median** = $\frac{magic\ sum}{3}$. • The 4 corners of a magic square are the numbers of 2nd, 4th, 6th, 8th of ordered numbers. **Example** Arrange 3, 6, 9, 10, 13, 16, 19, 20, 23 in 3 by 3 squares so that the sum of each row, column, and diagonal is the same. By using the following rainbow pairing method, we notice the middle-square number is 13. The sum of paired numbers is 26. The magic sum = 13 + 26 = 39 a1 a2 a3 a4 a5 a6 a7 a8 a9 3, 6, 9, 10, (13) 16, 17, 20, 23 Step 1, place the middle-square number. Step 2, place the 4-corner numbers 6, 10, 16, 20. $39 - 6 - 10 = 23$, $39 - 6 - 16 =17$, $39 - 10 - 20 = 9$

Student's name: _____ Assignment date: _____

4 by 4	• The **magic sum** (幻和) $= \dfrac{the\ sum\ of\ all\ numbers}{4}$.
	• To fill in numbers, we use a method called **Symmetric Rows and Columns Exchange method**.

Example 1

Place 3 to 11 into the following 3 by 3 square in such a way that it is a magic square.

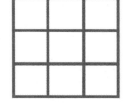

answer

The average is the middle number of 3, 4, 5, 6, 7, 8, 9, 10, 11, which is 7. So, the sum of each row, column, and diagonal is 21. Place 7 in the middle square. We need to figure out how to place other numbers around the 7.

21 − 7= 14 Which two numbers added to 14? 3+11, 4+10, 5+9, 6+8.
Place the 4 corner numbers first by calculating the sums of two diagonals to be 21.

Problem

Place numbers into the following 3 by 3 square in such a way that it is a magic square with magic sum 36.
To fill in a3 by 3 magic square, often two numbers given in chess knight moves and either the magic sum or the middle number is given.

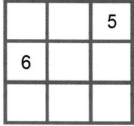
answer
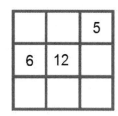

11	20	5
6	12	18
19	4	13

The average is $\frac{36}{3}$ = 12, which can be placed in the middle square. This is the key breakthrough.
After getting the middle square 12, all the other squares can be figured out with no difficulty.

Example 2

Place numbers from 2 to 17 in the following 4 by 4 magic square.

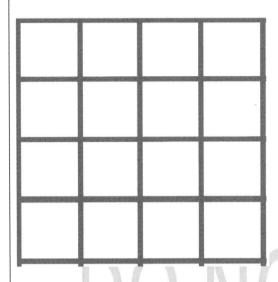

This kind of problem requires a special procedure to get answers quickly, so most likely will not appear in the international math contests.

The total sum $= \frac{2+17}{2} \times 16 = 19 \times 8$, the row sum (magic sum) $= \frac{19 \times 8}{4} = 38$

We use a method called **Symmetric Rows and Columns Exchange method**.

Step 1, Place numbers from 2 to 17 in the 4 by 4 square in order from top to down and left to right.

2	3	4	5
6	7	8	9
10	11	12	13
14	15	16	17

Step 2, Since the 4 cornet numbers added to 38 so they are okay, exchange the non-middle and non-corner numbers diagonally, as shown below.

2	16	15	5
13	7	8	10
9	11	12	6
14	4	3	17

The final answer is as follows:

2	16	15	5
13	7	8	10
9	11	12	6
14	4	3	17

Student's name: _____ Assignment date: _____

Problem

You should do the following problems with understanding of 2 basic concepts which are the magic sum and the middle-square number (the median or average), not try to memorize any formulas.

Complete the following incomplete magic square when its magic sum is 48.

The middle number is 48 divided by 3 = 16.

		15
11		
		12

20	13	15
11	16	21
17	19	12

answer

Arrange the whole numbers 3, 4, 5, 6, 7, 8, 9, 10, 11 in the following 3 by 3 squares so that the sum of the numbers in each row, column, and diagonal is the same.

1. The middle-square number is 7 (the median). The magic sum is 21 (11 + 3 + 7= 21)
2. The largest number 11, which cannot be at the corner because it will be added twice.
3. So, place 2 small numbers 4 and 6 around 11 to make the sum 21.
4. **4 11 6, 9 7 5, 8 3 10**

Student's name: _____ Assignment date: _____

Arrange the whole numbers 2, 3, 4, 5, 6, 7, 8, 9, 10 in the following 3 by 3 squares so that the sum of the numbers in each row, column, and diagonal is the same.

1. The middle-square number is 6 (the median). The magic sum is 18 (10 + 2 + 6= 18)
2. The largest number 10 which cannot be at the corner because it will be added twice.
3. So, place 2 small numbers 3 and 5 around 10 to make the sum 18.
4. **3 10 5, 8 6 4, 7 2 9**

Arrange the whole numbers 2, 4, 6, 8, 10, 12, 14, 16, 18 in the following 3 by 3 squares so that the sum of the numbers in each row, column, and diagonal is the same.

1. The middle-square number is 9 (the median). The magic sum is 27 (17 + 1 + 9= 27)
2. The largest number 18 cannot be at the corner because it will be added twice.
3. So, place 2 small numbers 4 and 8 around 18 to make the sum 30.
4. 4 18 8, 14 10 6, 12 2 16

Arrange the whole numbers 1, 3, 5, 7, 9, 11, 13, 15, 17 in the following 3 by 3 squares so that the sum of the numbers in each row, column, and diagonal is the same.

1. The middle-square number is 9. The magic sum is 27 (17 + 1 + 9= 27).
2. The largest number 17, which cannot be at the corner because it will be added twice.
3. So, place 2 small numbers 3 and 7 around 17 to make the magic sum 27.
4. The answer is 3 17 7, 13 9 5, 11 1 15.

Student's name: _____ Assignment date: _____

Place numbers 2, 6, 10, 11, 15, 19, 20, 24, 28 in the following 3 by 3 square in such a way that it is a magic square.

Since the middle is 15, so the magic sum is 45.

11	10	24
28	15	2
6	20	19

answer

Place numbers into the following 3 by 3 square in such a way that the magic sum is 30.

	8	
5		

The middle square is 10.

13	8	9
12	10	8
5	12	13

answer 1

16, 8, 6
9, 10, 11
5, 12, 13 answer 2

$+ - \times$ divide

Frankho ChessDoku 何数棋谜算独

Rule: All the digits 1 to 4 must appear exactly once in every row and column. The number appears in the bottom right-hand corner is the result calculated according to the arithmetic operator(s) and chess move(s) as indicated by the darker arrow(s).

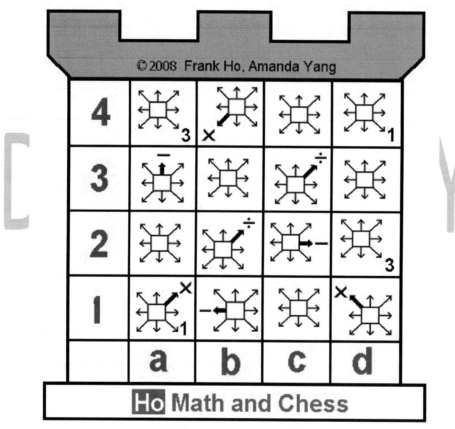

© 2008 Frank Ho, Amanda Yang

1243, 2134, 4321, 3412

只见棋谜不见题   劝君迷路不哭涕   数学象棋加谜题   健脑思维眞神奇
数学腦力棋力   三合一多功能   静心又增智力   神奇創新教材

4 (No calculator, show all your work on empty space.)

Matchstick arithmetic
0 to 9 digits can be written by using matchsticks (without heads) as follows:

0 1 2 3 4 5 6 7 8 9

The plus, minus, and equal signs are: + − =

A. Move one matchstick to make the following equation true.

2 + 5 = 3   12 + 5 = 3   12 − 9 = 3

B. Move one matchstick such that the following four-digit number will be the largest.

995   9951   9951

C. Move one matchstick such that the following four-digit number will be the smallest. 4-digit.

995   995   1095

Matchstick figure

The following is the upside-down chair with one missing leg in the front. Move two matchsticks so that the chair will stand upright with no missing chair leg.

 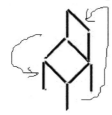

Matchstick figure

The following glass is opening up, move two matchsticks such that its opening will face down.

Student's name: _____ Assignment date: _____

Fill in the missing 4 squares.

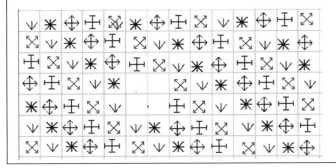

Observe each stickman and its pattern then fill in the empty circle with a number.

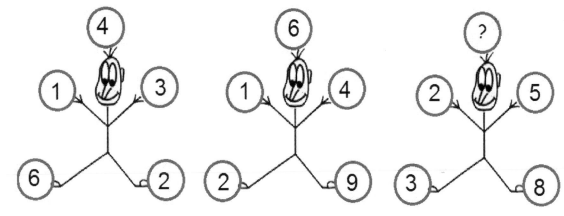

The sum of legs – the sum of hands. $8 + 3 - 5 - 2 = 4$

Triple mates	Diagram

Triple mates

Place black king on three squares marked A, B, and C where

- "A" square shows that the black king is checkmated.
- "B" square shows that the black king is stalemated.
- "C" square shows that the black king will be checkmated in one move.

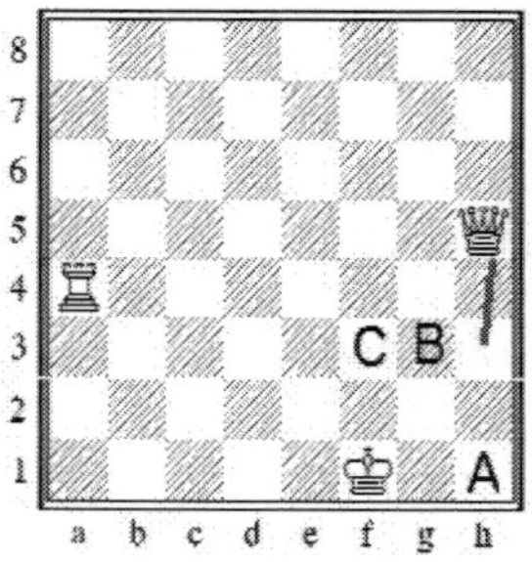

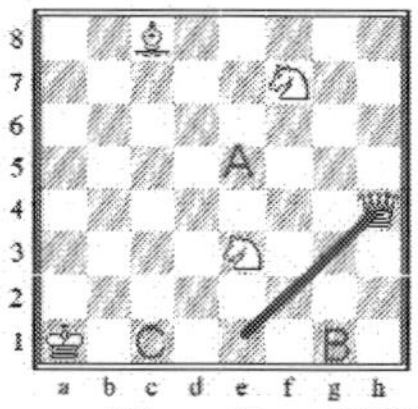

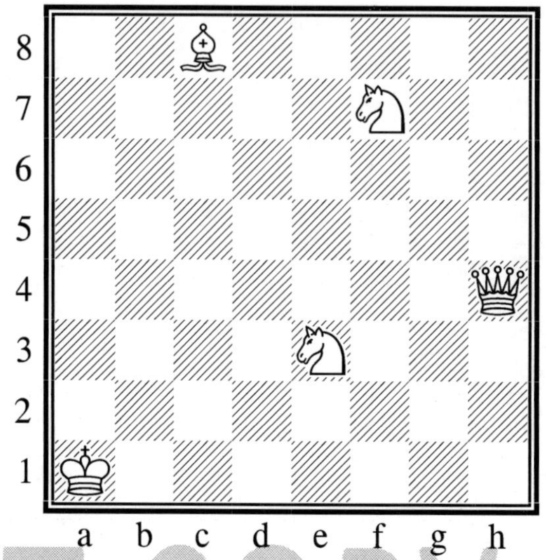

answer

Student's name: _____ Assignment date: _____

Frankho Rook Path Puzzle

Each rook's path is shown by either a vertical line ▌or horizontal line ▬ with the total number of vertical lines and horizontal lines equal to the number shown in the middle of each rook. No lines shall be crossed.

Example

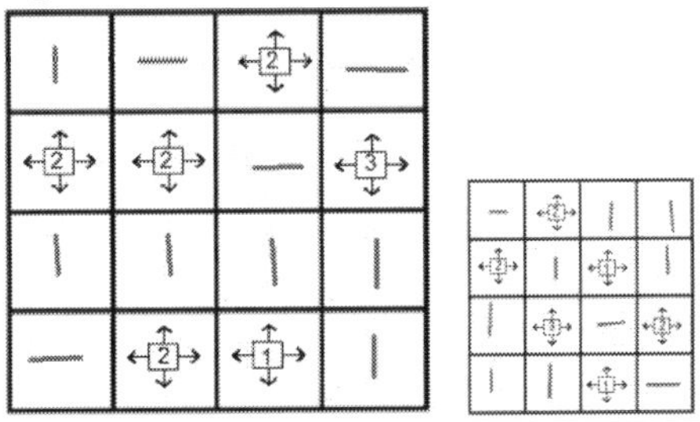

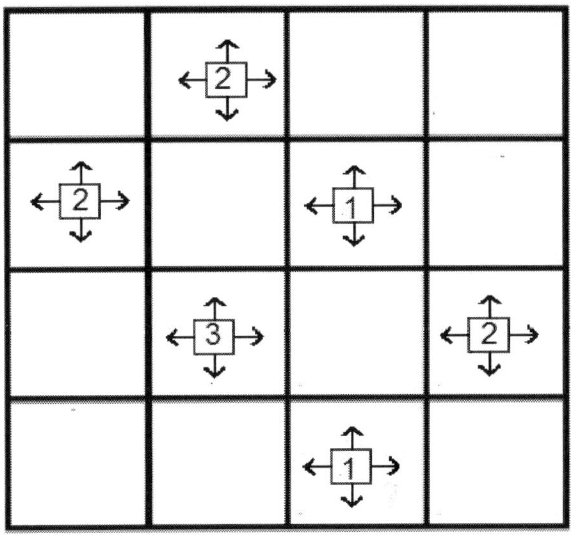

Draw line segments to show each rook's path.

Replace each ? with a number.

6+3=9, 4+8=12, 9+7=16, 7+12=**19**

Student's name: _____ Assignment date: _____

Frankho ChessMaze and Castle Math 何数棋谜迷官

Trace the path from Queen to King.

Transformation	Symbol	Example
Slide	$[- \leftrightarrow +, \updownarrow]$	[3, –2] Move right 3 squares and down 2 squartes. [0, 2] Move up 2 squares.
Rotation	⌐→ ←⌐	⊕ = ⊕, ⊕ = ⊕
Flip	⊕ flip	⊕ flip = ⊕ , ⊕ flip = ⊕

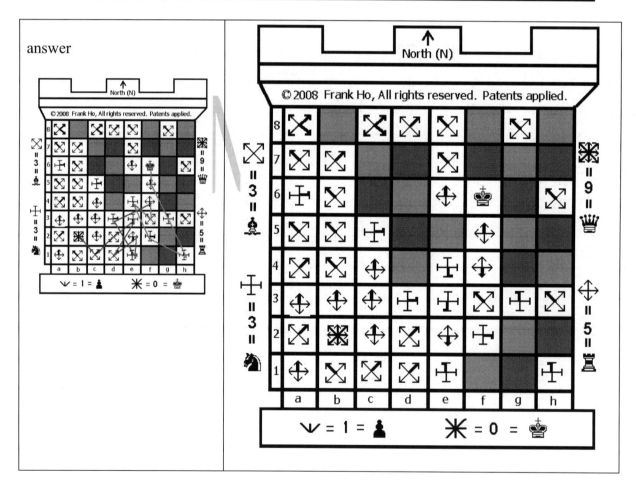

Student's name: _____ Assignment date: _____

Math and Chess Puzzle
You are at c3.

The points of chess pieces are as follows:

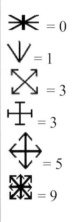

	a	b	c	d	e
5		⊞ (4 dots)	⬥ (arrows)	⊞ (4 dots)	
4	(3 dots)	⊥	1.99	⤬	⊞ (4 dots)
3	⊥	100−94		$2\frac{8}{9}$	✳
2	●	One dozen	10000 − 1	✸	(3 dots)
1		●	⤬	(3 dots)	

Points:
✳ = 0
⤋ = 1
⤬ = 3
⊥ = 3
⬥ = 5
✸ = 9

3.99, 4 8/9
10002, 10
5, 14
16, 6
9, 9

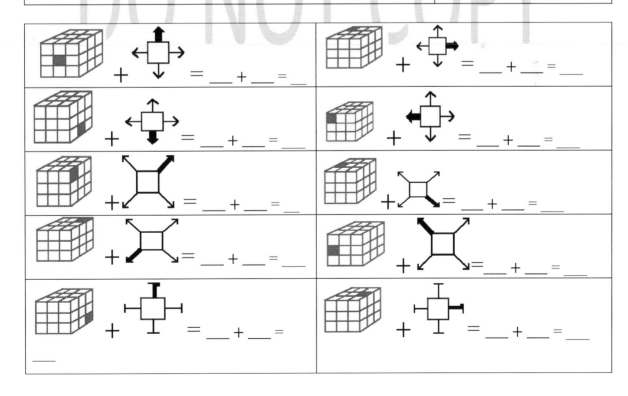

Student's name: _____ Assignment date: _____

Frankho Move Dots Puzzle ™

You are at c3.

Move some dots in b3, c4, c2, or d3 squares into c3 square such that the sum of dots + dots in each of rook's moves at c3 will be equal to the number shown on its destination square. See the following example.

Example

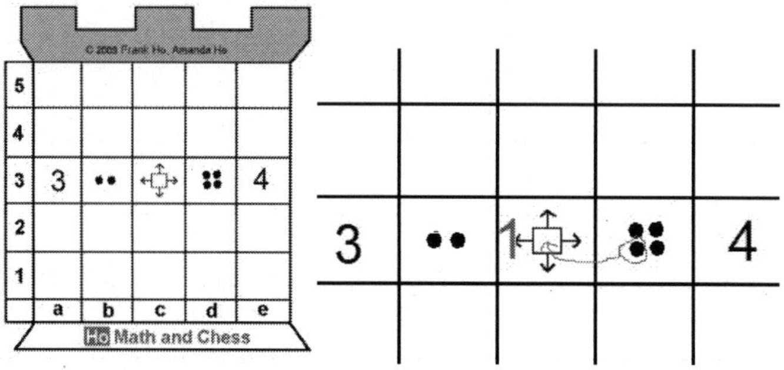

Problem

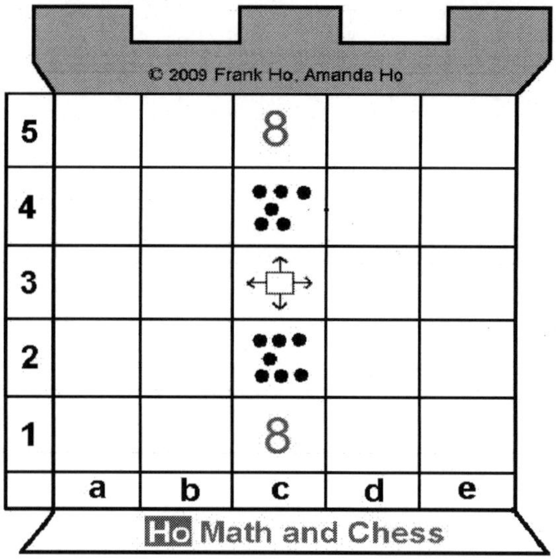

Move up 2 moves down 1. Move 3 in the middle.

Student's name: _____ Assignment date: _____

Unequal Sudoku

Every row and column must have only one number starting from 1 to the number of squares of each side (Sudoku), but all numbers must obey the inequality sign.

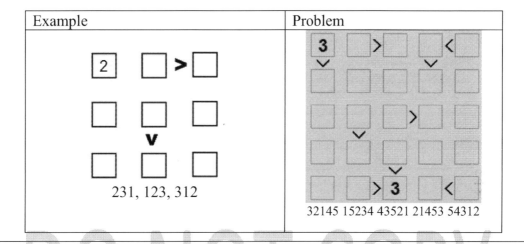

Fencing 盖围墙, 頭尾相连但不交义,不重複的循环围墙

Connect lines around each dot in such a way that each number indicates how many lines, connected by 4 dots only, surround it. The connected lines must form a single loop (like one rubber band) without lines crossed to each other.

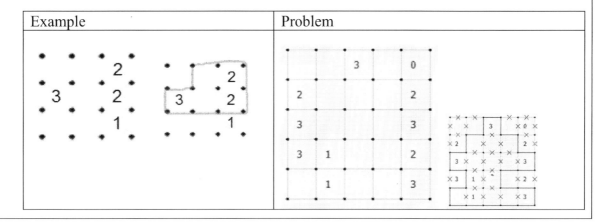

Triple mates

Place black king on three squares marked A, B, and C where

- "A" square shows that the black king is checkmated.
- "B" square shows that the black king is stalemated.
- "C" square shows that the black king will be checkmated in one move.

answer

Diagram

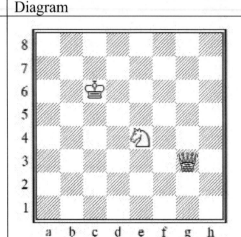

Frankho Maze

Diagram

Trace the path from ▨ to ♚.

Movement direction is shown by a darker line segment.

Answer

Student's name: _____ Assignment date: _____

Math and Chess Puzzle
You are at c3.

5		⸬		✳		⸬	
4	∴	$2\frac{2}{3}$		$3\frac{3}{5}$		$3\frac{1}{2}$	⸬
3	✳	$3\frac{4}{6}$				$2\frac{5}{7}$	✳
2	•	$1\frac{2}{3}$		$1\frac{7}{9}$		$1\frac{7}{9}$	∴
1		•		✳		∴	
	a	**b**		**c**		**d**	**e**

Inner box:

$1\frac{3}{8}$	$2\frac{5}{16}$
$1\frac{1}{2}$	$4\frac{1}{4}$

The points of chess pieces are as follows:

✳ = 0

↓ = 1

✕ = 3

✛ = 3

✦ = 5

✳ = 9

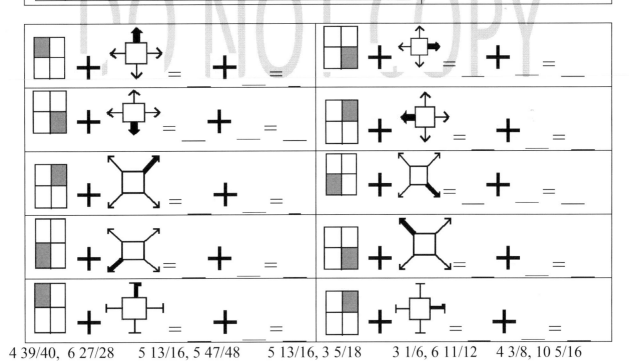

4 39/40, 6 27/28   5 13/16, 5 47/48   5 13/16, 3 5/18   3 1/6, 6 11/12   4 3/8, 10 5/16

Frankho Move Dots Puzzle ™

You are at c3.

Move some dots in b3, c4, c2, or d3 squares into c3 square such that the sum of dots + dots in each of rook's moves at c3 will be equal to the number shown on its destination square. See the following example.

Example

Problem

Move 1 up and move 1 down.

Maze

The answer to the previous maze.

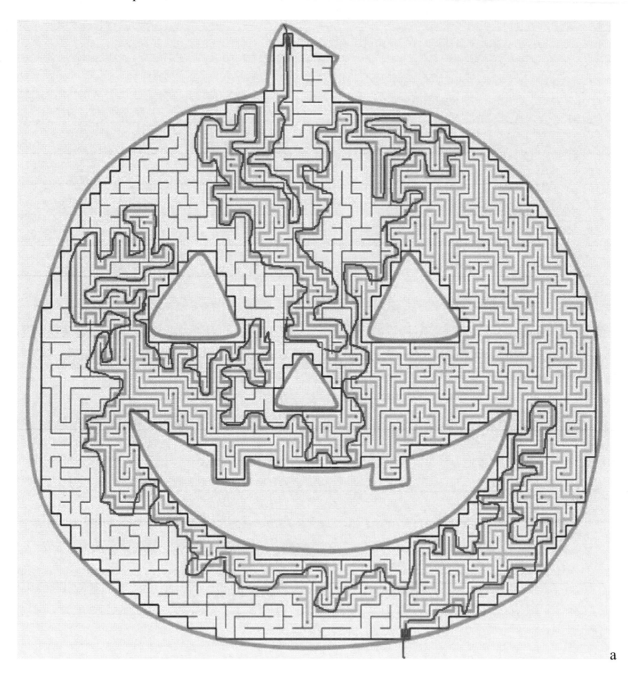

a

只见棋谜不见题   劝君迷路不哭涕   数学象棋加谜题   健脑思维眞神奇

2 (No calculator, show all your work on empty space.)

1	Evaluate $3\frac{1}{4} + \left(-5\frac{5}{6}\right) - \left(-2\frac{3}{4}\right) - \left(+3\frac{1}{6}\right) - \left(+9\frac{3}{7}\right) - \left(-2\frac{5}{7}\right) - \left(-3\frac{2}{7}\right) + 7$ $\dfrac{4}{7}$
2	Insert 3 fractions between $\frac{1}{4}$ and $\frac{1}{2}$. $\frac{1}{4}$. _____, _____, _____, $\frac{1}{2}$.

3	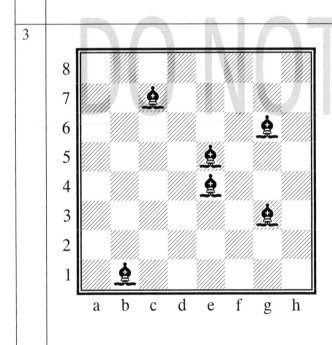 Look at the left chess diagram and Replace the ? by a number. **3 9 13** **10 10 ? 10** 3 9 13 refers to the vales of bishops on white squares. 10 10 10 refers to bishop on black squares under the condition that the horizontal axis is a = 1, b = 2, c= 3, d = 4, e = 5, f = 6, g= 7, h = 8. The bishops on black squares have the values of 10, 10, and 10.
4	Evaluate $\frac{4}{1\times3} + \frac{4}{3\times5} + \frac{4}{5\times7} + ... + \frac{4}{99\times101}$ $\frac{200}{101}$ answer

Triple mates

Place black king on three squares marked A, B, and C where

- "A" square shows that the black king is checkmated.
- "B" square shows that the black king is stalemated.
- "C" square shows that the black king will be checkmated in one move.

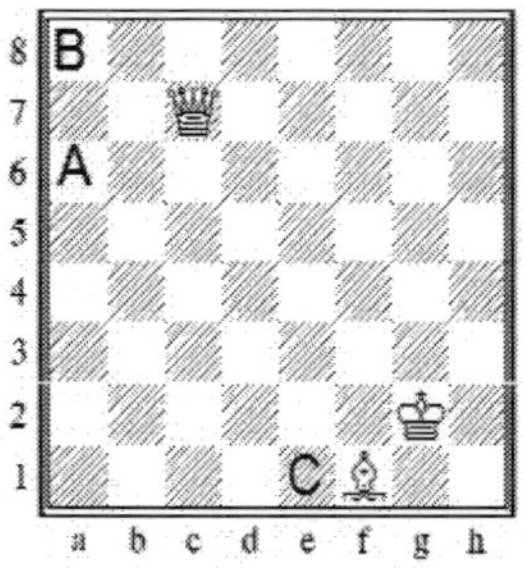

Diagram

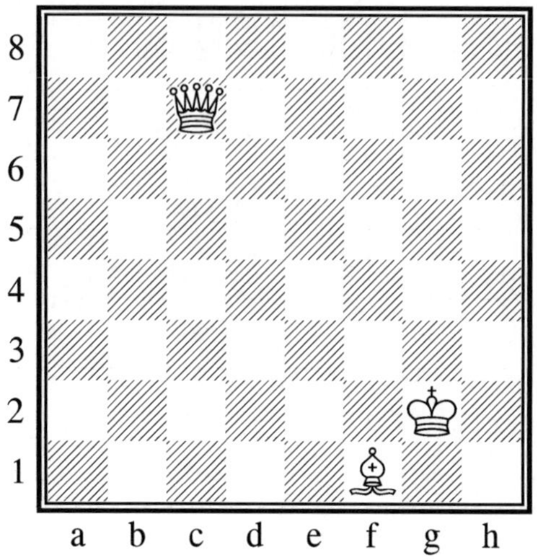

Frankho Rook Path Puzzle

Each rook's path is shown by either a vertical line ▮ or horizontal line ▬ with the total number of vertical lines and horizontal lines equal to the number shown in the middle of each rook. No lines shall be crossed.

Example

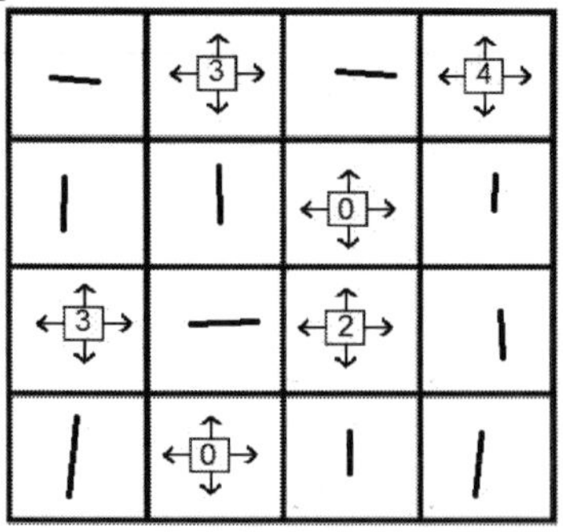

Draw line segments to show each rook's path.

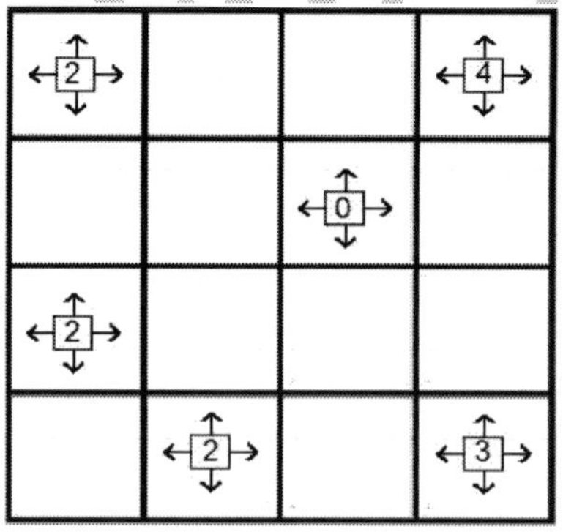

answer

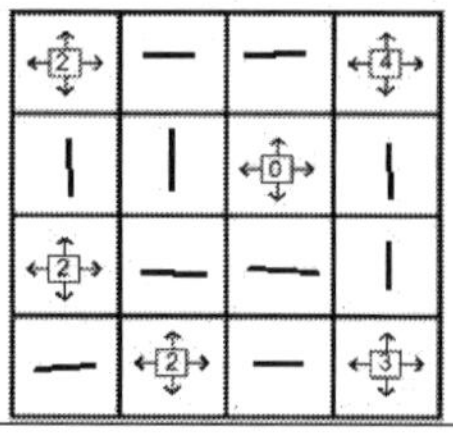

Student's name: _____   Assignment date: _____

Frankho ChessMaze 何数棋谜迷官

- Trace the path from ⊠ to ♔ ☐.
- Movement direction is shown by a darker line segment.

Transformation	Symbol	Example
Slide	[-↔+ , ↕̲]	[3, –2] Move right 3 squares and down 2 squartes. [0, 2] Move up 2 squares.
Rotation	⌐→ ←⌐	⟲ = ⬦, ⟳ = ⬥
Flip	⬦ flip	⬦ = ⬦ , ⬦ flip = ⬦

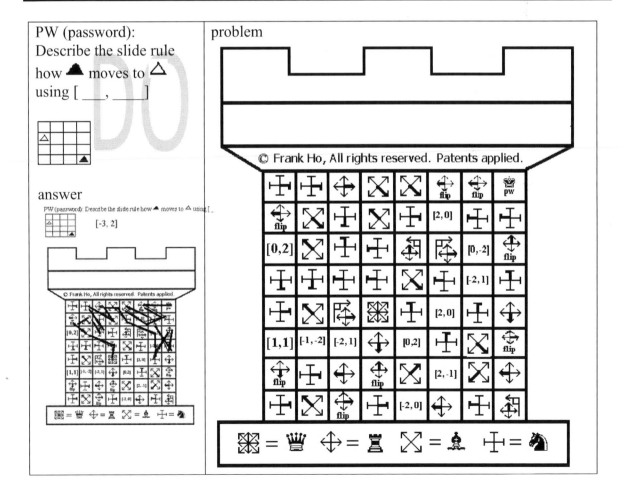

PW (password): Describe the slide rule how ▲ moves to △ using [___ , ___]

answer
PW (password): Describe the slide rule how ▲ moves to △ using [
[-3, 2]

Student's name: _____ Assignment date: _____

Math and Chess Puzzle

You are at c3.

The points of chess pieces are as follows:

$$\text{✳} = 0$$
$$\text{↓} = 1$$
$$\text{✕} = 3$$
$$\text{┼} = 3$$
$$\text{✛} = 5$$
$$\text{✾} = 9$$

	a	b	c	d	e
5		⣿	✳	⣿	
4	⣢	$2\frac{2}{3}$	$3\frac{3}{5}$	$3\frac{1}{2}$	⣿
3	✳	$3\frac{4}{6}$	$4\frac{3}{8}$, $5\frac{5}{16}$, $6\frac{1}{2}$, $7\frac{1}{4}$	$2\frac{5}{7}$	✳
2	●	$1\frac{2}{3}$	$1\frac{7}{9}$	$1\frac{7}{9}$	⣢
1		●	✳	⣢	

31/40, 4 15/28
5 11/36. 8 47/48
1 13/16, 4 13/18
4 5/6, 4 7/12
-5/8, 1 5/16   answer

Student's name: _____ Assignment date: _____

Frankho Move Dots Puzzle ™

You are at c3.

Move some dots in b3, c4, c2, or d3 squares into c3 square such that the sum of dots + dots in each of rook's moves at c3 will be equal to the number shown on its destination square. See the following example.

Example

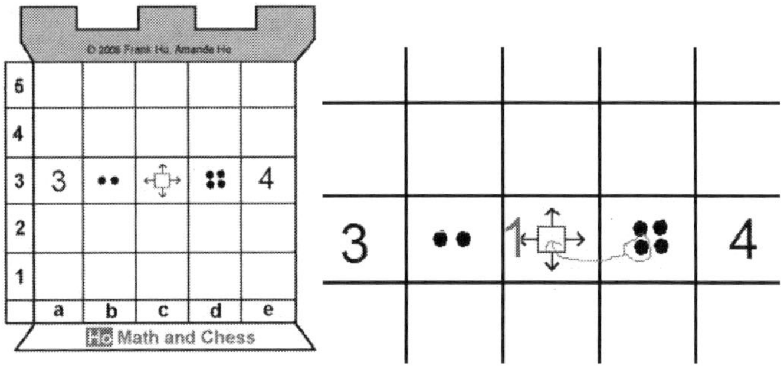

Problem

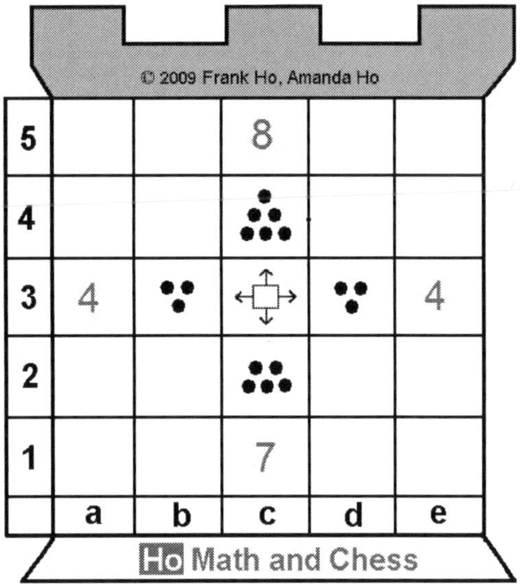

Move left 1. Move right 1.

Student's name: _____ Assignment date: _____

Unequal Sudoku

Every row and column must have only one number starting from 1 to the number of squares of each side (Sudoku), but all numbers must obey the inequality sign.

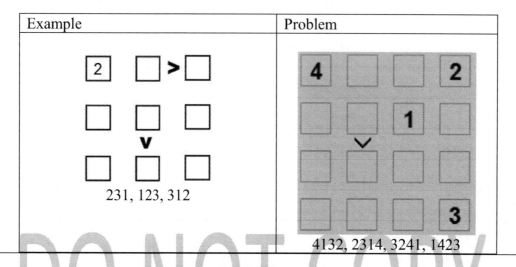

Example	Problem

231, 123, 312

4132, 2314, 3241, 1423

Fencing 盖围墙, 頭尾相连但不交义,不重複的循环围墙

Connect lines around each dot in such a way that each number indicates how many lines, connected by 4 dots only, surround it. The connected lines must form a single loop (like one rubber band) without lines crossed to each other.

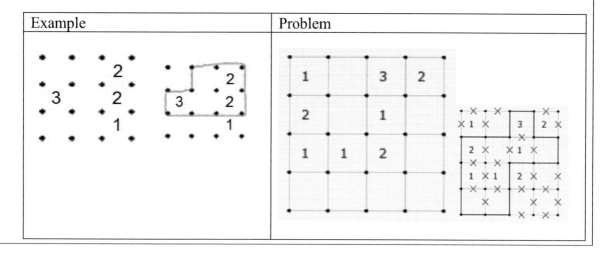

Example	Problem

Maze

Student's name: _____ Assignment date: _____

The answer to the previous maze.

a

Student's name: _____ Assignment date: _____

只见棋谜不见题　　劝君迷路不哭涕　　数学象棋加谜题　　健脑思维眞神奇

＃3 (No calculator, show all your work on empty space.)

1	Evaluate $\dfrac{\textit{The original price after paying purchase price \$6970 with 15\% discount}}{\textit{The after sale tax price after purchase price of \$8200 with 12\% tax}} \times \dfrac{0.012}{0.24} \div$ $\dfrac{0.036}{0.48}$ $= \dfrac{6970 \div 0.85}{8200 \times (1+0.12)} \times \dfrac{12}{240} \times \dfrac{480}{36}$ $= \dfrac{8200}{8200 \times 1.12} \times \dfrac{1}{20} \times \dfrac{40}{3}$ $= \dfrac{100}{112} \times \dfrac{1}{1} \times \dfrac{2}{3}$ $= \dfrac{25}{42}$
2	Eric read 15 pages per day. After 5 days, he still had $\dfrac{2}{5}$ to be read. How many pages were in the book? $15 \times 5 \div \dfrac{3}{5} = 125$ pages
3	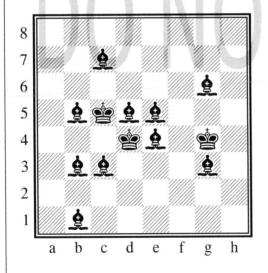 Take a look at the left chess diagram and Replace the ? by a number. **9 6 3 6 ?** 6 Add column-wise from the left to the right
4	Evaluate the following and find the value of x. $3 + x \div \left(2\frac{1}{2} \times 3\frac{3}{4}\right) - 6 + 4 \div 2 = 4$ $x = 2$

Triple mates

Place black king on three squares marked A, B, and C where

- "A" square shows that the black king is checkmated.
- "B" square shows that the black king is stalemated.
- "C" square shows that the black king will be checkmated in one move.

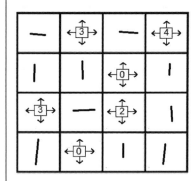

answer

Diagram

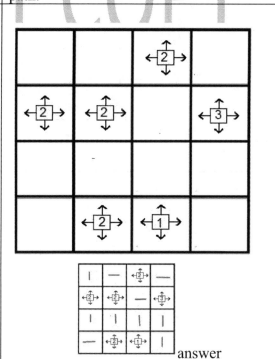

Frankho Rook Path Puzzle

Each rook's path is shown by either a vertical line ▎ or horizontal line ▬ with the total number of vertical lines and horizontal lines equal to the number shown in the middle of each rook. No lines shall be crossed.

Example

Draw line segments to show each rook's path.

Student's name: _____ Assignment date: _____

Frankho ChessMaze 何数棋谜迷官

1. Trace the path from ⊞ to ♔ □.
2. Movement direction is shown by a darker line segment.

Transformation	Symbol	Example
Slide	[- ↔ + , ↕]	[3, –2] Move right 3 squares and down 2 squartes. [0, 2] Move up 2 squares.
Rotation	↱ ↰	↻ = ↔, ↺ = ↔
Flip	↔ flip	↔ flip = ↔, ↕ flip = ↔

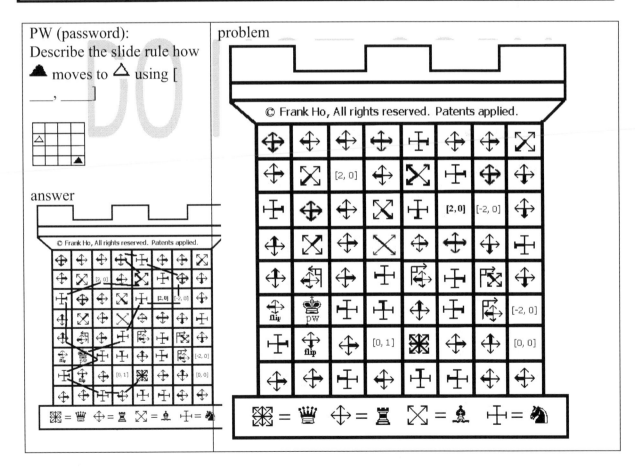

PW (password):
Describe the slide rule how ▲ moves to △ using [____ , ____]

answer

Math and Chess Puzzle

You are at c3.

	a	b	c	d	e
5		•• ••	✳	•• ••	
4	•• •	$2\frac{2}{3}$	$3\frac{3}{5}$	$3\frac{1}{2}$	••
3	✳	$3\frac{4}{6}$	$2\frac{1}{4}$ / $1\frac{2}{3}$ / $1\frac{1}{2}$ / $3\frac{1}{4}$	$2\frac{5}{7}$	✳
2	•	$1\frac{2}{3}$	$1\frac{7}{9}$	$1\frac{7}{9}$	•• •
1	•		✳	•• •	

The points of chess pieces are as follows:

✳ = 0

$\bigvee$ = 1

$\bigtimes$ = 3

$\boxplus$ = 3

$\bigoplus$ = 5

$\bigotimes$ = 9

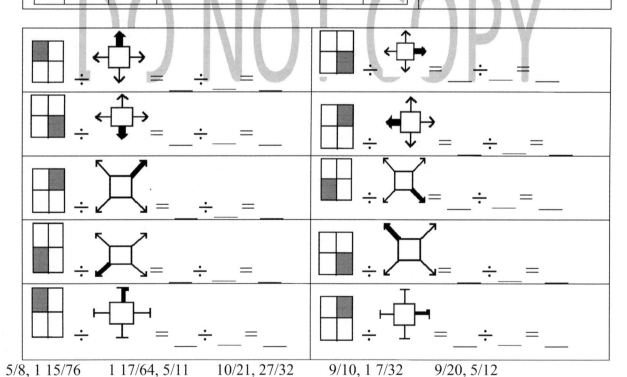

5/8, 1 15/76　　1 17/64, 5/11　　10/21, 27/32　　9/10, 1 7/32　　9/20, 5/12

Student's name: ______________________ Assignment date: ______________

Frankho Move Dots Puzzle ™

You are at c3.

Move some dots in b3, c4, c2, or d3 squares into c3 square such that the sum of dots + dots in each of rook's moves at c3 will be equal to the number shown on its destination square. See the following example.

Example

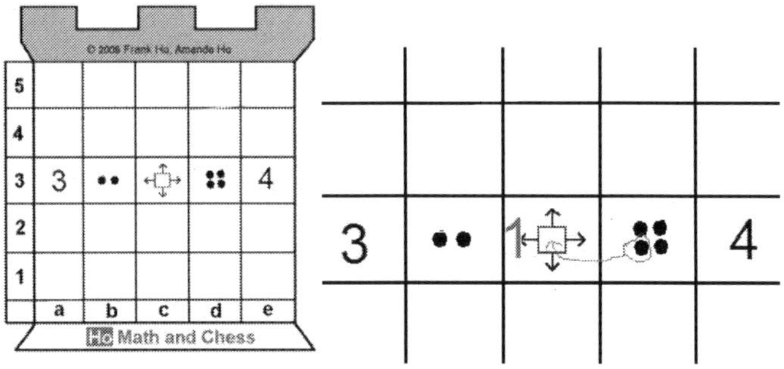

Problem

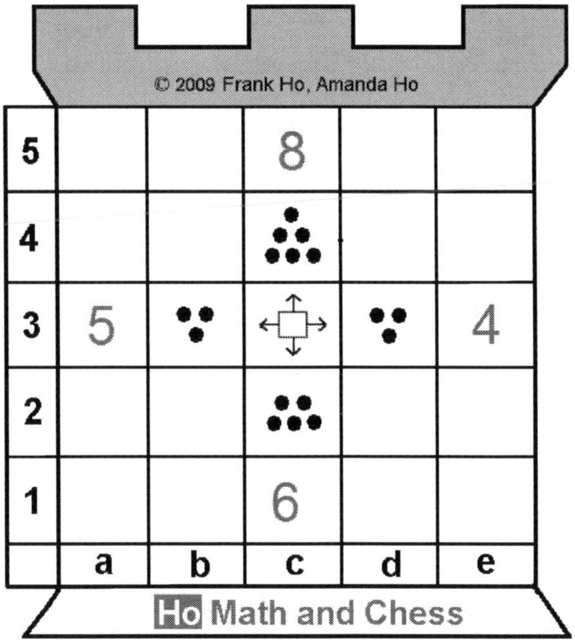

Move up 1. Move left 1.

Student's name: _____ Assignment date: _____

Unequal Sudoku

Every row and column must have only one number starting from 1 to the number of squares of each side (Sudoku), but all numbers must obey the inequality sign.

Example	Problem

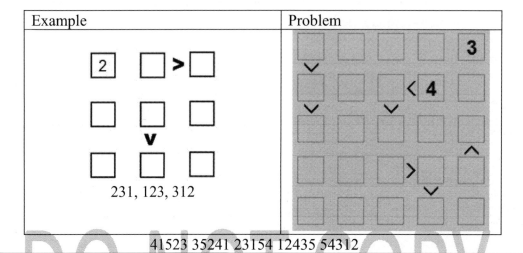

231, 123, 312

41523 35241 23154 12435 54312

Fencing 盖围墙, 頭尾相连但不交义,不重複的循环围墙

Connect lines around each dot in such a way that each number indicates how many lines, connected by 4 dots only, surround it. The connected lines must form a single loop (like one rubber band) without lines crossed to each other.

Example	Problem

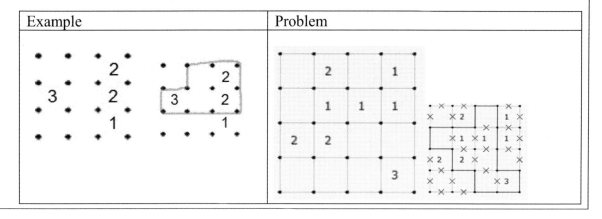

Maze

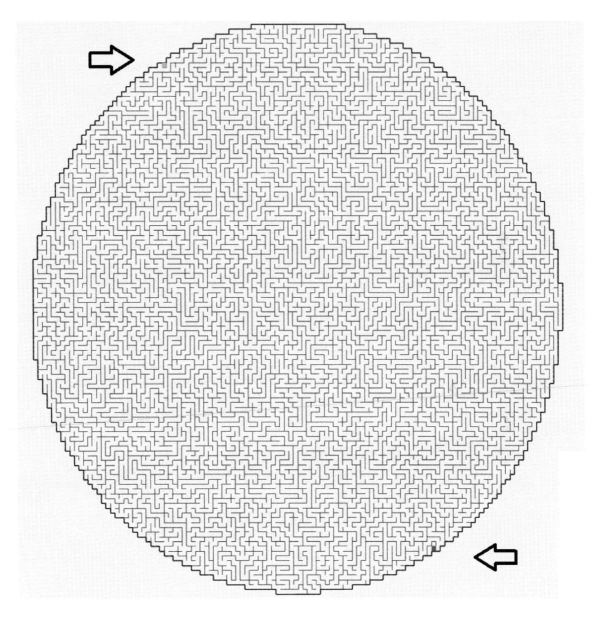

Student's name: _____ Assignment date: _____

Students! Please cover the answer below.

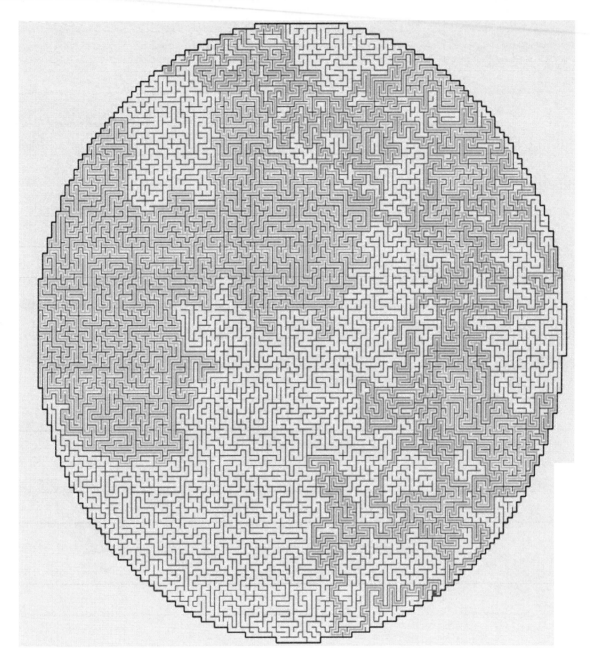

Student's name: _____ Assignment date: _____

只见棋谜不见题 劝君迷路不哭涕 数学象棋加谜题 健脑思维真神奇

5 (No calculator, show all your work on empty space.)

1	Evaluate $1\frac{8}{11} \div \left[\left(\frac{5}{6} - \frac{2}{3}\right) \div \frac{1}{4}\right] \times 2\frac{3}{4}$ = $$\frac{57}{8}$$
2	**3 Dimensional Frankho Puzzle™** Rule: All the digits 1 to 3 must appear exactly only once in every row and column of each layer, this same rule also applies to the same column of the multiple layers. Transfer the numbers of each layer of the following cube into the 3 by 3 tables below.

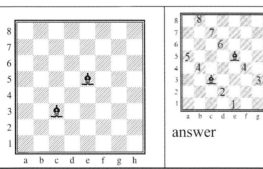

Cube	Bottom layer	Middle layer	Top layer
(cube diagram)	123 312 231	231 123 312	312 232 123

3	Take a look at the left chess diagram and Replace each ? with a number. ## 876432542? 1 The first bishop row values are 876432 from the top left to the right bottom and the second bishop has the value from left row 5421 answer
4	$0.5 \times [\blacksquare - 1.2345 \times 10^2 + 132.55] + 0.09 - 0.08 \times 9.0 = 0.01 \times 100$ $0.5 \times [\blacksquare - 123.45 + 132.55] + 0.09 - 0.072 = 1$ $0.5[\blacksquare + 9.1] + 0.018 = 1$ $0.5[\blacksquare + 9.1] = 0.982$ $\blacksquare + 9.1 = 1.964$ $\blacksquare = -7.136$

Student's name: _____ Assignment date: _____

Triple mates	Diagram
Place black king on three squares marked A, B, and C where • "A" square shows that the black king is checkmated. • "B" square shows that the black king is stalemated. • "C" square shows that the black king will be checkmated in one move.   <center>answer</center>	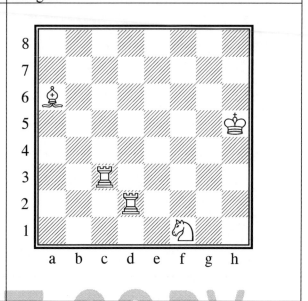

Frankho Rook Path Puzzle	Draw line segments to show each rook's path.
Each rook's path is shown by either a vertical line ▮ or horizontal line ▬ with the total number of vertical lines and horizontal lines equal to the number shown in the middle of each rook. No lines shall be crossed. Example 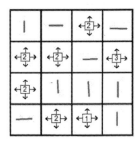	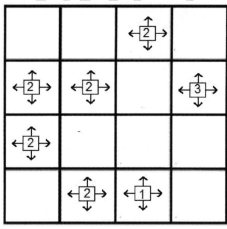 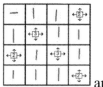 answer

Frankho ChessMaze 何数棋谜迷官

3. Trace the path from ⊠ to ♔.
4. Movement direction is shown by a darker line segment.

Transformation	Symbol	Example
Slide	$[\,-\leftrightarrow+\,,\ \updownarrow\,]$	**[3, –2]** Move right 3 squares and down 2 squartes. **[0, 2]** Move up 2 squares.
Rotation	⌐→ ⌐	⊕ = ⊕, ⊕ = ⊕
Flip	⊕ flip	⊕ = ⊕, ⊕ = ⊕ flip

PW (password): If rook is at e4 and queen is at g5 (take a look at the chessboard below), then name the squares, which are controlled both by rook and queen?

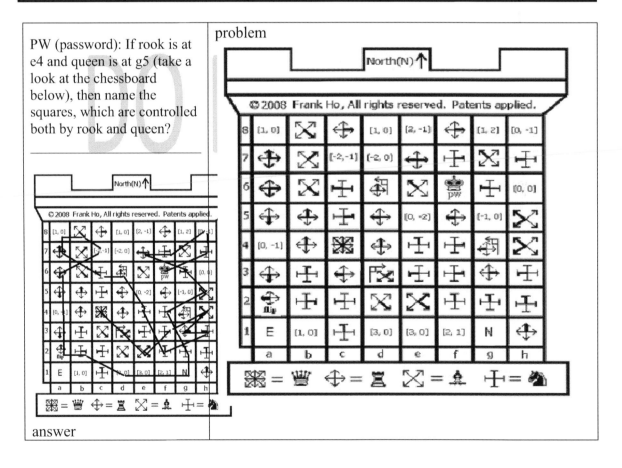

answer

Student's name: _____ Assignment date: _____

Ho Math Chess Puzzle

You are at c3.

	a	b	c	d	e
5		::	✳	∴	
4	∴	$2\frac{2}{3}$	$3\frac{3}{5}$	$3\frac{1}{2}$	::
3	✳	$3\frac{4}{6}$	$2\frac{1}{4}$ $1\frac{2}{3}$	$2\frac{5}{7}$	✳
			$1\frac{1}{2}$ $3\frac{1}{4}$		
2	•	$1\frac{2}{3}$	$1\frac{7}{9}$	$1\frac{7}{9}$	∴
1		•	✳	∴	

The points of chess pieces are as follows:

✳	= 0
↓	= 1
⤫	= 3
┼	= 3
✛	= 5
❋	= 9

Leave answers as improper fractions.

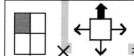 × = __ × __ = __

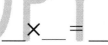 × = __ × __ = __

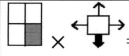 × = __ × __ = __

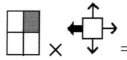 × = __ × __ = __

 × = __ × __ = __

 × = __ × __ = __

 × = __ × __ = __

 × = __ × __ = __

 × = __ × __ = __

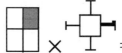 × = __ × __ = __

6, 247/28 (8 23/28)　　52/9, 110/18　　25/6, 8/3　　5/2, 104/9　　45/4, 20/3

Student's name: _____ Assignment date: _____

Frankho Move Dots Puzzle ™

You are at c3.

Move some dots in b3, c4, c2, or d3 squares into c3 square such that the sum of dots + dots in each of rook's moves at c3 will be equal to the number shown on its destination square. See the following example.

Example

Problem

Move up 2.

Student's name: _____ Assignment date: _____

Unequal Sudoku

Every row and column must have only one number starting from 1 to the number of squares of each side (Sudoku), but all numbers must obey the inequality sign.

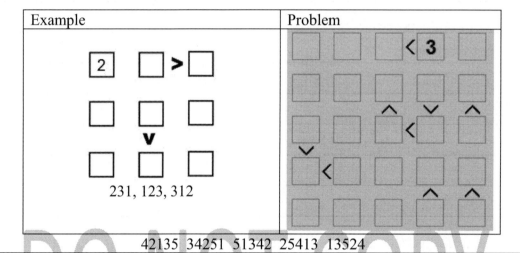

231, 123, 312

42135　34251　51342　25413　13524

Fencing 盖围墙, 頭尾相连但不交义,不重複的循环围墙

Connect lines around each dot in such a way that each number indicates how many lines, connected by 4 dots only, surround it. The connected lines must form a single loop (like one rubber band) without lines crossed to each other.

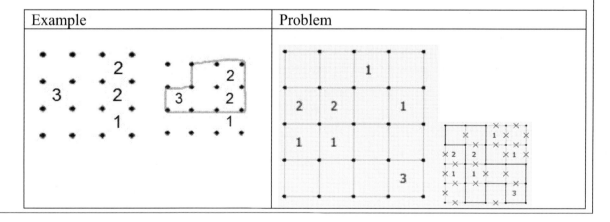

Student's name: _____ Assignment date: _____

Maze

Students! Please cover the following answer.

Answer

Ho Math Chess   何数棋谜   英文奥数, 解题策略, 及 IQ 思唯训练宝典

Frank Ho, Amanda Ho © 2020   All rights reserved.

Student's name: _____ Assignment date: _____

只见棋谜不见题   劝君迷路不哭涕   数学象棋加谜题   健脑思维眞神奇

5 (No calculator, show all your work on empty space.)

1	Evaluate $\dfrac{3\frac{1}{2} - 2\frac{2}{3}}{3\frac{3}{4} - 2\frac{1}{2}}$ $= \dfrac{\frac{7}{2} - \frac{8}{3}}{3\frac{3}{4} - 2\frac{2}{4}}$ $= \dfrac{\frac{21-16}{6}}{1\frac{1}{4}}$ $= \dfrac{\frac{5}{6}}{\frac{5}{4}}$ $= \dfrac{2}{3}$

2. **3 Dimensional Frankho Puzzle™**

Rule: All the digits 1 to 3 must appear exactly only once in every row and column of each layer, this same rule also applies to the same column of the multiple layers. Not all numbers on the cube are shown, and you must figure out the missing ones.

Transfer the numbers of each layer of the following cube into the 3 by 3 tables below.

Cube	Top layer	Middle layer	Bottom layer
	(empty 3×3 grid) 321 213 132	(empty 3×3 grid) 132 321 213	(empty 3×3 grid) 213 132 321

3	The following chess diagram gives a value of 7.5.	What chess value shall the following chess diagram give?
		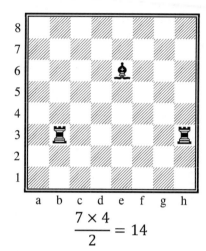
	Calculate the area of the triangle formed by 2 rooks and bishop. $\frac{5\times3}{2} = 7.5$	$\frac{7 \times 4}{2} = 14$
4	The purchase price after 15% off the asking price of $100. What is the original price after paying $21.95 with a 12.3% discount $= ?$ answer $\frac{100\times0.85}{21.95\div0.878} = \frac{85}{25} = \frac{17}{5}$	

Student's name: _____ Assignment date: _____

Triple mates	Diagram
Place black king on three squares marked A, B, and C where • "A" square shows that the black king is checkmated. • "B" square shows that the black king is stalemated. • "C" square shows that the black king will be checkmated in one move.  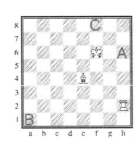	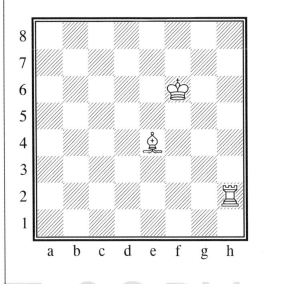

Frankho Rook Path Puzzle	Draw line segments to show each rook's path.
Each rook's path is shown by either a vertical line █ or horizontal line ▬ with the total number of vertical lines and horizontal lines equal to the number shown in the middle of each rook. No lines shall be crossed. Example 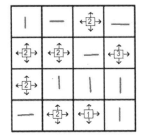 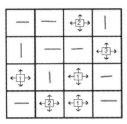 answer	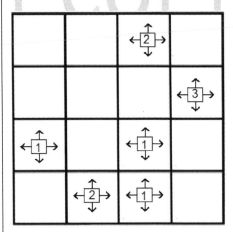

Frankho ChessMaze 何数棋谜迷官

1　Trace the path from ⬦ to ♛ .
2　Path direction is to move to a square with higher or equal value than the current one. Move one square at a time.

Transformation	Symbol	Example
Slide	$[\text{-} \leftrightarrow \text{+} , \updownarrow]$	[3, –2] Move right 3 squares and down 2 squartes. [0, 2] Move up 2 squares.
Rotation	⌐ ⌐	⬦ = ⬦ ,　⬦ = ⬦
Flip	⬦ flip	⬦ flip = ⬦ ,　⬦ flip = ⬦

It would be easier if students would just calculate the value of every square before making a move.

answer

problem

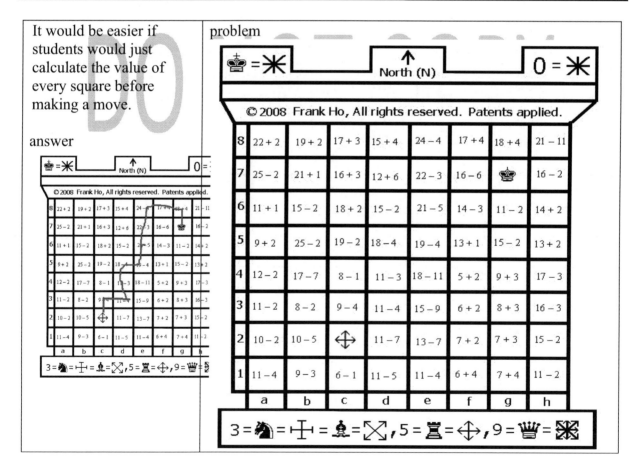

♚ = ✳　　　North (N)　　　0 = ✳

	a	b	c	d	e	f	g	h
8	22 + 2	19 + 2	17 + 3	15 + 4	24 – 4	17 + 4	18 + 4	21 – 11
7	25 – 2	21 + 1	16 + 3	12 + 6	22 – 3	16 – 6	♛	16 – 2
6	11 + 1	15 – 2	18 + 2	15 – 2	21 – 5	14 – 3	11 – 2	14 + 2
5	9 + 2	25 – 2	19 – 2	18 – 4	19 – 4	13 + 1	15 – 2	13 + 2
4	12 – 2	17 – 7	8 – 1	11 – 3	18 – 11	5 + 2	9 + 3	17 – 3
3	11 – 2	8 – 2	9 – 4	11 – 4	15 – 9	6 + 2	8 + 3	16 – 3
2	10 – 2	10 – 5	⬦	11 – 7	13 – 7	7 + 2	7 + 3	15 – 2
1	11 – 4	9 – 3	6 – 1	11 – 5	11 – 4	6 + 4	7 + 4	11 – 2

3 = ♞ = ⊥ = ♝ = ⤫ , 5 = ♜ = ⬦ , 9 = ♛ = ✳

Student's name: _____ Assignment date: _____

Frankho Move Dots Puzzle ™

You are at c3.

Move some dots in b3, c4, c2, or d3 squares into c3 square such that the sum of dots + dots in each of rook's moves at c3 will be equal to the number shown on its destination square. See the following example.

Example

Problem

Move up 1. Move left 1.

Unequal Sudoku

Every row and column must have only one number starting from 1 to the number of squares of each side (Sudoku), but all numbers must obey the inequality sign.

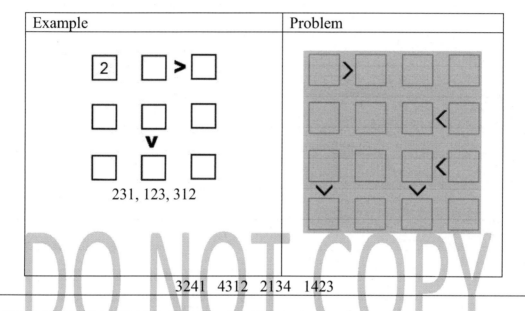

231, 123, 312

3241　4312　2134　1423

Fencing 盖围墙, 頭尾相连但不交义,不重複的循环围墙

Connect lines around each dot in such a way that each number indicates how many lines, connected by 4 dots only, surround it. The connected lines must form a single loop (like one rubber band) without lines crossed to each other.

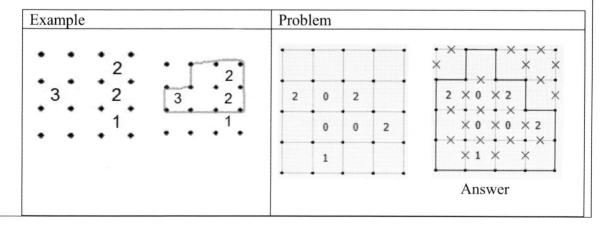

Answer

Frankho ChessMaze 何数棋谜迷官

1　Trace the path from ⟨symbol⟩ to ⟨symbol⟩.
2　Path direction is to move to a square with higher or equal value than the current one. Move one square at a time.

Transformation	Symbol	Example
Slide	$[-\leftrightarrow+ , \updownarrow]$	[3, –2] Move right 3 squares and down 2 squartes. [0, 2] Move up 2 squares.
Rotation	⟨symbol⟩ ⟨symbol⟩	⟨symbol⟩ = ⟨symbol⟩, ⟨symbol⟩ = ⟨symbol⟩
Flip	⟨symbol⟩ flip	⟨symbol⟩ = ⟨symbol⟩ , ⟨symbol⟩ = ⟨symbol⟩

It would be easier if students would just calculate the value of every square before making a move.

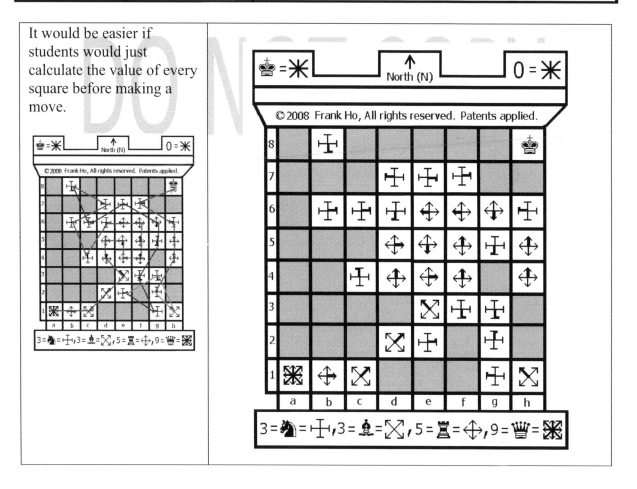

$3 = ♞ = ⊥, 3 = ♝ = ✕, 5 = ♜ = ⟨symbol⟩, 9 = ♛ = ✳$

Student's name: _____ Assignment date: _____

Math and Chess Puzzle
You are at c3.

The points of chess pieces are as follows:

	a	b	c	d	e
5		⸬	✳		⸬
4	⸪	12.29	0.003	0.37	⸬
3	✳	13.1	(0.23 / 49.12, 19.21 / 37.25)	0.21	✳
2	●	0.11	0.11	0.19	⸪
1		●	✳		⸪

Points:
✳ = 0
↓ (V) = 1
✕ = 3
╋ = 3
✥ = 5
✺ = 9

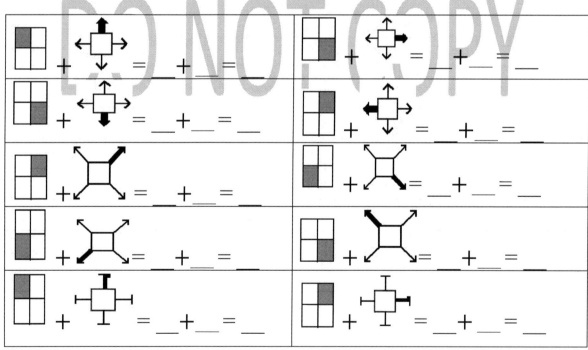

0.233, 37.46   37.36, 62.22   49.49, 19.40   19.32, 49.54   5.23, 53.12

Student's name: _____　Assignment date: _____

Fraction and Frankho ChessDoku

Ho Math Chess (何數棋谜 趣味數學)

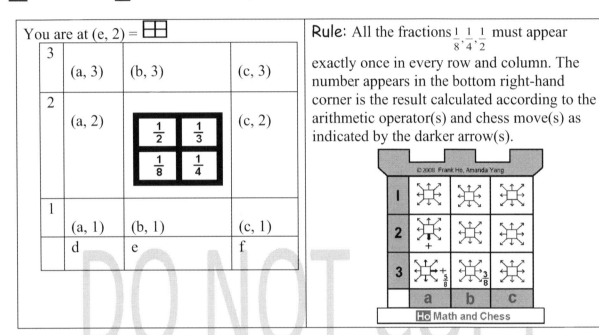

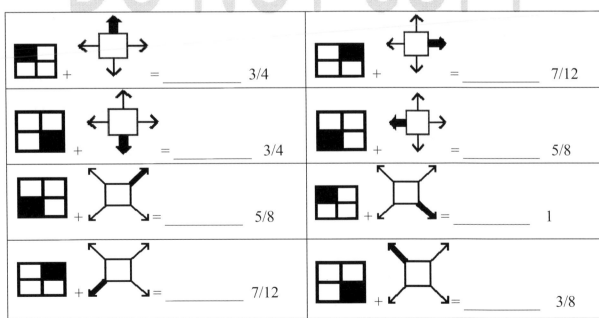

ChessDoku: ¼, ½, 1/8, ½, 1/8, ¼, 1/8, ¼, ½ (left to right, top to down)

Student's name: _____ Assignment date: _____

Introducing Ho Math Chess in Chinese 介紹何数棋谜

介紹何数棋谜

何数棋谜 = 奧数棋谜 + 思唯腦力開發
英文教材, 中英双语教学

什麼是何数棋谜?

上百篇科學論文已發表國際象棋可以提高兒童問題解答能力. 並且訓練他們的專心及耐力. 所以我們已經知道下國際象棋對兒童有好處. 但是因為國際象棋與計算能力並無直接開係, 所以如何讓兒童能在一個歡樂的環境下也能利用下棋來提高數學的計算呢? 何老師首創並發明有版权的幾何棋謎符號並利用此符號發明了世界第一的独特結合數學与棋謎教材. 何数棋谜讓兒童能利用幾何棋藝符號進行邏輯推理及數字的運算. 棋藝與算術的綜合題含蓋了整數, 幾何, 集合, 抽象數, 對比異同, 函數, 座標, 多空間圖形資料, 及規則性數字分析. 並且把棋藝的趣味性和數學的知識性結合在一起.

何数棋谜如何幫助兒童腦力思唯的開發?

很簡單的一個道理就是讓學生自願地同时去用左右腦. 何数棋谜棋謎式数学即是專为当達到此目的而研發的教法及教材.

訓練右腦
何数棋谜首創独一無二的融合數學與棋谜的独特趣味寓教於樂教材, 利用國際象棋訓練右腦的座標, 空間分析及圖形及表的處理.

訓練左腦
何数棋谜發明了整合棋子與數學的圖形語言, 讓兒童能利用抽象棋子符號圖形訓練左腦進行邏輯推理及數字的收集以創造題目並進行數字的運算.

國際象棋與算術的綜合題含蓋了整數, 幾何, 集合, 抽象數, 對比異同, 函數, 多空間圖形資料. 所以枯燥無味的計算題變成了謎題, 學生需要通過更多的思考. 能讓腦去思考愈多則腦力也愈開發. 處里訊息, 分析資料才能發掘出題目. 做這些謎題式數學時可以训练學生比較會專心及有耐心.

何数棋谜教学结果有科研报告吗?

何数棋谜融合數學與國際象棋的教學理論已在 BC 省數學教師刊物上發表. 科研報告已經證實何数棋谜教學法不但可以提高兒童數學解題及思維能力, 還可以開發兒童的腦力, 及分析問題的能力並且增加兒童學習的耐力, 學生的探索創造精神及求知欲. 判斷力, 及自信心等, 启發思維訓練機警靈巧及加強手腦眼的靈活運用.

Introducing Ho Math Chess™

Ho Math Chess™= math + puzzles + chess

Frank Ho, a Canadian math teacher, intrigued by the relationships between math and chess after teaching his son chess, started **Ho Math Chess™** in 1995. His long-term devotion to research has led his son to become a FIDE chess master and Frank's publications of over 20 math workbooks. Today **Ho Math Chess™** is the world's largest and the only franchised scholastic math, chess and puzzles specialty learning centre with worldwide locations. **Ho Math Chess™** is a leading research organization in the field of math, chess, and puzzles integrated teaching methodology.

There are hundreds of articles already published showing chess benefits children and that math puzzles are a very good way of improving brain power. So, by integrating chess and mathematical chess puzzles together, the learning effect is more significant.

Parents send their children to **Ho Math Chess™** because they like **Ho Math Chess™** teaching philosophy – offering children problem-solving questions in a variety of formats. The questions could be pure chess, chess puzzles or mathematical chess puzzles, logic, pattern, tree structure, Venn diagram, probability and many more math concepts.

Ho Math Chess™ has developed a series of unique and high-quality math, chess, and puzzles integrated workbooks. **Ho Math Chess™** produced the world's first workbook **Learning Chess to Improve Math.** This workbook is not only for learning chess but also for enriching math ability. This sets **Ho Math Chess** apart from other math learning centres, chess club, or chess classes.

The teaching method at **Ho Math Chess™** is to use math, chess, and puzzles integrated workbooks to teach children fun math. The purposes of **Ho Math Chess™** teaching method and workbooks are to:

- Improve math marks.
- Develop problem-solving and critical thinking skills.
- Improve logic thinking ability.
- Boost brainpower.

Testimonials, sample worksheets, reports, and franchise information can be found at www.homathchess.com.

More information about **Ho Math Chess™** can also be found from the following publications:

1. Why Buy a **Ho Math Chess™** Learning Centre Franchise: A Unique Learning Centre?
2. **Ho Math Chess™** Sudoku Puzzles Sample Worksheets
3. Introduction to **Ho Math Chess™** and its Founder Frank Ho

The above publications can be purchased from www.amazon.com.`

Made in the USA
Columbia, SC
17 June 2020